LOVE

LOVE
A HISTORY

SIMON MAY

YALE UNIVERSITY PRESS
NEW HAVEN AND LONDON

For information about this and other Yale University Press publications, please contact:
U.S. Office: sales.press@yale.edu www.yalebooks.com
Europe Office: sales@yaleup.co.uk www.yalebooks.co.uk

Set in Arno Pro by IDSUK (DataConnection) Ltd.
Printed in Great Britain by TJ International Ltd, Padstow, Cornwall.

Library of Congress Cataloging-in-Publication Data

May, Simon (Simon Philip Walter)
  Love : a history / Simon May.
    p. cm.
  ISBN 978–0–300–11830–8
  1. Love–History. I. Title.
  BD436.M375 2011
  128'.4609–dc22

2010049424

A catalogue record for this book is available from the British Library.

10 9 8 7 6 5 4 3 2 1

To MLM and ADG

Contents

Acknowledgements

I have benefited from the comments of many scholars, who gave so generously of their time, and I should like to record my great indebtedness to Rachel Adelman, Keith Ansell-Pearson, Liz Carmichael, Graham Davies, Nicholas Dent, Alison Finch, William Fitzgerald, Sebastian Gardner, Simon Gaunt, Ken Gemes, Lenn Goodman, Edward Harcourt, Philip Hardie, Michael Harris, Sandra Jacobs, Robert Jackson, Stephen Jaeger, Susan James, Chris Janaway, Werner Jeanrond, Menachem Kellner, Christopher Kelly, Duncan Large, Diana Lipton, Oliver O'Donovan, George Pattison, James Porter, Anthony Price, Bernard Reginster and Gudrun von Tevenar. Special appreciation goes to Michael Burdett, Meade McCloughan, Barnabas Palfrey and Chris Sykes, who provided invaluable help with research, checking citations, and pointing out sources that I had missed. I have enjoyed many fruitful conversations with Stephen Barber and Francis Pike and thank them for their interest and friendship.

Birkbeck College, University of London, was my philosophical home for many years and my heartfelt thanks go to my colleagues and students there for innumerable delightful and formative conversations, which have constituted an entire education. I am, as ever, grateful to my agent, Bill Hamilton, for his encouragement and support. Finally, it has been a tremendous pleasure to work with Robert Baldock and Rachael Lonsdale at Yale University Press. No author could wish for more stimulating, skilful and tenacious editors.

Preface

Isn't love indefinable – a matter of feeling, not thought? Worse: doesn't delving into this most spontaneous and mysterious emotion risk evicting its magic? And so end up killing precisely what we are trying to understand?

I have repeatedly encountered these questions, along with scepticism, even hostility, towards the very idea of a *philosophy* of love. A philosophy of love, so this view goes, is either futile (love cannot be defined) or self-defeating (to define it is to degrade it). The motive for such a project is not only naïve but suspect: one philosophises about love because one cannot experience it; but if one cannot experience it then how can one possibly philosophise about it?

Interestingly, these critics seldom see other emotions in the same way. Almost nobody believes that to philosophise about compassion, or generosity, or lust, or melancholy, or respect, or the yearning for immortality will destroy the capacity for those feelings; or that the motivation to do so betrays the inability to experience them – so that an interest in, say, hate would reflect one's inability to hate sufficiently, or one's having been hated too little, or one's failure to sustain a relationship of hate. If anything, they might suspect the opposite.

By contrast, attitudes towards a *psychology* of love seem much more positive. And especially towards an evolutionary psychology. Indeed, it isn't uncommon to find that those who despise attempts to philosophise about love are intrigued by, say, explanations of why and how we love in terms of mating strategies and evolutionary fitness, or brain states and neurotransmitters, or 'stories' about the various sorts of loving relationship that can exist, or patterns of attachment in childhood, or the workings of desire – for intimacy, for sex, for children.

Academic books, chat shows, pop lyrics, internet dating sites, self-help manuals – all buzz with curiosity about the conditions for successful love, the right partner, the challenges of fidelity and jealousy, or the virtues of intimacy such as empathy, respect and tolerance. Though one might think that these reductionist theories are likely to be at least as successful as philosophy in evicting the magic from love, it seems quite acceptable to describe people's emotions when they are in love or have recently been rejected; to map the feelings and histories that can obstruct intimacy and how they might be overcome; to explain why you, as the personality type you are, fall for one person rather than another; to explore gender differences in the brain and in courting or mating behaviour; and so on.

Why the inconsistency? Why is talk of love everywhere and yet in a certain sense it is also a no-go zone?

✦ ✦ ✦

Before venturing an answer it is worth reminding ourselves that it was not ever thus. If you had asked some of the greatest founders of Western love like Plato, Aristotle, Augustine and Thomas Aquinas, or philosophers like Spinoza in the seventeenth century and Schopenhauer in the nineteenth, whether it could be defined, or if uninhibited reflection on its nature could enable one to love better, they would have been amazed at the question. Not only could they all offer detailed definitions of it; it was also central to their philosophy and therefore to what are today considered, in most respects, distinct fields like ethics and meta-physics and aesthetics. For these thinkers, to get clear on what love is, what inspires it, what we seek in it, which qualities are most worth loving and which less, what prices are worth paying for it and what aren't, what virtues must be cultivated if we are successfully to pursue it, where we can fall into conceptual error and how we can educate ourselves to recognise and avoid such error – all this, they hold, doesn't stymie love but allows it to flourish. And in particular, allows us to love the right objects with the right sort of attention.

So what is going on today? The answer might be this: we are determined both to make traditional expectations of love come true *and* therefore to avoid questioning them. It is fine, indeed essential, to ask how love can be made to work, why it doesn't, what social or evolutionary purposes it might serve, what sorts of relationships express it. But the nature of love – what exactly it is; what we demand from it – is sacred territory. Is it really unconditional? Is it really spontaneous, and ultimately unfathomable in its motives? Do parents really love their children to equal degrees, if differently? Is love really our most personal and intimate emotion? Is it ever selfless? Is it, in its essence, about valuing the other person as a whole – and is it clear what this 'whole' is that we value? Is possessiveness really the enemy of successful love and the opposite of submitting to the reality of the loved one? Do we love the other for his or her[1] own sake?

The answer to these sorts of questions is widely assumed to be yes. Which in turn fixes the expectations of millions of lovers: when they feel delight, frustration, success, failure, reproachful, fulfilled, in their relationships. We are still dominated by a background picture of love that belongs to a certain sort of Romanticism and that hasn't changed in its essentials since the late nineteenth century. (In chapter 1, I will summarise what I take the key elements of this picture to be.) Indeed, when it comes to love, the 'long nineteenth century' extends not only into the twentieth, to 1914 or 1917, but well into the twenty-first.

✦ ✦ ✦

If this is right, then we are dealing with a fascinating paradox: the tremendous liberation of sex and marriage over the past hundred years has been accompanied by love's ossification, rather than by its reinvention. 'Free love' has not freed love – in the sense of giving us fresh conceptions of it. On the contrary, the new liberties – flowing, above all, from divorce, contraception, and the acceptance of gay love: three of the most far-reaching and still unfinished revolutions spawned by the twentieth century – have offered ever more opportunities for pursuing the same old ideal. Aided by abortion and feminism, they have meant that women and men are no longer committed to one another by pregnancy or traditional social relations but are free to go on and on searching for the 'right' person and the 'right' love. And that gays can, increasingly, do the same.

The search has also been fuelled by the spread of consumerism to love: the demand for quick satisfaction here, as in other areas of desire, and the urge repeatedly to move on to new partners if we don't find it. Indeed, to keep 'moving on' over a lifetime. It has been aided, too, by a steadily expanding pool of possible partners, thanks to greater mobility and the global reach of internet dating. And greater wealth, longer lives and better health have all made the search increasingly practicable by freeing people from bondage to poverty and war and dead marriages, so giving them that indispensable condition for great cultural achievements: leisure. Despite its hectic pace and process-driven spirit, contemporary life does allow more people than ever before the time and attention needed for the pursuit of love.

A returnee from the nineteenth century wouldn't recognise our everyday attitudes to morality, or freedom, or the position of women, or art, or race, or parenting, or homosexuality, or the Church, or travel. He would be astonished to witness ordinary social relations – how the sexes interact, how children behave towards their parents, how black and white talk to each other, how gays touch – but he would quickly identify with what we think love is, or ought to be. Alone among the great ideas that rule our lives, love seems to be frozen in time.

Why?

The similarities between the experience of religious belief and falling in love have often been noted. But in contemporary attitudes to love we are talking about something else: love itself as a religion. A religion that is all the more remarkable for being self-enforced by its votaries rather than supervised by a Church.

A religion must, among other things, posit some state of affairs which is venerated as supremely valuable, indeed as 'sacred', because through it salvation from whatever we most fear can in principle be found. And because it enables us to make sense of the most difficult questions about the nature and purpose of life. As a result, we feel awe for its power and grandeur, which we experience as far beyond the everyday. For many of a religion's votaries, therefore, fundamental questioning of the beliefs and practices by which it is upheld and pursued will seem absurd, if not perverse.

Indeed, anybody who really questions proves, by this very intent, that he is a stranger to what he is questioning. His attempt invalidates itself. His arguments are beside the point – even if they seem plausible. No religion could possibly regard someone who doesn't share its fundamental beliefs as qualified to criticise them.

I exaggerate – but only slightly. For these attitudes suggest that we must begin our investigation of the nature of love with a remarkable phenomenon: that for many in the Western world love has become a religion in just these senses – even (especially?) among those who consider themselves militantly irreligious.

Others might not have experienced such strong reactions. But I have found them so striking, and so powerful a symptom of contemporary attitudes towards love, that, in a sense, they have become part of the subject matter of this book. Indeed they have partly motivated its guiding questions: How did human love come to be modelled on divine love? What illusions about love has such hubris fostered? And how can we rethink love in a way that doesn't commit this error and sacrilege – against love? Precisely because there is no greater human need than love, which is, as St Paul put it, of great things 'the greatest', we need to ensure that it doesn't end up playing God.

1

Love plays God

'Almost two thousand years – and not a single new god!' cried Nietzsche in 1888.[1]

But he was wrong. The new god was there – indeed was right under his nose. That new god was love. Human love.

Human love, now even more than then, is widely tasked with achieving what once only divine love was thought capable of: to be our ultimate source of meaning and happiness, and of power over suffering and disappointment. Not as the rarest of exceptions but as a possibility open to practically all who have faith in it; not as the result of its being infused into us by a creator-God or after long and disciplined training, but as a spontaneous and intuitive power with which, to some degree, we are all endowed.

Though this faith in love as the one democratic, even universal, form of salvation open to us moderns is the result of a long religious history that saw divine love as the origin of human love and as the model to be imitated, it has paradoxically come into its own because of a *decline* in religious faith. It has been possible only because, since the end of the eighteenth century, love has increasingly filled the vacuum left by the retreat of Christianity. Around that time the formula 'God is love' became inverted into 'love is God',[2] so that it is now the West's undeclared religion – and perhaps its only generally accepted religion.

What does this really mean? It means that in cultures formed by the Christian tradition genuine love tends to get modelled on a certain picture of divine love, whether or not we are Christians. This picture has less to do with what Jesus is reported to have said – indeed, as we will see, he seldom mentions love (and almost never speaks of sex) – than with much later beliefs and practices. The key beliefs are these:

Love is unconditional: it is neither aroused nor diminished by the other's value or qualities; it is a spontaneous gift that seeks nothing for the giver. (Paradigm case: parents' love for their children.)

Love relates to and affirms the loved one in their full particularity, the 'bad' as well as the 'good'.

Love is fundamentally selfless: a disinterested concern for the flourishing of loved ones for their own sake.

Love is benevolent and harmonious – a haven of peace.

Love is eternal: it – or its blessings – will never die.

Love transports us beyond the messy imperfections of the everyday world into a superior state of purity and perfection.

Love redeems life's losses and sufferings: it delivers us from them; gives them meaning; overwhelms them with its own value; and reconciles us with that highest good from which they express our separation.

These sorts of ideas saturate the popular culture. They are also repeated by otherwise bold thinkers, who promulgate clichés such as love as 'disinterested concern for the well-being' of the loved one 'for their own sake', or love as the spontaneous 'bestowal of value', or love as directed at the loved one's 'full particularity' – and who are quick to chide great forebears like Plato and Proust for failing to subscribe to such worthy commonplaces.[3] Above all, these ideals fuel our expectations of romantic love and of parents' love for their children. To its immense cost, human love has usurped a role that only God's love used to play.

✦ ✦ ✦

This divinisation of human love becomes most obvious when we are personally confronted with severe loss – the sort that can abruptly drain our lives of meaning and security. Faced by the fragility of our achievements, possessions, health, jobs; by the helpless suffering of illness, poverty, bereavement, terrorism, or unemployment, love is enlisted as the one measure of value to which most Westerners, whether they are religious believers or not, can cling. Why me? Why the innocent child? To what end such calamity? Only love seems undefeated by such questions. Only love seems to have the all-conquering force to flood horrors with meaning – 'he didn't die in vain' – or, where even it cannot do that because he obviously did die in vain, then to give his life unquestionable value – 'he loved and was loved, and this vindicates his life, and this vindication of his life obliterates the meaninglessness of his death'.

The religion of love is no less attractive to the diehard atheist than to the agnostic or the believer. Many atheists find in love a taste of the absolute and the eternal that they rigorously deny to any other realm of life. There is hardly a humanist funeral that, having begun with a defiant statement that it is a godless celebration, doesn't seek comfort in the love that 'survives' the deceased person and thus gives him a measure of immortality: survives in his acts of loving and in his being loved; survives in the memories that the still-living have of that love.

If you then ask an atheist whether love, or its consequences, somehow lives on when even those touched by it have themselves died, he will, in many – perhaps most – cases, wish to say 'yes', as if love were a moral energy that, once expressed, can never be extinguished. For the inheritors and successors of Christianity, this belief is their last defence against despair. They would agree with St Paul that 'Love never ends' (1 Corinthians 13:8). The final line of Philip Larkin's poem of disenchantment, 'An Arundel Tomb', speaks for a whole civilisation: 'What will survive of us is love.'[4]

By contrast, since the West started losing its faith in God in the seventeenth and eighteenth centuries, all his substitutes – all those objects of worship that have, at one time or another, been seen as harbingers of human exaltation and redemption; as imbuing with value and meaning anything they structure – have, one by one, been found wanting. Reason, Progress, the Nation, the State, Communism, and the bevy of other idols and 'isms' that were, and in one or two cases – like nationalism and art – still sporadically are, elevated to religions of salvation to fill the void left by the slow 'death' of God, all failed to deliver the ultimate contentment or limitless promise expected of them.

For all the spiritual and moral significance attached to them, none could sustain that vision to which the Western imagination is still so addicted and for the sake of which it continually erects its idols: the vision of some final state of perfection where all good things harmoniously coexist. None could successfully serve as the master ideal or experience that gives meaning to life as a whole and, in the process, redeems, explains, justifies, washes away, or otherwise defeats suffering and injustice.

Freedom – the only other perennial candidate for a mass religion – will not do the trick, if only because it cannot be, even theoretically, unlimited in either extent or value. Though almost universally acclaimed in the contemporary world as a great good, including by its enemies (always a sign of how powerful a value has become), it cannot lend value to *anything* genuinely done in its name in the way that love can. Nor is every increase in freedom necessarily good in the sense that we think every increase in love is.

Art is better than freedom at meeting man's religious needs – but only for the few (and, as creators of art, for even fewer), quite apart from the fact that contemporary art has become too determinedly ironic, too intentionally everyday in tone, too scornful of the idea of salvation or ultimate meanings or the unconditional or the enduring, to be in a position to do the job reliably. Yet other ideals, such as racial and gender equality, or protection of the environment and animal rights, have sprung up; but, no matter how noble and vital and revolutionary they are, none provides the final justification of life's aim and meaning that the Western mind still craves. The more individualistic our societies become, the more we can expect the value of love, as the ultimate source of belonging and redemption, to keep rising. In the wasteland of Western idols, only love survives intact.

THE PERILS OF HUBRIS

To give any human ideal a divine character does it no favours. For the reality – of which so many ancient myths speak, from Adam and Eve eating from the tree of the knowledge of good and evil, to Prometheus's theft of divine fire, to the Babylonians' ambition to build a tower that would reach the heavens – is that any attempt to appropriate the powers of a god or to divinise the human ends in disaster.

Love is no exception. By imputing to human love features properly reserved for divine love, such as the unconditional and the eternal, we falsify the nature of this most conditional and time-bound and earthy emotion, and force it to labour under intolerable expectations. This divinisation of human love is the latest chapter in humanity's impulsive quest to steal the powers of its gods, and the longest-running such attempt to reach beyond our humanity. Like the others it must fail; for the moral of these stories is that the limits of the human can be ignored only at terrible cost.

But, one might object, the world is also full of scepticism about love as religion – or even as a story of Hollywood optimism in which, after the inevitable trials, soulmates find and cherish a perfect happiness for the rest of their lives. After all, there are many today – as there were in previous times – who do reject the divine model I sketched earlier; and who echo long traditions that see love in naturalistic terms, traditions which we will also consider in this book.

For example, there are hedonists like Ovid who advise us to enjoy the delights of courtship, sex and the amorous imagination for as long as they last; to cultivate them as a refined sport or art; to be cautious about the madness of 'falling in love'; and to be unmoved by the mirage of a higher meaning to love. There are deflationists like Schopenhauer who see passionate love, with all its ideals and illusions, as the machinations of a reproductive drive aimed at getting two people obsessed with each other for long enough to produce and raise the next generation. There are advocates of friendship-love, such as Aristotle or Montaigne, for whom devotion to the welfare of another whom we experience as our 'second self' is more conducive to our flourishing than love that strives to storm the heavens – and, for Montaigne at least, every bit as intense. There are, more recently, psychoanalysts, beginning with Freud, who depict love as a primal and often regressive search for physical gratification and protective union – and love's maturation as liberation from its infantile patterns. And there are those, like Proust, who regard most love between humans as a ruthless, fickle and often deluded mission to escape from ourselves into the security and novelty of someone else.

In the end, though, love plays too important a role in fulfilling our inescapable religious needs – today widely unsatisfied – to dislodge the divine model. And yet there is another way of thinking about love that, I hope to show, does justice to the powerful and universal needs behind it, while avoiding both the divine and the deflationary accounts of it. On this view love is neither an unconditional commitment to the welfare of others for their own sake, nor can it be reduced to drives for recognition, intimacy, procreation or sexual gratification.

So what, then, is it?

A THEORY OF LOVE: FIRST OUTLINES

Love, I will argue, is the rapture we feel for people and things that inspire in us the hope of an indestructible grounding for our life. It is a rapture that sets us off on – and sustains – the long search for a secure relationship between our being and theirs.

If we all have a need to love, it is because we all need to feel at home in the world: to root our life in the here and now; to give our existence solidity and validity; to deepen the sensation of being; to enable us to experience the reality of our life as indestructible (even if we also accept that our life is temporary and will end in death).

This is the feeling that I call 'ontological rootedness' – ontology being that branch of philosophy that deals with the nature and experience of existence. My suggestion is that we will love only those (very rare) people or things or ideas or disciplines or landscapes that can inspire in us a promise of ontological rootedness. If they can, we will love them regardless of their other qualities: regardless of how beautiful or good they are; of how (in the case of people we love) generous or altruistic or compassionate; of how interested in our life and projects. And regardless, even, of whether they value us. For love's overriding concern is to find a home for our life and being.

◆ ◆ ◆

At first, home is our mother and father; gradually its possibilities become larger and more complex: they might include our work, our friends, our children, nature, God. Or places, ideas, and ideals. Or – contrary to common prejudice – money or status and the people who offer us access to it. For these can also powerfully root, even if they are less noble and more obviously instrumental than other objects of love.

It is hardly surprising, then, that love can be so confusing. Its aim – groundedness, rootedness, at-homeness – is hard to define, and we can never be sure that we have attained it, let alone that we have stably attained it. It can be satisfied by different sorts of objects. Its faith in the loved one as the agent of this groundedness can never be 'deluded', though we can be deluded about their character and constancy, and how far they requite our love. It involves seemingly contradictory attitudes: submission and possessiveness; generosity and selfishness; intense gratitude and – not least – the disrespect that is easily fostered by need when it becomes overwhelming and even violent.

But one thing should already be clear: far from being unconditional, love is inescapably conditional on this promise of ontological rootedness. It might *seem* unconditional, if only because once we encounter people (or things) that can inspire in us this sense of grounding we will submit to them so unreservedly, desire to possess them so securely, wish to give to them so completely, ascribe to them such overwhelming goodness (even if we also think them morally bad in certain ways), delight so intensely in their presence, feel such gratitude and responsibility for their existence, and find their absence so unbearable that we will easily lose sight of the reality that all these feelings for them, which are traditionally associated with 'love', are entirely dependent on their power to hold out such a promise of making us feel at home in the world.

Indeed, as long as this sole condition for the existence of love is satisfied, it won't have any further conditions: it will, from that point on, be unconditional. The lover will affirm and rejoice in the existence of the loved one regardless of her other qualities: her powers, her looks, her intelligence, her status. Regardless, too, of complications in the lover's feelings and commitments to her. And to such a degree that he might be willing to die for her, for without her his life would be emptied of its ultimate 'meaning': the discovery of a home that gives validity and solidity to his existence. No destructiveness, betrayal, meanspiritedness, or decline on her part could then kill his love for her. Unless – and this is the *only* circumstance in which love can be killed – she no longer inspires in him the hope of ontological rootedness.

This hope is the 'something about her' that is decisive in all love. With it we will love her even if everything else is wrong about her or our relationship. Without it everything can be right but we will never love her.

✦ ✦ ✦

Everyone needs love; many find it; but few live it. Not because of a shortage of appropriate beings to love, which as I just suggested can be of many kinds. Rather because of the difficulty of attending to them in a manner that enables them to play this role in grounding our life. Without attentiveness of the right sort we will not recognise them in the first place, and even if we do we will fail to develop the dialogue between our two beings which turns that initial recognition into a home that can be the ground of our life. The difficulty of attending (and the many distractions from it, of which lust can be merely one – and perhaps an overrated one) is why most of our loves are false starts.

The complications begin, of course, with focusing on the right object – one whose capacity to ground us is genuine and stands the test of time. Usually this will be someone similar to us – someone whose being echoes the depths of our own; someone whose defining experiences and origins, self-conceptions and values, chime with ours; someone in whom we recognise ourselves and who we are sure could recognise us, even if they don't. Even if they don't love us back.

But attachments can become almost unmanageably complex when we have found the object and feel passionately bonded to it. For love involves a number of feelings that, if they are not cultivated in the right way, easily slip into insoluble tension.

One example, to which we will repeatedly return: how can we both submit to our loved one *and* possess him or her? Submission and possession are, as we will see, fundamental features of love; and they appear in almost every story about it, from Plato and Hebrew Scripture down to the present day. Yet it is easy to feel that the more there is of the one the less there must be of the other.

In fact, they exclude each other only when possession takes the crude form of experiencing another as totally at one's disposal, as entirely enclosed within one's world, and as an instrument of total attentiveness. In love of other people this sort of possession is out of the question: how can something as impossible to locate as the human self be taken hold of? And it is self-defeating: if we were to possess him in this way he would lose the sovereign independence that is crucial to his capacity to root us; quite apart from the destruction that such possessiveness, with its torments of jealousy and frustration, would inflict on any relationship.

But possession, I will suggest, can be something else entirely: the assimilation of another person's presence through attending to her and what she demands of you. Just as you 'possess' a piece of music only by listening over a sustained period to its innate structure and lawfulness, you 'take in' another person's reality only in surrendering to her. Contrary to most traditional thinking, whether religious or not, there is no necessary dichotomy between submission and possession, or giving and taking. These so-called rivals, expressed in stock formulae such as 'agape versus Eros', aren't rivals at all. Nor are they even competitors that can coexist. On the contrary, they are different modes of the same relation.

✦ ✦ ✦

Possession in the crude sense is even more nonsensical when we come to that great object of love which reappears in every age: origins. As we will see, love is deeply bound up with piety for our origins. Nothing gives us a more powerful sense of grounding in the world than finding a living relationship to what we take to be the source of our being. Here we can locate love for God: creator of our life; love for homeland: origin of our people; and love for ancestors: source of our lineage. Here we can also locate nostalgic longings for an 'authentic' past and the many myths that picture love as the desire to return to some primordial state where we will be whole again. And here too we can locate the feeling of lovers that they come from the same stable – that sense of having known each other forever, even if they have just met.

Ideas like this have been expressed in many different ways: in Hebrew Scripture, where Yahweh is the origin and rock of his people Israel; in Greek philosophy, where Plato, for example, tells us that the soul seeks to fly back to its spiritual source and, in another parable, speaks of two people seeking in each other their lost half; in a Christian thinker like Augustine, who sees the highest form of love – *caritas* – as the soul yearning to return to God, its creator; in Hindu texts that describe the saint as striving to free his soul from the lure of the sensory world by returning to *atman*, the ground or essence of his (and of all) selfhood; in Plotinus, the pagan thinker of the third century CE, later so central to Christianity, who speaks of merging with the highest good, the One – an experience in which the individual is taken out of himself in, literally, 'ecstasy' ('standing outside'); in those Muslim mystics, like Rumi, who sing of the individual soul returning to merge with God; and in a committed atheist like Schopenhauer for whom the highest love transcends the condition of individuality and sees that all living being is one. In all these cases (and like all great transformations of the self), love is experienced as both a recovery and a discovery – as a return and as a going forth.[5]

Why, though, can't one feel rooted in the world, at home in one's life, without someone or something *external* to one's own being to love? After all, we often hear that one can love others only if one first feels secure within oneself – only if one can first love oneself.

The answer lies in the intense sense of vulnerability of the individual, from the moment of birth. We cannot find the necessary grounding entirely within ourselves – in our feelings, our body, our 'subjectivity' – because the relation that is so vexing (as well as fruitful) to us, and to which love is the response, is our relation with an uncontrollable and alien world into which birth has thrown us. It is a relation of vulnerability that, unless we fantasise it away or otherwise conceal or stifle it, will be enriched and deepened over the course of our life. And it means that love will necessarily be directed outwards towards that very special person (or god, or thing, or country), or perhaps several of them, that can inspire ontological rootedness in us.

This outward relation succeeds in securing our life only if we experience the loved one as radically distinct from us. To feel rooted is to experience a relation to a ground beyond oneself, a ground that must seem insurmountably independent of us if it is to be a place in which we might anchor our being (which has nothing to do with loving the other person as 'an end in themselves' or 'for their own sake').

If we are simply looking to another to value us for our qualities, or give us a sense of status, or 'be there' for us in our loneliness – if, in other words, we are using them in a way that does not see them as a great unattainable power – then they will be unable to inspire in us a sense of our indestructible reality. To love them is necessarily to experience, even celebrate, their being as utterly sovereign and beyond our grasp. That is one reason why genuine love cannot be narcissistic. And why it evokes such fear.

There can of course be self-love: the joy of feeling oneself to be a rooted being – and of being *able* to be a rooted being. But because to feel rooted is to experience a relation to a ground beyond oneself, no one could love only himself. To love oneself is of a piece with loving a world or a person that affords such a grounding.

Self-love and love of another are therefore two sides of the same coin. There is a basic identity between them. It is as meaningless to say that one must be able to love oneself before one can love another as to say that one must be able to love another before one can love oneself. To love another as inspiring ontological rootedness is to love oneself. And to love oneself as a grounded being is to love the one who inspires – and to that extent is – this grounding of one's being.

✦ ✦ ✦

Since love is born in extreme vulnerability and seeks to overcome that condition through a correspondingly extreme invulnerability, it easily succumbs to its greatest temptation: to play God. To imagine it is unconditioned by the value of the loved one. To pretend that it is sovereign enough to be devoted disinterestedly to him 'for his own sake'. To pronounce itself eternal.

Such hubris can be, and has been, expressed in secular language as well as in religious beliefs. We will see Christians who say that we can become gods through love, just as we will encounter Romantics who believe that humans become divine through love and even through sex. In many ways the history of love is the history of this temptation to play God.

Which brings me back to my opening theme: how love has gone wrong by being modelled on the divine (a model perfectly expressed by Pope Benedict XVI in his first Encyclical: 'God's way of loving becomes the measure of human love'[6]). In order to understand how this happened, we need to reconstruct key steps in the history of Western love from its major sources: Hebrew Scripture and Greek philosophy. We need a history of love to give us the perspective to look afresh at ideas that have become rigidified by the weight of tradition. Such a history should re-examine knee-jerk assumptions at work in our relationships by recognising that those assumptions are not inscribed in stone, but are rather the outcome of a long and powerful cultural heritage. And it should seek to recover other, perhaps more fruitful, approaches to love that got lost on the way, especially, I will suggest, those modelled on how humanity is commanded to love God.

I assume throughout this book that the emotion of love is universal but that the way this emotion gets *interpreted* varies greatly from one society and epoch to another. In other words, individuals in all cultures and times are beset by passionate devotion to those others (be they conceived as natural or supernatural) whom the lovers experience as grounding their very existence, and whom they desire on that account – as well as by a battery of labours and hardships typically involved in pursuing that devotion. But the interpretation given to this mysterious attraction – why it exists, what it strives for, what its role is in a well-lived life, how it should be cultivated, under what conditions it is beautiful and ugly, good and bad – depends on time and place.

My history of love therefore tells the story of how this universal force of desire and devotion has been interpreted over the centuries in the particular collection of cultures that we call 'Western'. I suggest that this history is marked by four transformations, each of which evolves over several centuries. Like most revolutions, they have no clear beginning or end.

The first transformation concerns the *value* of love. Between Deuteronomy and Augustine – so for well over a thousand years, until the mid-fifth century CE – love is gradually made the supreme virtue. Hebrew Scripture commands that God be loved with 'all your heart, and with all your soul, and with all your might'; Jesus elevates love of God and neighbour to the most important biblical command-ments; John the Evangelist says that ultimate reality – God – is love; Paul and then Augustine see love as the root of all true virtue.

In the second transformation, spanning the fourth to the sixteenth centuries CE, from Augustine through Bernard of Clairvaux to Thomas Aquinas, and beyond him to Luther, human beings are given unprecedented – literally divine – *power* to love. By developing the idea of love as a gift of divine Grace, human beings can, at least in principle, become divine through love and even achieve friendship with God – though one's fellow human beings are still to be loved for the sake of God.

The third transformation, emerging in the eleventh century and culminating in the eighteenth, concerns the *object* of love. Now a single human being, or indeed nature more widely, can be experienced as embodying the greatest good and be worthy of the sort of love that was formerly reserved for God. And so the boundary between the divine and the earthly, between the supernatural and the natural, becomes ever more blurred.

This prepares the ground for a fourth transformation – beginning in the eighteenth century, with Rousseau, and still very much underway – which concerns *the lover*, who becomes authentic through love. In love he becomes not selfless but a self. He doesn't lose himself but finds himself. Far from striving to transcend nature he seeks to be guided by and in a sense to actualise his own nature. The true and the good lie not beyond the individual subject's experience but in an exploration of it. Indeed, as this transformation develops, the lover becomes the focus of love to such an extent that there are moments when the loved one almost drops out of the picture, reduced to a substitutable stage prop in the drama of the lover's life. Love comes to fall in love with itself.

Inevitably, much has been left out of my history. I have chosen to focus on those great voices which have, in my judgement, either said something radically new or expressed old ideas with fresh vigour. Several towering figures are conspicuous by their absence, most notably Dante, Petrarch, Shakespeare and Kierkegaard, because at least some of the ideas that inform their works appear elsewhere in my account, and because I lack the space and competence to cover them all. And though I treat Plato and Hebrew Scripture as the textual 'origins' of the dominant conception of love at work in the Western world today, they in turn have great predecessors about which I am silent – for example Hinduism and the Orphic mystery cults in the case of Plato; or the ancient Near Eastern love commandments, which prevailed in Hittite, Aramaic and Neo-Assyrian forms well before the traditions witnessed in the Jewish Bible.

In summary, this work has three principal aims. First, to show how love came to play God – and thus to be deprived, in key respects, of its humanity. (And, of course, like all gods, to be abused and misappropriated by its worshippers.) Second, to trace some of the debilitating illusions of this hubris: above all the belief that genuine love is unconditional. And third, to propose a way of looking at love that is truer to its fundamental nature – and so doesn't burden it with misconceived expectations. Here I will develop the idea, just sketched, that love is the intense desire for someone whom – or something which – we experience as grounding and affirming our own existence. And that this desire seeks two forms of intimacy, which, when we learn to practise them in accordance with their essential nature, we discover are opposite sides of the same coin: the intimacy of possessing another and the intimacy of making ourselves unreservedly available to them. It will present a picture of love as a harbinger of the sacred without pretending that it is an all-powerful solution to the problem of finding meaning, security and happiness in life.

The point of asking how love can be freed from its long imprisonment by vain and unreal expectations is not to downgrade it to something lukewarm like tender care or benevolent empathy, but, on the contrary, to reach a more successful understanding of this supreme emotion and its place in a well-lived life. My overall theme is that, especially in a secular age, we should model human love not on how God is said to love us but on how we are commanded to love God.

2

The foundation of Western love
Hebrew Scripture

THE TWO GREAT LOVE COMMANDS

If love in the Western world has a founding text, that text is Hebrew. Before Plato and Aristotle – the other dominant sources of Western concepts of love – and well before Jesus,[1] Hebrew Scripture provides, in two pithy sentences, ideas that have guided the course of love ever since:

> You shall love the Lord your God with all your heart, and with all your soul, and with all your might.[2]

and:

> You shall love your neighbour as yourself.[3]

The first idea, love for God, is characterised by intense devotion; absolute trust; fear of his power and presence; and rapturous, if often questioning, absorption in his will: its demands, meanings, vagaries and contradictions. Its moods are a combination of the piety of a vassal, the intimacy of friends, the fidelity of spouses, the dependence of a child, the passion of lovers, the intoxicated obedience of a hostage – and the terror aroused by all these forms of vulnerability.

The second – which has become a, if not the, central precept of Western morality – is a more sober relationship of care and respect for others in the community, based on their needs.

On the face of it, these great commandments speak of two sorts of love.[4] Love for God is an unbridled longing for the source of all being and value, a love to which every other love must necessarily be secondary, a love cultivated and expressed by ceaseless ritual and worship. Moses Maimonides (1138–1204), the medieval Jewish philosopher, sums it up as follows:

> What is the love of God that is befitting? It is to love God with a great and exceeding love, so strong that one's soul (*nafsho*) shall be knit up with the love of God such that it is continually enraptured by it, like love-sick individuals whose minds (*da'atam*) are at no time free from passion for a particular woman and are enraptured by her at all times . . . even intenser should be the love of God in the hearts of those who love Him; they should be enraptured by this love at all times.[5]

Love for neighbour, on the other hand, lacks this state of rapture. And just as well it does, for its great goals – respect, justice, even-handedness – aren't always best nourished by the emotion of lovesickness. Another mood is called for here, which is no less noble: scrupulous attention to the interests of others; a defence of their being that is as robust as our defence of our own; attention to their separateness and its sanctity.[6]

Indeed in the Hebrew Bible the command to love one's neighbour as oneself is preceded by a litany of kindnesses that one is to show one's fellows, such as: always leave part of your harvest for the poor and the stranger; do not steal from others or deal deceitfully or falsely; never place a stumbling block before those who are unable to see; do not hate or take vengeance or bear grudges. These are all special cases of loving kindness (חסד or *hesed*): devotion to the welfare of another that is akin to friendship-love.

To treat one's neighbour with respect and loyalty is not a favour one does him but a duty which is commanded by divine law and which stands in no further need of justification. As the Talmud elaborates it: 'One who exalts himself at his fellow's expense has no share in the World to Come'.[7] Similarly, the virtue of loving kindness is something we *owe* everyone in all our actions.[8]

But this doesn't mean that one has to deny one's own interests and desires. There is no presumption in the Torah (the first five books of the Hebrew Bible) that to love is, as some Jewish and Christian mystics later insisted, to empty the self, annihilate the will, and 'die to the world'.[9] On the contrary, it is not only legitimate to have interests, desires and needs – directed at enjoying the world rather than at negating it – but these are, according to the commandment, a benchmark for our treatment of others. The claims of our neighbour are on a level with ours and must be treated with the same moral seriousness. In early rabbinic literature, this is highlighted in the Mishnaic tractate, *Avot*: 'R. Eliezer said: Let the honour of thy fellow be as dear to thee as thine own'.[10] And the medieval exegete Nahmanides (1194–1270) comments that what is required 'is that one deem all of another's concerns as weighty as one's own'.[11]

Who are these others? Merely other Israelites, those who belong by lineage to one's nation? Certainly not. Love, in the Hebrew Bible, is also to embrace the alien.[12] The 'alien' is like today's naturalised immigrant or 'resident alien' – one who has joined the community and abides by its rules and customs.[13] Deuteronomy is explicit about this: 'You shall also love the stranger, for you were strangers in the land of Egypt' (10:19). Leviticus, shortly after commanding the Israelites that 'You shall not take vengeance or bear a grudge against any of your people, but you shall love your neighbour as yourself' (19:18), additionally insists: 'The alien who resides with you shall be to you as the citizen among you; you shall love the alien as yourself, for you were aliens in the land of Egypt' (19:34). And Exodus goes further: love is to be extended to your *enemy*; you are to love your neighbour equally whether he is friend or foe, native or alien, brother or stranger:

> When you come upon your enemy's ox or donkey going astray, you shall bring it back. When you see the donkey of one who hates you lying under its burden, and you would hold back from setting it free, you must help to set it free. (Exodus 23:4–5)

The wisdom of Proverbs similarly counsels us to generosity of feeling:

> If your enemies are hungry, give them bread to eat;
> and if they are thirsty, give them water to drink[.] (Proverbs 25:21)

Proverbs warns us, too, against delighting in the suffering or comeuppance of those who would harm us:

> Do not rejoice when your enemies fall
> and do not let your heart be glad when they stumble[.] (Proverbs 24:17)

With love for one's neighbour we have, therefore, the sort of impartiality and steadfastness that God – in one of his modes of being[14] – himself extends to his people as a whole: he 'is not partial and takes no bribe, executes justice for the orphan and the widow, and loves the strangers, providing them with food and clothing' (Deuteronomy 10:17–18). We are not to stand idly by if our neighbour's life is in danger (Leviticus 19:16),[15] nor to take advantage of others (Leviticus 25:17), but rather, in the words of the prophet Isaiah, to share what we have been given:

share your bread with the hungry,
and bring the homeless poor into your house;
when you see the naked . . . cover them[.] (Isaiah 58:7)

The 'neighbour' is to include the stranger and immigrant, but not necessarily all beyond the walls of community and nation.[16] Nor, as we will see, is love for neighbour in the Gospels necessarily aimed at all human beings. It is the modern world that reads strict universalism back into these texts, as their central feature. Indeed, not until the eighteenth century is a value regarded as having moral authority only if it is taken as a duty toward all people at all times.

I will return in subsequent chapters to the question of how universal the love commanded in Scripture – Jewish or Christian – really might be. But what we must note here, for it is fundamental to the history of Western love, is the remarkable and radical justice that underlies the love commandment of Leviticus. Not a cold justice in which due deserts are mechanically handed out, but a justice that brings the other, as an individual with needs and interests, into a relationship of respect. All our neighbours are to be recognised as equal to ourselves before the law of love. Justice and love therefore become inseparable.

HOW LOVE FOR GOD AND LOVE FOR NEIGHBOUR ARE RELATED

Love for God and neighbour, despite their strikingly different characters (including the different virtues internal to them), are intimately linked. The link arises from the idea, which we find in Genesis, that human beings are made in God's image:

So God created humankind in his image,
in the image of God he created them;
male and female he created them. (Genesis 1:27)[17]

Being made in God's image comes with the obligation to strive to imitate him. We are, as Deuteronomy repeatedly states, 'to walk in his ways' (28:9, 11:22 and 19:9).[18] And God himself commands: 'You shall be holy, for I the Lord your God am holy' (Leviticus 19:2). To love God is therefore to love whom God loves. It is to love our neighbour. And so immediately after we are told that God 'loves the strangers, providing them with food and clothing' we find humans exhorted to do likewise: 'You shall also love the stranger, for you were strangers in the land of Egypt' (Deuteronomy 10:18–19).

Indeed, only by imitating God are rituals of worship or the obeying of commandments filled with life and meaning. 'As God is merciful and compassionate, so too must you be merciful and compassionate'.[19] For if you treat others badly you offend not just them but God. 'Those who exploit the poor insult their Maker; but those who are kind to the needy honour Him' (Proverbs 14:31).[20] To deceive your neighbour about something entrusted to him is, at the same time, to be unfaithful to God.[21] The Talmud considers that even to call someone ugly is an insult to God, who is the designer and creator of the human form.[22] Again, we find this theme in the New Testament too, where at the day of judgement the King of Heaven tells sinners: 'Truly I tell you, just as you did it to one of the least of these who are members of my family, you did it to me' (Matthew 25:40).

The point of loving your neighbour as yourself is therefore, in the final analysis, not to create a more cohesive and efficient society, or to maximise happiness and contentment. It is simply to do as God does out of love for God, in whose image we – you and I and our neighbour in equal measure – are made. Love, we see here, has ethical force as a relation to the source of our being.

✦ ✦ ✦

Through these commandments – to love God 'with all your heart and with all your soul, and with all your might' and to 'love your neighbour as yourself' – Hebrew Scripture brings about three innovations of incalculable importance to the way we think about love today. One is to make love's goal divine: from now on the arrow of love shoots, as it were, for nothing less than God himself. Since the God of Hebrew Scripture is, or comes to be, the maximum possible God – the source and origin of everything that exists, and, unlike the Greek gods, without recognised rivals – this means that love for such a God is directed at the source and origin of all being and all value.

For this is what God is: the supreme, unknowable 'I am':

God said to Moses, 'I AM WHO I AM [or perhaps, more accurately translated, I WILL BE WHO I WILL BE[23]]. He said further, 'Thus you shall say to the Israelites, "I AM has sent me to you".' (Exodus 3:14)[24]

Indeed, God's very name, YHWH, comes to be explained by the Hebrew word meaning 'to be'.[25]

The second innovation of the Hebrew Bible lies in the command to imitate God: to walk in his ways, to love whom he loves: our neighbour. This is the principal source of the *imitatio dei*, which Christianity will so extensively develop.[26] But it is also the origin of that tremendous misunderstanding which led human beings to model their own loving on how they came to believe God loved them; for example, to think of their love for one another as unconditional and eternal and redemptive. It is a misunderstanding because God is radically different to us. His manner of loving us – and any unconditionality that we might see in it – cannot be ours. Our love is *always conditioned*: perhaps by God's love for us; perhaps by seeing our neighbour as God's creation; perhaps by secular conceptions of human dignity and human need.

And the third remarkable innovation brought about by the two love commandments is to turn love into a *moral duty* – something much more significant than a glorious feeling, a noble sentiment, a 'divine madness', a path to a flourishing life, or a force that 'makes the world go round'. Other pre-Christian systems of thought, such as Buddhism, Confucianism and Platonism, also made love – or expressions of love such as compassion, respect and desire for absolute beauty or goodness – a central value. But in none was it conceived as so overwhelming a command, issued by the one God in whom all power is concentrated. And so in none did it come to have the supreme significance that it has for the inheritors of Jewish monotheism: for the entire Christianised and Islamic worlds and their secular successors.

✦ ✦ ✦

The widespread belief that the Hebrew Bible is all about vengeance and 'an eye for an eye', while the Gospels supposedly invent love as an unconditional and universal value, must therefore count as one of the most extraordinary misunderstandings in all of Western history.[27] For the Hebrew Bible is the source not just of the two love commandments but of a larger moral vision inspired by wonder for love's power. 'Love covers all offences', says the Book of Proverbs (10:12).[28] 'Love is as strong as death',[29] exclaims the Song of Songs, the Bible's greatest erotic poem, and continues:

> passion fierce as the grave.
> Its flashes are flashes of fire,
> a raging flame.
> Many waters cannot quench love
> neither can floods drown it.
> If one offered for love all the wealth of one's house,
> it would be utterly scorned. (Song of Songs 8:6–7)

Generations of rabbis, in their extensive commentaries, elaborate on these themes. 'Do all that you do for the sake of love'.[30] 'By three things is the world sustained: by the Law, by the [Temple-]service, and by deeds of loving-kindness', says Simon the Righteous.[31] Rabbi Akiva teaches that love of neighbour is the supreme rule;[32] and the sage, Hillel, formulates the corresponding 'Golden Rule': 'What is hateful to you do not do to your neighbour; that is the whole *Torah*. The rest is commentary'.[33]

Hillel, it is said, formulates his sound bite only after a passing gentile challenges him to summarise the Torah while standing on one foot. But Hillel's instant response is hardly trite; it is directly echoed in the most famous formulation of the Golden Rule by a Jewish teacher, one born just a few decades later: Jesus of Nazareth.

> In everything do to others as you would have them do to you; for this is the law and the prophets. (Matthew 7:12)[34]

We see that, in this first formulation of the principle of love in the Gospels, Jesus explicitly acknowledges its origin in Jewish law. Through its dissemination by Christianity, Jewish Scripture gives the Western world both essential elements of what is later called 'Christian' love: on the one hand, altruistic love in which one gives of oneself to others without reserve or discrimination; on the other hand, passionate devotion to God and his commandments.

THE INVENTION OF 'AGAPE'

Yet this global dissemination of the moral law of a small nation might never have happened without the translation of the Torah into Greek, then the international language of much of the Mediterranean world – the world that we still think of as the cradle of Western civilisation. According to legend, in around 270 BCE the Egyptian pharaoh, Ptolemy II Philadelphus, invited a team of seventy-two Jewish scholars, six from each of the twelve tribes of ancient Israel, to undertake this vast translation. Though destined for the great library that he was establishing in Alexandria, its motive might have been political as well as literary: to recognise the importance of Jews in Egypt by conveying their biblical traditions in the only language that many of them understood, Greek.[35]

Translations are one of the great catalysts of world revolution. The epic pedantry and erudition of those who labour on them, sometimes for decades, have supplied the texts for many of history's upheavals. Without Bishop Ulfillas (c. 311–c. 383), an Aryan-Goth missionary in Constantinople who translated the Bible into Gothic, the German tribes might never have converted to Christianity and so we might have had no Holy Roman Empire and all the European history that followed it. Without Luther's German translation of the New Testament there might have been no Reformation and therefore, according to the sociologist Max Weber, no rise of capitalism (and hence no modern world) as we know it. And without the 'Septuagint', as this translation of the Torah into Greek became known because of its seventy-plus translators, the thought of the Hebrews might never have reached the various authors of the New Testament who wrote in Greek, and so the whole world that would become Christendom. Indeed, for most of the first century after Jesus's birth, the Christian Bible was nothing other than Hebrew Scriptures as translated in the Septuagint.[36] History, to paraphrase the philosopher Franz Rosenzweig, is sometimes looked up in a dictionary.

Crucially, the various Hebrew words for love – whether erotic or neighbourly, whether for God or for humans – were mostly translated in the Septuagint as 'agape', until then an infrequently used term.[37] As a result of its adoption by Christianity, agape becomes one of the most influential words ever coined. We will see in chapter 6 that – again contrary to widespread belief – Jesus himself is seldom reported as speaking of love, whether in terms of agape or not; and that agape is rather used by St Paul and other founders of Christianity who wrote, and quoted Hebrew Scripture, in Greek.[38] And so it gradually became

the word that refers to the unconditional, altruistic, obedient, humble selflessness with which 'Christian love' has become clearly – but, as I will argue in
chapter 7, far from accurately – identified.

Though its commands to love God and neighbour are the Hebrew Bible's
supreme statements on love, it has a lot more to say on the subject – including
on love as erotic passion and love in the sense of intimate friendship. In the
marvellous music of the Song of Songs, the young woman declaims:

> Let him kiss me with the kisses of his mouth!
> For your love is better than wine,
> your anointing oils are fragrant,
> your name is perfume poured out;
> therefore the maidens love you. (1:2–3)

And her lover answers:

> How fair and pleasant you are,
> O loved one, delectable maiden!
> You are stately as a palm tree
> and your breasts are like its clusters.
> I say I will climb the palm tree
> and lay hold of its branches.
> O may your breasts be like the clusters of the vine,
> and the scent of your breath like apples,
> and your kisses like the best wine . . . (Song of Songs 7:6–9)[39]

The language of erotic love that we encounter in this poem infuses human
love for God too. The Hebrew Bible nowhere expresses the enormous anxiety
about sex that is found in the Christian tradition (less in what Jesus is reported
as saying in the Gospels than in dogmas that developed after his death, especially with Augustine). Loving husbandry of nature – including our human
sexual nature – is far closer to the spirit of Hebrew Scripture than is denigration
of sex, the body, or the natural world more generally, which Christianity takes

primarily from *pagan* sources, especially Platonism. All creation is an emanation of God, and so can be loved as God's self-communication.[40] In Genesis, where we are told in detail of the stages in which God created the earth and light and sky and animals and humans and in each case 'saw that it was good' (Genesis 1:4–31), it is clear that nature is to be loved, if not to be clung to. Indeed, someone entering a temple must have an unblemished body: 'No one', Deuteronomy announces, 'whose testicles are crushed or whose penis is cut off shall be admitted to the assembly of the Lord' (Deuteronomy 23:1).[41]

✦ ✦ ✦

We also find in Hebrew Scripture instances of an almost erotic passion for friends. Two of history's most celebrated friendships – both of them same-sex – take place here. These are the friendships of Jonathan and David and of Ruth and Naomi, narrated in language whose tones are sensuous even if physical consummation is out of the question and indeed punishable by death.

David, the handsome young warrior who slays the Philistine giant Goliath with only a stone hurled from a sling, is received by King Saul after his triumph. The king's eldest son, Jonathan, sees David and is at once smitten: 'When David had finished speaking to Saul, the soul of Jonathan was bound to the soul of David, and Jonathan loved him as his own soul' (1 Samuel 18:1).

Nor was Jonathan bashful about declaring his love. He at once removed his robe and armour, and offered them to David.[42] He then swore eternal fidelity to David: 'Jonathan made a covenant with David, because he loved him as his own soul' (1 Samuel 18:3).[43]

Interestingly, David does not seem to reciprocate the intensity of Jonathan's love, which perhaps reflects the reality of most passionate relationships: that love isn't precisely requited. Nonetheless, when Jonathan is suddenly killed on Mount Gilboa by the Philistines (1 Samuel 31:2), David expresses intense grief, saying: 'I am distressed for you, my brother Jonathan; greatly beloved were you to me; your love to me was wonderful, [sur]passing the love of women' (2 Samuel 1:26).

Surpassing the love of the opposite sex. Loving another as one's own soul. Strikingly similar sentiments also enter Christianity (and Western love more widely) from the Greek world, especially in the form of Aristotle's concept of perfect *philia* or friendship-love; but, remaining with Hebrew Scripture, we see them too in Ruth's declaration of love for Naomi, which appears closer to a sworn vow of fidelity than any marriage between a man and a woman described in the Bible.

> Do not press me to leave you
> or to turn back from following you!
> Where you go I will go,
> where you lodge I will lodge;
> your people shall be my people,
> and your God my God;
> Where you die I will die – there will I be buried.
> May the Lord do thus and so to me,
> and more as well,
> if even death parts me from you. (Ruth 1:16–17)

They are far from being spouses. Naomi is Ruth's mother-in-law, the mother of her deceased husband. Ruth is also from another ethnic group, the Moabites, and movingly shows us a passionate friendship that transcends ethnic and religious and family origins, and that welcomes an outsider into the family as one of its own.

Not only as one of its own, but as the producer of an all-important heir. Ruth's devotion – as in a marriage vow 'till death do us part' – is expressed above all in her performance of a sacred duty, which is to provide Naomi, and Naomi's dead son, with a successor. She does this by marrying Boaz, a relative of her deceased husband, and giving Naomi a child named Obed. In doing so Ruth rescues Naomi from her grief, and even seems content for Naomi to regard the child as her own. The women of Bethlehem rejoice, and they congratulate Naomi as if she herself had just given birth: 'Then Naomi took the child and laid him in her bosom, and became his nurse' as the women declare 'A son has been born to Naomi' (Ruth 4:16–17).

Though Ruth and Naomi both gain something they want, their friendship-love is, or becomes, much more than that: uncompromising dedication to the welfare of the other; powerful identification with her life. Through such loyalty and kindness – *hesed* – one who was born a non-Jew founds a line that culminates in the most famous of all Israelite kings, King David, Ruth's great-grandson: poet, lover of women, harpist and singer, and the statesman who united Israel's twelve tribes and established its capital in Jerusalem.

+ + +

Many contemporary readers will recoil from the intensity of this devotion. Naomi seems to be 'crossing borders' here. Not even in secret, but to the crowd's applause. Family solidarity, parent-child intimacy, the sisterhood of strangers, and close friendship all blur into each other and seem marked with a passion that verges on the erotic – though there is no evidence that they, or Jonathan and David, had what we would today call an actively gay relationship.

But if we think that these friends are crossing borders this is because we are thinking of love in an artificially compartmentalised way. We tend (especially under the influence of Lutheran theology) to distinguish Eros-love – love as passionate desire, which longs for the delights of intimacy and even union with the loved one – from friendship-love – a more temperate, just and reciprocal devotion to the welfare of another whom we experience as a 'second self'; and to separate both these 'types' of love in turn from love as self-giving – the altru- istic and unreserved placing of oneself at the disposal of the other. We assign Eros-love to romantic lovers; we ask – it has become almost a cliché to do so – whether lovers can also be friends, or whether they lack the sobriety and concern for each other's well-being needed for friendship; and we think of self-giving love as typified by parents' relationships to their children, charity towards strangers, or genuine devotion to God.[44]

Yet, I argue in this book, these are not separate types of love but the three key modes of attention or engagement of *all* passionate love – whether for friends, children, parents, lovers or spouses. Though they might be expressed in different ways and to different degrees in these various relationships, they are always alive. We arguably see all three in the love of Jonathan for David and, in a more qualified way, of Ruth for Naomi. More importantly, we see all three modes of attention in Israel's love for God, sometimes spoken of in rapturous-erotic tones redolent of the Song of Songs, sometimes in terms of the devotion, favour and conversational intimacy of friendship, sometimes in terms of unre-served submission to the will of the loved one – a will that speaks of the laws of his being.

This means that in Hebrew Scripture love for God is very far from involving the debasement of the self, the destruction of the ego, that some later traditions,

Jewish and Christian, demand. The twentieth-century theologian and philosopher Martin Buber puts this point in modern terms when he says that all real
relationship 'is a bridge that spans across two firm pillars, man's "I" and the "I"
of his eternal partner.' Judaism, Buber continues,

> rejects the 'I' that connotes selfishness and pride, but it welcomes and affirms
> the 'I' of the real relationship, the 'I' of the partnership between I and Thou,
> the 'I' of love. For love does not invalidate the 'I'; on the contrary, it binds the
> 'I' more closely to the 'Thou'.[45]

This robustness of the loving 'I' is not surprising. Loving involves a relationship
of one's own self to another's in which every power of attention and affirmation
comes into play. How could such an orientation possibly involve crushing the self?
To submit to the laws of the other, whether it be God or another person; to favour
and praise their unique existence; to desire them in the language that we have seen
in the Song of Songs: this is the highest exercise of the will when purified of whatever destroys our capacity to attend to another being – and above all, of the
obstructions created by pride.

LOVE AND SUBMISSION

But now we need to take a deeper look at what we can learn from Hebrew
Scripture about this paradox of love to which I just alluded: that in love the
highest exercise of the will is to be found in submission to the other – to their
will; to the lawfulness of their being. For submission is central to the love for
God that Hebrew Scripture commands – and at the limit, after all interpretation
and interrogation of the meaning of God's will have been exhausted, this
submission is to be unquestioning. Israel's duty to love God, conceived as the
source of all being and value, involves absolute obedience to his law. One must
obey regardless of whether one finds his commands beneficial or even just.

Here Hebrew Scripture differs drastically from Greek thought, the other great
source of Western ideas about love. For Greeks like Plato and Aristotle love is a
natural desire to possess, or cultivate, or be united with, goodness or virtue.
Nature – including human nature and the conditions for its flourishing – is
the ultimate standard for laws and decisions about what is good and bad;
and for many Greeks nature in the widest sense constrains even the gods. In

contrast, for Hebrew Scripture (and Christian after it), the law is determined only by God and his revelation. One must love God irrespective of considerations of welfare and in defiance of any conflicting goods that nature might offer. To love God is also to fear and obey him – though, as I will suggest, the fear and obedience of a genuine agent involves making the other's law one's own: involves, that is, a profound engagement with what his presence demands of us. And this can, in the end, mean doing things one detests or finds immoral. It would make no sense to say that one loves God with all one's heart and soul and might, but nonetheless decides, case-by-case, whether to ignore or follow his will.

✦ ✦ ✦

The way in which obedience to God trumps every other value, including every other love, is epitomised by none other than the father of the Jewish people, Abraham, with whom God makes his first Covenant and to whom he promises the land of Israel. One day, and quite abruptly, God orders Abraham to sacrifice his son Isaac. He not only leaves Abraham in the dark about the purpose of this terrible order but rubs in the point that Isaac is Abraham's beloved and only son:

> After these things God tested Abraham. He said to him, 'Abraham!' And he said, 'Here I am.' He said, 'Take your son, your only son Isaac, whom you love, and go to the land of Moriah and offer him there as a burnt-offering on one of the mountains that I shall show you.' (Genesis 22:1–2)

Without, it seems, the slightest resistance, without any apparent search for explanations or justifications, Abraham takes his son to the place where God tells him the sacrifice must happen. It isn't as if Abraham has no time to agonise. God makes him travel to Mount Moriah, a three-day journey, bind Isaac, lay him upon an altar, and slay him. But then, just as Abraham raises his knife over his son, he finds his hand stayed by an angel, a messenger of God. Again, he obeys the divine order, without expressing surprise or even relief at the abrupt change of plan. And again he seeks neither to explain nor to justify.

But why does this make Abraham a hero? Isn't his obedience revolting? And what kind of God could it please? What kind of God could command a man to murder both his son and his sense of what it is right and just to do?[46] This sounds like religion at its most perverse, leading human beings, including great and noble human beings like Abraham, to do evil for the sake of what they take to be God's will and to imagine themselves blessed by doing so. This is the sort of faith that puts allegiance to God before humanity to our fellows, shows no remorse or compassion for the suffering it causes, and desires no explanation for its actions beyond the need, as it sees it, for obedience to supreme power. Worse, Abraham, unlike a Crusader, an Inquisitionist, or a suicide bomber, doesn't even consider his victim deficient or guilty. Isaac, for his part, is meekly compliant, travelling to his place of slaughter without ever questioning his father's actions. And God seems not only cruel but hypocritical, for this same God issues a command to all humanity not to murder and then demands that the Father of the Jewish people, indeed the Father of the three Abrahamic religions – Judaism, Christianity and Islam – a moral exemplar if ever there was one, do exactly that.

In ethical terms, these are all valid points. God *is* making it clear that, at the limit, obedience to him is to trump the very morality that he commands: you shall not kill. He *is* demanding the sacrifice of Abraham's will or spirit – and especially of what in modern terms would be called 'autonomous moral will'; and indeed this is precisely the sacrifice that Abraham actually ends up making and that God does not countermand. This points to one of the Torah's most radical innovations: that henceforth one is to offer up to God not so much material things, like animals or gold, as one's whole inner world – that labyrinth of intentions, desires and moral intuitions of which one's actions are merely very rough expressions. The Torah does not just prohibit such explicit actions as lying, stealing, incest, deception, and bearing false witness.[47] It also penetrates to one's most secret emotions and thoughts: 'You shall not hate in your heart anyone of your kin' (Leviticus 19:17); 'You shall not take vengeance or bear a grudge' (Leviticus 19:18); 'You shall not covet your neighbour's house' (Exodus 20:17). And dramatically in Proverbs: 'The human spirit is the lamp of the Lord,/ searching every inmost part' (Proverbs, 20:27).

This extraordinary demand to sacrifice will or spirit, rather than material goods, is perfectly expressed in Psalm 51, later cited with approval by St Augustine:

> O Lord, open my lips,
> and my mouth will declare your praise.
> For you have no delight in sacrifice;
> if I were to give a burnt-offering, you would not be pleased.

The sacrifice acceptable to God is a broken spirit;
a broken and contrite heart[.][48]

The prophet Samuel echoes this call for obedience – and listening:

Has the Lord as great delight in
burnt offerings and sacrifices,
as in obedience to the voice of the Lord?
Surely, to obey is better than sacrifice,
and to heed than the fat of rams. (1 Samuel 15:22)

Or as Psalm 40:6 states: 'Sacrifice and offering you do not desire,/but you have
given me an open ear.' (It is striking how listening seems to be the dominant
idiom in the Old Testament, unlike the New, where sight – seeing Jesus, seeing
miracles, and in general witnessing – is so prominent, perhaps as a result of
the latter's Greek influences.) The ultimate loyalty that Abraham shows is, of
course, rare and hard, as God laments:

What shall I do with you, O Ephraim?
What shall I do with you, O Judah?
Your love is like a morning cloud,
like the dew that goes away early. (Hosea 6:4)

And further:

For I desire steadfast love and not sacrifice,
the knowledge of God rather than burnt offerings. (Hosea 6:6)

✦ ✦ ✦

Abraham's obedience looks mindless. But is it?

If we look more carefully we will see that Abraham has sacrificed his will only
in the sense that he obeys God's command. In another sense, he has anything but
abandoned it: for he has assented – and assented in the deepest possible way,
with what today we would call his whole conscience – to this stance of obedience.
Conscience cannot obstruct obedience if conscience itself demands it.

To say that Abraham's obedience is dictated by his conscience is to say that it
is dictated by his deepest values. For what else is conscience but a hierarchy of

our own deepest values, those that structure us, define us, and cannot be substituted or argued away by us? And what else are the deliberations of conscience than attempts to understand the demands of this hierarchy in the concrete situations we face in our actual lives? So if conscience's highest value is always obedience to God's commandment then conscience itself, including all its powers of reflection and reasoning, will unhesitatingly endorse that obedience. (This has nothing to do with the obedience of the zombie, whose internalisation of a command is cold and lifeless and who has no conscience because he has no hierarchy of values that he has made his own.)

Hebrew Scripture in effect proclaims obedience to God as a supreme virtue, and so seems to advance the paradoxical formula: 'You will find freedom by abandoning your capricious will to the law of God. You will be powerful over the world by submission to the Absolute. You will find your self by sacrificing yourself'. This sacrifice, far from being resigned, makes God's command one that you assent and commit to 'with all your heart, and with all your soul, and with all your might' (Deuteronomy 6:5). To obey out of a deep assent of your whole being – including of your conscience and its capacity for reasoning and reflection – is to obey in freedom. Indeed, it is for obedience to become the path to freedom. And to selfhood.

Again we shouldn't dodge the dilemma: this can also be the road to moral perversity. Here the atheists are right: if piety trumps all, then however much theologians insist that we can 'interpret' biblical texts in the light of humane values, or inform our ideas of God with a morality of respect for the dignity, equal value, and diversity of all human life – ideas which can themselves be culled from some if not all passages of Scripture – the reality is that this morality will necessarily lose out if it happens to conflict with obedience to divine commands. Surrendering to absolute commands that are to be obeyed no matter what, is the womb of inhumanity and totalitarianism. Even if those commands have human welfare as their goal.

Theology can try to solve this unpleasant problem by either reinterpreting the offending biblical texts in the light of humane values or else sidelining them as 'products of their day' that speak in a language to which we can no longer connect. Or it can fudge the issue by declaring them 'mysteries' beyond human understanding. Religions will always claim that such solutions can be found. Atheists, citing the evil done in the name of religion from the Crusades to the Inquisition to September 11th, will always disagree. It is a debate without terminus.

But what the piety of monotheistic religion – beginning with Hebrew Scripture and its magnificent commandment to love God – does teach us and what cannot be argued away is that loving demands unreserved submission to the laws of the ultimately inscrutable loved one. That meaningful relationship to another presupposes obedience through which we make his law our own – even if it also involves much argument and sporadic turning away. If so, the conclusion is clear: love, precisely through its unlimited respect for the loved one, *is* potentially as immoral as the willingness of Abraham to kill his son – with the full assent of his conscience. Love *is* prepared to suspend humane morality and conscience towards others if the supreme beloved demands it. It will, like Abraham, be ready to kill whatever else is sacred to it.

But this very suspension enables love to be so creative of life: to unleash the will to value, defend, affirm, empathise with, and give to the supremely loved one in the most intense way possible. This terrible inner law of love – that it is prepared to suspend morality towards all in order to reach the highest morality towards one – is what Hebrew Scripture faces head on. From here leads the long thread to nineteenth-century Romanticism that I will trace through much of this book.

The sufferings of Job provide a possibly even more remarkable parable of what it is to submit – to sacrifice – one's will. For, unlike Abraham, Job's trials are tortuously long.[49] And though they might seem to have a happy ending – God finally gives Job peace and progeny in abundance: 'twice as much as he had before' (Job 42:10) – these gifts hardly erase Job's losses, above all of his children. This is no narrative of suffering made good.

Which is exactly the point that the story makes: submission, which is at the heart of the love-relationship, is not genuine if it expects just deserts or redemption from suffering. Job is not a deviant who is being punished for refusing to obey God's laws: on the contrary, he respects them scrupulously. God even lets it be known, *before* the misery starts, that Job is 'blameless and upright, one who feared God and turned away from evil' (Job 1:1). Moreover his anguish is 'for no reason' (Job 2:3). The misery is to lose almost everything he cherishes: his animals, his servants, and, worst of all, his seven sons and three daughters. As a coda to this treatment he is inflicted with painful sores that break out all over his body, at which he futilely scrapes away with pieces of broken pottery.

None of this unjustified suffering elicits the slightest sympathy from the God of Justice, who has, it would seem, allowed at least two of his own commandments to be broken in the process: against murder and theft. And yet, though Job protests his innocence, laments that his suffering has made his life worthless, wishes that he had never been born and longs for death, his immediate reaction is one of acceptance and piety: 'Naked I came from my mother's womb, and naked shall I return there; the Lord gave, and the Lord has taken away; blessed be the name of the Lord' (Job 1:21).

When Job's friends hear of his misfortunes they come to visit him, mourn his losses and strive to console him. For seven days and seven nights they remain by his side as he sits on an ash heap and scrapes his sores. But their consolations only worsen Job's anguish: he cries out that he doesn't deserve his punishment – and if he does God should tell him why; he questions God's justice and goodness; he laments that the innocent suffer calamities and that 'the earth is given into the hand of the wicked' (Job 9:24).

His friends tell him that this cannot be so. His suffering, they explain, must have a cause: he surely sinned to deserve all this. Since there is no meaningless suffering he must be guilty. Reward and punishment are central to God's order. As one of the friends, Eliphaz, asks: 'Think now, who that was innocent ever perished?/ Or where were the upright cut off?' (Job 4:7).

Yet Job's ordeal hints at some profound things about God, and so about how to love God – and how to love in general. We receive good – indeed we receive life itself – at the hands of this supremely loved one, but we also receive bad. We receive the greatest loving kindness but also the worst cruelty. We receive a promise to uphold our life and being, and at the same time we are meted out appalling 'injustice' – against which we have no recourse.

This, I suggest, is true of all genuine love. A real relationship with one whom we experience as grounding our being – or even as the source of our being, like God or a parent or a landscape or a nation – demands stubborn acceptance and offers no predictable or calculable benefits. Within a love-relationship negotiation is out of the question. As God says, 'I will be gracious to whom I will be gracious, and will show mercy on whom I will show mercy' (Exodus 33:19).[50] Questions about why the beloved deals us the hand that he does, or about whether he is morally justified in doing so, are pointless. We affirm the object of our love – be it God, another person, or life itself – most truly when we do not even *try* to justify its ways.

Job doesn't seek to justify or even explain what God does. Instead, as we have seen, he magnificently says: 'The Lord gave and the Lord has taken away; blessed be the name of the Lord' (Job 1:21). He could decide there is no God, for if God existed the world wouldn't be so unjust. Instead he affirms God's existence: 'I know that my Redeemer lives' (Job 19:25).[51] Or he could give up the struggle to live such a nightmarish life, curse God and die, as his wife at one point urges him to do.[52] But he answers her with one of his profoundest remarks about the acceptance that is at the heart of the genuine love-relationship: 'Shall we receive the good at the hand of God, not receive the bad?' (Job 2:10).

Above all, Job doesn't search for a 'meaning' to suffering. Instead he points to an ideal of how to be, *given* the existence of suffering. This is the ideal of doing without answers to the questions, 'Why suffering?', and 'What is the meaning of my suffering?' Indeed it is the still harder ideal of not *asking* the question in the first place – of being strong enough to live without clinging even to the unanswered question.

When God comes to speak he mocks the whole idea that anyone can fathom the universe deeply enough to determine what is justified and what isn't. And when he finally restores Job's fortunes and 'blesse[s] the latter days of Job more than his beginning' (Job 42:12), this appears not to be because Job has prayed for this outcome[53] or because any other conditions for happiness have now been fulfilled. On the contrary, the blessing, like the suffering, happens because it happens.

The question 'Why is there innocent suffering?' is the wrong question from within the standpoint of submission to, and fear of, God. Which means: from within the standpoint of love. To love God is to accept that. As Abraham also accepted it.

WHY LOVE GOD?

But what is it about God that evokes such love from his people – that causes them to respond, if sporadically and very imperfectly, to his command to love him?

The answer seems to be: it is his power over them, for good or ill – his power, as they perceive it, to give them life or to take it away, to enhance or to diminish their being, to give them or to deny them a place in the world (including the moral world). Scripture's injunction to love God is uninhibitedly linked to his absolute power over exactly these ultimate matters of existence.

This is why fear of God is so central to Hebrew Scripture. All great love involves fear (though, of course, not all fear involves love). For loss of the loved one is always a possibility, and so arouses fear even before the lover has actually suffered it. So too is our vulnerability to violence and vengeance by the loved one.[54] Especially when he is unpredictable.

But greater still than the fear of losing God is the fear of *seeing* him. One who possesses such immense power over our existence will inspire awe that easily threatens to overwhelm us, even if we believe he will never abandon or destroy us. As in Kant's concept of the 'sublime' we stand, exalted and humbled, before the '*absolutely great*'.[55] Its grandeur makes us feel both powerful and powerless – not just to possess the loved one – but in our existence itself: the existence which we yearn for love to anchor. To be in a relationship of love is, in other words, always to be in a relationship of fear; indeed, the greater the love the greater the fear.

✦ ✦ ✦

Much of this is not to our contemporary taste, for we are too deeply committed to the view, Greek in origin, that genuine love is evoked only by the good, that it pursues only the good, and that it fosters only the good. And that its attainment is marked by harmony and stability and understanding. On this view, if we love evil-doers it is for the specks of good that we see in them. Or, if we fall in love with destructive people, this is not genuine love but the result of a 'pathological' repetition of childhood relationships with destructive parents or of masochistic drives.

But if we look more carefully we will see that this isn't true. Why do hostages often end up not just sympathising and identifying with their captors (the so-called 'Stockholm Syndrome'), but actually loving them? Why does a child instinctively love and defend his parents before he is old enough to know whether they are good or bad – indeed before he has the concepts of good and bad? Why can the adult continue loving even a parent whom he discovers has seriously violated him or others? Why do many oppressed peoples love, rather than merely venerate, their murderous leaders – and weep in vast numbers, openly and genuinely, at their funerals – perhaps more than free peoples do? (Here we cannot ignore, for example, the extraordinary outpouring of feeling for Stalin by so many who lived through his Great Terror; the sincere grief of millions at his death cannot be put down merely to fear or propaganda or slavish loyalty, for it betrays many of the features of love: transformational devotion, self-sacrifice, submission, listening, affirmation, longing for closeness, tenderness of feeling, awe before his unreachable otherness.) If one says, 'Well, all this just isn't love,' then one ignores the great dangers inherent in human love at its most genuine.

Many of the conventional answers won't do here: it is not 'common humanity' that we love in such monsters; nor is it any ethical or cultural similarities to us that we detect in them; nor is it the ray of goodness in their dark souls; nor that they are also 'God's children'. It is, quite simply, our belief in their ontological power: their power to give or take away our life and being. Including power that arises from evil or does evil.

LOVE AND 'ONTOLOGICAL ROOTEDNESS'

Hebrew Scripture evokes a truer picture of the *motives* for love – not just for love's initial inspiration, but for its endurance and maturation – than any of the other traditions that have shaped Western conceptions of love. The people of Israel love God out of faith in his ontological *power*, though they can know him only dimly if at all: they love him as their creator and origin; as the arbiter of their survival and flourishing; and – by releasing them from slavery and bestowing law and land – as giving them a clear place in the world.

God loves them as the guardians of his law; and his 'choosing' of them to receive the law, given to Moses on Mount Sinai, is itself an act of his love, yet with the crucial proviso that it cannot be explained by any special merit on Israel's part.[56] Like the Creation, God's original act of love, it is an expression of his ultimately inscrutable and sovereign will – and to that extent unconditional. (Here is the origin of the idea of 'grace', later to be so central to Christian ideas of love.)

And, of course, this same God who gives life and law can also act with extraordinary cruelty and, on the face of it, injustice. He can be jealous, vindictive and vengeful.[57] He can vanish, leaving his people in the lurch in their moments of greatest peril, from the destruction of the second temple in the first century CE to the expulsion from Spain in the fifteenth to Hitler's Holocaust in the twentieth. He offers a love, in the form of the Covenant at Sinai, which is unconditional in the sense that his people do not and cannot deserve it, but which, after it has been given, can also be conditioned by their behaviour. (Indeed in the Torah it is hard to find clear instances where God reaches out spontaneously to Israel when it has failed him – and it often takes the intercession of a figure like Moses for God to renew his love for his people.[58]) They are nonetheless to love him with all their heart and soul and might, though they can never count on his presence when they need him. They must, in principle, be prepared for their love to be unrequited.

This is how all love works. Like Israel's love for God, love does not need deep knowledge of the other in order to be evoked and sustained – though, once inspired, it might seek such knowledge. Love is evoked not by beauty or moral goodness (in the sense of kindness) but by the mysterious promise of the loved one to anchor and sustain one's life, such that one can feel at home in the world. Love can never count on requital or justice – and it is perhaps most genuinely love if it doesn't. It is always a movement into a future made uncertain by the opaque and changeable nature of the loved one – and by the fact that any love he shows us always has its conditions, even if the magnitude of its gifts or the intensity of our response to them seems to suggest that it is unconditional. It seeks to affirm and obey the innate lawfulness of the loved one – the lawfulness that speaks of his being (what Heraclitus, speaking of the law of Being or Cosmos as a whole, called the *logos*).

✦ ✦ ✦

Here, in Israel's love for its God, we see the paradigm example of the search for what, in chapter 1, I called 'ontological rootedness'. The loved one has the power to inspire – or undermine – in the lover the sense that he exists as a real, legitimate and sustainable being; the sense that there is a place for him in the universe even if he will never manage to occupy it. In the extreme case, as with parents, hostage-takers, all-powerful rulers, very great romantic or friendship-loves, and, above all, the Hebrew God, this is the power over life or death itself.

Love, as I argue throughout this book, centrally involves the experience of being related to such a power – which is why religion, especially monotheism, and, even more especially, monotheism that hasn't been sweetened by the pretence that God is an all-good, all-forgiving, all-tolerant, all-protective father, has so much to teach us about it. Love involves the faith that the loved one can affirm, nourish and anchor our being (and so is always accompanied by the fear that he will disappear, or will fail to exercise this power, or will do so destructively). And it involves the willingness to pay a tremendously high price for this supreme good – a price that might seem perverse to an outsider but is of little consequence to one who experiences the promise of ontological rootedness.

There is no greater human need than to find such affirmation, nourishment and anchoring of one's being, and we can secure it only through relationships to a world in which we are embedded. This is why when we think we have discovered someone – or indeed something, like a vocation or art or nature – with ontological power over us we lunge at it with such overwhelming desire. It is also why we can fall (and remain) in love not only with those who would use their power to affirm and enhance our lives, but also – even precisely – with those who regard us as enemies, or with people whose wealth inspires a sense (robust or not) of ontological rootedness, or with fraudsters who give us illusory confidence in ourselves, or with others who might destroy us, or with those whose love for us we permanently doubt. The sorts of people whom we believe to have ontological power over us begin with our parents and extend in later life to all those at whose mercy our identity, our security, our flourishing, perhaps even our existence, seem to lie.[59] Our faith in the power of such people over us forges the *trust* at the heart of intense love: the trust to submit to a law whose inner workings – as Abraham and Job and the people of Israel knew all too well – we cannot ultimately understand or justify.

3

From physical desire to paradise
Plato

Plato conceived love for a beautiful body as the beginning of a long path that ends in paradise. He is responsible for one of the defining obsessions of the Western mind: that Eros can storm the heavens, ascending from physical desire to spiritual understanding, from the finite to the infinite, from the contingent to the absolute.

At the core of this obsession is an excruciating demand: spiritual love must overcome the very desires for bodily gratification in which it originates, and ultimately overcome the very conditions of life itself – time, space, and suffering. It is to overcome them *not* by suppressing or extirpating erotic desire – 'Platonic love' never does this – but by a refinement of desire that directs it from physical beauty towards divine beauty.

Through such refinement the lover attains godlike freedom from the deficiencies of raw Eros – or raw passionate desire: its capacity for jealousy, anger, neediness and vulnerability;[1] its demeaning crudeness; its contamination by time and flesh and mortality. From being the blindest of desires love becomes the most clear-sighted.

Ultimately, the lover sees his individual flourishing in a contemplation of beauty that transcends all individuality. Love becomes embroiled in a remarkable paradox: Eros, the great life force, desires nothing more than to transcend the fundamental conditions of life.

❖ ❖ ❖

Greeks before Plato had seen love as a great human and even cosmic force, but none of their surviving texts attributes such vast ethical significance to it.

Empedocles (*c.* 492–*c.* 432 BCE), for example, had claimed that love and strife govern the universe, whose four elements – earth, air, fire, and water – they keep in constant flux. When love dominates, these elements come together in an intimate commingling; when strife gets the upper hand they are dispersed again into four distinct masses.[2] The cycle of change is never-ending and though love can prevail for a period it will eventually be overwhelmed by strife:

> And they never will cease from continuous interchange,
> now by Love all coming together into one,
> now again each carried apart by the enmity of Strife.[3]

Others were in awe of love as a demonic force that overpowered gods as well as humans. 'Love . . . not even the deathless gods can flee your onset, nothing human born for a day – whoever feels your grip is driven mad', says the Chorus in Sophocles' *Antigone*. 'You wrench the minds of the righteous into outrage'.[4] But when – before Plato – people or gods succumbed to this force, sacrificed everything for love, or started wars for love, they didn't necessarily experience their desire sexually to possess the body of another person as the beginning of a spiritual quest for absolute beauty and goodness. The Trojan wars, recounted by Homer, were all about the overwhelming desire of one man (Paris) for a married woman (Helen of Troy) and the hell he was prepared to put whole peoples through in order to keep her. This playboy didn't, however, think of his love for Helen in ethical terms; nor did he see it as merely a pleasurable stopover on a more serious spiritual journey.

And then Plato, drawing on older traditions, probably including Orphism and other mystery religions, broke radically from this. He developed the idea that love, precisely as a spiritual endeavour, is key to becoming a flourishing individual. He prepared the ground for love to become the supreme virtue, trumping more traditional virtues like courage and honour – even if it would be left to others to take this next step. He gave love a privileged role in attaining that old human dream: an ideal realm of purity and peace free of life's messiness, its intractability, its wrecking of hard-won achievements, its indifference and cruelty.

✦ ✦ ✦

Plato made this radical move by (as was his custom) posing a seemingly innocuous question.

Isn't it a shame, he asks near the beginning of his great book on love, the *Symposium*, that 'not one in all the multitude of poets has ever composed a single panegyric of so ancient and mighty a god as Love?'[5] Though learned men have praised, sometimes at length, the usefulness of things like salt, they haven't had the courage to give love its due.

This question is a key moment in the history of love. For in the *Symposium* – the first extended discussion of love in Western philosophy and, together with the commands from Deuteronomy and Leviticus, the most influential text on love in the Western world – we find four powerful images of love, each of them easily recognisable by us today.

1. Love makes us 'whole' as individuals. I will not be myself without my 'other half'. (Plato effectively introduced these now hackneyed terms.)

2. Love is aroused by beauty. Beauty is not just about someone's physical charms: it is about their beauty of character, the beauty of their soul, the beauty of their virtuous deeds – and therefore about their goodness.[6] I can admire or appreciate or covet what I don't find beautiful, but I can't *love* it.[7]

3. Love enables us to get beyond a superficial relation to things – people, nature, objects – to what is absolutely valuable about them.

4. Love brings the best out of us as lovers – above all, virtue and wisdom. Though it begins in sexual attraction, the highest love enables us to give birth to what is noblest in us – to true virtue.

These ideas about love are articulated by various participants at the symposium, each of whom gives a short speech about love. In Greece, a symposium was not a meeting in a dank university lecture hall where thoughts secretly turn to sex, but rather a high-society dinner party, where food was followed by plentiful alcohol (*symposium* literally means 'drinking together'), and the guests, all of them men, reclined on couches, served by slaves and entertained by flute-girls who, not uncommonly, were also available for sex. It was also an occasion on which the guests might seek intellectual inspiration in erotic beauty and often in not only fantasising about, but actually fondling, a beautiful youth.

The beautiful youth is, of course, male. And the love that is discussed at this symposium tends to have homosexuality as its background. Most of the speakers take it for granted that only homosexual love between a man and a youth is conducive to the noblest aspirations, such as the pursuit of learning, politics and refined manners. Such love, we learn, can trigger a lifelong intellectual friendship between two people of similar nature, in which sex will be replaced by a 'pregnancy of the soul', a wide-ranging creativity from which virtuous acts, laws, poems, glorious deeds, and other immortal offspring can issue.[8]

By contrast, some of the speakers – but as we will see by no means all – regard heterosexual love as altogether inferior: a largely bodily impulse whose chief value is physical procreation. Love between a man and a woman, these speakers hold, is no starting point for spiritual growth. To the point where, if an older man were to desire a younger woman in this way – in other words for sexual intimacy leading to spiritual friendship and pregnancy of the soul – they might both need to pretend that she is a boy, or at least ignore the fact that she isn't.[9] Baudelaire might have been making such a Platonic point when he wrote that 'Loving intelligent women is a pederastic pleasure'.

Homosexual love existed mainly among the upper classes – those who had the freedom and leisure for pursuits like politics or philosophy or discussions at a symposium. And it was quite common for its devotees also to be heterosexual and to have wives at home, though marriage was rarely for love. Sex with another male, however, tended to be one-sided: an older, more experienced man could acceptably have an erotic attachment to an adolescent, whose face or genitals he might fondle; but the young man was supposed to respond only with *philia* – an attachment of admiring friendship – not physically.

According to Greek erotic convention, the junior party was to submit to the older man's advances only after a decent period of resistance. And he was not to enjoy the ensuing sex. Instead he was expected to lack – or failing that, to control – all erotic feelings of his own to the point where he was able to sustain a flaccid penis even in circumstances where this might be thought impossible.[10] He would smile charmingly and look demurely elsewhere while his lover was permitted to rub his penis between the young man's legs, but to avoid penetrating any bodily orifice. (Full-blown intercourse between men is seldom mentioned in Greek literature.[11])

Though Alcibiades, another participant at the symposium, loves Socrates so intensely that he is moved to go beyond an asymmetric relationship to one in which he is the active lover and even in which full emotional reciprocity will be possible, this is not the norm. In Greek convention, a relationship of equals that is genuinely reciprocal is one of *philia*, of wishing and doing well to another whom one experiences as a 'second self'. And though *philia* might develop out of a one-sided homosexual relationship between an older and a younger man, it is itself no longer sexual. Its chief aim is the subtler forms of intimacy as well as intellectual inspiration.

Yet the eroticism that triggers these refined pursuits is certainly not the luke-warm variety commonly (if mistakenly) associated with unworldly intellectuals – as Socrates makes abundantly clear in describing the stirrings awakened in him by a lovely boy called Charmides:

> Well, by then, my friend, I was in difficulties, and the self-assurance I'd felt earlier that I'd talk to him quite easily had been knocked out of me . . . he gave me a look that is impossible to describe and made ready to ask me something . . . when I saw what was inside his cloak. I was on fire, I lost my head . . .[12]

Needless to say, Socrates quickly brings his lust under control and proceeds to educate the young Charmides on – not coincidentally perhaps – the nature of temperance.

WHY LOVE MAKES US FEEL 'WHOLE'

The first major reason for taking love seriously that emerges from the *Symposium* – the idea that love makes us whole – is voiced by the comic playwright Aristophanes, whom Plato makes the mouthpiece for an extraordinary fantasy.

Aristophanes recounts a myth that he believes explains the intense attraction that we can suddenly feel for one person out of the thousands we encounter in our life – someone who might not even be particularly reliable or kind or otherwise suitable; but someone whom we at once feel that we 'recognise'.

A long time ago, he says, human beings were perfectly content and round, with two faces and two pairs of eyes, ears, arms and legs. (The circular form, so early Greek philosophy imagined, was the shape of a god. Perfection was a sphere, not a waif.)

These self-sufficient figures came in three sexes: male, female and hermaph-rodite. With all those limbs and senses they had a lot going for them, and they knew it. Eventually, they decided to challenge the power of the gods, leaving the celestial councils with a dilemma: whether to kill them or to curb them. The problem with the first option was that the gods wouldn't have any humans left to worship them – so, Greek gods being unashamed in their enjoyment of flattery and sacrifice, they decided to spare humanity. Zeus, their king, hit on the solution of cutting human beings down to size by chopping them in half. (And he warned that if this punishment didn't deter their arrogance, he would split them again, leaving them with a face as flat as a profile on a tombstone.)

Ever since that catastrophe, humans have forlornly wandered the earth searching for their unique other half, longing to become complete again and to discover a lost happiness.[13] Such a longing, Aristophanes says, is for more than companionship or sexual satisfaction. Love is 'simply the name for the desire and pursuit of the whole'[14] – a succinct definition of what we often take to be an indefinable emotion. Its goal is to fuse with a kindred spirit, so overcoming once and for all the vulnerability of the incomplete condition. 'The way to happiness for our race [men and women alike] lies in fulfilling the behests of Love'[15]: we must each find for ourselves the mate who properly belongs to us, so that we can recover our original nature.

So when one half finally meets up with the other, the pair become lost in amazed intimacy and yearn to spend their whole lives together. They refuse to separate even to seek food. And they are able to enjoy intercourse, courtesy of Zeus's compassionate decision to relocate human genitals to a more convenient, centre-forward position. (Previously, procreation happened without intercourse – 'by emission onto the ground, as is the case with grasshoppers'.[16])

This myth, like many myths, articulates deep human realities.[17] We still say that we have 'found ourselves' and feel 'whole' when we stumble across that unique person who can 'complete' us. We still believe that there must be a 'right' person for each of us – the perfect 'fit'. We see sex as expressing and celebrating the desire for union with her. We feel, as the myth suggests, that she is our 'lost' half. For we have a sense of (re-)gaining something that belongs to our very nature, of restoring something primal. (Equality for gays is built into this idea, as they are simply the halves of the original entirely male or female wholes; while heterosexuals are bisected androgynes. Not that Aristophanes envisaged exclusive sexual orientations.[18])

Over two thousand years later, we find Freud picturing the experience of the lovers' union in remarkably similar terms. He describes the desire to merge with our loved one – and the 'oceanic feeling' of lovers that the boundaries between them are melting away – as a regression to a primitive stage of development when the infant was united with its mother. She, like Aristophanes' original creatures, is the origin of our being; and love aims to restore that original condition, that lost unity, in which we were not yet a distinct individual, and in which the pain and powerlessness of separation had not yet been experienced. Love, says

Freud, 'strives to make the ego and the loved object one, to abolish all spatial barriers between them'.[19]

✦ ✦ ✦

Yet Aristophanes' myth raises powerful questions about love's search for 'completion'. Though his story appears to have a happy ending – men and women get to discover their other halves, at least if they are lucky – the picture that he paints is more complex. The fact is that love couldn't restore his bisected human beings to their original state of wholeness. It could, at best, attempt 'to come as near to it as our present circumstances allow'.[20] Only a god can restore wholeness. In the myth this is the god Hephaestus (Vulcan in Latin), the god of fire and a metal-smith who was said to have his forge below Mount Etna, the volcano in Sicily, and, perhaps significantly, was married to the goddess of love, Aphrodite (Venus in Latin). Only a god could join together what a god had put asunder.

But if a god were to enable us to achieve what love cannot – to become whole – would this really make us happy? The reality is that we don't know. As Aristophanes says, 'no one would refuse the offer' if the god were to say 'I am ready to melt and weld you together, so that, instead of two, you shall be one'. But when Hephaestus specifically asks the lovers: 'What is it, mortals, that you hope to gain from one another?' they can't answer. They know only that they want 'never to be separated from one another day or night', but they don't know why. Nor do they answer the question 'Would such a fate as this content you, and satisfy your longings?'[21]

And so the scale of love's ambition to restore a primal union quickly mires it in a dilemma, which Aristophanes leaves hanging in the air. On the one hand this ambition is so abstract that the lovers are confused about what they really want as well as frustrated that they aren't getting it. On the other hand the completeness they crave might never satisfy them anyway. For it would be a nightmare of perfect contentment, without appetite, desire, or motion. Not to be whole is torture; but once we have tasted desire and its delightful, if fleeting, satisfactions and torments, would it not also be torture to be whole? (This, too, is the dilemma of all Adam and Eve's successors in the Jewish and Christian stories: once we have been intoxicated by the endless variety of hope, danger, delight and novelty outside the Garden of Eden, would we really wish to return to a life in which there is no want?)

And yet the comic tragedy isn't over. All this assumes that there is a matching other half out there for us to want to fuse with. If we read the myth carefully, though, we realise that the only people who have lost halves to reclaim are those ancestors whom Zeus cut in two. All human beings since then have been born of already bisected individuals and don't have an actual other half to which they originally belonged (if we leave out, for the moment, our mothers – a point to which I will return in chapter 15). So while we all have the feeling that there is a perfect someone waiting to be discovered, there actually isn't. There is no single person – or type of person – who will fit us snugly and unproblematically. And so the whole which two loving individuals constitute will never be perfect; nor will it take us back to an original state of innocence.

But if the completeness that love craves is impossible or undesirable, and if there is no perfect other half to be had, then do we overrate it? And to what end sex, which becomes the servant of love once the original humans have been split and their genitals relocated? Aside from the pleasure of sex and its importance to reproduction, Aristophanes' myth invests with faint absurdity the toiling of human beings for so much of their lives to insert one not particularly attractive part of their anatomies into another – and their willingness to ruin families, fortunes, reputations, even countries, for the sake of it. Much like we might laugh when we see two dogs feverishly copulating by the side of the road or the ungainliness of a male elephant heaving himself onto his female.

So is there another approach to the question: What is the ultimate aim of love? The *Symposium* suggests there is: to possess beauty and goodness. Where Aristophanes said that love is motivated by the desire to find our other half, but implied that he or she could have any qualities so long as we found completion, Socrates, in his interventions, adds crucial provisos: love desires beauty (*kalon*[22]) and goodness (*agathon*[23]).

Here beauty and goodness seem to be merely two ways of describing the same quality that love seeks, so that ethically we see it as good and aesthetically as beautiful. There cannot, therefore, be love for the ugly;[24] nor will a lover seek his other half unless he knows it to be good.[25]

LOVE AS THE DESIRE TO POSSESS BEAUTY AND GOODNESS

Socrates' provisos might seem vague; but they are of momentous significance. We cannot, he suggests, genuinely love our other half, or anything about ourselves, or the whole which the two of us together make, unless we consider it good and beautiful. Love is, in this sense, anything but unconditional.

But what sort of beauty and goodness do we go for in others? What specifically attracts us to them? After all, there are innumerable instances of beauty and goodness in the world and we don't love all of them.

What we lack, answers Socrates. I find beautiful or good what I lack; you find beautiful or good what you lack.

The reasoning behind this is simple: love is a desire,[26] and desire is for what we don't already have.[27]

Since our lacks are often shown up most clearly by someone who is unlike us, perhaps we are attracted, after all, not to similarity but to difference. This possibility isn't entailed by Socrates' point about the logic of desire, but it is suggested. In which case love would flourish by alertness to precisely the beauty and goodness that we feel we don't have ourselves. And so the key to successful love would be continually to refresh our sense of our loved one's *difference* to us – not merely to tolerate difference but to crave it.

This idea that we are attracted to what we don't have also raises the intriguing possibility that part (but only part) of a man's attraction to women – both to their bodies and to their minds – arises from desire to possess a femininity that he doesn't have within himself. And conversely for a woman's attraction to men. On this theory, gay men would feel a lack of manliness or a surplus of femininity in themselves. They would be mainly attracted by the masculinity of their partners, rather than by their femininity. Similarly, lesbians would be attracted to the feminine – not the masculine – in other women.

Such speculation surfaces in our own times in both novels and psychological investigation. In *A la recherche du temps perdu* Proust's Narrator, Marcel, conceives of gay men as being psychologically feminine. Of Charlus, a thwarted gay lover, he says: 'He belonged to that race of beings, less paradoxical than they appear, whose ideal is manly simply because their temperament is feminine'.[28] The miserable dilemma of the Proustian gay man is that he tends to desire heterosexual men for their male temperament, but they, of course, desire only women; whereas he is repelled by other gay men on account of their feminine temperament, and so is doomed to loneliness. Socrates would say that he needn't be so doomed, as there will surely be other beautiful or good properties of a gay man that Charlus will lack, and to which he can therefore be attracted; but Proust seems to refuse this consolation and, as we will see in chapter 16, to regard erotic passion, gay or otherwise, as bound to be disappointed.

✦ ✦ ✦

Socrates thinks that love originates in lack, Aristophanes that love originates in loss. Socrates, now reporting the words of a wise (and almost certainly fictional) priestess called Diotima, then adds to this idea of love arising from want by depicting it as the child of Poverty (its other parent being Contrivance, the son of Invention – also translated as Plenty, son of Cunning[29]). In a brilliant passage, he articulates with merciless clarity the scheming nature of love:

> having Contrivance for his father and Poverty for his mother, he [Love] bears the following character. He is always poor, and, far from being sensitive and beautiful, as most people imagine, he is hard and weather-beaten, shoeless and homeless, always sleeping out for want of a bed, on the ground, on doorsteps, and in the street. So far he takes after his mother and lives in want. But, being also his father's son, he schemes to get for himself whatever is beautiful and good; he is bold and forward and strenuous, always devising tricks like a cunning huntsman; he yearns after knowledge and is full of resource and is a lover of wisdom all his life, a skilful magician, an alchemist, a true sophist.[30]

This image – that love is a crafty street urchin, that though love desires beauty it doesn't necessarily behave beautifully – is extremely suggestive. For can the experience of inherited poverty ever be overcome? Can it ever cease to drive our life or fuel our memories? Can it ever be made good – no matter how much good it motivates us to achieve? Whether it originates in loss or lack? In the realm of human love these questions boil down to one: can its needs ever be finally satisfied? The answer suggested by love's maternal lineage is no.

But its paternity hardly endows it with calm either. Plenty or Contrivance fuels the natural plenitude that, according to Socrates, we all have and that seeks release through love and specifically through love's desire to procreate.

This thought of procreation enables the claim that love desires beauty to be further nuanced. Love, Socrates now says, is the desire for 'procreation in what is beautiful'. And 'such procreation can be either physical or spiritual'.[31] In other words it can issue in either children or creations like art and philosophy and virtuous acts. Everyone has 'a procreative impulse, both physical and spiritual, and when they come to maturity they desire to beget children, but they can do so only in beauty and never in ugliness'.[32] In other words: in and through love we are able to create. And through these creations to be immortal.

So love springs both from deficit and plenty. It is both needy and resourceful. The lover feels both too empty – which spurs him to create – and too full – which enables him to create. I lack the other, but also have, so to speak, too much of myself – an excess of spirit that has not been manifested in creative achievements; and it is these that the loved one can help me deliver. There is a perpetual tension in love, or at least in the love that constantly searches: 'What he wins he always loses, and [he] is neither rich nor poor, neither wise nor ignorant'.[33] Love seems to be always unresolved, always on the way, without reaching a clear and final destination.

As with Aristophanes' myth, this again suggests that there might never come a point where we have attained a love which will be contented once and for all. Not because we have somehow failed to discover the formula for successful love; or because we haven't 'worked at it' hard enough. Even less because of external impediments – class barriers, ethnic prejudice, the strains of everyday living, rivals, and the like. But because love is, in its very origin and essence, insatiable. The desires that, according to Aristophanes and Socrates, fuel it – to restore a primal wholeness; to find a type of goodness and beauty that we lack in ourselves; to create out of plenitude – cannot be stably fulfilled. Or if they could be then, as Hephaestus implied in his question to lovers in search of wholeness, we might find ourselves fixed in a state of deadly perfection.

This is the tragic dilemma of all love between people, from which life offers no exit.

LOVE AS THE DESIRE TO POSSESS ABSOLUTE BEAUTY
AND GOODNESS – PERPETUALLY

We need, however, to pause at this point and ask a question that Socrates/Diotima has so far glossed over. What sort of beauty and goodness that we lack does love ultimately desire?

In the answer to this question Western love begins to store up serious trouble: to generate expectations which love in practice cannot meet.

Love's ultimate desire, Socrates reports, is to be 'in constant union' with the very essence of beauty, goodness and truth itself.[34] To be united with the essence of, say, beauty means not to be united with this or that beautiful thing, but to be united with beauty itself, with what it is to be beautiful, with what is common to all beautiful things and enables us to identify them as beautiful. This is a reality that is absolute and immortal and unchanging.

Socrates describes this vision of absolute beauty in the language of religious experience:

> This beauty is first of all eternal; it neither comes into being nor passes away, neither waxes nor wanes . . . [it is not] like the beauty of a face or hands or anything else corporeal, or like the beauty of a thought or science . . .; [we] will see it as absolute, existing alone with itself, unique, eternal, and all other beautiful things as partaking of it . . . What may we suppose to be the felicity of the man who sees absolute beauty in its essence, pure and unalloyed, who, instead of a beauty tainted by human flesh and colour and a mass of perishable rubbish, is able to apprehend divine beauty where it exists apart and alone?[35]

Seized by this vision of divine beauty, we look to love to take us from an imperfect, transient world to a realm of perfection and eternity. We expect love to culminate in an experience of absolute beauty and goodness – and our beloved to inspire in us such an experience. Its function, as Socrates reports, is 'to interpret and convey messages to the gods from men and to men from the gods'.[36] Indeed, love enables us humans to find a divine completion; to have 'the privilege of being beloved of God, and becoming, if ever a man can, immortal himself'.[37]

+ + +

But we don't become capable of such exalted love all of a sudden. It isn't purely spontaneous. Love, like a skill, needs education and training. We must cultivate the knowledge, maturity and virtues needed to ascend the ladder of love. And for that we require a teacher, a guide.

At first, love will naturally be directed towards one beautiful body. 'The man who would pursue the right way to this goal must begin, when he is young, by applying himself to the contemplation of physical beauty', says Diotima – adding that if love leads him aright, he should at this early stage 'fall in love with one particular beautiful person and beget noble sentiments in partnership with him'.[38]

As love matures, it progresses from loving one beautiful body to loving beautiful bodies in general. For the lover, focused as he is on beauty, quickly realises that 'physical beauty in any person is closely akin to physical beauty in any other',[39] so that to be fixated by the beauty of just one body is petty and to be despised.

Then the lover becomes capable of loving the beauty of souls, which seems to him nobler than the beauty of bodies, and he interests himself in 'such notions as may serve to make young people better', and then in the 'activities and institutions' which such ideas express. But these activities and institutions are themselves expressions of knowledge and the lover now desires the great sea of beauty, which inspires him to 'bring forth in the abundance of his love of wisdom many beautiful and magnificent sentiments and ideas'.[40]

Finally, we realise that the reason and driving force behind this ascent of love is desire for the very essence of beauty, for its own sake. As we have seen, the essence of beauty – or goodness – occupies a higher realm, like God's, abstracted from our ordinary everyday life and so from everything that derives its beauty from it. In this realm things aren't perishable, or dependent on other things for their existence and value, but rather exist and are valuable eternally and unconditionally. In this realm, therefore, the body and its desires, time and its ravages, become possible objects of disgust.

✦ ✦ ✦

This picture of love's ascent from the physical to the divine has shaped the history of Western love in such immense and varied ways that I can do no more here than pick out a few of its influences – though many others will become apparent as we consider other conceptions of love that, for all their seeming difference, crucially depend on Plato's thought (whether by adopting it or opposing it).

The first of these influences is to create the basis for making love the path to supreme value: to the blessings of the highest beauty and goodness; to true virtue; to what is pure and eternal. As Socrates says: 'in the acquisition of this blessing human nature can find no better helper than Love. I declare that it is the duty of every man to honour Love'.[41] Taken together with Hebrew Scripture's commands to love God and neighbour, the ground is prepared for Christianity to make love the supreme value of the Western world – life's ultimate virtue and meaning.

The second is to think that sexual desire can lie at the beginning of the path towards the highest love, but that it is *not* what the highest love is finally about or where it is really consummated. Whether in Socrates' report of love's ascent to absolute beauty or in Aristophanes' myth of finding our other half, sex is a means but not the end. Amazingly, no amount of sexual liberation has put this view to flight. Few regard love centred on sex as comparable in resilience or richness to love based on 'higher' things we share with our partners, like common values or ideals. Few figures in Western history have not, deep down, thought that sex ought to be servant rather than master in a loving relationship. The Marquis de Sade, after over two centuries, is still a celebrated exception, still an object of fascination, even in these liberated times.

The third Platonic idea still with us is the link between love and immortality. The highest love not only enables us to glimpse immortal things of eternal value, but through it we can become 'if ever a man can, immortal' ourselves.[42] The culminating vision of the *Symposium* – the vision of love as a passport to the unchanging essence of beauty and goodness and so to a world free of much that makes us human, such as transience, loss, suffering, chance, and evil, whether natural or man-made – comes to captivate the Western imagination as few other ideas ever have.

Yet, for all its majesty, this vision of love as ultimately directed to the timeless essence of beauty severely undermines the value of love between people. It makes a vice of one of love's greatest virtues: to attend precisely to the time-bound particularity of individuals. It makes people – indeed anything transient – less worthy of our love simply on account of their impermanence. It flattens out their individuality to the point where we could just as well swap our beloved for anyone else, providing they embody at least the same degree of beauty. It makes loved ones valuable only as stepping stones to our greater good as lovers, notably our creativity, our immortality, and our perception of absolute beauty – and otherwise gives us little or no interest in their lives or in deepening our relationship with them. Thus, for the sake of the lover's own flourishing, it ends up drawing the truest love from the personal to the impersonal, from the individual to the general, and from the human to the – literally – inhuman. A tendency which, as we will see, is powerfully fostered by the career of Platonism within Christianity and which culminates in the nineteenth-century celebration of *Liebestod*, or love-death.

Moreover, the idea that love is necessarily aroused by beauty doesn't seem credible. For one thing, we manifestly love fewer people and things than we consider beautiful. Someone might find many women beautiful, or indeed paintings or vases or landscapes, but really love only one. For another thing, the 'true' beauty that Plato has in mind is inseparable, in his account of it, from goodness – that is, ethical goodness; and it is obvious that people love many things that they themselves do not consider ethically good. The woman who falls in love with the murderer whom she acknowledges as bad (and indeed might even find attractive for his badness); the love of the hostage for his captor that we considered in chapter 2; the ease, discussed there too, with which love is aroused by power, indeed by brutal power; the love of a child for his parents before he has any developed sense of whether they are good or bad, and often after he has been abused by them – all these suggest that love is not aroused uniquely by the good.

Nor does love for the beautiful go together with love for the good. To see the music-loving Auschwitz camp guard as a contradiction and agonise over 'how this is possible' is a legacy of Plato. It is entirely possible: for a love of beauty does not entail a commitment to morality. (Here we will leave aside the question of whether there are circumstances in which a love of beauty, whether as creator of art or as interpreter of the works of others, could actually be inhibited by morality and fostered by freedom from it.)

If love is, as I have proposed, inspired by the hope of ontological rootedness – the hope of feeling that our life is indestructibly anchored in a reality whose value we take to be absolute – then beauty will be a consequence of love, not its cause. Similarly the joy of having found such a hope will cast a general light of goodness over the loved one – not a moral goodness, but a goodness akin to that which God found in the world he had created. In other words, a sense of delight, gratitude, even awe, at the existence of those we love.

I must leave the development of this thought for the concluding chapter – but it brings me back to ontological rootedness, possibly the deepest of all human needs after food, water, shelter, recognition and protection.

✦ ✦ ✦

The ruling myths of the *Symposium* – those attributed to Aristophanes and to Diotima – are two of the most powerful ways of picturing this need to be found in the Western heritage.

It is a need that can best be expressed in mythical terms. For the desire to experience our beingness, such that our individual existence feels securely rooted, is as hard to specify as it is powerful.

Aristophanes presents this ambition in terms of a 'return' to a primordial and immutable wholeness; Socrates/Diotima as a moving forward – or upward – towards a divine essence. Both do something that has governed Western sensibility ever since: they ascribe to love the role of securing the unchanging and the eternal.

But in characterising the object of love's striving as something unchanging and eternal, the ground is prepared for Eros, that greatest of life drives, to be – paradoxically – a death drive. For Eros then desires a fulfilment which, literally, involves the overcoming of human life in the only form in which we know it: as individuals whose lives are structured by time and transience, and by the possibility of loneliness and loss and incompleteness in every sense. In other words, the ground is prepared in Plato's texts for love to become an immense force for destruction – not out of mad anger, jealousy and possessiveness, but motivated and justified by nothing less than its noblest ideals; not in an overtly violent way but with a brutality that has been exquisitely sublimated.

Such ambitions are particularly dangerous when the ultimate arena of love is human relationships, as it definitely is not in the *Symposium*. When this happens – perhaps most strikingly within German Romanticism of the eighteenth to nineteenth centuries – human relationships inevitably become burdened with unrealisable expectations. They are given the job of enabling the lovers to come into touch with the divine and even to become divine; to strive, through their love, for immortality; and, ultimately, to annihilate their existence as embodied individuals.

This would be enough of a burden to place on any personal relationship, and indeed it will take over two thousand years to reach its apotheosis. But then we notice another thing, to which Hephaestus already gestured: the ultimate goal of love – the joy of completeness, of indestructibility – cannot be specified. Love cannot *know* precisely what it wants. When Plato's protagonists say that the goals of love are wholeness, beauty in itself, or the essence of the good that all particular good things instantiate, they speak of goals that are like the mystic's object of contemplation: no definitions or representations or purposes can capture them.[43] (In fact the word 'good', even if not used in this strict Platonic sense is, like the word 'truth', probably indefinable – and centuries of effort have not enabled philosophers to pin down either of these concepts.)

The problem – and a challenge I attempt to take up in this book – is this: how can the search for an indestructible grounding of our individual being through love, to which Plato gives such masterly expression, affirm human life, including human relationships, rather than seek to overcome it? In other words, how can love, *contra* Plato, become the privileged means of relating precisely to time and brevity and loss and suffering and imperfection and the particularity of embodied individuals – and so honour the very phenomena that Plato's highest love wants to transcend?

In this context we should return to something else which the myths of Aristophanes and Diotima tell us: Love is thoroughly conditional. Conditional upon finding a very particular 'other half' (Aristophanes' view) or upon the extent to which someone exemplifies beauty (Socrates'/Diotima's view) – or perhaps especially upon those aspects of beauty that each of us lack. If, as I just suggested, these are merely two ways, out of many, of picturing the human desire to achieve a fundamental relation to Being (expressed in Jewish and Christian traditions as a right relationship to God; a turn or re-turn to the source of our being), then love will be conditional upon someone or something appearing to us as the embodied promise of that paradise.

To suggest that love has such conditions hardly makes it capricious or narcissistic, for to live it demands sustained and scrupulous attention to our object of love and to the world beyond our individual concerns – an attention that is the opposite of narcissism and would be defeated by caprice.

Perhaps once love has been inspired by the satisfaction of these conditions it becomes 'unconditional' in that it will pursue and care for its object wholeheartedly and without provisos. But in no way is love, in its origin and aims, unconditioned, as many a cliché would have it.

✦ ✦ ✦

Finally, we can learn from Plato how love must be educated, precisely if its aims are so exalted. It is like a talent for anything – inborn but needing to be continuously developed if it is ever to flourish. Specifically, love's attentiveness to its object is too hard to master without prolonged effort. The capacity to seek the real presence of another and what he demands of us does not mature overnight. We quickly recognise our situation as that of the young man in W.H. Auden's *The Age of Anxiety*: 'So, learning to love, at length he is taught/ To know he does not.'[44]

Plato's insistence that the older person can teach the young a thing or two about love is overdue for a revival. So, too, is the idea that an erotically charged affection, and the special trust it fosters, should have a pedagogic role in such a relationship between an older man (or woman) and a younger person. Without, of course, the pederasty that was practised in Athens, and that cannot but be regarded as abhorrent by our own age. The mentoring relationship is, in other words, to be spiritual.

There is a related point here: the capacity to love is the fruit of age, not the monopoly of youth. There are prodigies of love – Baby in the movie *Dirty Dancing* might be one of them; Vladimir in Turgenev's *First Love* is another. But on the whole when we are young we lack the refined receptivity that makes love not blind, as is often thought, but, as Plato points out, potentially the clearest-sighted of passions; not chaotic and reckless but *the* exemplar of order and form; not wild glorification but discerning surrender; not unconditional but inescapably conditional; not deluded but knowing.

Nor in our youth have we yet discovered that love is a chancy business in which we might never find our real other half or, if we do find her, be unable to harmonise two, often inscrutable and uncontrollable, lives. Attempt rather than success – the journey more than the destination – is the point. The journey is to *learn* a passionate attentiveness that opens us to the lives of our loved ones. In the process we might ourselves come to creative fruition – or, to express a Platonic thought in a modern way, 'give birth to ourselves'.

Contrary to Socrates' intent, this gradual opening to the other's presence is likely to make us more vulnerable to loss and luck, not less. More thrown into the world of change and chance, not more insulated from it. We therefore need to explore what it might be to bring Socrates' world-transcending ambitions down to earth – not for the sake of it, but because love's first aim and need is to root our life in this world. The person to help us do so is Aristotle, Plato's most gifted student. And it is to him that we must now turn.

4

Love as perfect friendship
Aristotle

Aristotle (384–322 BCE) reclaims love for this world: for nature, time, and human character.

He sees it as a bond between individuals for the sake of their flourishing,[1] rather than, as we read in Plato's *Symposium*, a way of looking beyond individuals to a timeless reality of absolute beauty. He believes that humans are by nature social animals, so that living our lives in intimacy with select others is part of one's full flourishing – unlike Diotima's vision of human attachments as at best a stepping stone to a love that reaches for the heavens. Aristotle recognises, indeed celebrates, our need to value and be valued by loved ones.

Crucially, Aristotle makes friendship, rather than sexual relationships or contemplation of the Good, the supreme form of love. Indeed he so elevates the best sort of friendship-love – what he calls perfect *philia*: wishing and doing well to others for their own sake; intensely identifying with them as if they were 'a second self'; seeking deep mutual harmony – that all other forms of relationship, whether to spouses, siblings, children, parents, or sexual partners, are, for him, valuable mainly insofar as they exhibit the features of such *philia*.[2]

The last point is of great importance: *philia* is a form of devotion that is best translated as 'friendship-love', but that flourishes not only between what we normally think of as friends, but also in all these other sorts of relationship at their best. And so sexual intimacy, for example, isn't in principle opposed to friendship-love; but since it is motivated merely by the hope of pleasure, Aristotle regards it as no more important to a flourishing life (and possibly less) than, say, a good sense of humour, an adequate income, or handling your drink well.

This decisive elevation of *philia* fuelled one of the longest-running controversies in the history of Western love. The question is this: Is Aristotle right to suggest that friendship-love is more important to our flourishing, more constant, more harmonious, more reciprocal, and ultimately more ethical than sexual love? In this camp we find figures like Cicero, Plutarch, Montaigne, and in some ways Nietzsche. Or, by contrast, is friendship a feeble sort of love, lacking the *mania* and sensuality of erotic passion and its indifference to convention, as well as any powerful commitment to a transcendent ideal (God, spiritual union, art, and the like)? Those who would say yes form an odd coalition: romantics like Rousseau, who sees friendship as inferior to erotic love; Christians of many sorts, from St Augustine to Kierkegaard, for whom friendship is a distraction from spiritual love and ultimately selfish; and pessimists like Proust's Narrator, who damns friendship as 'an abdication of self . . . devoid of virtue'.[3] These divisions over the value and role of friendship have been running for two thousand years, and are still not resolved.

For Aristotle there is a lot at stake here. For him the purest love – love that is based on wishing and doing well to others for their own sake, and not merely on pleasure or gain to oneself – is, in its very essence, ethical. It is possible only between two individuals who are good – and indeed are good in similar ways. What Aristotle means by 'good' is much more than simply agreeing on rules like telling the truth, or not stealing, or keeping promises. He means that they share an entire conception of the best way to live life, of the right ends of life, and of the excellences of character with which our choices and actions must accord.[4] Only friendship-love, he maintains, can fully exemplify this sort of ethical relationship. Erotic associations are driven by desire for pleasure and gain; and though they can be accompanied by friendship-love that seeks the good of the other regardless of pleasure or gain to oneself, or even develop into friendship-love, they are not themselves founded on such love and so are not intrinsically ethical associations.

✦ ✦ ✦

This idea that friendship-love is necessarily an ethical relationship in a way that erotic love isn't chimes with certain contemporary intuitions. For example, you can fall in love with a murderer but you are unlikely to want to be friends with him. Erotic love, like ambition for power, can kill those who get in its way or refuse to submit. A certain possessive violence that cares nothing for morality, or at least for conventional mores, seems to belong to its nature, and, indeed, is often seen as proof of its authenticity and strength. We disapprove but aren't completely amazed when lovers stalk, or turn on, loved ones who fail to reciprocate.

Whereas if a friend started behaving to us like this, consumed with jealousy of our other friends, determined to possess us, and furious if we failed sufficiently to requite his affections, we would be impressed not by the power of his friendly feelings but by their poverty.

This isn't because friendship is an anaemic bond compared to erotic or romantic love. It is a very different sort of love. It is, in its essence, a two-way relationship. 'Unrequited friendship' can't exist; or if it can we don't think of it as particularly noble or beneficial. (Unlike Platonic Eros, in which I love the beautiful, not it me.[5]) And reciprocity in friendship doesn't involve possessing or 'merging' with the other. At least not in any manner that obliterates the independent agency of the loved one. Though in perfect *philia* one experiences one's friend as one's 'other self', and to that extent as continuous or even identical with oneself, one does so in a way that explicitly respects his integrity and agency and distinct life, and is dedicated to finding, nurturing and enjoying the good in him.

WHY FRIENDSHIP-LOVE IS CONDITIONAL

Aristotle's insistence that *philia* depends on – even essentially *is* – an ethical relation means that he is dead set against the first two myths about ideal love that I mentioned in chapter 1: that it is unconditional (it loves the other regardless of her qualities or of changes in her qualities); and that it totally affirms the beloved, her 'bad' as well as her 'good'.

Philia is inescapably conditional on the excellences of character that we perceive in the other person. Since character is realised in concrete acts and desires over the course of a lived life,[6] we love someone not just for dispositions that we detect in her but for how these dispositions are revealed, over time, in her actual life. Revealed in heroic actions or personal crises or pursuits like thinking, artistic creation and political leadership; and also revealed in ordinary everyday life: in eating, drinking, having sex, party-giving, even telling jokes – all of which can be pursued with varying degrees of excellence or baseness.[7] Hence for Aristotle ideal love 'is a thoroughgoing and unconstrained sharing in *all* activities that people judge to be pertinent to their human good living' – all activities, that is, 'according to the recognised excellences of character'.[8]

But if love is so conditional, then – contrary to another myth about ideal love – it isn't necessarily constant, let alone eternal. We don't go on loving someone regardless of whether they remain the same. Aristotle would disagree with Shakespeare that 'Love is not love/ Which alters when it alteration finds'.[9] Love will be undermined precisely to the degree that the loved one changes for the worse. Such as through a moral deterioration that isn't reversed. Or through the deterioration of old age, which can 'bring about a loss in sensitivity and in enjoyment that can lead to the dissolution or at least the diminution of love'.[10] Or through the departure of the loved one. This is how separation and death can, after sufficient time, help us to get over love.[11] (Nor is this far-fetched: some people do after all manage to find new loves when they are deserted or to marry again when a spouse dies.) Anything that seriously undermines trust can also destroy love: suspicion, jealousy, fear, self-protectiveness are all enemies of *philia*.[12]

It isn't just that *philia* cannot be expected to be constant if the other person becomes irreversibly bad. Aristotle seems to go further: one should drop a friend under these circumstances. For '[w]hat is evil neither can nor should be loved'.[13] A friendship, he implies, should be broken off even if one party has 'remained the same while the other became better and far outstripped him in excellence':[14]

> if one friend remained a child in intellect while the other became a fully developed man, how could they [continue to] be friends when they neither approved of the same things nor delighted in and were pained by the same things? For not even with regard to each other will their tastes agree, and without this . . . they cannot be friends . . .[15]

Normally, of course, we would expect *philia* to survive because it is based on something as robust as the friends' excellences of character ('their friendship lasts as long as they are good – and excellence is an enduring thing'[16]). These qualities are so fundamental to who someone is that to love him in this way is to love him 'for his sake'.[17] It is to love him for the person he is, and not merely because he is useful or pleasurable to us. When this happens, we identify so closely with him – with his virtues and choices and desires and values – that he seems to be 'another self'.[18]

We have already seen similar feelings at work – and even similar talk of loving the other as one's own soul – in the great friendships of the Old Testament, those of Jonathan for David and Ruth for Naomi, though without the explicit grounding of friendship in the excellences of character of the loved one.

✦ ✦ ✦

Friendship-love has a second condition: the goodness of the *lover*. It takes virtue to recognise virtue, to desire it, and to crave unity with another person who possesses it. Only lovers who are themselves virtuous are able, and motivated, to love the good in another. Only they can do what all genuine love must do: bear witness to the other's life and specifically to his quality as an ethical being.

So 'perfect' friendship-love, the sort that doesn't simply use the other for pleasure or utility, but wants the best for him for his own sake, is found only between two virtuous people.

Not just any virtuous people, though, but people of *similar* virtue. Like is attracted – and suited – to like. We bind to another through our love of similar ideals, through our possession of similar virtues. 'Perfect friendship is the friendship of men who are good, and alike in excellence'.[19]

Indeed likeness *is* friendship.[20] Aristotle's claim here is startlingly extreme. In his ideal friendship the likeness of the friends would encompass not only their virtue – and the key choices, desires, motivations, and tastes that it expresses – but also their social status as well as all the pleasures and advantages that they bestow on each other.

This rules quite a few relationships out of the running for friendship. Spouses, for example; or in general men and women. Since female virtue is, he thinks, naturally inferior to male virtue, the best a woman can be never matches the best a man can be. So perfect *philia* couldn't exist between a man and a woman, no matter how virtuous the woman.[21]

Nor can it exist between parents and their children[22] – for they too are unequal, at least until the children have reached ethical maturity. And certainly not between masters and those who, Aristotle believes, are slaves by nature, rather than merely in subservient positions through bad luck or birth. He adds that although one can be friends with such a person insofar as he is a man, one cannot be friends with the slave in their nature.[23]

But if we set aside these beliefs – to our modern egalitarian sensibility unacceptable and groundless – that women are ethically inferior and that some people are natural slaves, there remains a powerful kernel of truth in Aristotle's claim that the deepest and most enduring love thrives on likeness in the nature of two people – and especially in their ethical nature broadly conceived: what they think of as their highest goods or values or purposes.

We might, of course, also desire opposite types – those who bring something quite new and unknown to us – finding them fascinating and enchanting as well as a welcome escape from ourselves and from the difficulties of ploughing our own furrow in life. In particular, when pleasure or utility motivate our interest in another, we might expect to seek out delights and goods that we don't already have – and Aristotle himself supposes that 'Friendship for utility's sake seems to be that which most easily exists between contraries'.[24] But, ultimately, we tend to feel most at home – and we bond most deeply – with people whose nature is fundamentally kindred.

◆ ◆ ◆

Many other philosophers have agreed with this, from Empedocles, who went as far as saying that like cannot be known *except* by like (and whom Aristotle quotes as saying that 'like aims at like')[25] to Cicero, and from Montaigne to Nietzsche. Interestingly, dissenters such as Schopenhauer and Proust who picture love – or at least romantic-erotic love – as searching for difference rather than similarity are also less optimistic about its contribution to a rich and fulfilling life.

Of course, people's idea of their 'essential nature' – and even of whether there is such a thing – varies from one age or culture or person to another. Perhaps we no longer think of virtues of character, strictly speaking, as defining our nature, and instead regard other categories as crucial, such as taste, profession, ideals, interests, ethnic origins, nationality, or religion. However we define ourselves, though, we do tend to go for similarity – as many psychological studies on marriage, mating, and separation have confirmed.[26] Love is strikingly conservative, whether it is expressed in friendships, marriages, partnerships, parent–child relationships, or other close bonds. People who dedicate their lives to racial, economic, educational, and social equality, and who genuinely celebrate 'diversity', often, if not usually, go off and marry one of their own kind.

Probably with good reason. Not only does mirroring by another, essentially similar, person give us a powerful sense of being validated and anchored in the world; it might also be the best basis to perceive, understand, enjoy – and, if not always to enjoy, then wholeheartedly to tolerate – the uniqueness of our loved one. Just as, even with the best will, we cannot understand and savour the subtleties of a language unless we are fully one of its speakers, so we cannot understand and savour the particularity of another person unless they are, in a similar sense, native to us.

CAN WE BE FRIENDS WITH OUR LOVERS?

Aristotle's philosophy suggests a simple answer to this long-running question: friendship-love and erotic love are such different sorts of devotion that they can flourish within the same relationship only if we remember not to expect things from erotic love that don't properly belong to it, and similarly from friendship.

To summarise the features of friendship-love: It is mutual – friendship is reciprocal goodwill – and is seen by both parties as such.[27] It involves wishing the other what is good for his sake.[28] It requires clear mutual recognition of the independence of the two friends: despite thinking of one another as a 'second self', they do not expect to 'merge' into that indistinguishable union celebrated, as we will see, by much of the erotic-mystical tradition, from early Neoplatonism through Christian unity-mysticism to nineteenth-century Romanticism. Friendship takes time to develop: two lives and their myriad activities must be mutually intertwined for long enough to enable both parties to get to know and love each other's characters well and also to benefit from their joint activities. And it is durable to the extent that good qualities of character – the object of this sort of love – are stable. Whereas these conditions aren't necessary for erotic love, which can be both passionate and genuine without being reciprocated, or making the other's well-being a central goal, or scrupulously respecting his separateness, or taking much time to mature, or being particularly durable. Erotic relationships are fragile because they depend on expectations of beauty or sexual pleasure which are either unfulfilled or do not last:

> . . . in the friendship of lovers sometimes the lover complains that his excess of love is not met by love in return (though perhaps there is nothing lovable about him), while often the beloved complains that the lover who formerly promised everything now performs nothing. Such incidents happen when the lover loves the beloved for the sake of pleasure while the beloved loves the lover for the sake of utility, and they do not both possess the qualities expected of them . . .; for each did not love the other person himself but the qualities he had, and these were not enduring; this is why the friendships also are transient. But the love of characters, as has been said, endures because it is self-dependent.[29]

Aristotle is clear: sex is not necessary for the most fulfilling love.[30] So if sex 'gets in the way' of friendship-love, say by inducing intense possessiveness of the other at the expense of acting for the sake of his welfare, or an excessive emphasis on physical beauty rather than ethical attractiveness, or on spontaneity rather than constancy, then we can infer that the first of these pairs will always have to yield to the second. At least if we are to aim for 'perfect' *philia*, where two people love each other for their own sakes and not merely for pleasure or utility.

But where does that leave relationships that seek both *philia* and Eros – relationships like marriages and other forms of rich intimacy? The conclusion that Aristotle's philosophy suggests – though he doesn't explicitly reach it himself – is that *philia* and Eros, and therefore relationships embracing them both, will always be vulnerable to tensions, where respect for autonomy vies with possessiveness, an emphasis on character and virtue with a fixation on pleasure and physical beauty, the pleasures of reciprocation with the pain of unrequited desire, harmony with turbulence, trust with jealousy. The battles in all love of this sort are not so much between the sexes as between the different forms of love that a particular relationship encompasses.

SELF-LOVE AND SELF-KNOWLEDGE

But, for all Aristotle's talk of *philia* making the other's well-being an end in itself, isn't even 'perfect' *philia* extraordinarily self-regarding, given that we love people in this way only if their virtues of character are similar to ours – only if they feel like a 'second self' and so are, in a sense, us? Though Aristotle claims that *philia* is the highest form of love, isn't it essentially about loving oneself in another? About a rather self-conscious mutual admiration society?

To which the answer is unashamedly yes. This is not a problem for Aristotle. He sees no necessary conflict between loving another and loving oneself. Nor between altruism and self-interest. Unselfish altruism, where I do something for someone else because his needs or wants are a sufficient reason for helping him, is perfectly consistent with my benefiting from doing these things. It is even consistent with my also having a self-interested reason for doing them.

Indeed, Aristotle goes further: he believes that the highest love essentially involves the desire for *one's own* good. Since the natural and proper aim of life is to fulfil our human potential, our first concern in everything we do, including in loving others, *should* be our own flourishing.[31] Not in the sense that we look for a return from every good thing we do for another person. Rather in the sense that we flourish precisely by loving her for whom she is 'in herself'. As a 'second self' her flourishing is also my own flourishing. And so in caring for her life I care for mine.

What, then, are the blessings that flow to us by loving another? There are two main ones that we can broadly infer from Aristotle's discussion of *philia*.

First among them is self-love. In particular, close friendships deepen one's esteem for oneself,[32] and they dispose one to act in ways that express what is best in one – that are, as we would now say, 'true to oneself'. For loving others inspires the energy and tenacity to dedicate oneself to one's own flourishing. We are better at sticking with what we care about, at sustaining our motivation, if we share our life with a loved one:[33] 'by oneself it is not easy to be continuously active; but with others and towards others it is easier'.[34]

This doesn't mean that two friends need to live under the same roof, but it does involve the closest regular association in all the activities that they find necessary to living a good life, from ordinary things like eating, drinking, and giving parties, to thinking, reasoning, law-making, conversing, working, and confronting danger.[35] ('[F]or this is what living together would seem to mean in the case of man, and not, as in the case of cattle, feeding in the same place.'[36])

Such continuous association isn't therefore about meeting in order to take a break from life's weightier preoccupations. On the contrary, it involves spending time precisely on those activities that are most central to each other's lives and taking pains to avoid the prolonged separations that, Aristotle insists, endanger the firmness and trust of a friendship.[37]

Plainly, no contemporary man with a job, a mortgage and a family could have time for many friendships of this sort, and it is hard to imagine a wife who would be happy if her husband undertook everything he most cherished only with his friend. But if we jettison Aristotle's assumption that women are inferior to men, ethically as well as in terms of understanding, and therefore incapable of the same quality of friendship-love, it is clear that the ideal arena for this sort of continuous intimacy would be a marriage or other long-term partnership in which all the aspirations and values that make life most worth living for both parties are accommodated.

Aristotle insists that human flourishing needs such long-term intimacy, however it is achieved; and that this is precisely what distinguishes us from wild beasts – as well as from God, who requires no company to be fully himself:

... with us [humans] welfare involves a something beyond us, but the deity is his own well-being.[38]

... he who is unable to live in society, or who has no need because he is sufficient for himself, must be either a beast or a god . . .[39]

✦ ✦ ✦

This brings us to the second great blessing of loving for Aristotle: self-knowledge.[40] Self-knowledge was much prized by Greek thinkers and mystics – the Delphic Oracle famously charged its votaries to 'know thyself'; and Socrates, Plato's teacher, and so Aristotle's intellectual grandfather, went round Athens preaching that 'the unexamined life is not worth living'. But Aristotle thinks that one sort of self-knowledge is particularly essential to our flourishing: knowing our *motives* for acting in the ways we do. The point is this: our motives aren't arbitrary whims; they embody our inbuilt conceptions of what is good, they express our 'core values' (as we would put it nowadays). To understand what sort of life we are leading we need to study not only our actions but also what drives them; we need to know whether we have chosen the right actions out of the right motives.[41] Giving money to a hungry child, for example, has quite a different ethical quality if we accidentally drop a coin into his lap or if our motive is to stop him harassing us with his suffering, than if we give it to him out of genuine empathy and want to help him flourish. Leading a good life isn't about pursuing worthwhile things on autopilot.

And so only by examining our motives can we discover our hidden conceptions of what is good. Only by understanding what values drive us can we be sure that our actions are true to them, and so to who we are.

But why must we love *another* in order to get such self-knowledge? Why can't we obtain it just by looking inwards or by observing ourselves in action?

Because, Aristotle says, it is so hard to know ourselves. Which is, for example, 'plain from the way in which we blame others without being aware that we do the same things ourselves'.[42] Or in which we claim virtues that we don't have. As Nietzsche was to say over twenty-two centuries later: '. . . we are necessarily strangers to ourselves, we do not comprehend ourselves, we *have* to misunderstand ourselves, for us the law "Each is furthest from himself" applies to all eternity – we are not "men of knowledge" with respect to ourselves.'[43]

Nietzsche goes much further than Aristotle: he believes that we can never really understand our actions, let alone their motives; they are too complicated, too opaque. If we think we know precisely what we are about, we are almost certainly deluded. Aristotle thinks we *can* gain knowledge of ourselves emotionally, just as we can physically; but we need the aid of mirrors – in this case the mirror of someone who is just like us in his essential nature, a 'second self' whom we love; not an enemy (though, one might add, enemies – our choice of them and the behaviour they evoke – can surely give us valuable insight into ourselves):

> [Just as] when we wish to see our own face, we do so by looking into the mirror, in the same way when we wish to know ourselves we can obtain that knowledge by looking at our friend. For the friend is, as we assert, a second self. If, then, it is pleasant to know oneself, and it is not possible to know this without having someone else for a friend, the self-sufficing man will require friendship in order to know himself.[45]

In other words, we learn about ourselves from a loved one not so much because of what he tells us, but rather by observing our own reflections in him. By coming to know him as a 'second self', we come to know our own self. By discovering that our intuitions of kinship with him are reliable and well-founded, we discover our own character and why we choose and act as we do.

Aristotle's idea of friends as mirrors hardly exhausts the ways in which intimacy can foster self-knowledge. As important as mirroring is, surely, what we learn from the many unexpected ways in which a close relationship makes us feel secure or frightened, relaxed or uneasy, happy or angry, powerful or weak, sure or unsure of our own values and projects. But Aristotle offers us a crucial insight: that our idea of who we are is formed through intimate, sustained relations with others, based on a sense of deep affinity which has stood the test of time. In other words, individuality is fundamentally relational.

✦ ✦ ✦

Which brings us back to Aristotle's point that these benefits of love will flow only if lover and beloved are sufficiently virtuous. His idea that love is unjustified – and unjust – if it isn't rooted in appropriate excellences of character might seem distasteful. But it is more profound than meets the eye. It echoes an archaic Greek idea that the cosmos has an essential order – a 'just' order – to which everything, whether human or inanimate, must be attuned if it is to flourish. Justice, in the sense of such an attunement, is therefore not simply a matter of respecting rules, like keeping promises or not lying, that we hive off into an area of life called 'morality'. Instead, justice is acting in accordance with what are taken to be the deepest laws of the universe. Anything that disobeys them does so at its peril. Heraclitus remarks that this includes even the sun: 'The sun will not transgress his measures. If he does, the Furies, ministers of Justice, will find him out.'[46]

Aristotle is firmly within this tradition when he asserts that everything unfair is unlawful and everything fair is lawful. Greek has a special word for this lawfulness: *dikaios*, meaning 'fair', 'just', 'right' *or* 'in accordance with the laws'. Love is *dikaios* when it is in accordance with the laws of the other person's nature, when it is strictly justified by his character, when it gives him his due. If love isn't in such accordance it is inauthentic and hollow (as everything is ungenuine when untrue to the laws governing it).

Each of us can therefore only love – and be loved by – very particular people. The bond we feel with such people isn't the result of some mysterious 'chemistry', but is based on tangible and observable features of their character and of their conceptions of what is good. Love affirms only those features of the beloved that are virtuous and good, and otherwise is far from 'all-accepting'. And though we might 'fall' in love with inappropriate people – for Aristotle, those who lack virtue, or don't share similar ideals, or fail to wish and do each other well – it won't work. Such an urge will go against the laws of (human) nature: and so, with such people, no lasting intimacy will be possible.

The moral? We are probably much too casual in our choice of lovers; for the wrong choice can knock our life off a flourishing course. Passion and chemistry are no proof of love, let alone of whether a relationship will be good for us. Out of our powerful urge to become similar to those we are attracted to – to heed their advice, to emulate their values and tastes – we pay a real and often disastrous price for associating with the wrong people: those of insufficient virtue, those whose values are too different to our own. We become worse with a worse person, better with a better person; but the secret to durable love is two people who are not only virtuous, but *similarly* virtuous.

It is easy to underestimate how extraordinarily contrary Aristotle's thought is to those contemporary dogmas about love that I noted in chapter 1: for example that it is unconditional, spontaneous, selfless, affirming of the whole person, and, in its very nature, constant. Thus, where we might think that love sets no conditions, Aristotle tells us that it is absolutely conditional on both parties being good and alike in character. Where we might see altruistic love as competing with self-love, Aristotle suggests that loving another for his own sake is integral to the exercise of self-love. Where we might suppose that we must love ourselves before we can love another, Aristotle indicates the opposite. Where we might imagine that to have insight into others we should first be able to have insight into ourselves, Aristotle proposes the reverse. Where we might proclaim that true love is constant 'no matter what', Aristotle maintains that it can, even should, change if the loved one changes. Where we might assume that love is a spontaneous emotion for which there is no accounting, Aristotle sees it as a supremely reasonable and entirely explicable feeling. Where we might view love as innately unjust and possessive, Aristotle insists that it is necessarily just and flourishes only between two self-dependent individuals.

Though the dogmas about love to which *philia* is opposed are themselves inherited from various Christian traditions, *philia* is also taken up by Catholic Christianity, above all under the influence of Thomas Aquinas. Indeed Christianity's protean genius for co-opting the most diverse traditions – Hebrew Scripture; the 'paganism' of Plato, Aristotle and Ovid; the egalitarianism of the Enlightenment – means that radically different conceptions of love are going to collide, sowing confusion that lasts to this day. Yet before we turn to how this came to be so, and to how we might unravel so much confusion, we must pause in that 'eternal' city where Greek ideas and the newly formed Christian sect were to encounter each other so intimately: Rome.

5

Love as sexual desire
Lucretius and Ovid

In love, as in politics and engineering, Rome is home to pragmatists of genius. Among them we find two of the greatest exponents of love as a purely natural drive that is corrupted by being expected to redeem suffering and evil and death. They give love, and especially friendship, a central place in the flourishing life; but they refuse to deify passion, instead seeing it, as do many ancients, as a type of slavery and unhappy fate. They examine with unsparing precision the machinations of sexual desire and its overwhelming urge for procreation and pleasure, in the hope that we will control it rather than allow it to control us – and so will free ourselves from the fear, madness and delusion with which this desire can overwhelm us.[1]

For Lucretius and Ovid (respectively *c.* 99–*c.* 55 BCE and 43 BCE–*c.* 17 CE), what two people erotically besotted with each other call 'love' is merely the unwitting servant of the instinct for self-perpetuation. This is an instinct so fundamental that, on some conceptions of it, it can be identified with life-force itself. Its *modus operandi* is power and manipulation, warfare and illusion. Far from being a harbinger of virtue, it is a harbinger of ruin; and the art of love is to live this impulsive and heedless instinct without being harmed by it. There isn't much spirituality to be found in these Roman beds.

But from this common foundation the two poets draw very different conclusions, especially in the aesthetic *value* they attach to sexual love.

✦ ✦ ✦

Lucretius, a contemporary of Julius Caesar, is as unidealistic about sexual love as it is possible to be. In his great poem, 'On the Nature of Things' (*De Rerum*

Natura), he describes the spectacle of a man attracted to a woman: 'He runs at the person . . . and wants to copulate/ And to plant in that body the fluid from his own body;/ His dumb desire suggests it will give him pleasure'.[2]

Sex is addictive: desire is never finally satisfied, and – unlike other cravings, say for food and water – the more we feed it the more we inflame it.[3] Yet if we refuse it altogether it will torment us with fantasies. We should therefore gratify our sexual appetite temperately, but also free ourselves from its tyranny.

At the same time and entirely consistently, Lucretius worships Venus, the goddess of love and mother of the Roman people (called Aphrodite by the Greeks). He does so on account of the boundless procreation she inspires: '. . . everything under the stars/ . . . Is full of you: every living thing is conceived/ By your methods and so comes into the daylight'.[4]

He even asks Venus for help in writing his poem: 'Since you alone control the working of nature . . ./ And nothing is glad or amiable without you./ I seek your assistance as I write these verses'.[5]

There is neither ambivalence nor paradox here. Lucretius rejoices in the love-drive insofar as he identifies it with, or sees it as serving, Venus's vast generative power. Vitality thrills to itself. Vitality is the delight that keeps life wanting more of itself. Wanting, in other words, to procreate.

But, crucially, not because life is good in itself. Here again we must emphasise the strangeness to our modern ears of Lucretius and later of Ovid. Schopenhauer, for example, will also see sexual passion as expressing a cosmic erotic energy, a procreative life-force that pervades all of nature – which he calls 'will to life'. But its insatiability and the misery to which he thinks it, like all desire, leads will cause him to indict the value of life as such.

Whereas Lucretius seems to have no interest in judging the value of life as a whole. And rightly: for we living creatures cannot ourselves get outside of life – whether life as such or our own life – and take a view on whether, on balance, it is for the good or not. Whether its suffering, disappointment, fragility, vulnerability and certain death are somehow outweighed and justified by a supreme good, be it natural or supernatural.

Lucretius is therefore bleak, but not pessimistic. He portrays the horrors of life with relentless clarity; but without drawing the conclusion that it is, all things considered, 'bad' – the conclusion that would warrant calling him a pessimist. He knows that people can surrender to despair when the hope of life's continuation is overwhelmed by the forces of decay: illness, old age, bad luck. He offers ways of coping with despair – for example about death – but he doesn't think love should be given the job of redeeming it.

✦ ✦ ✦

The despairs of love attract his particular disdain, especially when they flow from idealising one's mate or the sexual act itself. Grand passion, Lucretius warns, begets grand stupidity. Lovers are seized by the impossible craving to merge, as if they each want their whole body to be absorbed into the other's.[6] They are beset by jealousy and envy. They dissipate their energies. And they easily turn sadistic:

> They squash the body they sought until it squeals
> And often their teeth make a gash on the lips
> In the course of affixing a kiss, which is hardly pure pleasure.
> They are indeed rather provoked to injure the object,
> Whatever it is, which causes this onset of lunacy.[7]

Where Ovid finds these illusions entertaining, if sometimes farcical, Lucretius finds the whole business of idealisation tedious:

> We often see mis-shapen, disgusting women
> Regarded as charming, indeed, you might say worshipped . . .
> A dark girl looks like honey; an unwashed one is natural;
> The cat-eyed bitch is a goddess; the stringy one is a sylph;
> The undersized, undergrown one a minute gem;
> The overgrown monster has an extraordinary dignity . . .[8]

✦ ✦ ✦

In the ancient world, Greek and Roman, it was a commonplace to warn of love's madness, including its tendency to idealise and, when disappointed, to demonise. But Lucretius regards these ills of love as merely in need of remedies, rather than as symptoms of a drive that, properly channelled, can bring us in touch with great ethical and spiritual goods.

In essence, he sees only three remedies, which in descending order of nobility are: contemplation, marriage and promiscuity.[9] The tyranny of sex can, he thinks, be calmed by contemplation, contained by marriage and, if all else fails, expended by promiscuity.

Contemplation, as Lucretius describes it, is meditation aimed at stilling our desires as well as enjoying simple and sociable pleasures. It is a less demanding, less spiritual, method of transcending sexual desire than most approaches in Western history, which tend to involve passionate attention to a reality conceived as supremely valuable, as in Plato's search for the essence of beauty, or the Christian's devotion to God, or Spinoza's *amor intellectualis Dei*, or Schopenhauer's contemplation of art and the aesthetic – although, as we will see, Schopenhauer comes close to Lucretius's position.

Meditation enables us to look at the world, and more particularly at sexually attractive people, without being overwhelmed by lust, fear, jealousy, possessiveness, or other dissipating emotions.

In all this Lucretius is faithful to Epicurus (341–270 BCE), the Greek philosopher whom he reveres with a passion redolent of his veneration of Venus. Indeed, Epicurus's influence on Lucretius is so immense that a very brief detour into his philosophy is necessary.

In the first place, Epicurus was no 'Epicurean'. He wasn't devoted to luxury and intoxication; nor to cultivating the delights of the senses: sex, wine, food and glamorous living. Though he wants to maximise pleasure, he insists that we do so by living a frugal life in which bodily desires in particular are strictly limited:

When, therefore, we maintain that pleasure is the end, we do not mean the pleasures of profligates and those that consist in sensuality, as is supposed by some who are either ignorant or disagree with us or do not understand, but freedom from pain in the body and from trouble in the mind.[10]

Basic necessities like food, drink, clothing and shelter should be as modest as possible, or they will bring us more sorrow than joy. Sexual satisfaction should be sought only in moderation: 'intercourse has never done a man good, and he is lucky if it has not harmed him'.[11] As for power and fame, Epicurus counsels against them. Desire for these sorts of thing is always insatiable. And unsatisfied desire causes pain, which it seeks to overcome by more desires and their satisfactions, and so on.

Real happiness, Epicurus insists, is tranquillity of mind. And this comes from freedom and friends. One must seek freedom from demanding entanglements in the world, including politics, spouses and children – as well as from fear of poverty, death, and the gods, and in general what the future might hold. And one must find like-minded friends with whom to enjoy bucolic pleasures. ('Of all the things which wisdom acquires to produce the blessedness of the complete life, [by] far the greatest is the possession of friendship.'[12])

Reflection is crucial to attaining such happiness, for it enables us to understand the absurdity of our anxieties. Thus we shouldn't fear death, Epicurus tells us, 'for that which is dissolved is without sensation; and that which lacks sensation is nothing to us'.[13] This was, after all, the case before we were born – so why should we worry that it will again be so after our demise?

And we needn't fear the gods, since, contrary to popular superstition, they do not interfere in the world, nor are they angry or violent. On the contrary, they possess just the self-sufficiency and happiness that we humans should make our own aim: 'The blessed and immortal nature knows no trouble itself nor causes trouble to any other, so that it is never constrained by anger or favour. For all such things exist only in the weak.'[14]

✦ ✦ ✦

So what should we do when we find ourselves powerfully desiring someone? We should focus on developing friendship with her, and on enjoying modest delights together – including modest sexual delights. Perhaps, like Epicurus himself, we should be part of a secluded group of friends: for this, and not the State, is his ideal society.

Yet, as Epicurus teaches and Lucretius echoes, it is extraordinarily hard to discipline our sexual drives – and in general our desire for intoxicating emotion. For those of us who can't do so Lucretius recommends marriage and children. That combination will soon put an end to delusions about our beloved and make both parties see each other realistically – the only basis for successful human relationships. Desire will be contained by occasional satisfaction as well as by the routines of conjugal life; and sex will be channelled to its proper end: producing offspring.

This advice isn't meant cynically, in the manner of those who see marriage as so dull that it can be counted on to douse the flames of passion ('One should always be in love. That is the reason one should never marry'[15]). On the contrary, Lucretius praises marriage as solving the eternal problem of how to socialise *and* to satisfy our unruly urges – and in the process to form a lasting and happy relationship.

But who is the right person to marry? Lucretius's answer is again biological: whoever has the most compatible seed – and in particular seed of the right consistency. If semen is too thick it 'comes out more solid than is suitable/ And either does not penetrate far enough up' to reach the woman's egg or is 'ill adapted to mix with the woman's seed'. On the other hand, if semen is too fluid it also fails to 'stick where it should/ But flows back at once before its work is done'.[16]

Two things can help here. One is the right diet: 'By some foods the seed is thickened in the body;/ By others it is thinned out and wasted away.'[17] The other is the coital position. Lucretius recommends doggy-style: 'The manner in which the female quadruped takes it/ Generally seems the best for securing conception./ The seed can get to its objective best/ If wives put their breasts down and behinds in the air.'[18] And he notes: 'No need for wives to engage in lascivious movements'. In fact conception is hindered if 'she wriggles her buttocks in pursuit of pleasure,/ And stimulates oceans by presenting a boneless front,/ She throws the furrow out from the right area,/ And stops the plough and the spurt of seed going home'. Whores might do this to please their men, but 'Nothing of that sort seems necessary for wives'.[19]

If all else fails, there is promiscuity. Those tortured by a futile obsession should get their imagination under control, remember that there are other attractive lovers out there, and seek release wherever they can find it:

> Keep off imagination and frighten away
> Whatever encourages love; turn your mind elsewhere,
> Get rid of the fluid in any body you can
> Instead of keeping it for a single person
> Which is bound to lead to trouble and end in grief.[20]

✦ ✦ ✦

Unsurprisingly, Christians were not always enamoured of Lucretius's thought, with its concern to maximise well-being in this life, its worship of nature, and its belief that the soul is material. Over four centuries after the poet's death, St Jerome (c. 347–c. 420) allegedly spread the story that far from escaping obsessive love Lucretius had been driven to suicide by – of all things – a love potion: 'The poet Titus Lucretius was born. In later life he was sent mad by a love-potion; in the intervals of his madness he composed a number of books, later edited by Cicero. He died by his own hand at the age of forty-four'.[21]

Though this story was never confirmed, Tennyson sets it to verse, adding that the love potion which brought about the poet's comeuppance had been administered by none other than his sexually frustrated wife Lucilla. Angered at his self-control and absorption in his work,

> She brook'd it not; but wrathful, petulant,
> Dreaming some rival, sought and found a witch
> Who brew'd the philtre which had power, they said,
> To lead an errant passion home again.
> And this, at times, she mingled with his drink,
> And this destroy'd him; for the wicked broth
> Confused the chemic labour of the blood,
> And tickling the brute brain within the man's
> Made havoc among those tender cells, and check'd
> His power to shape[.][22]

OVID: LOVE AS WAR AND DELIGHT

No such anger could be inspired by Ovid. He is too charming, too playful, to attract enmity. Where Lucretius warns, Ovid says 'enjoy!'

In his didactic poem – *Ars Amatoria*, or *The Art of Love* – one of the earliest guides to love in the West, Ovid recognises in humans the same impulsive, possessive, deluded erotic desire as does Lucretius – but he celebrates it. Love is a sport:[23] vigorous, delightful, and subtle. We should pursue it not just to win, but for its beauty. Where people today say that love shouldn't be about 'playing games', Ovid would answer 'Oh yes it should!' Love loses much of its point if it doesn't play games. It can certainly be dangerous: 'Love is a kind of war, and no assignment for cowards';[24] but one can excel at it given talent, skill, cunning, enthusiasm – and self-restraint.

Ovid gleefully probes love's opposites: attraction and contempt; tenderness and spite; trust and jealousy; the craving of our flesh for someone whom our reason condemns.[25] And he sees women's erotic power over men in even starker terms than does Lucretius, reflecting perhaps the way in which Roman women were often the chief players in romantic intrigue, despite their subservience to men in other respects. As Octavio Paz remarks:

> Women – more precisely, patrician women – occupy an outstanding place in
> the history of Rome, during both the Republic and the Empire . . . because to

an unprecedented degree they had the freedom to accept or reject their lovers.
They were the mistresses of their bodies and their souls.[26]

Sexual pleasure is central to the game. Here full reciprocity between men and
women can be found: 'Let the woman feel the act of love to her marrow,/ Let
the performance bring equal delight to the two'.[27]

Yet, Ovid observes, the constraining institution of marriage hardly fosters the
courtesy and consideration that may be found in a relationship enjoyed for love
alone:

Husbands and wives, by right, may harry each other with nagging;
Let them believe, as they must, this is their nature and law.
This is all right for wives: the dower of a wife is a quarrel;
Let your mistresses hear nothing but what they desire.
You have not come to one bed in the name of the law, but more freely.
Love is your warrant and bond, love holds the office of law.[28]

✦ ✦ ✦

Before all this can happen a lover needs to be ensnared. Here too there are
rules for winning the game and avoiding its pitfalls. Ovid begins with some very
practical advice for men:

1. Put in the effort: 'First, my raw recruit, my inexperienced soldier,/ Take
some trouble to find the girl whom you really can love.'[29]

2. Hunt in the right places: 'the theatre's curve is a very good place for your
hunting,/ More opportunity here, maybe, than anywhere else./ Here you may
find one to love, or possibly only have fun with,/ Someone to take for a night,
someone to have and to hold.'[30]

3. Don't be too coy: 'be a confident soul, and spread your nets with assurance./
Women can always be caught; that's the first rule of the game'.[31]

4. Get your timing right: 'It is worth making a try when she's grieving because
of a rival,/ Vengeance can quickly be hers if you're conveniently there'.[32]

5. Don't be too proud to implore or persist, and be eloquent in a relaxed way –
without attempting to look learned: 'Young men of Rome, I advise you to learn the
arts of the pleader,/ Not so much for the sake of some poor wretch at the bar,/ But
because women are moved, as much as the people or Senate,/ Possibly more than
a judge, conquered by eloquent words'.[33]

6. In appearance, make sure you are well-groomed but casual: 'Men should not care too much for good looks: neglect is becoming'. 'Let your person be clean, your body tanned by the sunshine, . . ./ Keep the little hairs out of your nose and your ears,/ Let your breath be sweet, and your body free from rank odours,/ Don't overdo it; a man isn't a fairy or tart.'[34]

7. If she's married get her husband onside: 'Also, make it your aim to get her husband to like you;/ If you can make him your friend, he will be useful, you'll find.'[35] 'Propose "A health to the lady! A health to the fellow she sleeps with!"/ Making your silent toast, "Damn her husband to hell!" '[36]

8. Emote if you can: 'Tears are a good thing, too; they move the most adamant natures./ Let her, if possible, see tears on your cheeks, in your eyes./ This is not easy: sometimes the eyes will not stream at your bidding./ What can be done about this? – get your hands wet, and apply.'[37]

9. Remember that though women are attracted to money and good looks, their love is more likely to last if the man also has some education: 'You might have all the good looks that appealed to the sea-nymphs, or Homer;/ That's not enough, you will find; add some distinction of mind . . . Culture is surely worth while, and the liberal arts are a blessing:/ Take some trouble to learn two great languages well./ Handsome, Ulysses was not, but his eloquence charmed with its power'.[38]

✦ ✦ ✦

Ovid says he would spare women his advice, but Venus has insisted that he also pass on to them some of her personal tips:

In the first place, don't be prudish – if you are you will regret it: 'So when a woman tells a man, "It doesn't seem proper!"/ What is she doing but waste what her own thirst will require?'[39]

Pay attention to personal hygiene and shave your legs: 'Should I warn you to keep the rank goat out of your armpits/ Warn you to keep your legs free of coarse bristling hair?'[40]

Disguise imperfections: 'Art supplies the means for patching an incomplete eyebrow'.[41]

If your teeth are stained or uneven, keep your mouth shut: 'Pay no attention to jokes; laughter might give you away.'[42]

Laugh and cry with restraint, cultivate the art of singing, and, of course, time your surrender carefully: 'Don't be a reckless girl, too quick with a promise, too easy/ Don't, on the other hand, absolutely refuse./ Keep him hoping and fearing'.[43]

Have a separate man to fulfil each need: 'Hold an inspection, and set each of us where he belongs./ Let the rich bring gifts; get legal advice from the lawyers'.[44]

Choose sexual positions that display your best features: 'Lie on your back, if your face and all of your features are pretty;/ If your posterior's cute, better be seen from behind . . ./ If you have beautiful legs, let them be lifted'.[45]

Talk dirty and moan: 'Coax and flatter and tease, with inarticulate murmurs,/ Even with sexual words, in the excitement of play'.[46]

But whatever happens, make sure he thinks he satisfied you: 'And if nature, alas! denies you the final sensation/ Cry out as if you had come, do your best to pretend'.[47]

✦ ✦ ✦

In Ovid's universe women are no less fixated on sex than are men. Indeed, women's lust can be 'fiercer, more wanton than ours'.[48] It can destroy men, or forcibly change them into creatures alien to their true nature.

Here Ovid draws on an ancient mythological tradition that speaks of the violence of female desire: the Sirens' seductive songs against which Odysseus protects himself by being tied to the mast of his ship, and defends his men by blocking their ears with wax; the obsessive goddess Circe, a beautiful sorceress who transforms men, especially those who reject her advances, into animals; the nymph Salmacis who so craves the beautiful youth Hermaphroditus that she pounces on him in a deep pond in whose clear and disorienting water she literally merges her body with his – and, in doing so, destroys them both as individuals:

> . . . so were these two bodies knit in close embrace: they were no longer two, nor such as to be called, one, woman, and one, man. They seemed neither, and yet both.[49]

Though Ovid wants erotic warfare to be as raw, resourceful and joyous as possible, lovers must give style to their passions by displaying charm, tact and civility towards each other. They must make their sometimes dangerous sport beautiful, imaginative and uplifting – an art.

✦ ✦ ✦

But there should be limits to wooing. To those in hopeless love matches, Ovid says: get out; move on. Don't stick at it regardless. Find a more promising match. And, if you just can't get your mind off her, though you know she's wrong for you, focus on her faults. Recall her misdeeds, itemise what she has cost you, and see her as she really is – just an ordinary, imperfect, replaceable woman.

And if that doesn't kick the addiction, exaggerate her failings. Do the opposite of what people falling in love do: use your imagination to play up her defects. After learning to un-love one woman (or man), one's imagination will be freed up to embrace and glorify another.

But if all else fails, escape.

The point of these diverse experiments in love – of repeatedly falling into and out of love – isn't that by trial and error we will eventually find a 'perfect' fit and stop there. Ovid, at least in his *Art of Love*, isn't concerned with the sort of search for an ideal love that still motivates so much skipping between partners today. His aim is rather to cultivate the joys of erotic experience; to create delight and beauty and style out of wild, unformed and sometimes unbecoming nature. Given skill and patience he believes that erotic desire's primal, pitiless, procreative force can and should be relished; and that the opposing elements of war and grace, brutality and tact, creativity and destructiveness, can coexist.

Ovid's motto is: recognise, master and then enjoy love's dangers. And do so with levity – an attitude that doesn't come easily to us, the inheritors of a tradition that takes love to be the most serious business of life.

✦ ✦ ✦

Lucretius and Ovid therefore belong to a powerful, but minority, voice in the Western tradition: they are uncompromising naturalists about love, who see it in exclusively earthly or material terms. But unlike almost all other naturalists, with the possible exception of Freud, they do not – one might say, they resist the temptation to – see love and its trials as figuring in a narrative of redemption: in other words as making possible a supreme good which overcomes or justifies life's suffering and evil.

As we have seen, they recognise – as their Greek forebears did and as most subsequent traditions will do – the madness, brutality and immorality of which sexual desire is capable. They warn – whether severely, cynically or humorously – that lovers' idealisations can deceive them and violate their loved ones. And they see the insatiability of passion and the impossibility of real possession. Yet their response to these dangers is to recommend practical ways of controlling them rather than to offer an 'ascent story' in which the crude energies of desire and misshapen human relationships might be transcended or sublimated. Though Lucretius and Ovid can be lyrical about love – for friends, for spouses, for Venus – they do not invest its role in human flourishing with the primacy and urgency that we see in much of the Western tradition. Still less do they deem love to be the supreme virtue, tasked with securing an absolute and immortal state of perfection that can vanquish the sorrows of the world.

Rome was, of course, to end up as a capital city of that religion which would go to the opposite extreme, and forge a bond between love and redemption so powerful that it becomes almost impossible to break. A bond that so permeates Western sensibility that even atheists like Schopenhauer, Nietzsche and Proust cannot entirely escape it – indeed, arguably strive to give it new form. This religion is of course Christianity, to whose central traditions we now turn.

6

Love as the supreme virtue
Christianity

The immensely diverse and adaptable group of related Churches that we call 'Christianity' brings about two innovations with which the Western world and many who have been influenced by it live to this day. It turns love into life's supreme virtue and moral principle; so that to the question 'Can we do anything better than to love and be loved?' the answer is clearly no.

And Christianity makes love a divine power that, if infused by God into the receptive human being, ordinary people can express. With the aid of this power and the relationships that celebrate it we can rise above the terrors and traps of earthly life and redeem suffering, pain, loss, anxiety, evil and death. In other words, the strange sacrilege which Christianity has encouraged – and which has been embraced with particular fervour by some of its secular successors – is that through love humans can become god-like, even if only imperfectly and fleetingly.[1]

These legacies are far more powerful determinants of how we think about love today than are, say, Christianity's strictures against sexuality. 'Just say no' is a sporadic fad; but 'All you need is love' is the motto that saves secular societies in the West from staring into an abyss of meaninglessness. The Christian idea that love is the absolute and eternal virtue by which all our other virtues are ultimately to be judged is everywhere at work, even (especially?) among many atheists who otherwise despise the very idea of 'the absolute' or 'the eternal'. If we learn that a course of action that instinctively repels us – perhaps a husband who assists his terminally ill wife to die; or parents who give their profoundly retarded daughter a hysterectomy so that she can never conceive – is motivated by love we at least pause to consider its merits. If we hear at a funeral that the deceased was a great statesman or inventor or artist or writer but sense that he never loved or was loved we are filled with unease – convinced that something was fundamentally lacking in his life that can be made good in no other way. If, by contrast, we hear that the dead man loved greatly but otherwise did little with his life we might be saddened by what was left undone, but we don't feel that it casts a shadow over his whole life – for love gives it an overriding value that can never be lost or reassessed. In having such thoughts we are merely echoing Augustine, one of the great founders of what would gradually become thought of as 'Christian love', who says: 'Where there is love . . . what is there that can be lacking? But where it is not, what is there that can be profitable?'[2]

✦ ✦ ✦

Yet we encounter something quite startling in the Synoptic Gospels[3]: Jesus hardly talks about love. He nowhere says that 'God is love'. Nor is he clear that love – even, as we will see, God's love – is necessarily unconditional (or 'spontaneous'), perhaps the first feature of 'Christian love' that many people think of. He certainly doesn't speak of love as a great mystical connection to the divine – as an erotic-spiritual force through which we come to union with God. He doesn't describe it as a creative, all-conquering power that enables us to transcend or redeem everyday life and suffering. As for sex, he barely mentions it – indeed he places no restrictions on it except, as we will see, in the context of adultery. When it comes to his reported sayings on love in the Synoptic Gospels, Jesus is not a 'good Christian'.

Such central features of 'Christian love', as it is widely thought of, first appear with St Paul and the last of the Evangelists, St John – and, for the most part, Paul and John do not attribute them to Jesus. On the few occasions when Jesus talks about love in the Synoptic Gospels his claims are much more restricted. In particular: love is the most important of the commandments that God issues to humans; and it is to be extended, to a hitherto unimagined extent, to one's enemies.

Both these claims are, as we saw in chapter 2, deeply rooted in Hebrew Scripture. Jesus himself acknowledges this origin by citing Deuteronomy and Leviticus – not surprisingly, perhaps, for a Jewish teacher interpreting Jewish faith:

Jesus answered, 'The first [commandment] is, "Hear, O Israel: the Lord our God, the Lord is one; you shall love the Lord your God with all your heart, and with all your soul, and with all your mind, and with all your strength." The second is this, "You shall love your neighbour as yourself." There is no other commandment greater than these.' (Mark 12:29–31)

And in the 'Sermon on the Mount'[4] he takes love of one's foes far beyond the scattered demands in the Old Testament to help an enemy in trouble (Exodus 23:4–5; Proverbs 25:21) and even beyond the general command to love one's neighbour. He demands that one actually bless one's tormentors and accept their hostility in a spirit of non-resistance:

But I say to you that listen, Love your enemies, do good to those who hate you, bless those who curse you, pray for those who abuse you. If anyone strikes you on the cheek, offer the other also; and from anyone who takes away your coat do not withhold even your shirt. Give to everyone who begs from you; and if anyone takes away your goods, do not ask for them again. (Luke 6:27–30; cf. Matthew 5:44)

Jesus's revolutionary call to love our enemies isn't distinct from the commandment to love God and neighbour; enemies aren't, so to speak, a third focus for love in addition to God and neighbour. To obey the commandment to love God and neighbour *is* to love the enemy: the neighbour includes the enemy.

Ultimately, Jesus says, the law depends on this commandment (Matthew 22:34–8). Elsewhere, in an echo of the 'Golden Rule' of the Jewish sage, Hillel, he says: 'In everything do to others as you would have them do to you; for this is the law and the prophets' (Matthew 7:12; cf. Luke 6:31).[5]

And the law, Jesus stipulates here, must be fulfilled.[6] He has not abolished the paradox that we encountered in Judaism: the paradox that love, the paradigm of an emotion that must be free to be genuine, is commanded.

Do not think that I have come to abolish the law or the prophets; I have come not to abolish but to fulfil. For truly I tell you, until heaven and earth pass away, not one letter, not one stroke of a letter, will pass from the law until all is accomplished. (Matthew 5:17–18)

Love is also commanded in John:

I give you a new commandment, that you love one another. Just as I have loved you, you also should love one another. By this everyone will know that you are my disciples, if you have love for one another. (John 13:34–35)

You are my friends if you do what I command you. (John 15:14)

And this is his [God's] commandment, that we should believe in the name of his Son Jesus Christ and love one another, just as he has commanded us. (1 John 3:23)

That love and law are here inseparable couldn't be clearer. Jesus in no way sees love as above the law. Nor – to use modern terms – does he locate love's essence in a freedom or spontaneity that lies beyond our duties and rights. And yet for centuries, and especially since Luther and the Reformation, Jesus has been seen as decisively 'liberating' love from the restraint of law. Indeed this has been defined as one of the great dividing lines between the New and Old Testaments. It has become a cliché to say that the New Testament invents love as a spontaneous gift free of law, whereas the Old is obsessed with a coldly legalistic fulfilling of the law. This is not only a popular conviction but taken as axiomatic by such an influential scholar of love as the Protestant Bishop and theologian Anders Nygren: 'The difference between the Jewish and the primitive Christian view of love can be formulated thus: *love set within the scheme of law – love breaking down the scheme of law.*'[7]

Love breaking down the scheme of law? How does that blanket claim take account even of the words of Jesus that we just heard? Or of the many others that clearly show Christian Scripture and tradition to be at one with Judaism on the commandment to love? Or on love for God presupposing obedience of one's whole being to God, who gave the law?

The highest expression of such obedience in the New Testament is Jesus's sacrifice of his own life on the Cross. He knows he must die to fulfil God's purpose, and predicts his own death (Mark 8:31). He is, as St Paul says, 'obedient to the point of death' (Philippians 2:8). Yet his last words – 'My God, my God, why have you forsaken me?' (Mark 15:34) – suggest precisely the inscrutability of the beloved that makes submission to the lawfulness of his being not only heroic, but a genuine mark of love. These words capture the essence of the lover offering himself unreservedly: you know what the loved one commands but not why; you open yourself maximally to his powerful but, to you, incomprehensible, and even seemingly perverse, purpose; you embrace willingly a fate that you did not will; you acknowledge in attitude and action your often painful lack of control, self-sufficiency, and understanding.

+ + +

The way Jesus talks of love in the Synoptic Gospels is therefore far more modest in scope than some of the claims with which Christianity came to be associated, such as that God is love or that all true virtue is motivated by love – or can even be reduced to love. If we want to find the Scriptural origins of these more ambitious claims we have to look elsewhere – and in particular to the following utterances:

> If I speak in the tongues of mortals and of angels, but do not have love, I am a noisy gong or a clanging cymbal. And if I have prophetic powers, and understand all mysteries and all knowledge, and if I have all faith, so as to remove mountains, but do not have love, I am nothing. If I give away all my possessions, and if I hand over my body so that I may boast, but do not have love, I gain nothing. . . . Love is patient; love is kind; love is not envious or boastful or arrogant or rude . . . It bears all things, believes all things, hopes all things, endures all things. . . . And now faith, hope, and love abide, these three; and the greatest of these is love. (1 Corinthians 13:1, 2, 4, 7, 13)

> Beloved, let us love one another, because love is from God; everyone who loves is born of God and knows God. Whoever does not love does not know God, for God is love. God's love was revealed among us in this way: God sent his only Son into the world so that we might live through him. In this is love, not that we loved God but that he loved us and sent his Son to be the atoning sacrifice for our sins. Beloved, since God loved us so much, we also ought to love one another . . . God is love, and those who abide in love abide in God, and God abides in them. (1 John 4:7–11 and 16)

The authors of these seminal statements – the staple of weddings and funerals to this day – are St Paul and St John the Evangelist. Here, for the first time in Western history, love is clearly named as the essence of the divine. If God, the highest possible being and the source of all other beings, *is* love then love must be the highest possible value and, in key respects, the source of all other value.

St John's way of making the point – 'God is love' – is mystical; St Paul's – 'the greatest of these is love' – is more practical. Combined, they will establish love as the fundamental principle of the moral universe.

John: Love is how God shows himself. It is the way in which he shows 'how' he is – or differently put: the way in which he reveals his essence. It is, in some sense, his supreme principle – more important than omnipotence or wisdom or eternity. And so love should be the supreme principle of how we, as beings created by God, relate to others.

Paul: Love is the binding force of a brotherhood of believers in Christ; it is the practice, attitude and art of being together as members of the one 'body of Christ' in the world (1 Corinthians 12); it is first among the 'fruit[s] of the Spirit': love, joy, peace, patience, kindness, generosity, faithfulness, gentleness, and self-control (Galatians 5:22–3). Only in such practice of love can Christians be renewed together in Christ.

Because love is the foundation of all good, it isn't just the highest virtue. It is also the virtue, the supreme practical excellence, which must inspire and imbue all others – such as courage, faith, hope, and forgiveness – if they are to be really valuable. As Augustine will put it: 'no fruit is good which does not grow from the root of love [caritas]'.[8] All good actions and intentions are rooted in love. All virtues – courage, generosity, hard work – are therefore forms of love, or as Augustine claims, virtue is 'nothing other' than the supreme love of God.[9] While Thomas Aquinas, for his part, tells us that there is no true virtue without caritas.[10]

In this vein, Paul boldly claims that Jewish law is fulfilled in love of neighbour. The great commandments speak of different ways of loving:

> Owe no one anything, except to love one another; for the one who loves another has fulfilled the law. The commandments, 'You shall not commit adultery; You shall not murder; You shall not steal; You shall not covet'; and any other commandment, are summed up in this word, 'Love your neighbour as yourself.' Love does no wrong to a neighbour; therefore, love is the fulfilling of the law. (Romans 13:8–10)

The value of love had never before been so extravagant. Though neither Paul nor John talks of a love that is romantic or particularly individual – in the modern sense that its essence is to recognise and affirm the specific nature of the other 'for who they are' – nonetheless we find here the foundation stone of our deep belief that a life without great love, whether directed at a romantic lover, our children, God, or a stranger in need, is impoverished in a way for which no heroic deeds or original achievements can ever compensate. 'If I . . . do not have love, I gain nothing' (1 Corinthians 13:3). 'Whoever does not love abides in death' (1 John 3:14). You can do whatever else you want. If you do not love, everything else you do is weightless; your existence is a living death.

✦ ✦ ✦

It is worth pausing to see what is happening here. One thing that is obviously happening is the creation of a new morality – based on so great an intensification of Old Testament morality that a genuine revolution in values has occurred. The ancient Hebrew commands to love God and neighbour have culminated in the idea that love is the measure of all virtue, the standard by which the worth of all other virtues and all the actions that express them are ultimately to be gauged. As Augustine puts it: our 'actions . . . are . . . judged not on the basis of what each of us knows but on the basis of what each of us loves'.[11] All true virtues are forms of love.[12]

But morality is concerned with more than helping us reach practical decisions about good and bad; more than answering the question 'What is the right thing to do?', or 'How should I behave to others?', or 'How should I rank my values?', or even 'How can I lead the most flourishing life?' A morality that compels us has to appear to answer another set of questions: How can I stand with firm self-respect in the world? How do I command and rely on the recognition of others? How do I interpret the meaning of events – such as what other people do and say, or strokes of fortune and misfortune? Ultimately: How can I find a home in the world, an anchorage in existence, which feels indestructible? Deep down all morality is a grab for safety and significance.

In Christianity's morality of love the ground is prepared, inadvertently or not, for fulfilling one of mankind's oldest dreams: to possess the power of gods. Love, now deemed to be not just one divine feature among many, but the defining essence of God, the real ground and purpose of his actions, can be infused into us humans. Love is to be the lodestar of our lives and, if blessed with the capacity to exercise it, we can aspire to imitate God. It was only a matter of time before the outrageous conclusion was drawn that through love we, ordinary men and women, can ourselves become divine.

Martin Luther (1483–1546), the great Protestant reformer, quite explicitly drew this conclusion:[13] 'we are gods through love',[14] he says. Love is the means by which God 'produces a divine man, who is one . . . with Him; a man who, when he loves his neighbour . . . can glory that he has acted like a God'.[15] God's loving descent into us humans is 'a true "bestowal of [divine] being", a sharing of the nature of the divine with the creature'.[16] And so when we love properly we are acting as God's agent and performing nothing less than divine work. Such a person is no longer 'a mere man, but a god . . . for God Himself is in him and does such things as no man nor creature can do'.[17]

Here, Luther, for all his railing against the Catholic Church, is simply developing an ancient tradition that goes back at least as far as Augustine. Echoing Athanasius, Augustine says: 'in order to make gods of those who were merely human, one who was God made himself human'.[18] The Holy Spirit (who is one of the 'persons' of the Trinity in which God reveals himself, the others being the Father and Jesus Christ), dwells in us as love and enables us to participate in divine love. Since a peculiar feature of love, Augustine points out, is that we become like the objects of our love – a reality surely to be seen in many a couple? – 'by loving God we are made into gods'.[19] Or as Thomas Aquinas puts it, to attain fellowship with God is to assume divine form: to become, in his vivid word, 'deiformis'.

Building on Augustine, the Franciscan mystical theologian St Bonaventure identifies six preparatory steps by which we can mount to God. Each of these steps brings us closer to divine love and perfection, until, in a final ascent through Christ, we encounter the completeness of being that is God. In the typical manner of medieval mysticism, St Bonaventure pictures the whole universe as a ladder reaching to God, traces of whose love and goodness can be seen in all creation, from the lowest rung to the highest. And yet this hierarchy of existence, this ladder that stretches from earth to God, each level of which is more perfect, pure and enlightened than the previous one, is not just a feature of the universe as a whole. It is reflected within us, in our own individual spirit. This means that in order to come close to God we need to enter into ourselves in self-love, and to recognise and achieve in ourselves just such a hierarchy:[20] 'Enter into yourself . . . and see that your soul loves itself most fervently'.[21] In a thought of great profundity Bonaventure seems to do away with the old question, still much debated today: Do we need to love ourselves before we can love others? Or, on the contrary, must we be able to love others before we can love ourselves? The two are simultaneous, for one journey of love is being taken: in striving to love God our spirit is striving to love itself. And conversely: in loving ourselves we are also moving towards God.

✦ ✦ ✦

Theology needed, of course, to be careful at this point. Human beings, mired in selfishness and sin, cannot be God. As always, when we walk on sacred territory we are one step from sacrilege. So a powerful doctrine of humility had to accompany – indeed was inseparable from – the conceit that humans could express divine love. Christian thinkers enlisted the concept of 'grace' to deem that men and women are incapable of genuine love without God's help – for which they must wait with longing and patience and prayer.

In other words: if we can love like God this is only because God has flooded our hearts with his love – or will to love. This caution is already there in St John the Evangelist, with whom the idea that God is love originates: '. . . love is from God; everyone who loves is born of God and knows God' (1 John 4:7). St Paul, too, says that '. . . God's love has been poured into our hearts through the Holy Spirit . . .' (Romans 5:5); indeed that all salvation 'depends not on human will or exertion, but on God who shows mercy' (Romans 9:16).

There is fierce debate in the history of Christianity about how exactly to characterise the relation between God's power and humanity's helplessness in love. Do humans, after the Fall, possess at least a basic power to love – which can then be inspired to genuine love by God's intervention? Or do we have no inbuilt power to love – not even a latent one?

Thomas Aquinas espouses the first of these positions. We are capable of 'friendship' with God in a minimal sense because we are created in God's image,[22] which, despite the Fall, we retain to some extent. But full friendship with God – and so with our neighbour, whom we love for the sake of God – isn't possible without grace.[23] (By 'full friendship' he means something similar to Aristotle's perfect *philia*.)

For Thomas, as for most thinkers in the Christian tradition, genuine love ultimately depends on God. Love, the supreme of the three theological virtues – faith, hope and love – is infused into us by him. But we are not mere vessels for God's work; we have an innate will that, with grace, can develop and grow throughout life as we strive for spiritual perfection. Like Aristotelian *philia*, this striving demands patient and meticulous cultivation of virtue. And so by responding to grace through such moral development, the human will comes increasingly to resemble the Holy Spirit and applies itself 'chiefly to the work of cleaving to God'.[24]

Augustine, by contrast, doesn't believe that human beings have any innate capacity for genuine love. Only God can love genuinely, and when we experience such love we are really experiencing God's love.[25] Yet, unlike some of his followers, he holds that human desire (*appetitus*) naturally strives for the origin of our being – namely for God ('. . . you have made us and drawn us to yourself, and our heart is unquiet until it rests in you'[26]). For unlike God, we are not self-sufficient, most fundamentally in regard to our beingness – and so must always want a good that we do not possess. To long for our 'sufficiency' is to love – an idea that we already saw in Plato's *Symposium* – though as long as we are alive we will, of course, never achieve perfect sufficiency.

And so nothing, Augustine continues in his Platonic vein, is more important than whether love seeks the right object – God, the source and sustainer of our being: the only object of love that can ultimately satisfy human needs – or whether it settles for the easier, more obvious, more immediately pleasing, but ultimately unsatisfactory, realm of the worldly.[27] Since all genuine love is for God, when we love another person we are really loving God in her – and loving her for the sake of God. We never truly love her for anything else about her. Indeed, everything that is merely worldly is to be despised.

Only grace enables us to make the right choice: to love God. 'The Grace of God makes a willing man out of an unwilling one'.[28] 'By grace we are commanded to imitate the life of the Godhead with respect both to God himself and to one another'.[29] Thus, through grace, desire can be directed upwards to the divine, which is eternal and unchanging and all good (thus becoming '*caritas*': love for the sake of God; a selfless love, marked by dispossession of the ego, that is fruitful also for human relationships), rather than downwards to the merely human and earthly and transient (so remaining '*cupiditas*': love without reference to God).[30] Since *caritas* is itself divine, to claim that we could love without God's grace would be, in effect, to claim that we have it in us to reach for divinity[31] – 'Whoever, then, asserts that it is possible to possess the love of God without the help of God, what else is he asserting than that God can be possessed without God?'[32] – which would be pride of the highest order.

Not surprisingly, perhaps, Luther, who thinks 'we are gods through love', takes this opposing humility to its extreme. He, and the Protestant tradition he inspires, insists that we have no inbuilt capacity whatsoever for genuine – in other words, divine – love. We are so base that we can merely be vessels for God's love 'through which the fountain of divine blessings continuously flows to other individuals.'[33]

In contrast to Thomas Aquinas, who thinks that as a result of God's gift humans can love in the sense of *caritas*, Luther sees divine and human love as absolutely distinct – and reconcilable, if at all, only through Jesus Christ. He is also utterly opposed to Augustine's view that human desire and its possessive strivings can play any part in loving God. All desire, even if directed towards God, still seeks our own good, bound up as it is with the search for satisfaction. To that extent many of the greatest saints and mystics remain trapped in self-preoccupation. There is no ladder to God up which we can climb; God will meet us only by reaching down to our human level – through his love in Christ.

Luther's insistence on the deficiency of human love is so intense that he ends up challenging the feasibility of the first and second commandments – to love God and neighbour: 'No-one is able to love God from his whole heart, etc, and his neighbour as himself.'[34] This, Luther fumes, is 'an impossible law'.[35] Love of this order cannot originate in man 'for such love is not a natural art, nor grown in our garden'.[36] If a person loves well it is because he is 'a medium between God and his neighbour, to receive from above and distribute below.'[37]

Clearly, the last thing Luther wants to do is to deify human beings in themselves; but his theology of humility (*humilitas*), which demands the total destruction of one's will, is in fact of a piece with the conceit that a human being can become 'a divine man . . . [who] has acted like a God'.[38] Humility and will-to-power are two sides of the same coin. It is precisely the grandness of one's conception of what one could be (given the right relation to God, the source of all power), precisely the loftiness of the tasks to which one feels oneself called, that induces a – genuine – sense of awe. Humility makes the human dream to become gods plausible.

Perhaps that is why so many myths that speak of this dream warn that it will founder if men and women try, arrogantly, to grab divine powers. In Greek myth there is Prometheus, who stole fire for humankind against the will of Zeus, the king of the gods. There are the original whole human beings who, we read in Plato's *Symposium*, insolently challenged the power of the gods. In the biblical tradition, there are Adam and Eve – also original human beings – who picked the forbidden fruit from the tree of knowledge of good and evil. All failed – even the semi-divine Prometheus. And not merely failed but were punished horribly for their presumption: Prometheus was chained naked to a pillar where a vulture could feast forever on his liver, which grew back every night and was eaten again by day. The original humans in the *Symposium* were cut in half by Zeus. Adam and Eve were expelled from their paradise and every generation after them blighted at birth by their 'original sin'.

Christianity was shrewder. It knew that to partake – without hubris – in divine power you have to submit to it, in total self-abasement and without expectations of receiving it, or of keeping it if you receive it. If humans have the potential to love genuinely this is because we are open to the work of God in Christ by the in-dwelling of the Holy Spirit.

This view of love expresses the reality that exaltation and abasement are related to each other in a profound dialectic – a dialectic incomparably revealed in the incarnation and crucifixion of Christ. 'Wanting to be as gods' is inseparable from readiness to go the way of the Cross. The crucifixion of the incarnate God is not a gruesome paradox, as Nietzsche was to characterise it, but rather speaks a deep truth: if you want to be 'Gods and Saviours of the world'[39] you have to *be* (and not merely appear) humble. Or as the German mystic Meister Eckhart puts it, in his more oblique way:

> Ours to know all and deify ourselves with all. Ours to be God by grace as God is God by nature; ours to resign the same to God and be as poor as when we were not.[40]

✦ ✦ ✦

The optimistic side of Christianity's ideal of love remains, in its essentials, entrenched in Western culture. Great love, like God's, unexpectedly 'takes us over', endowing us with world-conquering power that can triumph even over the fundamental facts of death and time. Love, like the divine grace that bestows it, is a unique source of freedom from the limitations of ordinary life. Love exists in a higher realm than the everyday world. Love is a great creative force, as it is for the Christian God, who created the world out of love. Love 'redeems' suffering and loss and absurdity in our lives – just as Christ's love does on an infinitely vaster scale. Love is the source and measure of all true virtue – just as for Augustine this was true of love for God. Love, like God, is eternal: it is the one residue of any human life that feels indestructible.

This is why our idea of love is so bound up with the sacred: for wherever we locate ultimate value and power, there we experience the sacred. We all, including diehard atheists and materialists, need the sacred; for we all need to ascribe ultimate value and power to something – if not to God then to freedom, art, nation, landscape, truth, ancestors, leaders, ethnic group, family, language, love, evil, the Devil, even money: to whatever we believe (delusionally or not; durably or not) can give our existence unassailable meaning.

This realm of supreme value can ground all other things but doesn't itself stand in need of grounding – and mustn't if it is to retain its power. It is, in other words, the object of faith; its value is not up for proof or disproof. As supreme, it demands that all other values – perhaps even that of life itself – be subordinated to it.

And the sacred is always accompanied by fears of desecration. When the stakes are so high lapses of devotion are ominous. And easy: dedication is readily threatened by simple pleasures, doubt, laziness and less demanding idols. Sacrilege is just a step from reverence.

+ + +

The problem for love in a secular world is that the two sides of the Christian view – the sanctification of love and what I have called the 'doctrine of humility' – have come unstuck. Without an all-powerful God to hold them together and to serve as a standing reminder of how severely hard love is, as well as how fundamentally beyond our control, they have simply gone their own separate ways, producing extremes of optimism and pessimism about love, both of which have damaged it.

The optimists never cease to believe that love can be all-conquering, unconditional, redeeming, constant, eternal, and creative. The pessimists, on the other hand, have observed the obvious: such expectations are repeatedly disappointed. And they have drawn the opposite conclusion: human nature doesn't allow the hopes of love to be realised. Or, in a similar vein: human love, bogged down in illusion, narcissism, misunderstanding and selfish or possessive manipulation, can never stably attain its ideals; it is a prisoner of our individual past as well as of present loved ones in ways that cannot be more than partially overcome. Freud, Proust and others run the gamut of this pessimism. And yet it is strikingly similar in form to the Christian conception of man (or rather to one side of it) that such thinkers reject. Though for the old religious categories of human depravity such as pride, lust and wrath they substitute contemporary notions like narcissism, projection and instrumentalisation of the 'Other', their doubts that human nature can ever allow a love that really attends and gives to the other person bear striking similarities to those of the ageing Augustine.

Christian teaching is closer to the truth than are either the optimists or the pessimists on their own. It reminds us that love can be our highest virtue, but that this presupposes a severe doctrine of humility, grounded in the reality that we do not know how to love and have little control over the progress of any relationship of love. Where Christianity's doctrine of humility claims that human love is a gift of God's mysterious grace conferred unequally on human beings, and insists on an absolute distinction between the creator and his creatures, a secular doctrine of humility needs to recognise that, far from being a capacity possessed by all, love is among the rarest of all talents. The ability to recognise those few beings who enable one to find ontological rootedness and then to attend and give to them with all one's might – which, I suggested in chapter 1, is constitutive of love – is as exceptional as the great artist's or scientist's capacity to let herself be flooded by the world and then recreate it through an act of individual conception. And, far from being ready-formed, love demands as long and meticulous an apprenticeship, as much willingness to learn and experience, as any other discipline.

Though we all desire to love – in other words to find ontological rootedness – we don't all have sufficient talent and will to do so. Talent is all-important: our failure to love isn't due only, or even mainly, to earlier circumstances of our lives – such as cold parents, sexual abuse, loss of loved ones – that have aroused an unconquerable 'fear of intimacy'. Few are capable of excelling at love, as few perhaps as are capable of excelling as an engineer or musician or golfer or tycoon or politician or gardener or writer. To embrace one side of the Christian inheritance – that love is a divine gift, capable of redeeming human suffering – while jettisoning the other – the humility to see this love as something to which we have no birthright and over which we have little control except to cultivate our ability to attend and wait – is to court disaster. The disaster of all who lunge presumptuously at divine powers. The disaster of Prometheus, of Aristophanes' original humans, of Adam, and of Eve.

7

Why Christian love isn't unconditional

Christianity didn't make love the Western world's supreme virtue just by proclaiming it so. At the same time as reminding human beings of how inadequately they could love without divine grace, it had to make that greatest good seem genuinely accessible to ordinary mortals who are open to it. Otherwise the exhortations to love of Paul, Augustine, Bonaventure, Thomas Aquinas, Luther, and their followers, far from being the basis for a world-conquering morality, would have become demoralising and eventually lost their power to guide human lives.

To make love of this order appear accessible is no easy matter. We are not talking here of virtues like courage or moderation or honesty – difficult virtues but, unlike love, not ones that Christianity singles out as the essence of God, nor as needing to inform all our actions and even our most private thoughts, feelings and intentions. The stakes are so high with love that extraordinary help needs to be at hand.

That help is no less than the incarnated God, Jesus Christ. He is the great intermediary who can bring God to humanity and so humanity to God. Through Jesus Christ, the highest love is transmitted to men and women; and through him they are, in turn, capable of the highest love: 'No one comes to the Father except through me' (John 14:6). 'I am in my Father, and you in me, and I in you' (John 14:20).

Jesus's presence in the world, his Incarnation, is itself an act of divine love – indeed it is a defining act.[1] God's love, bestowed undeserved and mysteriously as a gift of grace, is epitomised by Jesus's life – and death: 'God so loved the world that he gave his only Son . . .' (John 3:16; cf. 1 John 4:9vv.).

The Christian revolution is not about creating a new God or even a new law. Nor does Christianity create any new conception of love. The Jesus of the Gospels proclaims the same God and, in a core sense, the same law as Judaism.

Instead Christianity inaugurates a new relationship with that God, a more universal faith focused on the person, death and resurrection of Jesus – and on his unique status in expressing God's love for man and in enabling our love for God and neighbour.

This faith in turn founds dramatic new possibilities for realising an already existing conception of love. From the perspective of later doctrine, Jesus's dual status as God-man offers human beings unprecedented power to attempt to love in a divine way. To return to an image of medieval mystics that we saw in the previous chapter, not only is Jesus our 'ladder' to God, but his life and death offer us the ultimate model of love to follow.

Again, we see how submission occupies centre stage in the nature of love: 'Therefore be imitators of God, as beloved children, and live in love, as Christ loved us and gave himself up for us, a fragrant offering and sacrifice to God' (Ephesians 5:1–2).

As in biblical Judaism, such submission is an obedient self-giving that places oneself entirely at the disposal of the loved one. Only thus is a transformative relationship to God and neighbour possible.

EROS COLLIDES WITH JESUS

Christianity's promise that (some) ordinary mortals can be infused with divine love and even become one with God through love is aided by a second tremendous development. This is the integration into early Christianity, to a more far-reaching degree than anything seen in the Hellenised Judaism that immediately precedes it, of the pagan idea of spiritual Eros: that immense desire, described by Plato and his followers, to rise above the transient, imperfect world into which we are born, the earthly flesh of which we are made, and, through increasing levels of spiritual attainment, to gain intimacy with the highest goodness, beauty and truth – which, in Christianity, is of course God himself.

In particular, Augustine (354–430) brings together in an entirely original way what is distinct about the spirits of Christ and Eros, Jerusalem and Athens. In him we see combined, on the one hand, the sense of genuine human love as utterly dependent on the inscrutable grace of God and the indwelling of the Holy Spirit; and, on the other, the Eros-mysticism of Plato and his followers, based on the intense desire to ascend towards the supreme good. Through the idea of the universe ordered in this upwardly striving and divinely inspired way, the human soul can be seen as having the opportunity progressively to approach a loving union with God.

Eros poeticises love; it gives biblical Judaism's image of Israel's love-relationship with God, though already passionate and often argumentative, a richer, more sensual, more seductive range of tonalities. It alters the quality of love between man and God by making it less a relationship of filial piety and more one of a bride to her groom. Though we read of God's betrothal to his people in the Old Testament – 'I will take you for my wife ... in steadfast love ... and you shall know the Lord' (Hosea 2:19–20); 'as the bridegroom rejoices over the bride,/ So shall your God rejoice over you' (Isaiah 62:5) – the metaphor of marriage or union becomes far more developed in Christianity. And it profoundly influences our modern ideas of romantic love as a sacred union of two people – who are, for each other, the world.

Thus St John of the Cross (1542–1591) proclaims: 'in the spiritual marriage between God and the soul there are two natures in one spirit and love ... He that cleaveth to the Lord is one spirit.'[2] God 'in the omnipotence of His unfathomable love absorbs the soul with greater violence and efficacy than a torrent of fire a single drop of the morning dew'.[3] And St Teresa of Ávila (1515–1582) speaks of a mixing of the human with the divine that comes close to total unity: 'like rain falling from heaven into a river or a stream, becoming one and the same liquid, so that the river and rain water cannot be divided'.[4]

St John of the Cross and St Teresa of Ávila belong to the great sixteenth-century Spanish school of love-mysticism. This mysticism is no orgy of swooning, however much its language might suggest so to the contemporary ear. Nor can it be reduced to worship of the irrational, let alone to a mere channel for unfulfilled sexual desire – any more than Platonic Eros itself can be so reduced. Rather it is the most disciplined striving, using all one's powers, rational and non-rational, for direct communion with the ground of one's being: with God. A striving that demands precisely the self-command – the attentiveness and patience – needed for the Platonic ascent.

How much patience is required for the mystical ascent, and how far it is from formless intoxication, is clear from the 'dark night of the soul', the desolation and emptiness, which, St John of the Cross tells us, must be endured by one who longs for God.

> For indeed, when this purgative contemplation is most severe, the soul feels very keenly the shadow of death and the lamentations of death and the pains of hell, which consist in its feeling itself to be without God, and chastised and cast out, and unworthy of Him; and it feels that He is wroth with it. All this is felt by the soul in this condition – yea, and more, for it believes that it is so with it for ever.[5]

The sense of abandonment and loneliness pummels the soul until it is emptied of its vanity and finery and other crudities of spirit:

> [Souls in search of union are] as powerless in this case as one who has been imprisoned in a dark dungeon, and is bound hand and foot, and can neither move nor see, nor feel any favour whether from above or from below, until the spirit is humbled, softened and purified, and grows so keen and delicate and pure that it can become one with the Spirit of God, according to the degree of union of love which His mercy is pleased to grant it; in proportion to this the purgation is of greater or less severity and of greater or less duration.[6]

Though religious mysticisms are traditionally divided into those that preserve the essential separateness of the human and the divine and others that contemplate a total unity in which all human agency disappears, in reality they tend to involve a dialectic between the two. Thus Meister Eckhart (*c.* 1260–*c.* 1328) is notorious – and was condemned by the Church authorities – for seeming to claim that the human soul could be indissolubly fused with God: 'We shall all be transformed totally into God and changed into him. In the same way, when in the sacrament bread is changed into Christ's Body, I am so changed into him that he makes me his one existence . . . there is no distinction there.'[7]

And yet Eckhart also insists that '*Minne einigt nicht*' – 'Love does not unite'; indeed '*Sie einigt wohl an einem Werk, nicht an einem Wesen*' – '[Love] unites in act and not in essence'.[8] Elsewhere, he adds: 'In dying to her [the soul's] own nature and her being and her life the soul is born in her divinity . . . She becomes so wholly one that there is no distinction except that he [God] stays God and she stays soul.'[9]

So even for a mystic like Eckhart, the ideal of unity with God exists alongside an insistence on the responsibility and so distinctiveness of the individual human being before God: 'two natures in one spirit', as St John puts it. Indeed if unity with God and the dissolving of selfhood that it involves is to be a real ideal, rather than a sentimental hope, it must be pursued by a self able to withstand repeated defeat, waiting, banishment and a sense of its own inadequacy at the hands of the loved one – a self that is strong enough, in other words, to bear the dark night of the soul. Such endurance is a mark of the moral agent – not of one who considers himself to be, or yearns to be, merely a passive drop in the infinite ocean of being that is God.

LOVE AND DEATH

The promise of coming to God that both Eros and Christ offer, and that the mystics take up with such eloquent passion, brings us back to two of Western love's greatest obsessions: death and sex.

Like the divinisation of human love, these obsessions don't peak until the nineteenth century, with the *decline* of religious authority. Devotion to *Liebestod* and, indeed, to sexual prurience attains its apogee with the 'death of God'. Yet the roots of these obsessions are obviously in Christian tradition. And specifically in its intense ambivalence about the value of this world, including the body and its sexual desires. From one of its points of view, to merge with God, who is fundamentally distinct from the world – to seek the eschatological promise of the Kingdom of God – we must keep at bay all desire that is not directed to God, and particularly that most potent expression of our earthly nature: sexual desire. If God is love, so this view goes, genuine love is beyond this world, and we cannot find it if we get bogged down in attachments to ordinary life. 'Beyond this world' easily comes to mean: to be reached via death.

Or via a living death. 'Put to death . . . whatever in you is earthly' (Colossians 3:5), says St Paul. 'Set your minds on things that are above, not on things that are on earth, for you have died, and your life is hidden with Christ in God' (Colossians 3:2–3). In other words: see worldly things and desire for them as the enemy of the heavenly realm to which we should be aspiring. For friendship with the world is nothing other than enmity toward God (James 4:4).[10]

Such 'dying to the world' was, for its devotees, how one could best live *this* life – while waiting for the ultimate union with God that is possible only in physical death. The suicide of worldly desire frees the spirit to live – in the here and now.

Dying to the world could, in extreme cases, employ the symbolism of being buried alive. Thus, the ceremony that initiated the life of an anchorite (or anchoress) would involve a service of enclosure, conducted with severe formality after Mass. The novice would be taken in procession from the church to a cell, which was to be thought of as a tomb. He then prostrated himself upon a bier, and was sprinkled with holy water and earth, as if he were actually being buried. Finally he would be left alone and the entrance to his dwelling ritually walled up[11] – his needs from then on met by helpers.

✦ ✦ ✦

The problem to which death, or dying to the world, is the solution is not, however, the body as such – but only the body's earthly desires. Since traditional Christianity holds that in Christ God has assumed human flesh and therefore that the physical is a site for God's self-manifestation, outright repudiation of it is a heresy – a heresy for which sects like the Gnostics and the Manichees, who deemed matter the source of evil, were repeatedly persecuted.

Indeed there have been Christian mystics, like the towering monastic reformer Bernard, Abbot of Clairvaux (1090–1153), who have seen the body as central to salvation. The body is where the human and the divine originally met and it remains so despite its corruption in the Fall.[12] It is a 'good and faithful companion'[13] to the soul in life and after death, and helps point it to its highest spiritual goals. Bernard even insists that after death the soul on its own can't fully love God unless it gets its body back – a 'perfect body' now freed of its earthly desires, and immortal, 'beautiful and at peace'.[14]

Such themes are then reworked in the thirteenth century by Thomas Aquinas and Bonaventure. Here is Thomas on why we ought to love our body:

Now our bodily nature, far from issuing from an evil principle, as the Manichees imagine, is from God. We can therefore use it for God's service . . . Accordingly, with the same love of charity by which we love God, we ought also to love our body, though not the taint of sin and the corruption that punishment brings it . . .[15]

It is a fine line to tread: to repudiate the body altogether would be heresy; to affirm its earthly desires would be unholy. The body is to be valued for the sake of God while its desires for purely earthly ends are to be denied, or at least strictly circumscribed. Not least: its desire for sex.

JESUS AND SEX

Yet when it comes to sex, Jesus will once again surprise many modern readers, accustomed as we are to Christianity's preoccupation with this subject, especially since the nineteenth century. For just as he says little about love in the Synoptic Gospels so he says even less about sex.

As he is reported in the Gospels, Jesus never condemns sex as such. He never demands that sex serve spiritual love. And he never says that it must be accompanied by the intention to procreate. On premarital sex, homosexuality, contraception, and abortion – topics central to modern religious and especially Christian debate – he is silent.

In the New Testament it is above all with St Paul that sex plays a larger role – though, contrary to the reputation he has acquired, it is hardly a major theme for him either. Paul condemns the lawless carnality that he sees around him (1 Corinthians 5); rails against untamed desires of the flesh, which he sees as emblems of unredeemed man's sinfulness, in sharp contrast to 'the Spirit' and its 'new creation' in Christ;[16] and condemns homosexuality as God's punishment for gentile idolatry (Romans 1:24). In a tone very unlike that of Jesus of the Gospels he says:

> Do you not know that wrongdoers will not inherit the kingdom of God? Do not be deceived! Fornicators, idolaters, adulterers, male prostitutes, sodomites, thieves, the greedy, drunkards, revilers, robbers – none of these will inherit the kingdom of God. And this is what some of you used to be. But you were washed, you were sanctified, you were justified in the name of the Lord Jesus Christ and in the Spirit of our God. (1 Corinthians 6:9–11)

Since Paul expects the impending end of the world and the second coming of Jesus,[17] he worries about the commitment involved in getting married and raising a family. Time is short; and the effort a married man expends on practical affairs – not to mention on trying to please his wife – inevitably distracts him from the serious business of spiritual renewal: 'The unmarried man is anxious about the affairs of the Lord, how to please the Lord; but the married man is anxious about the affairs of the world, how to please his wife, and his interests are divided' (1 Corinthians 7:32–4).

Nonetheless, Paul also values the uniting power of sex, marriage and family, arguing that 'the unbelieving husband is made holy through his wife, and the unbelieving wife is made holy through her husband' (1 Corinthians 7:14). Moreover, while waiting for the end of the world, marriage also has value as a way of reining in the urge to fornicate, and he encourages husbands and wives to have sex often enough to keep their desires in check:

> Now concerning the matters about which you wrote: 'It is well for a man not to touch a woman.' But because of cases of sexual immorality, each man should have his own wife and each woman her own husband. The husband should give to his wife her conjugal rights, and likewise the wife to her husband. For the wife does not have authority over her own body, but the husband does; likewise the husband does not have authority over his own body, but the wife does. Do not deprive one another except perhaps by agreement for a set time, to devote yourselves to prayer, and then come together again, so that Satan may not tempt you because of your lack of self-control. This I say by way of concession, not of command. I wish that all were as I myself am [i.e. unmarried]. But each has a particular gift from God, one having one kind and another a different kind. (1 Corinthians 7:1–7)

Paul is a single man, who neither believes that marriage is always noble, nor insists that it is needed to consummate the love of a man and a woman, nor celebrates the having of children.[18] Though his hymn to love as the supreme value – 'of all these things love is the greatest' – is a fixture of Christian and even atheist weddings, there are few where you would be likely to hear what he also says: '. . . those who marry will experience distress in this life, and I would spare you that' (1 Corinthians 7:28).

✦ ✦ ✦

So, when it comes to sex, what is Jesus's real concern? Probably, above all, to uphold the marriage bond. He takes a very hard line on adultery and divorce, and goes out of his way in the Sermon on the Mount to distance himself from what he takes to be the more tolerant contemporary Jewish teaching on those subjects:

You have heard that it was said,[19] 'You shall not commit adultery.' But I say to you that anyone who looks at a woman lustfully has already committed adultery with her in his heart. If your right eye causes you to sin, tear it out and throw it away. It is better for you to lose one of your members than for your whole body to be thrown into hell. (Matthew 5:27–9)

The penalty meted out for adultery in the Old Testament seems draconian enough: death by public stoning for both parties.[20] It is hard to judge whether Jesus considers the punishment he moots – consignment to Hell – to be more drastic. Nor is it obvious how he reconciles it with his message of forgiveness of sins, which on one occasion he extends even towards an adulteress.[21] In Matthew's Gospel he is clear that to remarry or to marry a divorced woman is to be an adulterer:

It was also said, 'Whoever divorces his wife, let him give her a certificate of divorce.' But I say to you that anyone who divorces his wife, except on the ground of unchastity, causes her to commit adultery; and whoever marries a divorced woman commits adultery. (Matthew 5:31–2)

That a man who glances lustfully at a woman has already committed adultery in his heart is of the greatest significance for the development of morality. For with Christianity, intentions – and not merely actions – become crime scenes: the stage is set for the entire inner world of human beings to be the focus of moral scrutiny. As Matthew puts it: 'nothing is covered up that will not be uncovered, and nothing secret that will not become known' (Matthew 10:26; cf. Mark 4:22).

✦ ✦ ✦

Yet for all his strictures against divorce and adultery, Jesus's greatest enemies have nothing to do with sex. They are money, pride and hypocrisy. His repudiation of them is overwhelming. Money is the absolute enemy of closeness to God; it separates us from God more surely than sex ever could. 'How hard it will be for those who have wealth to enter the kingdom of God' (Mark 10:23), he says to his disciples. 'No one can serve two masters . . . You cannot serve God and wealth' (Matthew 6:24). 'Do not store up for yourselves treasures on earth, where moth and rust consume . . . but store up for yourselves treasures in heaven' (Matthew 6:19–20). Or as St Paul puts it: 'the love of money is a root of all kinds of evil' (1 Timothy 6:10).

Material pursuits must take second place to a right orientation to God and his justice: '. . . do not worry, saying, "What will we eat?" or "What will we drink?" or "What will we wear?" For it is the Gentiles who strive for all these things; and indeed your heavenly Father knows that you need all these things. But strive first for the kingdom of God and his righteousness,[22] and all these things will be given to you as well' (Matthew 6:31–3).

And, in the end, the greedy shall not gain even earthly things, let alone intimacy with God: 'But woe to you who are rich, for you have received your consolation. Woe to you who are full now, for you will be hungry' (Luke 6:24–5). Rather: 'Blessed are you who are poor, for yours is the Kingdom of God. Blessed are you who are hungry now, for you will be filled' (Luke 6:20–1). Or as Matthew reports: 'Blessed are the meek, for they will inherit the earth' (Matthew 5:5).[23]

As to pride and hypocrisy, there can never have been a more uncompromising opponent than Jesus. His loathing – this is not too strong a word – for people who lord it over others is hard to overstate. He despises moralisers who enjoy strutting in public and care only for their prestige. '[T]hey do not practise what they teach,' he cries. 'They tie up heavy burdens, hard to bear, and lay them on the shoulders of others; but they themselves are unwilling to lift a finger to move them. They do all their deeds to be seen by others' (Matthew 23:3–5).

But it is not just hypocrisy that Jesus repudiates; not just the fact that these people on their high horses fail to do what they demand of others. He detects something even worse: their preaching isn't aimed at the good of others at all. 'But woe to you, scribes and Pharisees, hypocrites! For you lock people out of the kingdom of heaven. For you do not go in yourselves, and when others are going in, you stop them' (Matthew 23:13). And in an extraordinary sentence that could stand as a warning to all today who seek to foist their superior values on far-away peoples whom they see as morally benighted, Jesus shouts: 'Woe to you . . . hypocrites! For you cross sea and land to make a single convert, and you make the new convert twice as much a child of hell as yourselves' (Matthew 23:15).

For in the end this moralising is vanity – a show to make the moralisers feel good. Inside they are sordid and evil:

> Woe to you . . . hypocrites! For you clean the outside of the cup and of the plate, but inside they are full of greed and self-indulgence.

Woe to you . . . hypocrites! For you are like whitewashed tombs, which on the outside look beautiful but inside they are full of the bones of the dead and all kinds of fifth. So you also on the outside look righteous to others, but inside you are full of hypocrisy and lawlessness . . .

You snakes! You brood of vipers! How can you escape being sentenced to hell? (Matthew 23:25–33; cf. Luke 6:37–42)

Jesus's tremendous focus on money and the vices of pride – hypocrisy and self-righteousness – returns us to a central theme of this book: the precondition for love – as a dialogical relationship to one whom we experience as the ground of our being, or as leading us to the ground of our being – is submission to the real presence of the other; submission to her individual lawfulness and what she calls on us to do.

Sex, or erotic desire generally, is no necessary impediment to such submission. On the contrary it can confront one suddenly and overwhelmingly with the vividness of the other as both object and subject. But pride and some of the conditions of wealth-accumulation can be huge impediments. Pride is about self-protection, self-sufficiency, barricading oneself against one's neighbour, absorption in the business of self-esteem, a myopic dedication to one's own prestige and power that darkens the mind to the reality of others – all attitudes that exclude submission; while the pursuit of wealth necessarily places the impersonal demands of utility at the centre of our relations with those caught up in this ambition – a far cry from the attentiveness that is at the heart of love. (And it is notable that virtually every version of 'the seven deadly sins' regards pride and greed as far more serious than lust.[24])

Why then has Jesus's message been so perverted? Why has Christianised civilisation been so concerned with sex, and so much less inhibited by Jesus's preaching against pride, possessions and power? Whether we are talking about the historical Church, the 'civilising mission' of Victorian Britain, the Communist Party of the Soviet Union (the atheistic embodiment of the deeply religious Russian nation) and its unspeakable vanity of bringing revolution to the whole world, the 'manifest destiny' with which American 'Anglo-Protestantism'[25] dignifies itself, or the Christian fundamentalism that gives it such strident voice today – in all these cases intense sexual prudery is combined with ruthless pursuit of power and property, flaunted with the very pride, the very self-congratulatory lording it over others, to which Jesus's whole life and death are a standing reproach.[26] 'It is easier for a camel to go through the eye of a needle than for someone who is rich to enter the kingdom of God' (Mark 10:25). 'All who exalt themselves will be humbled' (Matthew 23:12). It is remarkable how often people who seek to civilise the world by force, often in the name of Christianity and with a sense of being guided by God, themselves profess a hierarchy of values so completely at variance with those of Jesus.

Is 'Christian love' universal?

The myths about what Jesus really says on sex and love to which I have pointed hardly begin to account for the misconceptions that have grown up around Christian love. One might readily accept that it is the exact opposite of the truth to claim that Jesus is hostile to sex as such but has no problem with money-making or with the pride that people indulge in when they believe themselves superior to others. But surely it is undeniable that the New Testament and, following it, the Fathers of the Church preach universal love? Surely it is clearly promised that God's love is impartially and equally available for the salvation of all, or at least of all who seek him? Surely God will always love and forgive human beings, even when they turn away from him? Surely Christianity, as the religion of universal love, is distinguished from Judaism by decisively abandoning the idea that any particular people are 'elected' by God, and in that sense loved by him over others. Surely it unambiguously commands us to love everyone as a 'neighbour', in virtue of their being human and a child of God. All this must be the case since it deems genuine love – God's love for human beings and their love for their neighbour – to be unconditional.

Wrong on all counts. If these myths are believed today – and even preached by Christian ministers – that is testimony not just to the extreme difficulty of seeing the past except through the lens of current values, but to the extraordinary adaptability of Christianity, which is arguably the most inclusive political party in all Western history, capable of appearing dogmatic and consistent while blowing hard with the winds of the times. It is as if Christianity has deliberately deceived itself about what its own Scripture has to say on love.

In fact the New Testament is, at best, ambivalent on whether God's saving love is addressed to all human beings – let alone to all of them equally. As against the remark that 'God so loved the world that he gave his only son . . .'[27] (which does *not* entail that he loves everyone equally), we find two ideas that make any guarantee of God's universal love hollow: merit and grace.

Worse, these ideas are, in crucial respects, contradictory. Merit means that salvation must be earned by good deeds; that our spiritual strivings count in God's eyes and can influence whether or when we come to him. To this extent God's saving love will be fully bestowed only on those who have deserved it – a view that in fact dignifies human beings by placing great weight on their moral agency.

Grace, by contrast, means that God elects some of us over others for mysterious purposes of his own – and to that extent we cannot, after all, earn salvation by good deeds. Though there is a great spectrum of views in Christian tradition about how far merit and grace are independent, and if not how to characterise their dialectic, nonetheless there is a core sense in which, taken together, merit and grace make it impossible that God's love can be conferred impartially and equally on everyone – even on everyone who seeks him.

✦ ✦ ✦

On merit, Jesus says 'If you wish to enter into life, keep the commandments' (Matthew 19:17; cf. Mark 10:17vv., Luke 18:18vv.). When he finds himself at a Sabbath meal he advises the host to invite the poor and lowly, and promises that this charity 'will be repaid at the resurrection of the righteous' (Luke 14:14). Above all, he assures his disciples that anyone who follows him will be amply recognised by God, both in this life and in the next:

> Truly I tell you, there is no one who has left house or brothers or sisters or mother or father or children or fields, for my sake and for the sake of the good news, who will not receive a hundredfold now in this age . . . and in the age to come eternal life. (Mark 10:29–30; cf. Matthew 19:29)

St Paul, for his part, embellishes this with unmistakeable clarity:

> For he will repay according to each one's deeds . . . There will be anguish and distress for everyone who does evil, the Jew first and also the Greek, but glory and honour and peace for everyone who does good, the Jew first and also the Greek. For God shows no partiality. (Romans 2:6–11)

Thomas Aquinas sums up this view: 'Man . . . reaches it [happiness] through many motions of activity, which are called his merits.'[28] In other words, we had better not take God's indulgence towards sinners for granted; salvation is conditional on our obeying his commandments, on good works, and on faith in him.

And yet, as Paul also tells us, God is absolutely sovereign in loving and choosing (Romans 9:13, 25). Human beings cannot presume to determine his choices merely by following or flouting his laws.

We see, at the receiving end of grace, how baffled and afraid Mary is when the angel Gabriel addresses her as 'favoured one . . . for you have found favour with God' (Luke 1:28, 30) and announces that she is chosen to be Jesus's mother. Though she cannot understand what she has done to merit such favour, she submits to its mystery, undeterred by the difficulty of receiving what she cannot comprehend or deserve. This is precisely what grace speaks of: the sense in which genuine love cannot be either evoked or earned.

✦ ✦ ✦

Two parables particular to Matthew's Gospel illustrate the sovereignty of grace. One tells of various labourers who are hired for a day's work in a vineyard (Matthew 20:1–16). Some of them work longer hours than others, but they are all paid the same. Indeed, those who started work last get paid first.

The labourers who were hired earliest in the day, and who had worked right through it, complain to the landowner: 'These last worked only one hour, and you have made them equal to us who have borne the burden of the day and the scorching heat.' But the landowner replies: 'I am doing you no wrong; did you not agree with me for the usual daily wage? Take what belongs to you and go; I choose to give to this last [labourer] the same as I give to you. Am I not allowed to do what I choose with what belongs to me? Or are you envious because I am generous?' (Matthew 20:1–15)

We are to learn that the ways of God are like the landowner. Though they are not capricious, they are inscrutable and therefore unpredictable. As is the moral of the labourers' story: 'the last will be first, and the first will be last' (Matthew 20:16).

A closely related point is made, more chillingly, by the parable of the marriage feast thrown by a king: 'when the king came in to the guests, he noticed a man there who was not wearing a wedding robe; and he said to him, "Friend, how did you get in here without a wedding robe?" And he [the guest] was speechless. Then the king said to the attendants, "Bind him hand and foot, and throw him into the outer darkness, where there will be weeping and gnashing of teeth." For many are called, but few are chosen' (Matthew 22:11–14).

Grace is about being chosen. Like the wedding guests, you are either included or you are not. It is about the undeserved nature of love.

But the seeming perversity of grace – its inequality; its cruel incomprehensibility: why him? why not the other? – is still deeper than this. It turns out that the very merits that can – if anything can – earn us salvation, might themselves depend on grace. In other words, you can't obey God's will . . . without God willing that you obey it.

We saw in the previous chapter how this was the case for genuine love: how without grace we cannot fulfil God's commandment to love him in the sense of *caritas*. Nearly all traditions in Christianity agree that faith in the mysteries of revelation, such as the Trinity and the Incarnation, also cannot be achieved without grace.[29] The author of St Paul's letter to the Ephesians says: 'For by grace you have been saved through faith, and this is not your own doing; it is the gift of God' (Ephesians 2:8–9). Augustine writes that 'when God crowns our merits, he only crowns his own gifts'.[30] The love for God that is commanded of us is also, he says, a 'gift' of the Holy Spirit.[31] Aquinas, for his part, argues that the unqualified virtues – those that alone can earn us salvation, in other words eternity with God – are dispositions to act well that God must have infused into us, even when they feel like second nature. While for Luther the faith that enables us to have a relationship with God – indeed that drives the process of becoming gods through love or of union with God – is entirely a divine gift and cannot be chosen by human beings.

✦ ✦ ✦

If grace is God's free and unfathomable bestowal of his plenitude, this is even truer of 'predestination' – that extreme development of the idea of grace which sees certain souls as elected before birth for salvation, while the majority is doomed to be kept at arm's length from God for eternity, indeed to burn in Hell. God elects a person before birth and so before they have had a chance to do anything good or bad, as St Paul says God elected him: 'God . . . set me apart before I was born and called me through his grace'(Galatians 1:15).

But Paul isn't just thinking of himself here:

We know that all things work together for good for those who love God, who are called according to his purpose. For those whom he foreknew he also predestined to be conformed to the image of his Son, in order that he might be

the firstborn within a large family. And those whom he predestined he also
called; and those whom he called he also justified; and those whom he justified
he also glorified. (Romans 8:28–30)

St Paul is no maverick: a whole tradition relies on him, both Catholic and
Protestant, which claims that people are either predestined for salvation or not.
It culminates in the grim edicts of the Protestant reformer John Calvin:

Before the first man was created, God in his eternal counsel had determined
what he willed to be done with the whole human race.

   In the hidden counsel of God it was determined that Adam should fall from
the unimpaired condition of his nature, and by his defection should involve all
his posterity in sentence of eternal death.

   Upon the same decree depends the distinction between elect and reprobate:
as he adopted some for himself for salvation, he destined others for eternal ruin.[32]

It is remarkable that Christianity is widely seen as the religion of universal
love – of a divine love equally available to all – in spite of the fact that the New
Testament and the theology of nearly two millennia is shot through with warnings that God doesn't confer his favours equally and impartially on all, including
the ability to love him and to be loved by him. God might bestow grace on
someone who would, by nature, tend to flout his commandments and lack faith
in him, and yet fail to bestow grace on another who pleases him.

   That is the whole point of divine love: we can't be sure that our virtue will
arouse it or our vice undermine it; it is a free, spontaneous gift that obeys only
God's inscrutable purposes. Though God's actions are neither arbitrary nor
incoherent – indeed he has sometimes been equated with rationality and intellect – they are unconstrained by any laws, including laws that he himself issues.
All three Synoptic Gospels agree on this: that 'all things are possible with God.'[33]

   Such warnings about the nature of divine love speak of hard truths about
all genuine love: that it cannot be reliably earned or evoked; that it reflects the
deepest purposes of the lover in relation to the world he faces (to this extent
it is like grace, though these purposes are clearly less mysterious in the case
of human beings than in the case of God – indeed, as I suggested in chapters 1 and
2, they turn on the lover's need to experience his being as indestructibly grounded
in a world into which he has been cast); that the loved one can, nonetheless, 'merit'

love to a degree – by conforming to the innermost laws of the lover; that we cannot reliably predict whom – what type of person – we will love, or who will love us; and that we cannot expect to be loved, however patiently we wait and however much we strive to delight our loved one. Grace is a metaphor for how precisely the most genuine love can be horrendously selective, inscrutable and 'unjust'.

✦ ✦ ✦

But what does Christian tradition have to say on love between humans? Surely its demand here is unambiguous: I am to love *all* others like myself? Surely all my neighbours are equally entitled to my love, irrespective of who they are or what they believe?

That, after all, is the moral of the Good Samaritan: he helps a neighbour who doesn't belong to his community and who has no special ties to him, and he does so purely out of empathy for the stranger's plight. Jesus concludes the parable by telling his listeners: 'Go and do likewise' (Luke 10:37); your neighbour is whoever needs you. And only just before this we find his famous command to love your enemies and do good to those who hate you.

But, again, matters are not so simple. In tension with this command to help all according to their needs and to love the enemy are traditions within Christianity, once again founded in Scripture itself, that explicitly treat some neighbours as more equal than others – and in particular neighbours who happen to share your faith. The first circle of love, as St Paul suggests, is to be reserved for fellow Christians: '. . . whenever we have an opportunity, let us work for the good of all, and especially for those of the family of faith' (Galatians 6:10).

The famous line from St Paul that is often used to show how Christian love is universal and unselective – 'There is no longer Jew or Greek, there is no longer slave or free, there is no longer male and female . . .' (Galatians 3:28) – is usually torn from its context, which stipulates that this equality is to apply to those who are believers in Jesus Christ. The paragraph from which it comes is specifically addressed to baptised believers:

> for in Christ Jesus you are all children of God through faith. As many of you as were baptised into Christ have clothed yourselves with Christ. There is no longer Jew or Greek, there is no longer slave or free, there is no longer male and female; for all of you are one in Christ Jesus. And if you belong to Christ, then you are Abraham's offspring, heirs according to the promise. (Galatians 3:26–9)

Thomas Aquinas puts the same point with extraordinary bluntness:

Not all our neighbours are equally close to God, but the greater goodness of some makes them closer to him than others, and so more entitled to be loved in charity [in other words: with genuine love].[34]

Thomas appears to allow that non-Christians, such as Jews and Muslims, are less worthy of love. And that we should calibrate our love according to a person's goodness.

In John, too, the principal arena for love is the community of believers – and *not* humanity as a whole. Love is inward-looking: it is a sign of common identity, and binds a community to Jesus and the Father – though it is also the highest, even eschatological, reality. Jesus himself is spoken of as 'having loved *his own* who were in the world . . .' (John 13:1, my italics); while even in Luke's Gospel, which, as we just saw, commands love of the stranger and enemy, Jesus is nonetheless reported as restricting the scope of his brothers to 'those who hear the word of God and do it' (Luke 8:21).[35]

Much later, in monastic tradition, the circle would come to be drawn still more closely: now the 'brothers' in the Order, and not even all Christians, are the primary objects of love.

✦ ✦ ✦

Seen in this light, the Catholic Church's timidity in opposing Hitler's persecution and destruction of the Jews does not seem so bizarre – or even hypocritical. Though it is untrue that the Vatican did nothing to protect Jews during Hitler's rule, and though numerous ordinary clergy and laymen saved Jews from deportation,[36] many of them no doubt inspired by the love commandments of Christian tradition, the reality is that no clear protest by the Church against such events as the Nuremberg race laws of 1935 or the State-sponsored pogrom of November 1938 was ever forthcoming; and that in the nearly decade-long build-up to the Holocaust itself, not to mention once it had got underway, the Jews were largely abandoned by the universal Church to fend for themselves.

The Opus Dei priest and philosopher, Martin Rhonheimer, makes the point bluntly: 'Even when we have taken full account of the enmity between the Catholic Church and National Socialism, the Church's "silence" – the astonishing fact that no Church statement about Nazism ever mentioned Jews explicitly or defended them – cries out for explanation.'[37]

But the explanation might not be so hard to find. The silence on the Jews – the Church's 'astonishing' failure, from local parishes up to the Vatican itself, to behave as the Good Samaritan and to respect this side of its own teaching – cannot be put down merely to cowardice, or to the need to protect itself, or to the delicate diplomatic manoeuvring that the Vatican felt forced to pursue, which included its 'concordat' with Hitler in 1933, or to any other demands of pragmatism in a situation in which there is only a choice between bad alternatives. Nor even does the Church's long history of anti-Semitism – of despising Jews as Christ-killers and perverters of morality and society – partly documented by Father Rhonheimer, account for the failure of so many, whether churchmen or laity, to treat a people facing social death and then genocide as neighbours.

The cause is more fundamental than anti-Semitism or pragmatism:[38] Christian love is *not* unambiguously universal; it therefore doesn't provide, even in principle, as robust a defence against barbarism as might be imagined. Doctrines of divine grace, of predestination, and of the priority of the community of believers, are shot through with the inequality of Christian love: inequality in how God loves us, in how he enables us to love him, and in how we are expected to love our fellow human beings. The intrinsic tension between the universalism of the Good Samaritan and the localism of love in parts of John and Paul has never been resolved – and is perhaps irresolvable. (So, too, the tension between a God of love who never abandons humanity and a God who, according to Jesus, consigns sinners to the eternal damnation of Hell.)

Moreover, from the New Testament onwards the Church is identified with Christ himself – as both his body and his bride (Revelation 19:7). In Catholic tradition the Church – as a concrete community and as a hierarchically-ordered institution – represents the presence and authority of Christ in the world. This means that if the first duty of Catholics is to Christ, as it necessarily is, then it is all too tempting, and in many ways warranted, to conclude that their moral responsibility is to place the Church and its members above the rest of humanity. (And similar moves are possible in Eastern Orthodox and Protestant churches.) So that the power of this identification of the Christian community with Christ can dwarf any contrary demand to love the non-Christian and the heretic.

The reality is that Christianity is a rainbow tribe which defines its borders by faith alone – rather than by ethnic or cultural belonging. The 'new covenant'[39] sets apart the faithful from the rest of humanity, as 'a chosen race, a royal priest-hood, a holy nation, God's own people' (1 Peter 2:9), just as the old Covenant at Sinai sets Israel apart from the rest of humanity. This is why many Catholics and Protestants had little difficulty despising Nazism – a pagan creed to which ethnic and cultural belonging were paramount – while remaining ambivalent, at best, about their obligations towards Jews and others who lay beyond the borders of their faith.

And it is why it would be superficial to put the bloodthirsty history of Christian peoples – burnings of heretics, forced conversions, and murderous Crusades – down to 'human frailty'.[40] Quite apart from the fact that cruelty isn't one of the seven deadly sins (indeed, many traditional texts do not regard it as a sin at all), Christian Scripture and tradition offer no clear answer to these ques-tions: 'Are those who do not share our faith loved as much by God as those who do? And are they to be loved as much by Christians themselves?' Christianity, notwithstanding the God of Love and the Good Samaritan, has always been – and remains today – fatally unclear about who our neighbour or 'nearest' ulti-mately is.

IS CHRISTIAN LOVE UNCONDITIONAL?

But if Christian love is not clearly universal it cannot be clearly unconditional either. In other words, it cannot be that nothing conditions God's love for us. Or that, in imitation of his ways, nothing should condition our love for our neigh-bour – or indeed for God himself.

As we have just seen, love for neighbour can be conditioned by whether he is a fellow Christian. Whereas God's love is conditioned by his mysterious purposes – whom, for example, he chooses to favour with grace – and, for some Christian thinkers, by our merit, which, as we saw, can itself depend on grace.

Moreover, Jesus himself, in key parables, gives the lie to any idea that God will necessarily continue to love human beings, even when they sin and turn against him. On the contrary, he is clear that there isn't always the offer of forgiveness and restored relationship.

Thomas Aquinas puts the conditionality of love bluntly: 'one thing naturally loves another only as good for itself'.[41] This rule extends even to our love for God. If we love God, Thomas unsentimentally tells us, we do so because he is the 'supreme Being' who is 'the universal good on whom depends all the goodness found in nature'.[42] And Thomas adds, as if to leave no doubt that love is conditional on the goodness of its object: 'Assuming what is impossible, that God were not man's bonum [good], then there would be no reason for man to love Him.'[43]

This is not a maverick view but a position that stretches back to St Paul – who is easily misunderstood to be the architect of unconditional love because of how he makes it the supreme value. Yet Paul says this:

> Do not be deceived; God is not mocked, for you reap whatever you sow. If you sow to your own flesh, you will reap corruption from the flesh; but if you sow to the Spirit, you will reap eternal life from the Spirit. So let us not grow weary in doing what is right, for we will reap at harvest time, if we do not give up. (Galatians 6:7–9)

If we return to Jesus's life we see that here too love is by no means clearly presented as unconditional. It is true that in the 'Sermon on the Plain' Jesus tells us to turn the other cheek and to 'love your enemies, do good, and lend, expecting nothing in return' (Luke 6:35). But he means only that we should expect nothing in return from those to whom we have given. For a much higher reward than that is in the offing, namely from God himself, as Jesus says in the very next sentence: 'Your reward will be great, and you will be children of the Most High . . .' (Luke 6:35).

As we have already seen, Jesus frequently insists that God's saving love must be merited, and to that extent has its conditions. When asked by a passing man what good deed he must do to achieve eternal life with God, Jesus doesn't say: 'God will take you to him regardless of what you do because he loves all men and women unconditionally.' Instead Jesus says: 'If you wish to enter into life, keep the commandments' (Matthew 19:17; cf. Mark 10:17vv., Luke 18:18vv.). Those who have renounced the world for his sake will be rewarded with both earthly goods and eternal life (Mark 10:29–30).

In the 'Parable of the Talents' (Matthew 25:14–30; Luke 19:12–28) love seems even more obviously conditional. Here Jesus explains that the Kingdom of Heaven is like the master who, before going on a journey, entrusts each of his three servants with money, strictly according to their abilities: the smartest gets five talents, the next receives two, and the last just one. When the master returns, he demands to see what the three servants have achieved with his money. The two ablest have each worked hard to double their money. He congratulates these two, saying 'I will put you in charge of many things. Come and share your master's happiness!' But the third has, un-enterprisingly, hidden his one talent in the ground and now simply returns it with the words, 'See, here is what belongs to you.' To which his master replies: 'You wicked, lazy servant . . . you should have put my money on deposit with the bankers, so that when I returned I would have received it back with interest.' And he orders that the talent be taken from him and given to the ablest servant: 'For to all those who have, more will be given, and they will have an abundance; but from those who have nothing, even what they have will be taken away.' Not content with this rough justice he then proceeds to cast the 'worthless slave . . . into the outer darkness, where there will be weeping and gnashing of teeth' (Matthew 25:29–30).

The idea that love's very essence is to be unconditional is, in fact, not present anywhere in Christian Scripture.

IS GOD'S FORGIVENESS UNCONDITIONAL?

One might reply that what is unconditional is God's forgiveness: that even those cast into outer darkness will ultimately be forgiven. And that forgiveness is a sign of love, or perhaps tantamount to love.

But God's forgiveness seems far from unconditional, and by no means always on offer. It can depend on the sinner repenting: 'unless you repent, you will all perish' (Luke 13:3). It can depend, too, on our forgiving those who have wronged us, as Jesus clearly warns: '. . . if you forgive others their trespasses, your heavenly Father will also forgive you; but if you do not forgive others, neither will your Father forgive your trespasses' (Matthew 6:14–15; cf. Luke 11:2vv.). Or: 'Forgive, and you will be forgiven; give, and it will be given to you . . . the measure you give will be the measure you get back' (Luke 6:37–8). Even John, whose first letter is the only place in the New Testament to contain the famous phrase 'God is Love', could not be clearer that divine forgiveness isn't to be assumed:

Whoever believes in the Son has eternal life; whoever disobeys the Son will not see life, but must endure God's wrath. (John 3:36; cf. John 3:16)

These are not maverick statements. If the parables of the Marriage Feast ('many are called but few are chosen'), or of the Talents ('from him who has not, even what he has will be taken away'), or of the Debtor Servant ('So also my heavenly Father will do to every one of you, if you do not forgive your brother from your heart') do not make the point sufficiently strongly, then we need only listen to what Jesus has to say about the Day of Judgement itself, when the sheep shall be separated from the goats. The righteous, who have acted well, will be rewarded with the Kingdom of God and eternal life. But, Jesus warns, those who failed to act well in their lives will hear this from the Heavenly Judge: 'You that are accursed, depart from me into the eternal fire prepared for the devil and his angels'. And, he adds: 'these will go away into eternal punishment' (Matthew 25:31–46).

This place – in case we are in any doubt about it – is Hell. It is the scene of last judgement that we see in countless paintings: the saved to the right of the Son of Man; the damned to the left. The punishment is, as Jesus says, eternal; there is to be no forgiveness, no redemption, no last chance, no restored relationship. Elsewhere he adds: 'The Son of Man will send his angels, and they will collect out of his kingdom all causes of sin and all evildoers, and they will throw them into the furnace of fire . . .' (Matthew 13:41–2). For there are sins which cannot be forgiven: 'people will be forgiven for every sin and blasphemy, but blasphemy against the Spirit will not be forgiven' (Matthew 12:31).

That is as final as it gets. Given how deeply Hell and eternal damnation are built into the fabric of the Religion of Love from its very beginnings, it is a public relations coup of staggering proportions that the Catholic Church, which for centuries burned heretics, killed believers of other religions, sponsored wars, and threatened its own flock with awe-inspiring punishments beyond death, has managed to transform itself into the religion of universal love and forgiveness, in which the successor of the popes who condoned and often sponsored such outrages, tours the world, clad in pure white, preaching tolerance and non-violence towards all peoples. The Machiavellian manoeuvrings of popes in eras when they still collaborated with earthly authorities to destroy their supposed enemies – popes such as Urban II, who called for the first Crusade and promised, in return, to forgive the sins of the crusaders – are dwarfed by the extraordinary dexterity of the Vatican in reinventing itself as God's Ambassador for love and forgiveness. Without, it should be added, abolishing the concept of Hell and eternal damnation, which remain very much part of Catholic doctrine. (Protestantism's various reinventions of itself, since the Enlightenment and especially since the mid-twentieth century, to suit the temper of more tolerant and transparent times have been barely less remarkable.)

So how could it have become conventional wisdom that 'Christian love' is intrinsically unconditional? How could the conclusion have been drawn that this is love's defining feature? Part of the explanation could be a mistaken starting point: if God is indeed unconditioned by anything and if God is love, then it might follow that genuine love is unconditioned by anything. But we have just seen that Christian Scripture is hardly clear that this is the case: God's saving love can be conditioned by human merit. And anyway, humans are not gods: so even if divine love were obviously unconditioned, it would be hubris to imagine that human love could be likewise. The whole notion of *imitatio dei* – be merciful as God is merciful; be perfect as God is perfect; love each other as I have loved you – easily becomes sacrilegious.

But more is at work here than a forgetful reading of Scripture. The idea that human love, unaided by God, can be unconditional is actually a modern invention. We have seen that even a great Christian thinker like Thomas Aquinas doesn't believe it. Everything that human beings do is conditioned. So why might we have come to believe that love is somehow different?

One possible answer is this: we moderns are desperate to preserve an indestructible residue of the divine in a world powerfully dedicated to the abolition of the divine – but unable, in reality, to give up this most fundamental human need. Ironically, we owe the conviction that love is unconditional less to Christian authority than to the decline of Christian authority, which really gathers momentum from the late eighteenth century onwards. In particular, the sanctification of human love by some forms of Romanticism was possible only because the world was becoming ever more emptied of God. Something had to fill his place – and love quickly presented itself as an ideal candidate.

8

Women as ideals
love and the troubadours

For all the argument within medieval Christianity about the extent to which human beings could love without divine grace, or about the scope of the command to love one's neighbour, or about the nature of love within marriage, or about the value of desire for earthly goods, certain things were not in dispute. One of them was that genuine love for another human being is necessarily love for the sake of God and experienced as such; another was that adulterous desire, never mind consummation, is taboo.

It therefore seems scarcely conceivable that there could be a corner of medieval Europe where love between Christian men and women was celebrated in an utterly different spirit: as a pageant of refined and often adulterous passion, devoted to its own earthly flourishing even when its subject also praises and fears God; passion which isn't experienced as dependent on God if it is to issue in genuine love, or as directed ultimately at God; passion which, precisely at its purest, can be seen as incompatible with marriage; passion which is intensely serious about itself yet can also be ironic, playful and even bawdy; passion which is taken to rejuvenate a suitor and perfect his virtue, provided he serves his mistress with appropriate devotion and patience, courtesy and proportion.

Yet that is what happened in the twelfth and thirteenth centuries in Provence and more widely in the vast region of southern France, including the Pyrenees and northern Spain, known in modern times as 'Occitania'. The troubadours of the region wrote and set to music numerous poems in praise of *fin' amor*, or, literally, 'refined love' – widely regarded since the late nineteenth century as the first flowering of 'courtly love'.[1] Their greatness is *not* that they invented love as passion – as many, like Nietzsche,[2] think – for this quite obviously existed and was celebrated before: we have seen it, for example, in love for God from the Hebrews to Augustine, especially when expressed as the love of a bride for her groom; in the Song of Songs; and in the friendship of Jonathan and David. Indeed, passionate love for the Virgin Mary flowers at the same time as the troubadours pay homage to their married mistresses – and so is hardly their preserve.[3] Nor, of course, were they the first to see love as a school in virtue, a way for the lover to strive for ethical perfection – for Plato and Aristotle had already articulated such thoughts in great detail. Instead, their radical innovation is to institute a cult of love for an *earthly woman*, through which her suitor (and sometimes she too) can attain to a nobility, freshness, and above all joy that are available in no other way.[4]

ADULTEROUS DESIRE

Like every great and innovative sensibility, *fin' amor* is tremendously complex. Some troubadours, such as the first of whom we know, Guilhem de Peitieu[5] (1071–1126), seem to celebrate not merely adulterous desire but also sexual consummation: 'God let me live long enough to get my hands under her cloak!',[6] Guilhem sings, in a style pilloried by some later troubadours as crude and uncourtly. He can be torn between his different loves, though his anguish is seldom unmixed with play: 'Knights, give me counsel in a problem!/ . . . I don't know at all with which one I should stay, with Lady Agnes or with Lady Arsen.'[7] His style is magnificently high-spirited, whether he is praising love's enhancement of health and life, bemoaning his amorous failures or mocking a lady whose professed expectations of courtliness in a suitor won't stop her settling for whatever man she can get:

> I never saw a lady of such great faith who,
> if one refuses her plea or her entreaty,
> excluded from true valour, does not make her peace with baseness.
>
> If for her you set good company at high price,
> she provides herself with what she finds at hand;
> if she cannot have a horse, she'll buy a hack.[8]

Other troubadours, especially after Guilhem and his generation, repudiate adulterous acts on ethical grounds (though some might do so because they are socially too far beneath their ladies to hope for sexual intimacy).[9] One of these is Marcabru (active 1130–1149), thought to have been a Gascon clerk, who insists that love cannot be a school for virtue if it isn't monogamous and rails against the sexual licence of courtly men and women. At times he sounds like a voice from Scripture,[10] chiding human folly and immorality; and yet, like his fellow troubadours, his voice is predominantly secular. The wages of vice lie less in divine punishment than in human degradation: adultery, Marcabru declares, pollutes the noble bloodline with degenerate offspring.[11] Wrong love – and Marcabru recognises that no area of life is more littered with false coinage – results in decadence: a decadence that is not a merely an ethical 'Fall', but a social and biological corruption.

Yet others, like Bernart Marti, are less clear either way about adultery – but insist that a married lady should confine herself to one lover: 'A lady is perfidious towards her lover if she feeds three men with her love . . . I allow her one courtly, worthy friend as well as her husband'.[12]

Not that love within marriage was regarded as impossible. But marriage tended not to embody the love celebrated by the troubadours: the sort that, whether or not sexually consummated, purifies and rejuvenates the lover through the practice of the virtues of *fin' amor*. It is said that in a celebrated judgement of 1174 a Court of Love under the Countess of Champagne clearly distinguished between the affection that belongs to marriage and the superior possibilities for love that are available outside it:

> We declare and hold as firmly established that love cannot exert its powers between two people who are married to each other. For lovers give each other everything freely, under no compulsion or necessity, but married people are in duty bound to give in to each other's desires and deny themselves to each other in nothing.[13]

The troubadours who espoused these views weren't studs strumming their lutes below innocent girls' balconies. Nor were they dandies like the inarticulate soldier, Christian, who wooed Roxane with verses supplied by Cyrano de Bergerac. They were skilled court poets and often, like Guilhem de Peitieu, aristocrats themselves, though a few were also of merchant or even peasant birth. Writing in a language called *lenga d'Oc*, more commonly known as Provençal or Occitan, they invented a way of loving suffused with the ideals of erotic delight, grace, proportion, play and service.

WOMAN AS VIRTUE-INSPIRING IDEAL

Apart from sanctifying adulterous desire, a second revolution of *fin' amor* strikes us straightaway: a woman is now worshipped as a privileged repository of virtue, and as inspiring in her suitor an ennobling and virtue-giving love.[14] In effect, if not self-consciously, the troubadours challenge a centuries-old view of woman as temptress who leads men to sin, on the model of Eve and Adam: of woman as the path of wickedness and the devil's gateway.

The extraordinary reversal of roles, in which even a supremely powerful feudal lord subordinates himself to a lady who by all the social and political authority of the times is vastly his inferior, is perfectly illustrated by Guilhem's verse. As Duke of Aquitaine and Count of Poitiers (and a direct ancestor of King Richard the Lionheart of England), Guilhem was right at the top of the hierarchy. Yet here he is speaking of himself – a ruler of vast territories – as love's supplicant:

> No man will ever be gracious to love unless he is submissive to it, and unless he is humble to strangers and those near by, and obedient to all those dwelling within its bounds.[15]

A later troubadour, Bernart de Ventadorn (*c.* 1147–1170), sings in similar terms:

> I love and can fear nothing more than her,
> and nothing would ever be hardship for me,
> provided only it come to please my lady . . .[16]

At the same time, Bernart laments that a woman can also betray and be base; that she can falsely accuse the virtuous suitor and fall at the feet of the wealthy one. Indeed he might venerate and scorn her in the same poem.[17] Argument, reproach and frustration are often found in his verse; and just as the Hebrew prophets might argue with God, so there is no reason to suppose that reproach is incompatible, indeed doesn't go together, with veneration. In any event, for Bernart the joys that the lady inspires surpass all others:

> When the fresh grass and the leaf appear,
> and the flower blossoms on the bough,
> and the nightingale raises high and clear
> its voice and pours out its song,

joy have I for it, and joy for the flower,
and joy for myself and for my lady *yet more*: . . .
[for] *that* is joy which all other joys overwhelms.[18]

Nor do Guilhem and Bernart leave us in any doubt about the stakes of
winning – or forfeiting – a lady's acceptance:

For joy of her a sick man can be cured,
and from her anger a healthy man can die,
and a wise man go mad,
and a handsome man lose his good looks,
and the most courtly one become a boor,
and the totally boorish one turn courtly.[19]

Guilhem de Peitieu

Since with my lady neither prayer nor mercy,
nor the right that I have can avail me,
and it comes not to please her that I love her,
I'll never more tell her so . . .
she has caused my death and by death I answer her
and go away . . . into exile, I know not where.[20]

Bernart de Ventadorn

Thus a lady's decision to recognise and accept her suitor's love – or not to do
so – is experienced by him as a matter of life and death, if not physical then spiritual
and moral. If she withholds her recognition he will undergo a living death. And if
she grants it he will be rejuvenated in body and spirit, and even a boor will somehow
become refined.

It is by no means clear, though, that a lady's acceptance involves genuine
reciprocation. Sometimes it seems to, as when Bernart de Ventadorn says 'In
accord and in assent is the love of two noble lovers'.[21] But for Bernart the lady's
acceptance might also be signalled merely by some 'honour and good'[22] that she
is pleased to bestow upon her suitor – a response that seems to fall short of
anything like full requital.

✦ ✦ ✦

Even if adulterous *desire* is fundamental to the affective structure of *fin' amor*, the real end of the troubadours, especially after the first generation represented by Guilhem, is not sexual possession. Rather, it is the ethical and spiritual enrichment of the suitor, and perhaps of both parties.[23] With or without requital, the very act of loving his lady with courtesy, service and measure, benefits him:

> Each day I improve and grow more pure,
> for I serve and worship the most noble [lady]
> in the world – this I can tell you openly.
> Hers I am from head right down to foot . . .[24]
>
> *Arnaut Daniel (active 1180–1200)*

Elsewhere Arnaut says that in all his travels and in all the women he has encountered 'I find not thus in one person alone all such qualities, for in her God chose to display and establish them fast.'[25] To love such a woman is an apprenticeship in virtue and the source of all good deeds:

> Noble and true and more constant than is my wont
> am I towards love for my Fair Delight. . . .
> For this I love nobly, that by loving I am enhanced. . . .
> Love causes all good, seemly deeds to be done,
> and bestows those qualities which pertain to merit.
> Thus love is a school of valour,
> for no man is so stupid but, provided he love,
> love guides him to valorous port.[26]
>
> *Guiraut Riquier (1254–1292)*

Love as the source of good deeds; as a schooling in virtue; as the path to purity; as seeking out a loved object that instantiates divine qualities: here again the long arm of Plato (extended largely through Neoplatonism) is unmistakeable. In many of the later courtly poems the lady personally embodies the perfection sought by the highest love. In other words, she exhibits in one person the goodness or beauty that is to be found, though in lesser ways, in anything or anyone we could call good or beautiful – and that inspires its lover to become virtuous and to give birth to great deeds and works. For these troubadours, just as for Plato's Diotima, movement towards perfection is the supreme aim of love and central to a flourishing life. They sing of a love whose eroticism has nothing to do with physical reproduction and everything to do with a search for beauty that is also a search for moral goodness.

All of which is why *fin' amor* might not be finally fulfillable. Not because lovers are riveted to the search for obstacles and suffering for their own sake, as Denis de Rougemont insists in his influential study of Western love;[27] rather because spiritual enrichment and the perfection of virtue have no end point where they are fully attained. Progress is its own reward – and, as troubadours like Arnaut Daniel make plain, the cause of infinite happiness. *Der Weg ist das Ziel*: the path is the goal.

FIDELITY AND JEALOUSY

But one can't in practice be absorbed in more than one beloved at a time. Nor can one easily think of more than one lady as embodying the essence of beauty or virtue. And so a golden rule of courtly love is that a suitor may not cheat on his lady – even if he does on his wife. He might be married and have lovers, but in its very structure *fin' amor* is serially monogamous.

This might mean leading a double life; yet, being clearly out in the open, it is hardly a furtive one. And nobody lived it more flamboyantly than Guilhem de Peitieu. He venerated his lady as passionately as any troubadour; yet he was also a prodigious seducer, according to a thirteenth-century biographer:

> The count of Poitou was one of the most courtly men in the world as well as one of the greatest deceivers of ladies, and a fine knight in deeds of arms, and generous in wooing; and he knew well how to compose and sing. And he trav-elled for a long time throughout the world in order to deceive ladies . . .[28]

Guilhem's reported double life is matched, indeed outshone, by his complex lyrical style. On the one hand, he evinces the idealising, erudite, and subtle passion of *fin' amor*. On the other hand, he is brutal, impatient, and deceitful. He yearns to worship women, and also to conquer them (not that these urges are inconsistent). He enjoys desire to the full and yet also deems it to be vain. His moods can be playful, satirising and lampooning; yet they are also intensely serious – and, behind the fun, seem threaded with suffering. It is hard to know exactly where one is with him, as if he has no 'true' face or, differently (but no more adequately) put, as if all is mask.

So too, but in a very different style, with Arnaut Daniel. On the one hand, he wants to serve his lady and become more virtuous. On the other hand, he wants to be in her bedroom – which, he is clear, is no Platonic nook: 'Would I were hers in body, not in soul!/ and that she let me, secretly, into her bedroom!'[29] Like Guilhem, but less bawdily, he embodies the joyful 'immoralism' of the Ovid of *The Art of Love* – which preaches thorough delight in sensual pursuits, whether in the chase or the quarry. And, again like Guilhem, but now much more overtly, we see traces of the idealism of Plato and Christianity, which seeks a high-minded transcendence of physical desire. In the character of his verse these (in many ways unnecessarily) warring traditions in the history of Western love are allowed to harmonise fruitfully. As if in the bedroom love's virtue finds its confirmation and reward.

✦ ✦ ✦

One emotion that *fin' amor* did need to regulate was jealousy. Even when its eroticism is largely spiritualised or its ends are primarily ethical, jealousy is bound to be on the cards. And, again, its position is fairly clear: husbands are not allowed to be jealous of rivals; suitors are. Indeed, a suitor's jealousy is admirable. It reflects his uncompromising devotion to his lady. And it fosters a love that makes both parties finer.[30]

Whereas a husband's jealousy has a crude motive: possessiveness. Worse, it is an implicit attack on courtly behaviour. Here is the troubadour Uc de Mataplana urging his colleague, Raimon de Miraval, to overcome jealousy of his wife's suitors for the sake of upholding *fin' amor*:

> Let him not be worried about her,
> Nor grieved if his dwelling is frequented by courtly wooers,
> For in this way he will be pleasing to us who are courtly
> And repulsive to those who are jealous.[31]

Not surprisingly, the sort of jealousy we encounter least in troubadour poetry is that of suitors towards their ladies. The lady, elevated on her pedestal of virtue, is implicitly trusted to remain constant to her lover; and, if she strays a little, he, as her vassal in love, is hardly in a position to chide her – quite apart from the fact that her life is usually too private to be observed. Even when Guilhem de Peitieu fantasises about a lady he has never met and whose life is entirely unknown to him, he claims to be confident of her fidelity – unless, that is, she finds herself in the company of the feckless northern French (neighbours whom southerners had always regarded with the highest suspicion):

> I have a lady love, I know not who she is,
> For I never saw her, by my faith;
> Nor did she do anything to please or vex me,
> Nor do I worry about this,
> For there was never any Norman or Frenchman in my dwelling.[32]

✦ ✦ ✦

The passionate love celebrated by the troubadours seeks and is steeped in 'jois': intense joy that heals suffering and self-doubt; the delight in life and its rejuvenation that is to be found through love for a lady.[33] As Peire Vidal says, 'in her joy is born and has its beginning'.[34] In jois, as Bernart de Ventadorn tells us, a noble person has his dwelling:

> Any man is indeed of base life
> who has not his dwelling with joy,
> and who directs not towards love his heart
> and his desiring,
> since all that is, gives itself up
> to joy, and rings and is full of song:
> meadows and parklands and orchards,
> heathlands and plains and woods.[35]

For all their praise of jois, however, in our own day the troubadours' veneration of their ladies has sometimes been viewed as expressing a masochistic fantasy enacted by men longing to submit to what Goethe mysteriously called 'the eternal feminine' – indeed to make an interminable ordeal of their submission. Thus the sweet torture of this ordeal is heightened by picturing a remote lady who is more an impersonal archetype than a real human being. The adulterous desire that the troubadours praise but seldom consummate is, on this view, a way of intensifying their ardour – to the satisfaction of which they then generate one obstacle after another, as if fulfilment is the last thing they want. And the idealised lady of *fin' amor* is (like most idols) constructed narcissistically by the worshipper for his own delectation, so denying her actual nature – as well as preserving male dominance after all by making the worshipped lady merely a prop in his ritual of self-punishment. Seen in such terms, courtly love is a prime instance of how love's very nature is to crave unreachable ideals and thus its own frustration.[36]

But even if this masochistic-narcissistic picture is useful in understanding why, or one reason why, human beings might delight in submitting to an idealised object of desire, pictured as removed from our grasp by numberless obstacles, it will apply to *any* such structure of love, including one where the ideal object is in heaven. In other words it will fail to explain what is peculiar to courtly love: the *lady* (rather than God or absolute beauty or any other ultimate reality) as the ideal; the sanctification of *earthly* and sometimes adulterous desire (rather than exclusively of desire for God); the celebration of joy in *worldly* goods.

Indeed, if unfulfilment is crucial to love's development, this is not because love is a masochistic drive that craves obstacles to its own flourishing or delights in its own unhappiness; nor because it feels genuine only if endangered. Rather it is because unfulfilment keeps love focused on cultivating those dispositions that are essential to its success: the 'courtly' dispositions of service and courtesy, patience and proportion. Then love will be a nobility of the heart that rejuvenates its practitioners with the vitality of *jois*, whether they suffer or not, and whether they win their beloveds or lose them.[37]

9

How human nature became loveable
from the high Middle Ages to the Renaissance

After the twelfth and thirteenth centuries Western love is left with a revolutionary thought: a single human being might be worthy of the sort of love that was formerly reserved for God. She might be seen as embodying the greatest good and so evoke reverence fitting for a divine being. Though the universe is still conceived as an order of love leading up to God, and all love as ultimately subordinate to love for God, devotion to another person – or indeed to nature in general – is freer to take on a life of its own.

This chapter will trace some key developments of this thought up to the dawn of the seventeenth century – the first century of the modern world; the century in which Baruch Spinoza (1632–1677) effectively eliminates the distinction between nature as a whole and a God beyond it, so that it is no longer meaningful to think of loving the natural world for the sake of God. For with this philosopher nature and God become one.

But even before it is proclaimed in a new philosophy, the idea that love for nature, including human nature, might assume a sacredness of its own is alive in poetry and song. The troubadours are at the head of a procession of 'great lovers' who start to fill the stage of Western love from the twelfth century, among them Abelard and Heloise – the Parisian philosophy professor, and his student, fifteen to thirty years his junior – whose passionate affair, intense sex, love-child and secret marriage are documented in an extraordinary exchange of letters.[1] As Heloise says in an early letter to Abelard, 'Surely I have discovered in you – and thus I love you – undoubtedly the greatest and most outstanding good of all'.[2] And she writes with some, but not it seems wholehearted, regret,

'At every stage of my life up to now, as God knows, I have feared to offend you rather than God, and tried to please you more than him'.[3]

Abelard, for his part, recalls that 'our desires left no stage of lovemaking untried, and if love could devise something new, we welcomed it'.[4] And he adds: 'Separation drew our hearts still closer while frustration inflamed our passion even more; then we became more abandoned as we lost all sense of shame and, indeed, shame diminished as we found more opportunities for lovemaking.'[5] By which he means to provide evidence for his and Heloise's total devotion to one another, and for the central place of carnal bliss in that love (for which he was eventually punished with castration, at the instigation of Heloise's uncle, Canon Fulbert). Their love was – to use the cliché justifiably – all-consuming: at once physical, intellectual and spiritual.

In a similar vein, the illicit love of Tristan and Isolde is presented by the poet Gottfried von Strassburg, writing around 1210, as a supreme good,[6] which they can find only in a secluded forest, in other words in pristine earthly nature. Here their overwhelming desire, including their sexual desire, for one another becomes a sacred dedication. They address each other, as Roger Scruton suggests, 'in hushed, liturgical words',[7] a liturgy of love similar to the religious liturgy, but – and this is the new element – without them experiencing their love as constantly drawing its legitimacy and vitality from God. Without, in other words, Augustine's 'for the sake of' dominating their awareness of love and its sacredness. As Gottfried tells us, they needed nothing apart from each other:

> They looked at one another and nourished themselves with that! Their sustenance was the eye's increase. They fed . . . on nothing but love and desire. . . . Hidden away in their hearts they carried the best nutriment to be had anywhere in the world . . . I mean pure devotion, love made sweet as balm that consoles body and sense so tenderly, and sustains the heart and spirit – this was their best nourishment. Truly, they never considered any good but that from which the heart drew desire, the eyes delight, and which the body, too, found agreeable. With this they had enough.[8]

Erotic passion is now a way not of reaching beyond the human, but of being fully (even heroically) human. With love that fuses the sensuous and the spiritual one can achieve blessedness in this life. Without defying God, it makes 'heaven on earth'.[9]

And this becoming more perfectly human is expressed, in turn, by a setting that is strikingly natural – the forest – and within the forest and its blossoms and leaves and brooks and singing birds, the further seclusion of a lovers' grotto, where Tristan and Isolde can consummate their desires free from the impure dealings of everyday life. That the grotto resembles a gothic cathedral only enhances the sense we have that the lovers' exchanges are a form of erotic liturgy. Its architectural features seem to be allegories of love's virtues:

> Its roundness inside betokens Love's Simplicity: Simplicity is most fitting for Love which must have no corners, that is, Cunning or Treachery. Breadth signifies Love's Power, for her Power is without end. Height is Aspiration that mounts aloft to the clouds: nothing is too great for it so long as it means to climb, up and up, to where the molten Crown of the Virtues gathers the vault to the keystone.[10]

At the centre of the cave is a bed – in the same position in which one might find an altar in a church – and this bed is made of crystal, which, Gottfried says, is 'unerringly' accurate to love's real nature: 'Love *should* be of crystal – transparent and translucent!'

Crystal is unyielding, and Gottfried might be alluding here to this quality in love – to the steeliness that love must have in order to master the sorrows and sacrifices and obstacles that are inseparable from loving.[11] As he says elsewhere in his poem: 'He that never had sorrow of love never had joy of it either'.[12] But the transparency of crystal makes another point: genuine love strives to be clear-sighted, undeluded. (Echoes again of Diotima in Plato's *Symposium*.) Though love's desires all too easily lead one to fantasy and obscurity, the highest love achieves the opposite. It is neither destructive itself, nor does it have truck with those who would destroy it. 'Deceit or Force', says Gottfried, 'cannot be accounted Love'. And so the cave has a 'door of bronze' that bars the way to anyone who seeks to enter using such means: 'it is made of bronze so that no tool, whether of force or of violence, cunning or artifice, treachery or falsehood should ever have power to harm it.'[13]

Behind this protective door their love is consummated 'as their hearts prompted them ... and as they felt inclined'.[14] 'Instead of the eucharistic miracle, instead of the transubstantiation of the material kinds and the divinisation of him who receives these' – in other words instead of the rituals of the

Catholic Mass – 'flesh commingles with spirit in transcendental unity', as Denis de Rougemont puts it.[15] The yearning of sexual desire to fuse with one other person is sanctified in tones redolent of love for God in the Christian mystical tradition.

✦ ✦ ✦

This new language of love for the natural – and set in the natural – doesn't find expression just in romantic and sexual love. It is also to be seen in the passionate love for all of nature – for wind, sun and air, as well as for the animals – of Francis of Assisi (1182–1226). Francis calls birds and moon 'sister', and fire and wind 'brother'; and he praises God for their existence:

> Praised be You, my Lord, with all your creatures,
> especially Sir Brother Sun,
> Who is the day and through whom You give us light.

> Praised be You, my Lord, through Brother Wind,
> and through the air, cloudy and serene, and every kind of weather
> through which You give sustenance to Your creatures.

> Praised be You, my Lord, through Sister Water,
> which is very useful and humble and precious and chaste.

> Praised be You, my Lord, through our Sister Mother Earth,
> who sustains and governs us,
> and who produces varied fruits with colored flowers and herbs.[16]

If we knew nothing about its author, we might think this poem the work of a pagan: of a nature worshipper or a pantheist. Its language neither accuses nature of corruption, nor shrinks it into a bridge that must be crossed to reach the world beyond, nor deems friendship with the world to be enmity toward God. 'Sister Mother Earth . . . sustains and governs' us; she is not beneath man in the order of Creation, but, as both sister and mother, at least an equal.

More remarkable still is how Francis goes about seeking intimacy with nature. Unrelentingly, he forsakes all comforts, including any, except temporary, lodging in houses and churches. Even churches have walls that divide us from the world outside and provide solace that dulls our senses. We should be no more than passing strangers in them.

Francis's rejection of the material, like his love of nature, seems artless and dreamy, as if he were a hippy-figure marinated in his own benevolence and letting it all go. But anybody with the discipline to see through a programme as strict and unconventional as his is possessed of a powerful, even a brutal, will. None of the saints and great benefactors of humanity is likely to have been particularly gentle or tolerant.

This willpower seems to have been on open display when, after recovering from a life-changing illness, Francis first abjured the comforts into which he had been born. Rather than making a private vow of poverty, he publicly humiliated his father, a prosperous local merchant, in the main square of Assisi, berating him for his greed, ostentation, and self-satisfaction. In front of a crowd that was gathering at the sound of the young man's rising fury he stripped naked and hurled his clothes at his father with the words 'Now I owe you nothing!'[17]

Yet there is nothing gloomy or world-denying in Francis's spirit of poverty. He rejects possessions not to flee the world, but on the contrary to come close to a world uncluttered by their demands and distractions. He helps us see that to call money 'worldly' is a misnomer; for it *obstructs intimacy* with the world rather than expresses it. He provokes the thought that the seeker after wealth is not too bound up with ordinary things but not bound up enough. He has seen that although riches help protect us from the harshness of reality, they also protect us from the richness of reality.

You cannot love what you have concealed from yourself. This is surely why money and pride – those great tools of concealment – are major targets for Jesus, while sex isn't. And why asceticism needn't be world-repudiating, but can powerfully open us to the world, and in particular to that intense experience of its 'there-ness' that we call 'sacred'. (Indeed, the supreme Epicurean is the ascetic. Sensitivity to pleasure and delight is greatest in those who have mind and body under the most refined control.) Francis, with his open-hearted spirit, evokes with incomparable power and simplicity this joy and sanctity of the worldly, this sense of nature made holy by God's presence in it as its creator and value-giver.

Francis's strict simplicity was, however, not to the taste of most of his followers, let alone of the medieval Church hierarchy with its immense wealth and ambition for power. His immediate successor as head of the Franciscans, the order of friars that he founded, lived in ostentatious luxury. Only twenty years after he died, a prominent Franciscan, Archbishop Rigaud of Rouen, boasted that he possessed three palaces together with huge estates.[18] Worse, the Inquisition, which was set in motion shortly after Francis's death, was manned by Franciscans who, in a further twist of perversity, burnt as heretics several fellow members of their Order for excessive belief in frugality. In 1323 Pope John XXII condemned as heretical the doctrine, preached by this small minority, which proclaimed that Jesus and his Apostles had possessed nothing – not even the clothes they wore – a doctrine that Francis himself had, in effect, upheld when he flung his clothes back at his father.

Yet the Church, despite persecuting many who criticised its opulence, was shrewd enough to see that it needed Francis. Its brutality, greed and corruption threatened to ignite a revolt of the sort that would, three centuries later, hasten the Reformation; and the attractiveness to ordinary people of Francis's philosophy of love, his saintly life, and his easygoing rapport with all of nature was not lost on the authorities. Even while he was alive his new order of friars was officially recognised, subject to certain restrictions, and after his death he was swiftly canonised.

✦ ✦ ✦

It would be categorically wrong to see love for the natural or physical – of the sort articulated by Abelard and Heloise, Tristan and Isolde, and Francis himself – as opposed, in principle, to mainstream Christian traditions. Though, in the nineteenth and twentieth centuries, thinkers like Nietzsche present 'Christianity' (and even the imaginary construct 'Judeo-Christianity') as monolithically contemptuous of nature and flesh, and as instilling in men and women 'hatred of the human, and even more of the animal',[19] this is an error. Indeed, as I mentioned in chapter 7, such unqualified contempt for body and nature would run up against a central Christian tenet, which is that the world is a site for God's self-manifestation, beginning with the Creation and then with Christ, in whom God assumes human flesh. Which is precisely why sects like the Gnostics and Manichees, who regarded matter as the source of evil, were so brutally persecuted.

Rather, the break with convention wrought by this diverse cast of characters, from the troubadours to Francis, is to do with the nature of their *experience*. Though the formal background picture stays the same – love for God remains, as Augustine had put it, the end to which all other love is to be ultimately referred[20] – yet all this other love can now be lived without either constant reference to him or constant mindfulness of its imperfection. Human loving can be less besieged by the awareness that none of us has value independent of God, or that we are 'fallen' creatures. We can enjoy others (to use Augustine's language again) without remembering that we really enjoy them only as they are related to God.

So if Heloise says that Abelard is 'the greatest and most outstanding good of all', she in no way devalues God, who unquestionably remains at the apex of the hierarchy of love; nor does she see Abelard as a substitute for God. But the background picture doesn't intrude as vividly into her living experience of Abelard; her love for *him* does not lead her beyond him but can linger with him.

Two hundred years after the high Middle Ages, in which these naturalisers of passionate love write, a pageant of great minds, beginning in fifteenth-century Florence, continuing in sixteenth-century Gascony, and culminating in seventeenth-century Holland, takes this revolution radically further. So that the human, the physical, and the natural are increasingly experienced as places of divine revelation – places that, far from being mere bridges to a realm beyond this world, or being overwhelmed by sin and delusion, we are called on to love, study, enjoy and live in to the full.

PLATONIC LOVE AND THE ITALIAN RENAISSANCE

Once again Platonic insights are central to the story. In fifteenth-century Florence, the key idea about love is that God's beauty and goodness infuse nature, from the stars to plants to human bodies, and to that extent make it loveable. Rather than being just a nest of temptation that leads us away from God, nature is a garden of riches in which God has placed us. To love and study its numinous beauty is to love and study God himself. This is the philosophical justification for the veneration of beauty in the Italian Renaissance.

Any notion that the so-called 'humanism' of the Italian Renaissance is fundamentally materialistic, pagan and anti-Christian would therefore be entirely inaccurate. The Renaissance's fascination with natural things like the body and its anatomy cannot be separated from their relation to the divine; indeed these things derive their spiritual quality from their participation in the divine.

This deep religiosity of nature sustains, perhaps even enhances, the sovereignty of humanity over the rest of nature that had been enshrined in the Bible.

Endowed with quasi-divine powers of intellect and will, and themselves exem-
plars of physical and spiritual beauty, human beings can now revere not only their
inner world, itself a microcosm and image of Godhood, but also the whole world
in which they have been set. Love is the language of their longing, whether for the
form of another human body or for the harmony and order of the universe. And
because God's presence in the physical world glorifies it, the physical can also be
employed to glorify God.[21]

Marsilio Ficino (1433–1499), a deeply Christian philosopher who founded
a Platonic Academy in Florence in the second half of the fifteenth century,
modelled on Plato's Academy in Athens, expresses this new optimism by saying
that humanity is 'the vicar of God' in his earthly powers. More than that, the
human soul is able 'By means of the intellect . . . [and] by means of the will . . .
to become in a sense all things, and even a god.'[22]

Indeed, this is man's duty. Man has no higher task than to use his power and
freedom in the service of his own self-creation. Ficino's younger contemporary,
Giovanni Pico della Mirandola (1463–1494), polymath, mystic, scholar of
Kabbalism, aristocrat, and sometime playboy, wrote an *Oration on the Dignity of
Man* in which he has God speak to Adam in terms that are also a call to humanity
as a whole to strive for its exaltation:

> You, who are confined by no limits, shall determine for yourself your own
> nature, in accordance with your own free will, in whose hand I have placed you
> . . . We have made you neither heavenly nor earthly, neither mortal nor
> immortal, so that, more freely and more honourably the moulder and maker
> of yourself, you may fashion yourself in whatever form you shall prefer. You
> shall be able to descend among the lower forms of being, which are brute
> beasts; you shall be able to be reborn out of the judgement of your own soul
> into the higher beings, which are divine.[23]

At the heart of these powers are imagination and knowledge. Through them
man can become aware of those eternal truths that order the universe, and in
doing so become a creator himself. Through them humans should strive to
become angels and ultimately to become one with the divine essence. And, in
true Platonic style, the royal route to such illumination, such knowing and
understanding, such mystical achievement, is in turn . . . love. Man is to *love* the
grandeur of God's creation, which is to be seen wherever we look, whether

inside ourselves or outside, in the workings of the human body or in the stars above. And through love he is to be united with it.

✦ ✦ ✦

For the development of Western love, this was heady stuff. Nature as divine manifestation; man as a free and self-transforming creator; human understanding as able, through love, to apprehend the world, and thence to achieve a mystical union with the divine; love of earthly beauty as a celebration of God.

Ficino is clear that human love ('amore umano') is not in fundamental conflict with love of divine beauty ('amore divino'), which can come from studying philosophy, practising justice, devotion to religion, and other spiritual-intellectual pursuits.[24] And yet in his philosophy, as for the most part in the Renaissance, the divinity that permeates nature still stops decisively short of that cursed old territory: sex. (Territory onto which it will refuse to move for at least another three centuries.)

A truly valuable relationship between two people, says Ficino, can take place only on a spiritual-intellectual level. And sex simply cannot be considered as in any sense spiritual – except as a means to creating beautiful children. The body might be venerated for its beauty but its capacity for sexual enjoyment is not. Indeed Ficino lambasts the desire to touch for the sake of sensuous pleasure alone as 'amore bestiale', and he regards all craving for voluptuous delight as a 'disease' and a form of 'insanity'.[25] He wants men and women to relate to each other through asexual friendship of a sort that resembles Aristotle's *philia*, in which individuals of similar quality would develop reciprocal love based on their appreciation of each other – except Ficino's Platonic influence means that this mutual appreciation is founded on intellectual enjoyment of each other's beauty of soul, mind and body, rather than strictly on their excellences of character. He calls this sort of relation 'amore platonico', a term that we still use when we speak of 'Platonic love'.[26]

In 'amore platonico' God and nature might not be pitted against one another, but spirit continues to bear grudges against matter – and we see shadows of this even in Ficino's illustrious student, Michelangelo. In celebrating the beauty of the human body, Michelangelo, especially in his later years, loves it as an emanation and embodiment of the realm of spirit for which he yearns. Nowhere does God show himself 'more clearly than in human form sublime,/ which, since they image Him, alone I love.'[27] His tremendous desire 'to soar alive among the chosen spirits' expresses not just his often-remarked melancholy, but also the powerful melancholy that colours the Italian Renaissance despite its brilliant optimism – and is perhaps inseparable from it. (For how much insight into the horrors of the world must be needed, and so how much melancholy, to motivate such a defiant will to see its beauty and harmony?)

It is a stark paradox: the human body can be exalted to a point that has perhaps never been surpassed; but physical sex can be denigrated with equal vehemence. By seeing God so clearly in the human body, the body becomes an object of intense study, fascination and devotion. But, precisely for this reason, the greatest suspicion is reserved for desire that is deemed not to be aimed at the divinity in nature. Carnal desire, in particular, remains the enemy of enemies: *the* obstacle to apprehending the body as spiritual.

MONTAIGNE'S DEFIANT HUMANISM

The next step in this revolution in how we experience the object of love was to go further still towards making love for another human being independent of what I called the 'background picture': the picture of God as the source of loveable qualities in the world; of God as the end to which all love is to be ultimately referred. The picture is still there, but – in contrast to Ficino – it is absent from the lover's experience of delight in the other, which is entirely focused on his natural and individual qualities. Nor does the lover feel the need to invoke it to explain his love for the other. 'If you press me to say why I loved him, I feel that it cannot be expressed except by replying: "Because it was him: because it was me".'

So says Michel de Montaigne[28] (1533–1592), the most humane thinker of the French Renaissance and among the most attractive in Western history. He is speaking of his friendship with an older man, Etienne de la Boétie – one of the great friendship-loves in literary history, on a par with Jonathan and David or Ruth and Naomi, in which from the moment of meeting 'we discovered ourselves to be so seized by each other, so known to each other and so bound together that from then on none was so close as each was to the other.'[29]

This bond is at the opposite extreme to one that is explicitly based on loving God in the other, or in loving the other for the sake of God. It is rooted entirely in what is specific about the two friends and their interaction. It isn't grounded even in some general quality of human nature that is loveable, such as benevolence or generosity. In its uniqueness it has 'no ideal to follow other than itself; no comparison but with itself.' Though fostered by two people's similarity – their 'congruity and affinity'[30] – when Montaigne reflects on his friendship he concludes that he can't really say what it is about Etienne that provokes such a passionate response in him:

> There is no one particular consideration – nor two nor three nor four nor a thousand of them – but rather some inexplicable quintessence of them all mixed up together which, having captured my will, brought it to plunge into his and lose itself and which, having captured his will, brought it to plunge and lose itself in mine with an equal hunger and emulation. I say 'lose itself' in very truth; we kept nothing back for ourselves: nothing was his or mine.[31]

Such soul-friendship necessarily cannot exist with more than one other person:

> If anyone suggests that I can love each of two friends as much as the other, and that they can love each other and love me as much as I love them, he is turning into a plural . . . that which is the most 'one', the most bound into one.[32]

Nor does Montaigne shrink from the consequences of this fanatical exclusivity. Above all, it trumps all our other loves – for our country, spouse, and even children. Each friend gives himself and whatever he values so totally to the other that 'he has nothing left to share with another'. If our friend were to command us to set fire to our temple or to kill a daughter, we would obey[33] – though, Montaigne adds, we know that he would in practice be too scrupulous a guardian of our interests to go this far. Equally if he demands that I reveal to him secrets which I have sworn to tell no one, I can do so with impunity because, as a second self, he is in effect me: 'The unique, highest friendship loosens all other bonds. That secret which I have sworn to reveal to no other, I can reveal without perjury to him who is not another: he *is* me.'[34]

The magnificent corollary of this idea that two souls and wills are fused is that it makes no more sense for him to reckon up, or even be grateful to me for, 'the services and good turns' I perform for him than for me to thank myself for actions I take that benefit my own life. Soul friends not only refuse to calculate the costs and benefits of friendship, they cease even to be aware of them. The *very idea* of 'a good turn', or 'duty', or 'gratitude' is divisive; these are all concepts that presuppose differences and separation between people. And as such they are repugnant to a true union of souls.

Moreover, friends who have become one interwoven soul must clearly share everything about their lives: not only fortune and misfortune, secrets and thoughts, but also 'their wills, goods, wives, children, honour'.[35] Because they are now one, there can be no division of anything. If such a friend gives you money, he is therefore merely giving you your own money back!

Montaigne is not presenting a merely theoretical ideal of friendship. Throughout he is drawing on his own 'loving friendship' for Etienne, compared with which all the rest of his life – blessed as it was with talent, pleasure, and achievement – was 'but smoke and ashes, a night dark and dreary'; so that after Etienne's early death, Montaigne says that he felt 'no more than a half' person.[36] Theirs is a love in which sexual desire seems to play no part. (Indeed sex doesn't feature in the friendship that interests Montaigne – and he is generally relaxed about homosexuality, despite at one point dismissing 'that alternative licence of the Greeks' as 'abhorrent'.[37]) It is a love that shows how wrong it is to think that friendship is a less committed or passionate bond than 'romantic' relationships, for it was 'so perfect and so entire that it is certain that few such can even be read about, and no trace at all of it can be found among men of today. So many fortuitous circumstances are needed to make it, that it is already something if Fortune can achieve it once in three centuries'.[38]

✦ ✦ ✦

Montaigne's friendship-love strikingly resembles Aristotle's perfect *philia*, a resemblance which he acknowledges. For both these thinkers friendship is fostered by similarity; it is uncontaminated by any interest in 'pleasure or profit' beyond enjoying the other for his own sake; it is undermined by inequality, such as exists between parents and their children; it demands a real intertwining of two lives through living together; and, for all its intensity, it is a devotion of sobriety, characterised by measure, naturalness, patience and realism. Only such devotion, Montaigne and Aristotle agree, can yield love's greatest delights.

Above all: it celebrates the natural. Montaigne is very much a believing Christian and a loyal Catholic; and he wants to live – and love – in the world in which God has set us, which means to discover and fulfil the natural conditions in which our humanity can flourish. One of his favourite mottos, which he had painted onto the wall of his study, was from the Roman playwright Terence (*c.* 195–159 BCE): 'I am a man, I consider nothing human to be alien to me'.[39] And late in his life he wrote: 'Anything which goes against the current of Nature is capable of being harmful, but everything which accords with her cannot but be pleasant.'[40]

We are here at the culmination of the revolution which began with the troubadours and in the love of Gottfried's Tristan and Isolde, the revolution in which nature and the human can be affirmed as objects of love without keeping half an eye on rising above them. For Montaigne it is an achievement of great moral beauty to be able to live life naturally.[41] Unlike Ficino, he despises any ambition in human beings to transcend their own nature. For he sees in such ambition not the exaltation of man but his bestialisation: 'They want to be beside themselves, want to escape from their humanity. That *is* madness: instead of changing their Form into an angel's, they change it into a beast's; they crash down instead of winding high.'[42]

In contrast to all who would glorify man as able, indeed duty-bound, to overcome his natural condition, Montaigne sees 'this miserable and wretched creature, who is not even master of himself . . . and yet dares to call himself lord and emperor of this universe.'[43] He doesn't care whether such self-glorification takes the form of mystical ambitions like Pico della Mirandola's or whether it comes from the opposite vanity: that, as the Greek thinker Protagoras put it, 'man is the measure of all things'. Secular and religious vanity are equally absurd.

How much nobler it is to be the person we actually are; to understand and affirm the limits of our own nature. 'Greatness of soul consists not so much in striving upwards and forwards as in knowing how to find one's ⌈natural⌉ place and to draw the line' – 'knowing how to live this life naturally'.[44] And so the first thing a child should learn is 'to know himself, to know how to die well and how to live well'.[45] After all, however high anyone sits, he always remain human: 'upon the highest throne in the world, we are seated, still, upon our arses'.[46]

To know ourselves is also to enjoy ourselves. The one is not fully possible without the other. Montaigne magnificently remarks that it is 'an accomplishment, absolute and as it were God-like, to know how to enjoy our being as we ought'.[47] He seems to suggest, almost in the vein of Heraclitus, that a flourishing life is an attunement to the *logos* of nature – in other words, accordance with immutable and inescapable cosmic laws.

Nothing is harder to achieve. It is so much easier, in love as in other strivings, to flee into the intoxicating extremes of either exalting oneself unrealistically or else debasing oneself unnecessarily. Montaigne despises both extremes. Raising oneself up is 'madness', but its opposite is also crude and unseemly: '. . . the most uncouth of our afflictions is to despise our being'.[48]

Montaigne's indictment of heaven-storming ambitions applies with particular force to love. The stakes are so high in love and our mastery of them so fragile that we readily seek qualities that our loved one doesn't have because we can't assimilate those she does. Instead of understanding and enjoying her as she is we falsely set her up as the saviour who can banish all our insecurity and incompleteness, magically replacing them with safety and wholeness. Instead of the vulnerability of relating in the here-and-now to her as an individual whose life we cannot control, we delude ourselves that an ideal union exists in which we can possess her perfectly. And in exalting our love we brutalise both our loved one and our love. '[S]upercelestial opinions: subterranean morals': these, as Montaigne pithily puts it, all too often go together.[49]

The *really* godlike achievement is to affirm what actually lies before us. 'You are a god insofar as you recognise that you are a man!'[50] he writes, citing the 'noble inscription' by which the Athenians honoured Pompey's visit to their city. But he could just as well have said, concerning love and all who want, hubristically, to model it on the divine: you would be a god if only you would recognise that you are human!

10

Love as joyful understanding of the whole
Spinoza

Montaigne had translated human beings back into nature through ceaseless study of what they – beginning with himself – actually do, in times of peace, war, crisis, triumph, banality, health and sickness. To vault beyond our own nature and use love as a springboard to the divine was, for him, hubristic and contemptible. Yet through it all he preserved the absolute distinction between human nature and God. God, as the creator, is a transcendent being, beyond nature and not bound by it.

It took the genius of Baruch Spinoza to place man so indissolubly in nature that the *very idea* of transcending it – and so the very idea of heaven-storming love – would make no sense. It wouldn't just be vain and self-defeating and denying of our proper place in nature: it would actually be nonsensical.

Spinoza does this by going further than any great thinker before him in repudiating the distinction between nature and God. For Spinoza nature, conceived as a whole, and God are one and the same. They are merely two different words for describing the totality of things. To love God *is* therefore to love nature as a whole.

For such heretical thoughts Spinoza was ostracised from the community of Portuguese-Jewish refugees in Amsterdam in which he had been born, raised and educated. His refusal to admit a fundamental distinction between God and nature conceived as a whole has dramatic implications for love, all of them incompatible with the religious orthodoxy of his day, whether Jewish or Christian. For in Spinoza's philosophy love cannot 'ascend' from the natural to the supernatural, from world to God, from body to soul, from the material to the purely spiritual, from a life of earthbound fate to a life of heavenly freedom, and from a world of evil to a realm of pure good. Spinoza sweeps away all these time-honoured dichotomies and so the entire picture of love that trades on them: the picture that gives love the task of overcoming the first element in each of these pairs for the sake of the second. In his hands love still offers us salvation, but this salvation is *not* to turn our backs on nature or matter or – still controversially today – evil. On the contrary, love affirms their reality – including the reality of evil – as part of nature taken as a whole.

The revolution in how we think about love that Spinoza makes possible therefore depends on – and can be understood only by looking at – his larger picture of the cosmos, to which we must turn.

✦ ✦ ✦

It is an extraordinary picture: God is no longer the figure of perfection who resides outside nature, which is at best imbued with his being. No longer the father who loves and protects and promises and judges and forgives and saves. No longer a creator fundamentally distinct from his creation. No longer a meddler who inscrutably intervenes in the world of cause and effect, or else mysteriously disappears. Now God *is* nature. Nature, that is, conceived as an intelligible whole.

Moreover, this whole that, according to Spinoza, we can call either God or nature can be viewed in both physical and mental terms: we can see it as a system of material bodies and their causal relations; or we can see it as a system of pure thought. Mental and physical aren't two different sorts of thing (as they are for Descartes); they are two ways of understanding one all-encompassing, borderless, self-creating reality.

Similarly, at the level of us individuals, mind and body aren't distinct substances, but two ways of grasping what we are. Every bodily event is a mental event, and every mental event is a bodily event. Those formerly sacrosanct distinctions that made the body, the material world, and the natural world of such questionable value, and that saw salvation in repudiating, transcending or at least perfecting them, are all gone.

And in the process of banishing these distinctions another one has been jettisoned: the idea of a human 'free will' independent of the chains of cause-and-effect that determine events in the rest of nature. We do *not* have a will that is free from causes and that could have chosen otherwise than it did. The illusion that we do arises because the *sensation* that decisions are up to us is so powerful (even when we vacillate) that we are sure there must be some faculty of free will behind them. And the illusion arises also because the real causes of what we do are shrouded in our ignorance. In reality,

> the mind is determined for willing this or that by a cause which is determined in its turn by another cause, and this one again by another, and so on to infinity.[1]

To know this infinite chain of causes would demand complete knowledge of the whole order of nature. Since that order of nature is another word for God, to understand any event is to infer how it inevitably results from the nature of God: 'all things are determined by the necessity of the divine nature to exist and operate in a certain way.'[2] If we take this moment – and whatever we are doing or thinking right now – nothing else could occur than what is occurring. The history that led up to now leaves no scope for anything to exist or happen except what does exist and happen.

For God, too, everything is determined. God did not freely decide to create this world, establish its laws of nature, and dispense its moral laws, as in the Jewish and Christian pictures. God couldn't have done otherwise: 'Things could not have been produced by God in any other way or order than that in which they were produced.'[3] And so the old question 'How can an all-good God allow evil to happen?' – the moral evil of people inflicting terrible cruelty on innocents – makes no sense in Spinoza's thought. Nor does the related puzzle: why did God choose to create a world full of natural disasters, such as earthquakes, droughts and tsunamis? There is, in other words, no 'problem of suffering' for Spinoza: no need to justify 'undeserved' anguish.

If God lacks the power to choose in the sense of an undetermined free will, and indeed is just another name for nature as a whole, then such questions are absurd. As are all those convoluted attempts to answer them: for example, to explain natural disasters as punishment for our transgressions, or moral evil as the price we pay for the gift of free will, or this world as 'the best of all possible worlds' (ridiculed by Voltaire in *Candide*).

In Spinoza's system, God not only 'permits' evil to happen, but, as present in everything that occurs, God actually *causes* the things that we find evil as well as those that we find good. Evil is an expression of God's essential nature.

And so there isn't much point praying to God to change things. Petitional prayer will have no effect. Miracles are impossible because there can be no departure from necessity – and if people believe in them this speaks only of their ignorance of the real causes of things.

As it happens, God isn't in the least 'worried' by evil or 'pleased' by good. Nor does he punish us for doing bad and reward us for being virtuous. To attribute such emotions to God, as if he were a human being writ large, is a fundamental error, which has been exploited by preachers and priests down the ages to aggrandise themselves and subdue the gullible.

✦ ✦ ✦

So is there any room in Spinoza's system for freedom? What could be free in a universe where everything is determined?

The answer is, perhaps, surprising: freedom is the greatest of all ethical goals for Spinoza.

Here too his thinking is remarkable. Freedom no longer lies in the power to stand back and choose without external influence, but rather in the opposite: to affirm the necessity of how things are. To be free is to understand and accept the causes that have made us the individuals we are, and that have made the world we inhabit what it is. Freedom is to affirm our life – and its fatedness – through the most active possible understanding of it.

A key object of this understanding is our emotions. Reflection liberates. By understanding and accepting our feelings, and the experiences that have shaped them, our beliefs can evolve – or else be abandoned. Since all events are interconnected, the ideal end point of this attempt at self-understanding would be to comprehend, by an effort of pure thought, nature as a whole – which means to understand God, the cause of all things.[4] 'The more we understand particular things the more we understand God.'[5]

Which brings us back to love. For to understand nature taken as a whole is the highest form of love: *amor intellectualis Dei* – the intellectual love of God.

To our contemporary ear the word 'intellectual' sounds too dry to do justice to what Spinoza intends here. He still has one foot in the medieval world of Thomas Aquinas where intellect and reason are seen as the essence of God and as the means by which human beings might seek to reach him – in other words, might seek salvation. This tradition goes back to Plato, for whom the divine can be glimpsed only through directing passionate Eros upwards towards eternal goodness and beauty, and to Aristotle, for whom *nous*, or pure thought, is the divine element in man, in the use of which he imitates God. For Spinoza understanding therefore lies at the heart of love. And love itself can have no nobler goal than joyful comprehension – and so affirmation – of nature as a whole.

✦ ✦ ✦

All this has fascinating implications for love, many of which Spinoza didn't tease out. Perhaps the most remarkable implication is also the simplest: genuinely to love someone is to love her as an entirely natural being. It is in no way to love her for spiritual qualities that are somehow distinct from her physical nature, let alone for the sake of a divine being that transcends the natural order. Nor is it to repudiate the wicked world for the obstacles it creates to loving her and to her loving you back; or to imagine that love can be more perfectly fulfilled in some supernatural realm, free of such obstacles. For no such realm exists.

Next – and more controversially: we are to strive to affirm what we find evil in our loved ones as well as what we find good. In other words: to affirm them not merely in spite of their evil, but *including* it.

Such affirmation can't be achieved by passion alone, which will never love anything that it experiences as bad, meaning anything that we experience as disempowering – for *this*, according to Spinoza, is what we really think of as evil. But insofar as we are capable of that larger understanding which strives to affirm the necessity of nature taken as a whole, and insofar as we grasp that our loved ones are inextricably part of this nature, we will be able to affirm the evil we see in them as well as the good. Against the whole of official Christianity, and the Platonic and Aristotelian traditions that nourish it, Spinoza's philosophy suggests that intellectual love necessarily fastens not only on the good it perceives but also on what seems bad, perverse, destructive.

And Spinoza's philosophy suggests a further radical conclusion for love: if the old distinction between mind and body is collapsed, physical love between individuals is no longer merely a way station to their 'spiritual' love. Instead, your physical relationship with someone else is one aspect under which your entire relationship with her can be viewed. Physical intimacy is intimacy with the whole person.

And the other way around. A spiritual or mental relationship to another person is also a bodily relationship. Which, in turn, cannot be reduced to sex and the communication afforded by sexual love. One thing we regularly underestimate, even in an era when we think of ourselves as uninhibited about the body, is the power of the physical in our relations to others – colleagues, friends, parents, strangers – even, or precisely, when there is no overt sexual agenda. We tend to notice the physical only when besieged by extreme feelings either about their bodies: disgust or admiration, repulsion or desire; or about ours: shame or pride, awkwardness or superiority. At such moments, these feelings threaten to overwhelm us and to colour how we see and value everything else about them.

But these extreme cases illustrate a more general rule, which Spinoza inspires us to think about though he doesn't actually state it. It is artificial to subdivide our relationships, whether romantic or not, into 'dimensions' like the physical and the mental. It is also wrong to imagine that the physical only intrudes strongly in human relationships when it is sexual or evokes powerful emotions. The bodily is *always* present in our relations with others; indeed it is an aspect under which a person's entire existence can be viewed. And our relationship to their body involves a communication and a language that go far beyond the sexual.

✦ ✦ ✦

As it happens Spinoza is hostile to sexual desire. His worry is that, whether satisfied or not, it can dangerously unbalance our life. Like the urge for riches or fame, it can consume our attention at the expense of our larger well-being. It provides intense but fleeting delight, which easily leaves a residue of melancholy and even madness. Its obsessiveness shrinks our concerns to one narrow aim and prevents us from multiplying our interests and loves and understanding, which is where real happiness is to be found.

Spinoza's problem with sex isn't therefore rooted in hostility to the body, let alone to pleasure as such. On the contrary, in a rounded, well-balanced life, there cannot be too much joy: 'it is always good' and 'melancholy [or pain] is always bad'.[6] He advocates cheerfulness and self-esteem (so long as the latter is grounded in a rational idea of one's power), and despises ascetic feelings, such as guilt, self-denial or remorse, as products of the superstition that pleasure, in itself, will somehow damage us. It is even a sign of *wisdom* to be able to find pleasure in things. But we shouldn't become so absorbed in a few satisfactions, like sex, that we unhinge our lives and lose the rich enjoyment to be found in many and diverse delights.

Which brings us to Spinoza's remedy for love, especially when it gets obsessive. Ordinary love, Spinoza says, is 'pleasure accompanied by the idea of an external cause'. In other words you associate pleasure with just *her* presence (pleasure that will arise, in particular, if you experience her as empowering). In which case you will wish to possess and be close to her. But if she abandons you or otherwise causes you pain (again, especially if you experience her as disempowering), love will quickly turn to hate, which is nothing but 'pain accompanied by the idea of an external cause'.[7] In which case you will wish to destroy her. It is almost as simple as that.

Ordinary love is inherently fragile because we can never rule out the possibility of loss, rivals, and therefore pain. She might abandon us or another might come to love her too. And so love is menaced, always and often invisibly, by the spectre of hate, jealousy and a desire to destroy – reason enough, one might add, for anyone overtly sensitive to these dangers to avoid it altogether.

The only way to liberate yourself from love's intrinsic instability and ambivalence – and the dreadful feeling of helplessness that they foster – is to understand that your loved one's actions are not free but a product of causes that stretch back in time further than you can see. You must abandon the belief that she is solely responsible for your pleasure and pain. She isn't. Thinking of her as free in this way causes so much suffering and illusion in our relationships. We know from common experience that if we think she 'freely chose' to harm us we will resent her more than if we think she didn't know or couldn't help what she was doing.

And so we must learn to see and affirm the necessity that governs her life. For this is freedom, in love as in everything else: to embrace necessity – not to deny it.

✦ ✦ ✦

The key object of such therapy is, however, not your loved one, but yourself. Only understanding your own history – the events that led up to you being just the person you now are – will liberate you from what Spinoza calls 'passive' love. This is the worst sort of love, in which your reactions to someone are driven by confused associations of ideas and emotions, ingrained by your past experience.

Your loved one merely triggers these confused associations, though you are convinced that she is the original cause of your pleasure and pain. For example, she might have become linked in your mind with someone else whom you once loved, either by resembling this other person (in which case you will love her) or by being quite different (in which case you will hate her) or both (in which case you will love and hate her at once). As we have seen since Aristophanes' myth of the two halves finding each other, love has a strongly conservative streak: it not only wishes to possess someone who is similar to you, but it tends to love the same sort of qualities it has always loved and hate the same sort of qualities it has always hated.

On top of this repetitive nature of love and hate, Spinoza tells us, they also have an unnerving tendency to follow the herd. So if we feel stirrings of love for someone and see that we are not alone in this our feelings will immediately be reinforced. But if we notice that others hate him we might begin to waver. Worse, we might come to love or hate someone to whom we were up to now indifferent merely because we imagine other people do so:

> From the very fact that we imagine any one to love anything, we shall also love it ourselves . . . Again, from the fact that we imagine any one to turn away from anything, we also shall turn away from it[.][8]

As Spinoza shrewdly notes, this tendency to imitate arises not merely from a sheepish desire to follow fashion, but also from the tyranny of others, who demand that we ape their likes and dislikes: 'every one endeavours as much as he can to cause every one to love what he himself loves, and to hate what he himself hates'.[9]

The herd instinct – the terror of feeling differently to others and the demand that others feel the same as one does oneself – moves stock markets, leads to gold rushes, and fuels mass hysteria in everything from the idolisation of the pop stars to ethnic cleansing. The fact that people who have never caused us either pleasure or pain can suddenly appear to do so accounts for the remarkable consensus at any one time of what is considered attractive or loveable or deserving of compassion. And, more ominously, it also underlies the horrors of race hatred in which whole groups which had formerly been considered neigh-bours can overnight become objects of murderous intent. Nothing is harder than resisting the urge to conform to the preferences of others or to demand that they conform to yours. As Ovid, quoted by Spinoza, says: 'of iron is he who loves what the other leaves'.[10]

✦ ✦ ✦

The task then is to convert passive love – with its susceptibility to hatred, resent-ment, blame, jealousy and other emotions of pain – into 'active' love, where the lovers experience the necessity that drives each other's lives and so take charge of their own chaotic emotions:

> In so far as the mind understands all things as necessary it has more power over the emotions, or, is less passive in regard to them.[11]

Instead of merely reacting to external triggers with confused associations of ideas, we shall have knowledge, and so power, over our emotions:

> the more an emotion becomes known to us, the more it is within our power and the less the mind is passive in regard to it.[12]

Two lovers who can achieve such understanding – of themselves and of each other – will have achieved real freedom.

If you take this understanding far enough it will lead beyond our narrow concerns to all the causes that have made us who we are, and beyond that to the whole order of nature in which these more distant causes are embedded. But this, as we saw before, is to love God. And so, says Spinoza: 'He who understands himself and his emotions clearly and distinctly loves God, and the more so the more he understands himself and his emotions.'[13] Genuine love therefore seeks to apprehend the loved one in relation to God – now understood as nature as a whole. And so, instead of aggrandising our loved one as godlike, love does the opposite: it affirms her infinitesimal but unique place in the vast, impersonal order of nature.

Spinoza's conception of human beings as embedded in the infinite order of nature, and of God as merely a name for that order, was regarded as so shocking that he was not only excommunicated by the Jewish community of Amsterdam but also widely shunned, as an agent of the devil and a saboteur of good order, by Christians and civic authorities. Though he fell into relative obscurity for a century after his death – regarded even by many of his sympathisers as a dangerous figure to be associated with – he became a crucial inspiration for the two great movements that were to shape the modern world, and that are often, but not entirely accurately, seen as warring sensibilities. On the one hand he catalysed seminal ideas of the Enlightenment: equality, democracy, tolerance, liberty of conscience, and universal rights, and was the hero of figures such as Lessing. On the other hand, he was claimed as a champion by the camp of those, like the late eighteenth-century German poet Novalis, who saw in Spinoza's thought their own sense of nature as a mystical whole, infused by an immanent metaphysical reality which manifests itself in everything. This is the large and diverse camp of Romantics to whose sensibility love was to become central, urgent and redemptive.[14] And it is to the first great standard bearer of this camp, Jean-Jacques Rousseau, that we now turn.

11

Love as Enlightened Romanticism
Rousseau

In concluding his final book, *The Reveries of the Solitary Walker*, the Swiss philosopher Jean-Jacques Rousseau (1712–1778) remembers his love as a young man for an older (married) woman, Mme de Warens, whom he called 'Mama':

> I recall with joy and tenderness this unique and brief time of my life when I was myself, fully, without admixture and without obstacle, and when I can genuinely say that I lived. . . . Without this short but precious time I would perhaps have remained uncertain about myself . . . I would have difficulty unraveling what there is of my own in my own conduct.[1]

These words foreshadow that elusive, thrilling and still pervasive sensibility that we call 'Romanticism' – a sensibility so complex and diverse that it is easy to doubt that any one such thing exists.

But it does exist. Two motifs define it and underlie all its expressions in the realm of love. We have just glimpsed the first of them: the discovery of what comes to be called personal 'authenticity' through love; the quest to become yourself in dedicating yourself to a loved one and in being loved. This is a self whose commitments are self-legislated: they speak of your inner nature and its integrity, whether that nature is conceived as unique to you, or as a great current of life to which you give voice, or as a Providential order of nature. And in speaking of your inner nature, or of your willed alignment to a larger order of nature, they express your freedom.

The other new motif is the nobility of passion itself – and, for some Romantics, of sexual desire. Passion is a – maybe the – great source of goodness and truth, far superior to reason. And no passion is greater than love between two human beings; here, in their enacted love, we might glimpse the sacred.

Both motifs often speak in a tone of exalted, even ecstatic, melancholy; a tone epitomised by the words of Rousseau that we have just heard.

Both, too, are related to the decline in the authority of religion and traditional social hierarchies. For they depend on the gathering conviction – overwhelming by the end of the eighteenth century – that humans are not assigned a position in an inherited hierarchy, whether a divine hierarchy defined by God at its apex or a social hierarchy with an absolute monarch at its head. Instead we have the right, even the duty, to be self-determining. Which means to create, or at least assent to, who we are. The greatest good, in other words, is legislated not in a heavenly sphere but deep within us as individuals, or in an organic relationship between each of us and our community.

Thus a new preoccupation is born: with personal identity. My identity comprises my own values, commitments and desires. For some thinkers this includes sexual desire and its powers of expression. And identity is governed by laws that I autonomously endorse. It isn't purely a gift of God. Nor is it determined by my social role – carpenter, aristocrat, singer. To be genuinely related to the world beyond my self is also to be genuinely related to that self.

These seemingly diverse themes are all related. To live in accordance with our own nature; to discover our inner voice; to conceive of ourselves as having an individual identity rather than an inherited role; to be self-determining; to regard passion as noble, even sacred – these belong to a family of concepts that cannot be understood except in relation to the decline in the authority of religion.

The tone of ecstatic melancholy that marks so much Romanticism is, I suggest, grounded in this dual sense of loss and gain. On the one hand, mourning and terror are natural reactions to the irretrievable loss of a divine world order and the firm moorings it afforded – or that many supposed it had afforded. On the other hand, the construction by human beings of a new order, founded on their own autonomy and its vast creative possibilities, evokes the rapture of a new dawn. And both – the destruction and the creation – speak of human freedom, indeed exaltation.

And so, just as love was conceived from early Judaism as our highest duty to God, so the ground is now laid for love to be conceived as our highest duty to ourselves. To love is to discover and obey one's own law – or, for some Romantics, the law of nature as it speaks through one. It is to express an inner voice.

Though the love of which Romanticism speaks is often, even usually, romantic –
that is, sexual love between two people directed at their spiritual union – its
sensibility can pervade love of almost any sort: for friends, nature, art, family,
nation, and any other object of passionate dedication. The point is that in the
mystery of such dedication I become alive to who I am. And by being loved in turn,
a man 'has new reasons to be himself'.[2]

✦ ✦ ✦

But isn't this, one might ask, an extraordinarily selfish attitude to love? Even a
betrayal of love's essence, which is to attend and submit to the other?

It is true that some Romantics seem in love with their exalted feelings. As if,
for them, the loved one is merely an emotional echo chamber in which the lover
gets to hear his own authentic voice. Rousseau can sound like this:

> during those few years, loved by a woman full of desire to please and of gentle-
> ness, I did what I wanted to do, I was what I wanted to be; and through the use
> I made of my leisure, aided by her lessons and example, I was able to give to
> my still simple and new soul the form which better suited it and which it has
> always kept.[3]

But for Rousseau there is a more serious, even moral, purpose to self-discovery
through the good fortune of loving and being loved. And that is to foster the inner
purity of feeling and motivation that belongs to human nature 'without admix-
ture and without obstacle'. This purity, like the rustic setting of his last Reverie, is
naïve and unsophisticated. In cultivating it you uncover and listen to your inner
voice, and so are in a position to listen more sensitively to the voice of a loved one
(or indeed of nature as a whole).

Human beings are, Rousseau thinks, naturally good. Before, that is, they have
become slaves to the rivalries, hatreds, and artificial needs that living in organised
societies stimulates. In the original 'state of nature' they were

> more untamed than evil, and more attentive to protecting themselves from
> harm they could receive than tempted to harm others . . . Since they had no
> kind of commerce among themselves; since they consequently knew neither
> vanity, nor consideration, nor esteem, nor contempt; . . . since they regarded
> the violences they might suffer as harm easy to redress and not as an insult

which must be punished, and since they did not even dream of vengeance, except perhaps mechanically and on the spot, like the dog that bites the stone thrown at him, their disputes would rarely have had bloody consequences . . .[4]

Conflict between these natural human beings is quickly resolved, leaving no residue of bitterness. The innate sentiment of pity (*pitié*) repels them from the sight of others' suffering and prevents them from inflicting it, except with good reason. Such pity, Rousseau says, 'precedes . . . the use of all reflection; and [is] so Natural that even Beasts sometimes give perceptible signs of it.'[5]

Such lack of resentment and aggression is possible only when people are free from emotional or economic subjection to others. Free from dependence on masters and slaves. Free, most importantly, from craving admiration. For that craving easily drives us to subjugate and humiliate our fellows:

> everyone must see that, since the bonds of servitude are formed only from the mutual dependence of men and the reciprocal needs that unite them, it is impossible to enslave a man without first putting him in the position of being unable to do without another; a situation which, as it did not exist in the state of Nature, leaves each man there free of the yoke, and renders vain the Law of the stronger.[6]

Rousseau identifies a natural self-respect, which he calls *amour de soi*, sometimes translated as 'love of oneself'. *Amour de soi* is also the inborn drive of all living creatures to persist as the kind of creature they are; it is the drive for self-preservation that is 'The source of our passions, the origin and the principle of all the others'.[7] Even if this drive leads individuals to conflict with one another, it is not malicious, nor does it seek to negate or diminish others. It is, he considers, 'always good'.[8]

By contrast, in society we all too easily live only to secure the recognition of others – to the point where we can't achieve a sense of our own worth without external affirmation, and so become alienated from our natural selves. Status is everything and to pursue it we must seek superiority over our fellows. As a result, human relations become provisional, uncertain, suspicious. Calculation, deception and concealment are their currency. The natural disposition to *pitié* is overwhelmed.

Status is addictive. The hunger for power, position, honours, luxuries and everything that is valued chiefly because others don't have it – what, today, are sometimes called 'positional goods' – is insatiable. (Driving a Ferrari would be a lot less satisfying if most people had one.) The dejection of feeling left out of the rat race is too debilitating to allow any let-up and even trivial gains or losses of prestige seem absurdly significant. The logical end point is the desire for total domination – the impossible aim of commanding unlimited obeisance from everyone at all times. Social man, Rousseau declares, will 'end by ruining every-thing [*tout égorger*] until he is sole Master of the Universe'.[9] (In which case, it wouldn't be a paradox that an advanced civilisation, with its complex networks of status-dependence, should be capable of genocide.)

Rousseau's name for this desire for others' admiration – and inferiority – is '*amour propre*', often translated into English as 'pride'. He contrasts the social ills it foments when out of control with the *amour de soi* that flourishes in the 'savage' condition:

> *Amour-propre* and love of oneself [*amour de soi*], two passions very different in their Nature and their effects, must not be confused. Love of onself is a natural sentiment which inclines every animal to watch over its own preservation, and which, directed in man by reason and modified by pity, produces humanity and virtue. Amour-propre is only a relative sentiment, artificial and born in Society, which inclines each individual to have a greater esteem for himself than for anyone else, inspires in men all the harm they do to one another, and is the true source of honour.[10]

There are two things that Rousseau is emphatically not saying here. He is not advising us to 'return' to a primitive state and abolish all society. Nor is he saying that *amour propre* is always bad or that it cannot fruitfully coexist with *amour de soi*. Instead he wants us to build a society on the basis of a rediscovery of our natural goodness and its uncorrupted will. And to respect ourselves without excessive dependence on others' good opinion. Appropriate desire for recognition isn't bad; indeed, it unleashes our ambitions and talents and fosters many of humanity's great achievements:

> to this ardour to be talked about, to this furore to distinguish oneself, which nearly always keeps us outside of ourselves, we owe what is best and worst among men, our virtues and our vices, our Sciences and our errors, our Conquerors and our Philosophers . . .[11]

✦ ✦ ✦

The implications for love of all this, though Rousseau doesn't spell them all out, are fascinating and dramatic. For love involves intense dependence. Love relationships, from couples up to large families, are microcosms of *amour propre*, closed societies in which people become crucial, and even irreplaceable, sources of recognition for each other.

If so, then nowhere are we likely to see the horrors of *amour propre* more brutally, if covertly, enacted. Love will be constantly threatened by hatred, fear, cruelty, resentment, servitude, and envy – open or concealed. The threat is constant because recognition and possession – the latter seen, since Plato, as a key aim of love – are always partial and reversible.

And in conflict: if we possess someone too securely will their recognition of us be free and therefore genuine? But if our influence over their recognition of us is too weak, won't our vulnerability be unbearable? The danger is that our mania to possess the recognition of loved ones will lead us to annihilate them. (Which, as Rousseau suggests in discussing *amour propre*, is the gruesome self-contradiction at the heart of all lust for status: that it seeks to destroy the freedom and even the lives of the very people upon whom its fulfilment depends.)

This is why a committed bond like marriage can so easily destroy freedom. Not because it demands monogamy or compromise, but because through it we are able to institutionalise the perilous expectation that one person will underwrite our needs to possess and to be recognised.

These needs have elusive aims. What is it to possess someone? How do we know when they are ours? Do they really recognise us? If so, what do they recognise, and who are we to them? There are few clear answers here; and even fewer ways of knowing what is happening in the inscrutable soul that is the other person.

Freedom in love, Rousseau's theory of *amour propre* suggests, is possible only where we can moderate these urges. Otherwise, in fostering *amour propre's* worst vices, love will make us helpless, bitter, alienated from ourselves, and so all too eager to inflict hurt precisely on our loved one. In a word: ungenuine.

✦ ✦ ✦

Now Rousseau hints at an extraordinary thought: the hurt that we ourselves inflict is the hurt for which we feel no pity. People who weep at suffering they haven't caused will be stone hard in the face of harm that they have intended:

daily in our theatres one sees, moved and crying for the troubles of an unfor-
tunate person, a man who, if he were in the Tyrant's place [in the play], would
aggravate his enemy's torments even more[.][12]

In a later revision of the *Discourse* he adds that they are

like bloodthirsty Sulla, so sensitive to ills he had not caused, or like Alexander
of Pherae, who did not dare attend the performance of any tragedy, lest he be
seen moaning with Andromache and Priam, whereas he listened without
emotion to the cries of so many citizens murdered daily on his orders.[13]

Rousseau's main concern here might be to express his contempt for the theatre
and the false emotions that he believes it cultivates.[14] But his words point, even if
entirely unintentionally, to a reality that has been amply confirmed: the cruellest
human beings – tyrants who send millions to their deaths – are also prone (especially prone?) to weep over an injured child or animal. Indeed, as Rousseau reminds
us, pity is so natural a disposition that even the greatest moral depravity can't
entirely destroy it.[15] (We might speculate further: depravity is not only unable to
destroy pity, but able to strengthen it in a perverted form. Because pity, to the
delight of the depraved person, stamps the pitied one with absolute inferiority.
Under, of course, the guise of kindness.)

If we indeed feel the least pity for the suffering that we ourselves inflict, then,
again, the love relationship will be especially vulnerable. The suffering that
lovers so easily cause one another as a result of their intense mutual dependence
will, according to this logic, be suffering for which they have no pity. Or at least
less pity than they will show for the suffering that they cause others, outside their
relationship.

✦ ✦ ✦

For Rousseau the aspect of love that gives rise to much of its ardour and cruelty
is not raw sexual desire – the 'general desire which inclines one sex to unite with
the other', which he calls 'the physical'. Rather it is 'the moral':

that which determines this [physical] desire and fixes it exclusively on a single
object, or which at least gives it a greater degree of energy . . . This feeling,
founded on certain notions of merit and beauty that a Savage is not capable of

having, and on comparisons he is not capable of making, must be almost null for him . . . any woman is good for him.[16]

The 'moral' clearly isn't the same as morality: those general ends or rules or principles that tell us what we ought and ought not to do. Rather it concerns the qualities of beauty and goodness that we think are most worthy of desire. By interpreting a visceral desire for copulation and intimacy as a soaring ambition for beauty and goodness, the 'moral' intensifies sexual desire, focuses it on one particular person in whom we see those qualities embodied, and so gives love its rich meaning.

And yet by having such specific ideas about what is and isn't attractive the moral makes sexual desire itself much more difficult to satisfy. For a merely physical urge, Rousseau says, 'any woman is good'; but for the moral, only some – or one, or perhaps none – will be acceptable.

Though the qualities we seek, and claim to find, in those we love feel intensely personal, they are often, Rousseau rightly observes, merely conventional: we largely inherit these preferences from the society in which we live. (La Rochefoucauld, the seventeenth-century French moralist, makes the point more generally when he says that 'Some people would never have fallen in love if they had never heard of love'.[17]) Most of our 'needs' are not natural at all but implanted in us by habit and custom:

With the sole exception of the Physically necessary, which Nature itself demands, all our other needs are such only by habit, having previously not been needs, or by our desires; and one does not desire that which he is not capable of knowing.[18]

And yet Rousseau, ever the complex thinker, does not favour the physical over the moral. Here, too, he is not advocating a return to some original state of nature where people roam as lone savages, quickly satisfying their sexual urges without seeking anything else in each other. He despises any vilification of sexual longing, but he in no way thinks that we will find fulfilment in mere sexual licence.

Rather, in line with the long Platonic tradition, he urges us to direct our sexual energy to spiritual satisfaction – to a drive for ethical perfection which harnesses rather than excludes passion. The twist, though, is that, unlike the

Platonic tradition, he believes that spiritual perfection will *intensify* physical satisfaction. Sexual desire and pleasure are healthy; to repress them, he effectively says, is a crime against our God-given nature. The challenge is for sex to find a new innocence and a new intensity – nothing to do with facile 'liberation' or promiscuity. In his picture of fulfilled love – which has become part of our contemporary picture – sexual intercourse and its culmination in orgasm have special delight and value because achieved with the one person in whom we see embodied the true, the beautiful and the good.

In other words, to seek a spiritual union with our lover is not only to turn physical desire for her into love. It is also to intensify that physical desire. Indeed, by doing so love is the best guarantor of monogamy that we have – far better than all the world's prohibitions against infidelity.[19]

+ + +

'Romanticism' is often thought of as celebrating the impulsive and intuitive – as admiring the person who emotes spontaneously; who falls in love on the spur of the moment; who blinks their way into life's great decisions.

But, according to Rousseau, impulsiveness is just what we should avoid if we are to discover love's higher possibilities. In his novel, *Julie, ou La Nouvelle Héloïse* (1761), a huge popular hit in his lifetime, the heroine, Julie, resists the ardent advances of her former tutor Saint-Preux and her gathering attraction to him; for the match has been forbidden by her father on account of Saint-Preux's inferior social standing. Though she does succumb to Saint-Preux on discovering that her father has betrothed her to the Baron de Wolmar, their intensely erotic affair is not to last. She weds Wolmar, the voice of reason and order, out of deeply felt duty to the contracts and institutions – above all, marriage – that foster the most genuine human relationship and that provide the conditions for the flourishing of individuals' natural goodness. (And she does so out of guilt too: for her mother, Julie is sure, died from the shock of her illicit love for Saint-Preux.) At the same time, she cannot help seeing herself as spiritually bound to Saint-Preux, and confesses shortly before her own death that she has always loved him.

Passionate erotic love between two individuals, the novel seems to be saying, cannot be complete and satisfactory. The voluptuous charge between Julie and Saint-Preux is not without virtue and nobility, but more virtuous still is her painful renunciation of that passion for the sake of dedication to children, husband and the higher moral and spiritual order. This is the order of nature created by God, and she prays that she will be dutiful to it:

> I will everything that belongs to the order of nature thou hast established, and to the rules of reason thou gavest me ... Make all my acts conform to my constant will which is thine, and no longer allow the error of a moment to prevail over the choice of my entire life.[20]

It is evident here how Romanticism can also speak in the idiom of Enlightenment: how sentiment is to conform to the rule of reason; how love, convulsively erotic at the source, is fulfilled not in febrile spontaneity but in a quest for spiritual perfection that requires the individual to be closely aligned to the deep order of nature. As Rousseau says in *Emile*, goodness and justice 'are true affections of the soul enlightened by reason' – the 'ordered development of our primitive affections'.[21]

But, he maintains throughout his writing, if we are to be true to nature, and if we are to cultivate the pure will needed to be so, improvisation isn't enough. Education is essential. In love, as in anything else, we need to discover and develop our powers. As we might put it today, perfunctory lessons in 'the facts of life' and the dangers of unsafe sex or adult predators are nowhere near adequate.

Sex education, says Rousseau, needs to have a much more ambitious agenda, covering both the physical and the moral aspects of love. Adolescents should be taught how to detect qualities and people worth loving; how to minimise conflict between desire and duty; how to achieve a permanent relationship and a stable family life; and how to moderate contradictory urges, such as for novelty and constancy, as well as destructive anxieties like jealousy and resentment.[22]

Nor should the training of physical desire be neglected. Masturbation, for example, is to be avoided at all costs. It encourages a life of isolation and depletes body and heart of vigour. Emile's educator is enjoined not to leave the young man the slightest opportunity to indulge in this 'dangerous supplement':

> Therefore watch the young man carefully. He can protect himself from everything else, but it is up to you to protect him from himself. Do not leave him alone, day or night. At the very least, sleep in his room. . . . It would be very dangerous if instinct taught your pupil to trick his senses and to find a substitute for the opportunity of satisfying them. Once he knows this dangerous

supplement, he is lost. From then on he will always have an enervated body and heart. He will suffer until his death the sad effects of this habit, the most fatal to which a man can be subject.[23]

It seems to be a case of 'Do as I say, not as I do', given that Rousseau admits in his *Confessions* to being addicted to this 'vice, which shame and timidity find so convenient'.[24] Though he complains that masturbation enervates him, he suggests that it can be valuable as a way of imagining partners more perfect than might be found in real life.[25] Practised to this end, he implies, masturbation will tactfully divert excessive expectations away from our lovers.[26] (Though, of course, it could end up making them all seem second-rate by comparison with the solitary pleasure.)

Interestingly, Rousseau insists that a lover's education centrally involves cultivating our capacity for pity – which, as we have seen, he regards as a natural sentiment. The adolescent's sexual awakening extends his feelings outwards, from preoccupation with his own preservation to imaginative identification with the sentiments and lives of others. With a good education he becomes intensely sensitive to the reality that bad luck can hit any of us – that we form a community of the vulnerable. But he also becomes aware that pity can destroy intimacy when, under the pressure of *amour propre*, the giver of it feels power over the recipient. When he uses it to manipulate or humiliate her. When he wants to keep her unhappy in order to confirm (to them both) his importance and merit. When her suffering makes him feel safe, and he is unable to relate to her unless she is enfeebled by pain. And conversely, when she, as the sufferer, exploits his pity to weaken and control him.

Again, the point of education is to alert us – to refine our sensibility – to the dangers inherent in even the noblest values and dispositions. We are to learn how pity can relieve the other's pain while modestly benefiting the giver's self-esteem. Then it can be both just and generous – and enable us to build that mutual trust in one another's care and respect which is central to all love.[27]

✦ ✦ ✦

The eyes of pity see through imaginative identification with the other. But the eyes of love see through imaginative idealisation of the other – and to that extent they create, even invent, the loved one:

And what is true love itself if it is not chimera, lie, and illusion? We love the image we make for ourselves far more than we love the object to which we apply it.[28]

In love everything is only illusion. I admit it. But what is real are the sentiments for the truly beautiful with which love animates us and which it makes us love. This beauty is not in the object one loves; it is the work of our errors. So, what of it?[29]

In other words, we create the ideal woman (or man) in our imagination and then, having found someone who 'feels right', in whom we recognise our ideal, we devote ourselves to her real needs and desires as if they were our own. On the one hand, then, love endows the other person with illusory qualities; it colonises her with the lover's expectations. On the other hand, love also inspires the pity which sees her needs for what they are and treats her with the dignity of a free individual.

Again, imagination is to be educated and refined over a long period; it isn't merely about whims or flights of fancy. With the aid of a cultivated imagination our conception of the beloved becomes genuinely ours rather than merely a product of social convention. It becomes a law that we give ourselves and that we can obey. It speaks of who we are as individuals.

Love might therefore start in genital arousal. But its education opens our imagination to those qualities whose attractiveness can endure; helps us to see perfection in the beloved without, in the process, subordinating her to our fantasies; encourages us to care for her without the care itself becoming a weapon in a destructive struggle for power; and, through striving beyond physical satisfaction for spiritual intimacy, intensifies our enjoyment of those sexual desires with which love began.

No one is more aware than Rousseau of the struggle between the good and the corrupt in love, and especially of how easily love can be hijacked by pride and vanity. He wants love to explore our innermost impulses, and also to uphold a wider natural order binding human beings, to which he sees the marriage bond as central. He wants us to listen to the dictates of our individual conscience, which flourishes in independence, yet also to harness it in the creation of a wholesome social life. He is key to our contemporary obsession with sincerity and passion – with expressing our feelings truthfully and intensely; and with seeing such expression as a moral achievement. Yet he would be appalled if passion and sincerity became so prized that they were, as sometimes happens today, faked; or if they were taken to be merely about spontaneous expression – about letting everything 'hang out'. For Rousseau, nothing is harder than for civilised man to be natural; nothing harder than for us to know and express ourselves genuinely.

✦ ✦ ✦

Late eighteenth-century Romanticism – and Rousseau in particular – is the culmination of the third great transformation in Western love to which I referred in chapter 1. This transformation begins in the eleventh century and allows a single human being, or indeed nature in general, to be seen as embodying the greatest good and to be worthy of the sort of love that was formerly reserved for God.

The first transformation, we recall, was about the value of love. Between Deuteronomy and Augustine – so until the middle of the fifth century CE – love was made the supreme virtue.

In the second transformation, spanning the fourth to the sixteenth centuries CE, from Augustine through Bernard of Clairvaux to Thomas Aquinas, and beyond him to Luther, human beings had been given unprecedented – literally divine – power to love through God's grace. But one's fellow human beings were, of course, still to be loved for the sake of God.

In completing the third transformation – about the object of love, now allowing a human being to be loved as a good in themselves – the ground is prepared for a fourth, which is the real child of Romanticism, and of which Rousseau is the guiding spirit.

This transformation, in which we still live, concerns the lover, who becomes authentic through love. In love he becomes not selfless but a self. He doesn't lose himself but finds himself. Even when he strives to transcend nature he seeks to be guided by, and in a sense to actualise, his own nature. The true and the good lie not beyond feeling, but in an exploration of feeling.

Indeed the lover becomes the focus of love to such an extent that, as we will see, the loved one is in danger of dropping out of the picture. At the limit, love falls in love with itself – and so, as the ultimate good, comes to hold the position once occupied by God.

12

Love as religion
Schlegel and Novalis

By the turn of the nineteenth century the Western spirit is beset by upheavals in its world view of perhaps unprecedented speed and cumulative scope. Within a mere three hundred years, from 1500 to 1800, people begin conceiving the earth as going round the sun rather than as the centre of the universe; human beings as self-determining rather than as bound by fixed social roles and the religious diktat of a single church; and politics as the pursuit of liberty, equality, and other individual rights, rather than as the government of absolute monarchy. In addition the basis is laid for thinking that life evolved rather than was created, and that we are alone in an impersonal universe.

All this turmoil serves to make love ever more important as a source and guarantor of precisely what such developments seem to undermine: man's significance in the universe; his sense of security and safety; his need for the sacred – that is for a repository of indestructible value and meaning; his hopes for eternity; his unquenchable thirst for redemption from loss, suffering, and ultimately death. These were of course precisely the things of which God alone had been the ultimate underwriter and that, in all these storms, love was increasingly called upon to vouchsafe.

This is most obvious in those successors of Rousseau who openly develop romantic love as a religion – plus or minus the Christian God. Most are German. Hardly by coincidence: for in the modern world no people has been remotely as concerned to rediscover the sacred in the ordinary. No people has had such a will (and ability) to foster an earthy spirituality with eyes to see and ears to hear and a mind to formulate the presence of the absolute in everyday things and events. No people has suffered more painfully from the death of God or striven more ardently to re-enchant the world without his direct help. The mood of this spirituality is at once enthusiastic and melancholic, ecstatically engaged and morosely detached.

Like so much longing for the absolute, this spirituality is shot through with nostalgia for a lost wholesomeness. Nonetheless, its deepest yearning is for the renewal of man through the emancipation, intoxication and sanctification of desire, especially erotic desire. It venerates the past – in order to love the future.

Friedrich Schlegel (1772–1829) sees love – for other people, for nature, for the ground of all being – as a great unifying and redeeming force. Though love isn't a master concept that organises his whole world view, in the sense that it is, say, for Empedocles, nonetheless he sees only it as able to transcend the tradition-ally rigid distinctions that separate off reason from feeling, male from female, humanity from nature, sensual from spiritual, body from mind, classical from progressive, and, as we will see, life from death. It doesn't abolish these distinct realms or strive for some vague holistic paradise, but allows them to inspire and enrich each other.

The place where this really happens is in erotic relationships between men and women. Though Schlegel, like other German Romantics, draws on an illus-trious tradition of Christian mysticism reaching back at least to Meister Eckhart, he gives an unprecedented role to sex, not merely as a means of creating a family and affirming marriage, but, above all, as sanctifying and purifying in its own right. 'In the solitary embrace of lovers,' Schlegel says, 'sensual pleasure becomes once more what it basically is – the holiest miracle of nature'.[1]

The sensual and the spiritual can reach their highest pitch only through one another. As one lover says to the other in Schlegel's novel *Lucinde* (a thinly disguised account of his affair with a married woman, Dorothea, daughter of the Enlightenment philosopher Moses Mendelssohn):

> The farthest reaches of unbridled lust and silent intimation exist simultane-ously in me. . . . You're at my side at every stage of human experience, from the most passionate sensuality to the most spiritual spirituality[.][2]

Sexual love, with its unifying power, paradoxically enables us to overcome our differentiation into male and female and to rediscover an androgynous condition – that original state in which humanity had not yet been split into man and woman. Where sex had once been associated with banishment from the Garden of Eden or, in Aristophanes' myth, had been brought into being by Zeus's revenge upon the original human beings, now it is the medium for the return to paradise, and for undoing the split between man and woman.

For two lovers to become more like each other and so to overcome the limitations of gender is, Schlegel suggests, to enlarge the possibilities of their individuality; it is to be more fully human:

> only gentle masculinity, only independent femininity is proper, true, and beautiful. If it is so, one must by no means further exaggerate the characteristics of gender, which is nothing more than an innate and natural profession, but rather seek to temper it through strong counterbalances so that individuality may find a potentially unlimited space and freely move about the entire realm of human existence[.][3]

This obscure language is code for sexual role playing. A man should experiment with taking on characteristics of a woman – and vice versa – if the barriers between lovers are to be broken down:

> when we exchange roles and in childish high spirits compete to see who can mimic the other more convincingly, whether you are better at imitating the protective intensity of the man, or I the appealing devotion of the woman. But are you aware that this sweet game still has quite other attractions for me than its own . . . I see here a wonderful, deeply meaningful allegory of the development of man and woman to full and complete humanity.[4]

Experimenting, Schlegel says, should be part of our love life from its beginning. We can't expect to find the partner best suited to us if we haven't tried out different sorts of relationships. This is particularly the case for men, whose egoism casts them so strongly in their male identity that they find it hard to come to share in female characteristics. Most marriages occur before such maturation has taken place. Consequently 'Almost all marriages are simply concubinages, liaisons, or rather provisional experiments and distant approximations of a true marriage'.[5]

When we finally find the 'right one', our relationship with him or her will be enriched not only by the maturity we have gained from this experimentation, but also by integrating our past loves into our present one. Far from repudiating these old loves as 'behind us' and no longer relevant, or merely as learning experiences that have taught us what we want and what to avoid, Schlegel wisely suggests that they become part of the fabric of our being. They make each of us 'complete and harmonious'[6] as individuals, and so as lovers.

Indeed, marriages might benefit by being open to other partners. Given that the essence of marriage 'consists of the fusion of a number of persons into one person' it is 'hard to imagine what basic objection there could be to a marriage à quatre'; any marriage 'might be helped by means of new and possibly more successful experiments'.[7] To love well, he implies, is to integrate as many different loves as possible into a single relationship – just as to experience anything most intensely is to experience it in as many ways and from as many angles as possible.

All this experimenting sounds saucy, but the guiding idea is that love – like God – is one; and so genuine love aims at the maximum unity with the world around us. Rather than shielding us from the world, love opens us to it. Rather than causing us to forget the world and our past, love is how we incorporate them. As one of the lovers in *Lucinde* proclaims: 'the sanctity of marriage has given me citizenship in the state of nature'.[8] To be able to love one person with an exclusive love one must already be able to love the world beyond him:

> Do you truly love if you don't find the world in your lover? To be able to find it and situate it in him, one must already possess the world, love it, or at least have a disposition, a sense, a capacity for loving it . . . The more completely one can love or form an individual, the more harmony one finds in the world[.][9]

In a profound thought, Schlegel says of a great love relationship: 'Everything that we loved before [it], we love even more warmly now. *It's only now that a feeling for the world has really dawned on us.*'[10]

✦ ✦ ✦

The chaotic sentimentality of Schlegel's prose, slammed by Schiller as 'the pinnacle of modern un-form and un-nature' (*der Gipfel moderner Unform und Unnatur*),[11] need not detain us here. What matters is its perfect expression of the Romantic idea that erotic love's power to overcome division and draw us towards the infinite makes it life's great salvation. Through love 'human nature returns to its original state of divinity'[12] and propels us towards a union that is eternal and absolute:

> we, like love, are immortal . . . I can no longer say *my* love or *your* love: both are identical and perfectly united, as much love on one side as on the other. This is marriage, the timeless union and conjunction of our spirits, not simply for what we call this world or the world beyond death, but for the one, true, indivisible, nameless, unending world, for our whole eternal life and being.[13]

It is worth pausing to take stock. We have here many of the key elements of Western love that we have so far considered – now freed, by the declining authority of official Christianity, to recombine in new ways.

From Plato there is the idea of love as a desire for absolute and eternal reality; or, in a modern echo of Aristophanes' myth, for a primordial condition of purity and wholeness in which gender and incompleteness are overcome.

From Christianity, there is the idea of love as a path to the divine; of humans becoming gods through love; of a return to a state of paradise before the Fall. From Christian mysticism we recognise the idea of losing our limited and transient existence in an ecstatic merging with the Godhead.

From Renaissance Neoplatonism, there is the idea of God infusing nature with his own being, and so with love.

From Spinoza, there is the idea of love as striving for union with nature as a whole, considered as divine. To love is to affirm the participation of our individual life in Being as a whole.

From Rousseau, there is the idea of love as a means of becoming the individual I really am – of finding myself through losing myself in the other. And, in particular, there is the idea of sexual desire as the driving will behind love – a will that finds completion in the attainment of spiritual union between two people.

Schlegel follows all these traditions in his immense valuation of love. But the mystical Romanticism to which he gives such impetus will, in the hands of others, go on to draw the final – and to mainstream Judaism and Christianity, heretical – conclusion: human love *is* God. It is not only a *means* to God, or to the supreme Good, or to the source of all things, or to Being. Now it *is* all those things. Where once God was love, now love is God.[14] It is itself the supreme Good; the creative source of all things; absolute Being; immortal; true; nameless.

As Schlegel himself says, we are embarked here on a 'religion of love'.[15] Though, like many Romantic (and Enlightenment) thinkers he remains a Christian, he can claim both to believe in the supremacy of the traditional God and also to set human beings on a journey to their own divinity – a divinity to which love is as defining a characteristic as it is for the Christian God. This journey is a pilgrimage; and the lovers who undertake it are the priests of the new religion and responsible for its rites, including confession and consummation. Thus the ground is prepared for that peculiarly modern phenomenon where love comes to be in love with itself as well as with its object – examining, revering, and nurturing itself as much as the one it loves. Or even more.

This magnificent and at the same time questionable development will end up making anyone and anything in the world loveable. In this democracy of love the aristocrat may be united with his maid; the merchant's daughter might hope to find a prince; the animal kingdom can be loved as much as human beings; and the sufferings and emotions of all creatures are regarded as deserving of compassion. Gone are those rigid hierarchies of lovability, which reflected not just the social strata of worldly power but the larger 'order of being' of the cosmos, with God at its head. Gone, too, is the ancient emphasis – that we saw in Plato, Aristotle, Augustine, Thomas Aquinas and much of the Christian tradition – on the objective qualities of goodness or beauty that deserve to be loved: on qualities that are not merely in the eye of the beholder or created by the act of loving but are entirely independent of beholders and their lovings. Instead, other images are used to explain attraction, such as 'chemical bonds', 'elective affinities' and more generally the vocabulary of 'chemistry' that is still much in vogue today. And love, increasingly unshackled from any need to be objectively merited, is the overcoming of separateness between a self and other selves or things in the world; and its sacred ideal is a primal unity that is also the highest reality.[16]

✦ ✦ ✦

But there is a dark side to all this. When love becomes an end in itself, its own object of infatuation, it can quickly incubate the seeds of inhumanity. The beloved is then a means to love, rather than love a means to the beloved. Love is no longer disciplined by the overriding need to serve a good apart from itself and so, in a bizarre turn of events, can cease to notice or even care for the actual person it loves. This most personal of emotions becomes the most impersonal, for it hardly matters any more who the lovers are: apart from their passion for one another, and their courage and persistence in pursuing it, their particular natures or characters play little role in their love story.

Indeed the lovers might relate in a more impersonal way to each other than to someone who isn't the object of their longing. Other people's individuality really can matter, if only because it can get in the way of the love story and so must be understood and reckoned with. But the lovers' individuality is, in the limiting situation, beside the point. Worse: it obstructs their desire for union. As a result, their own selves and the world to which they belong – this world of time and space and loss and suffering – become contemptible to them. And so they crave a realm beyond the world – beyond their imprisonment in their own individuality.

This striving for a realm beyond individuality has, of course, a very ancient pedigree, and we have repeatedly encountered it in this book. Nineteenth-century Romanticism hardly invented it.

For Plato it is a realm of light. It can be pictured as a sun that illuminates the everyday world of individuals.

For Christianity it is the realm of God – conceived as the origin of all light and life. Though God, almost by definition, is the Being of whom humans cannot know and therefore speak, as so-called 'negative theology' teaches, much has in practice been said of his doings and judgements, beginning with Scripture.

But with the slow retreat of God, which becomes earnest in the seventeenth century, and was already prepared in courtly love, the nature of this realm beyond individuals and their existence in time becomes steadily more opaque.

Since Kant, it is characterised as one of which nothing could be known though a lot could be said – especially that it was the realm of freedom: the realm presupposed by morality. For many who follow him, it is a realm from which light gradually vanishes, to be replaced by darkness.

When Dante mourned the dead Beatrice and praised her as a divine emanation, his songs were addressed to a dazzling apparition in a heaven flooded with light. By contrast, when the German Romantic poet Novalis[17] (1772–1801) mourns and praises Sophie von Kühn, the fifteen-year-old girl whom he too loved and lost, and whom he too saw as an outpouring of the divine, his hymns are addressed to the night:

> How paltry and childish seems now the Light to me! How comforting and
> blessed the day's departure! . . . More heavenly than these flashing stars seems

to us the infinite eyes which the Night has opened within us. They see further than the palest of those countless hosts; without need of the Light they penetrate the depths of a loving heart, a feat which fills a higher realm with unutterable delight.[18]

In these *Hymns to the Night* (1799–1800), inspired by a mystical vision that Novalis had while visiting Sophie's grave, the highest intimacy is possible only in darkness, the unclear, the uncanny. Love is a child of the night: 'faithful unto the Night will my private heart remain, and unto creative Love, her daughter'.[19]

The spirit of Novalis is one in which despair and hope, pain and ecstasy, are inseparable. In this there is nothing remarkable: we don't need Romanticism to remind us that these seeming opposites are inseparable and their struggle unending. What is remarkable are the extremes to which Novalis takes them and his portrayal of their flourishing in the night. From night comes new light; from eternal night new life.

Eternal night is, of course, death. And in death is found the truest love:

In death is love most sweet; for the lover, death is a bridal night, a secret full of sweet mysteries.[20]

What bliss, what sensual delight does thy life provide which would outweigh Death's ecstasies? Does not all that enraptures us wear the colour of the Night? She bears thee maternally, and to her dost thou owe all thy splendour. Thou wouldst burst asunder within thyself, in endless space wouldst thou crumble away, were it not that she held thee, bound thee, that thou mightest become warm and, flaming, mightest give birth to the world.[21]

Death is the goal towards which all life moves. It is – here anticipating Heidegger in the twentieth century – the indispensable horizon: the horizon in relation to which we can experience the reality of this life most intensively, that is to say most spiritually. Death: not the demoraliser of life, but, in Emily Dickinson's pregnant phrase, its 'hinge': 'Life is death we're lengthy at, death the hinge to life.'[22]

✦ ✦ ✦

This certainly does not mean – as it almost never means for traditional Christianity – that life is without any value. Nor does Novalis deny that love is possible within its realm. On the contrary, the world is a magnificent place, worth loving (Novalis was deeply interested in science and studied nature avidly). Daylight has its beauties and wonders, all of them expressions of God's presence in nature. Life's sensual joys and especially the sanctity of marriage are to be celebrated. Community, even politics, should be domains of love. There will, he predicts, be a 'time of eternal peace', when 'All humanity will melt together like a pair of lovers'.[23]

Nor does passionate love for another person necessarily conflict with love for the world. Indeed in loving this person I *also* love the world – I not only see her in the world; I also see the world in her:

What one loves one finds everywhere and sees similarities to it everywhere. The greater the love the wider and more varied the resembling world. My beloved is the abbreviation of the universe, the universe the elongation of my beloved.[24]

And yet the sharp definition in which daylight casts everything – our projects, goals, emotions, thoughts – is impoverished compared with the night, where alone the true depths and ends of human experience can be found. Night is when Christ's redemptive death took place, the death that reconciles man and God. Night is the realm of the great Mother, Mary the Virgin. And night is when Novalis visits Sophie's grave and imagines he can become one with her:

Praise be unto the world's queen, the high herald of sacred worlds, the fostering nurse of blessed love! She sends thee to me, tender Beloved, lovely sun of the Night. I wake now, for I am thine and mine: thou hast proclaimed to me the Night as life and made me human. Consume my body with spirit-fire that I may ethereally commingle more intensely with thee and that the bridal night may last then forever.[25]

And so Novalis is impatient for daylight to cease altogether so that love may claim the eternity to which it rightly belongs:

Must morning ever return? Does the power of earthly things never end? Unholy activity consumes the heavenly descent of the Night. Will the secret sacrifice of love never burn eternally? Apportioned to the Light was its time, but timeless and spaceless is the Night's dominion.[26]

An essentially similar thought had already been expressed by Friedrich Schlegel:

> Oh eternal yearning! Still at last the fruitless yearning and vain brilliance of the day shall vanish and expire, and a great night of love make itself felt in eternal peace.[27]

We see foreshadowed here the world of *Liebestod* – love-death – the world that Richard Wagner was to set to music in his *Tristan und Isolde*. It is quintessentially German – or, rather, late German Romantic – in its metaphysical striving that sees consummation in death, its yearning for the darkness in which alone the depths will be revealed, its ecstatic affirmation of the obstacles to its own fulfilment, its grandiloquent melancholy, its exquisite subtlety, its hearty bombast, and its tender intimacy. Nonetheless, it is *not* a world that grows primarily out of German myth or folk traditions. Nor is it essentially a revival of courtly love in a nineteenth-century setting. Rather it is the ultimate development of Greek thought on love, and specifically of Platonic Eros-love, whose inescapable paradox it celebrates. This is the paradox that when lovers strive for the absolute – for a good conceived as eternal and perfect – they end up willing their own destruction. Indeed, when love's desire itself comes to be thought of as godlike, love – that greatest expression of life-force – becomes a death drive.

In *Tristan und Isolde* Wagner's music affirms life by rapturously celebrating the will to love. Given love's paradox, to will love – and so life – in this extreme way is to have the courage to will its consequence: death. The individual expresses his life-energy not by magpie-like efforts to preserve himself but by readiness to sacrifice himself.

In this sense the will to life is, at the limit, a will to death – a will that is capable of charging life with such extraordinary energy. Translated into the medium of politics – where we recognise unmistakeable signs of Nazi ideology – this idea must be odious, among other reasons because politics is a collective business that can be hijacked by an uncontrollable medley of base and pragmatic interests. But as an individual and spiritual discipline, and as art, it is an ideal of incomparable vitality and meaning.

Precisely because *Liebestod* is the culmination of a paradox whose seed is sown by Plato we could also be here in a much earlier world than the eighteenth or nineteenth centuries – such as the world of Abelard and Heloise or of St John of the Cross and St Teresa of Ávila. With one crucial difference: love has now dispensed with the need for God. It needs neither God's grace to inspire it, nor God as its ultimate goal.

This focus on a human love that does not make constant reference to God had already begun when, in the years around 1100, Guilhem de Peitieu wrote the revolutionary lyrics that would found courtly love. It is clearly present in Gottfried von Strassburg's *Tristan* poem, composed in the thirteenth century – a poem condemned by many, right into the twentieth, as blasphemous and immoral. But by the time Wagner writes *Tristan und Isolde* in the nineteenth, human desire itself has become godlike – and, as importantly, the consummation it seeks is with another mortal individual, with God now irrelevant to the picture.

Such is the confidence of these late-Romantic lovers in their capacity to love, and so overwhelming is their dedication to each other, that if God were really present there would be three in the marriage. They bask in their self-sufficiency and aloneness with one another; they are oblivious to God, even if they still profess reverence for him. So greatly do they trust their union that they welcome, rather than fear, the unknowable void into which they hurl themselves. This is a new moment in the courage – and hubris – of Western love.

We still live in that moment, and it casts its light and its shadow over almost every 'passionate relationship' in the Western world and perhaps beyond. When even those who dismiss the idea of transcending life as unintelligible say 'love redeems all' or 'love is what remains of us after we die' – or when love is invoked to justify the destruction of marriages or the abandonment of families or anything else that we otherwise hold precious – we remain children of the Romanticism of Schlegel, Novalis, and, in his much more extreme way, Wagner. In summing up a litany of ideas about love that can be traced back to Plato, this Romanticism is peculiarly hard to define and impossible to reduce to any one motif. It prepares the conclusion that would until then have been sacrilege, but that was the next step in their logic: through love and in love man finally becomes God.

As I indicated in chapter 1, many other attempts at the deification of man take place in the nineteenth and twentieth centuries: freedom, reason, communism, imperialism, statesmanship, art, technology, and other forms of creativity are, at different times, all advanced as vehicles for human exaltation. But none mimics the features of the Christian God as precisely and democratically as love can – and, partly for that reason, has anything like love's staying power.

13

Love as the urge to procreate
Schopenhauer

In idolising erotic love between human beings and seeing in their union the salvation and eternity that were once to be found exclusively in coming to God, late German Romanticism had thrown down a powerful challenge to its own Christian origins at the same time as it remained powerfully tethered to them. 'For the sake of God' had been forgotten or sidelined. Love of neighbour was irrelevant to the passion between two people, even if it was otherwise to be commended. Likewise sympathy for suffering humanity. The Good Samaritan would have been a joker at the court of Tristan and Isolde.

In doing this, Romanticism had also given fresh impetus to that most resilient of Christian motifs: the way of love must be travelled if life's sufferings are to be redeemed; the trials of love and its losses are central to the highest spiritual achievements.

Atheism offers no guarantee of escape from this motif, or even necessarily seeks one. And its emperors mostly seem unaware of how thickly they are clad in Christian vestments. Many who see in love a natural and often brutal drive in search of self-interested gratification, such as Proust, end up offering a narrative of redemption that is, in many respects, Christian in form.

Indeed, no thinker more impressively articulates an essentially Christian view of love than that curmudgeonly atheist Arthur Schopenhauer (1788–1860). He is able to think of love, variously, as a longing for the infinite; as selfless devotion to the needs of our neighbour for his own sake; as compassion for everything living, very much including animals; and as a ruthless drive aimed at procreation and self-gratification.

Schopenhauer's key move, in effect if not in intent, is to revive and give new meaning to the fundamental division between *cupiditas* and *caritas* that we encountered in Augustine and that pervades so much Christian theology. In line with his Protestant heritage he characterises this division in terms of a certain opposition of Eros and agape. Eros-love as he sees it – the 'selfish' love that desires, idealises, possesses, seeks sexual union, and is focused on finding satisfaction in this world of individuals living in time – can never bring final satisfaction, let alone salvation. Only agape – the 'selfless' love that says no to all such striving, indeed that leads to the surrender of willing – is pure, and only it can save. This love is compassionate and giving: the love of neighbour shown by the Good Samaritan.

As an atheist, Schopenhauer doesn't see such a division in terms of heaven and earth, God and man. For him agape doesn't have a divine source or inspiration. It doesn't, for example, need to be activated by God's grace or by some other higher power. Instead it becomes the purely human capacity for compassion or sympathy. It rests, as we will see, on the axiom that there is no essential distinction between myself and everyone else: my essential being is also expressed in them; their concerns and pains are also mine. Individuality is ultimately an illusion.

Schopenhauer therefore regards the disinterestedness and self-sacrifice of agape-love as diametrically opposed to the selfishness of romantic love. Yet agape, as he presents it, achieves exactly what erotic love ultimately does in the Romantic picture we just sketched: it overcomes the (illusory) separateness between oneself and others, and draws us towards unity with them. Thus it redeems us from the constant suffering that individuality necessarily engenders – constant because, as we will see, the desire that is intrinsic to the life of the individual will always lead to pain, whether it is satisfied or not.

Schopenhauer's humanisation of agape is so clearly a rehearsal of Christian themes in atheist language that it cannot be regarded as saying anything particularly new about love. By contrast, his account of romantic love – and in general of what Christianity sees as earthly love – is of stunning originality. Indeed the way he dethrones the idealistic claims of passionate love has no equal since Lucretius – that is, not since the birth of Christianity.

✦ ✦ ✦

Like Lucretius, but in a much more radical and rigorous way, Schopenhauer sees all passionate desire for another – and beyond that all desire-driven action – as propelled by sex. Anticipating Freud, he claims that sex is 'the invisible central

point of all action and conduct, and peeps up everywhere, in spite of all the veils
thrown over it'.[1] It is the force behind war and peace, as well as wit and ribaldry.[2]
It produces the idealisations of passionate love, and of course its illusions and
frenzy. The way sex is now used to advertise almost anything would not surprise
Schopenhauer at all.

Sexual desire, he claims, is not only the strongest of our desires; it 'constitutes
even the very nature of man'.[3] This is so because

> the sexual impulse is the kernel of the will-to-live [or will-to-life], and conse-
> quently the concentration of all willing . . . Indeed, it may be said that man is
> concrete sexual impulse, for his origin is an act of copulation, and the desire of
> his desires is an act of copulation[.][4]

In a nutshell: the genitals are the focus of the will. No other impulse can conflict
with their urgings and be sure of victory. Nor can any other pleasure make up for
sexual frustration. Its tyranny drives us, like the animals, to 'undertake every peril
and conflict'.[5] For its sake, men and women will impulsively discard everything
else they value: honour; goods; family; friends; the achievements of a lifetime.
Sexual love

> is the ultimate goal of almost all human effort; it has an unfavourable influ-
> ence on the most important affairs, interrupts every hour the most serious
> occupations . . . It knows how to slip its love-notes and ringlets even into
> ministerial portfolios and philosophical manuscripts. Every day it brews and
> hatches the worst and most perplexing quarrels and disputes, destroys the
> most valuable relationships, and breaks the strongest bonds. It demands the
> sacrifice sometimes of life or health, sometimes of wealth, position, and happi-
> ness. Indeed, it robs of all conscience those who were previously honourable
> and upright, and makes traitors of those who have hitherto been loyal and
> faithful.[6]

This behaviour might be disastrous for the individual, as State governors,
world-beating athletes, or presidents of great corporations, all with picture-
perfect families and seemingly scrupulous consciences, find their lives destroyed,
literally overnight. But for the species as a whole it makes perfect sense. For the
species, an evening with a prostitute or a married man does trump income, career,

respectability, and conscience. Without offspring nothing has a future – no social order, no spiritual love, no art, no Church, no industry.

Of course when we crave someone we might *believe* that we are after physical pleasure for its own sake, or the excitement of the 'illicit', or the nobility of a great passion, or a hunger for goodness that cannot be satisfied, or – for those with great wealth and prestige – the banquet of delights that life offers at every turn. Or else we might imagine that we are after a soulmate, a kindly refuge from the world, or a source of much-needed intimacy. We might see our love as a spiritual quest capable of storming the heavens; or we might see it as motivated by a desire for money or status. Powerful desire never fails to explain itself.

Schopenhauer in no way dismisses such convictions. They are genuine and their power in human affairs is immense. Which is why they dominate poetry and drama, tragedy and comedy. Anyone like La Rochefoucauld who quips that love doesn't really exist though everyone talks about it is 'greatly mistaken'.[7] But the real purpose of sexual desire and the grand passions and ideals it inspires is quite different. It is to produce and raise children.

Since this is the sole purpose of the 'collected *love-affairs* of the present generation, taken together',[8] it is perfectly natural for a man, after sex with a woman, to be sated with her and look around for other partners. And it is natural for a woman to have the opposite reaction: for sex to increase her attachment to just this lover, whom she will want to ensnare as provider for her and their offspring. While orgasm makes him want to flee, it makes her want to stay:

> The man's love diminishes perceptibly from the moment it has obtained satisfaction; almost every other woman charms him more than the one he already possesses; he longs for variety. On the other hand, the woman's love increases from that very moment . . . The man, therefore, always looks around for other women; the woman, on the contrary, cleaves firmly to the one man; for nature urges her, instinctively and without reflection, to retain the nourisher and supporter of the future offspring.[9]

Similarly the qualities that most powerfully attract men and women to each other have to do with their fitness as propagators of the species – and not with their ability to provide other satisfactions: to be interesting or witty or athletic or empathetic or good at 'relating'. When you fall helplessly in love with one person out of the many you meet – and perhaps precisely with someone who otherwise makes you unhappy – the question 'Why her?' or 'Why him?' is answered entirely by his or her suitability to be a parent for *your* offspring. (Here Schopenhauer speaks a language remarkably similar to that of contemporary evolutionary psychology.) And so, he implies, the search for mates will go on and on, unless by a rare stroke of fortune we find just the right person.

✦ ✦ ✦

So when you post a description of your ideal partner on a dating site you are speaking, Schopenhauer would say, in two voices. One expresses the qualities that are unconsciously sought by the reproductive instinct and that trigger 'the wholly immediate, instinctive attraction, from which alone springs the condition of *being in love*'.[10] And the other gives vent to conscious values, such as cultural sophistication or ethical qualities or wealth or whatever will command the admiration of others in your particular culture – values which don't in fact determine whether or not you have instant chemistry with the candidates you end up meeting. Though you might imagine they do: *I am attracted only to people who give as much as they receive. Only to someone who can make me laugh and is caring and sensitive, as well as being confident and worldly. I am looking for common values, a sense of humour, professional success, and above all passion. Every relationship helps you to become yourself so hold out for what you believe in and be true to who you really are!*

A wish list like this, publicly posted on the internet, is immensely revealing – both for what it says and for what it doesn't say. Many, perhaps most, of the qualities sought by the instinct to procreate aren't voiced here at all. Partly because they are unconscious; partly because the aspiring dater will wish those reading his profile to think well of him. (In the priority attached to passion and being true to who you really are, we can recognise two of Romanticism's defining ideas.)

When it comes to the actual date, however, things will be very different. A man, Schopenhauer says, looks for the right age (basically the best years for procreation), health (acute diseases are acceptable, chronic ones repugnant), fine stature, fullness of flesh, and beauty of face. In terms of 'psychic' characteristics he is attracted to intellect more than to character.

Why intellect? Because, Schopenhauer suggests against most conventional wisdom, intellect is a female characteristic. The conscious mind is feminine. Emotion, character and will are more developed in *men*. Since we are attracted above all to qualities that we don't have – so that our offspring will get as many (compatible) qualities as possible from both their parents – men will often go for brilliant harridans, just as Socrates chose the terrifying but undeniably smart Xanthippe. And women, being the repositories of intellect and most forms of beauty, will on the whole not regard these as essential in a man.

In fact intellect might put her off – and genius will positively revolt her. 'Hence we often see an ugly, stupid, and coarse fellow get the better of a cultured, clever, and amiable man when dealing with women.'[11] Apart from the fact that she can pass her own intellectual qualities to the child and doesn't need them in a man, the point of marriage

> is not intellectual entertainment, but the procreation of children; it is an alliance of hearts, not of heads. It is a vain and ridiculous pretence when women assert that they have fallen in love with a man's mind[.][12]

Instead women will be attracted by character, 'especially by firmness of will, resoluteness, and courage, perhaps also by honesty and kindness of heart'.[13] They will want a man who is both youthful *and* experienced – so not under thirty or over thirty-five.

On Schopenhauer's own argument, however, it seems possible (and common experience confirms) that a woman could be genuinely attracted to intellect in a man if she experiences it as a form of strength and courage. And especially if she sees him use it fearlessly – not least against her (a sign of boldness if he also fears losing her).

Similarly, I suggest that it is plausible, *contra* Schopenhauer, that she will look for beauty in a man, not for its own sake, but to the extent that it strikes her as evidence of reproductive fitness. Or to put the point the other way around: she might experience as beautiful those physical features that she associates with good reproductive potential.

✦ ✦ ✦

We needn't spend more time on Schopenhauer's exhaustive list of qualities that draw men and women to each other. What matters is the path-breaking way in which he shifts the entire debate about the real goal of love's desire from intimacy with one who embodies goodness, truth and beauty or otherwise brings us to a harmonious completion – which is the focus of so much of the Platonic tradition and its expression in Christianity – to the search for a mate with an optimal biological and psychological make-up:

we feel most strongly every want of proportion in the *skeleton*; for example, a
stunted, dumpy, short-legged figure . . .; also a limping gait, where this is not the
result of an external accident. On the other hand, a strikingly fine stature can
make up for every defect; it enchants us. Here also we see the great value that
all attach to smallness of the feet; this rests on their being an essential characteristic of the species, since no animal has so small a tarsus and metatarsus taken
together as man has . . .[14]

In thus shifting the debate about the goal of Eros-love, Schopenhauer also
implies a clear distinction between lust and love. Both are driven by sexual
desire; but whereas lust is the desire to copulate with anyone attractive, love is
that obsessive attention to one person who intuition tells us is the right mate for
reproduction. His genius is to see romantic love as having a wholly biological
purpose – producing and raising children – while also doing justice to the
experience of being in love, with its willingness to sacrifice everything for the
loved one.

The fantasies that love cooks up might seem mad and destructive, but they
too serve the aim of reproducing. When I tell myself a story about the meaning
of love – for example, that it is a spiritual bond of supreme ethical value that
brings me to my authentic self and is blessed by God – this spurs me to make the
immense effort needed to find the right mate. When I find her and believe that
fate or God has led me to her, and deem our love more important than anything
else, this stiffens my resolve to keep just her; it generates the powerful commitment to raise and provide for a family; and it vindicates all the conflicts and costs
of the relationship.

For these reproductive purposes we are tricked into ascribing the most
fanciful meanings to love.

But tricked by whom or what?

By the will, Schopenhauer answers. By the largely unconscious 'will-to-life'
(*Wille zum Leben*)[15] of the species, of which I – like any individual living being,
whether human, animal or plant – am merely a manifestation. This will is focused
above all on the sexual impulse and its satisfaction, symbolised by the fact that
each of us – conceived as 'individualised will' – enters the world 'through the
portal of the sexual organs'.[16] Every time we fancy someone, or write her a love
poem, or declare that she is 'the one', we are merely the plaything of unconscious
instinct that is directing us, through trial and error, to the right mate. As a result

of this instinct we imagine that what is in fact an utterly impersonal and unspiritual drive is instead *the* most personal and spiritual of all drives.

So marked is the 'sense of the species, striving to maintain its type'[17] that, Schopenhauer bafflingly suggests, children in effect select their parents. We choose our families, he might say, more than we choose our friends.

> For it is the future generation in the whole of its individual definiteness which is pressing into existence by means of these efforts and exertions [of passionate love]. In fact, it is itself already astir in that far-sighted, definite, and capricious selection for the satisfaction of the sexual impulse which is called love. The growing attachment of two lovers is in itself in reality the will-to-live [or, will-to-life] of the new individual, an individual they can and want to produce.[18]

What we *consciously* think we are doing when we are in love is, in the last analysis, irrelevant. Indeed, to propagate the species it might even help for our real motives to remain unconscious.

◆ ◆ ◆

In the history of ideas this is a major moment: for it is when the idea of the unconscious as the seat of our ruling instincts and drives really gets off the ground. But for Schopenhauer the unconscious isn't just the source of what we think and feel; it determines the *whole person*, including the body. 'The *organism* is the will itself, embodied will';[19] whereas intellect is 'a mere tool in the service of the will',[20] from whose 'secret' and prior decisions it has been firmly excluded.[21]

But what if the intellect fails to find in the world what the unconscious will has 'ordered' it to find? Then, says Schopenhauer – and every lover will recognise the truth of this – the unconscious ensures that its wishes are fulfilled in fantasy 'with fairy-tales', and it will deck these fairy tales out 'so that they obtain an appearance of verisimilitude'.[22] The intellect is then required, like an obliging entertainer, to evoke whatever scenarios – happy, sad, confident, triumphant, and so on – the will wishes to believe are the case.

It is of no concern to the will that in the process 'the intellect is bound to do violence to its own nature, which is aimed at truth, since it is compelled . . . to regard as true things that are neither true nor probable, and often scarcely possible, merely in order to pacify, soothe, and send to sleep for a while the restless and unmanageable *will*'.[23] In love, as in much of life, the unconscious has no such scruples; it will accept only the evidence that it is already looking for, while denying or ignoring everything else:

> Love and hatred entirely falsify our judgement; in our enemies we see nothing but shortcomings, in our favourites nothing but merits . . . Our advantage, of whatever kind it may be, exercises a similar secret power over our judgement; what is in agreement with it at once seems to us fair, just, and reasonable; what runs counter to it is presented to us in all seriousness as unjust and outrageous . . . A hypothesis, conceived and formed, makes us lynx-eyed for everything that confirms it, and blind to everything that contradicts it.[24]

And, again anticipating Freud, Schopenhauer suggests that unconscious will can censor feelings or thoughts that would conflict with how we see ourselves or wish to be seen by others:

> For years we can have a desire without admitting it to ourselves or even letting it come to clear consciousness, because the intellect is not to know anything about it, since the good opinion we have of ourselves would inevitably suffer thereby. But if the wish is fulfilled, we get to know from our joy, not without a feeling of shame, that this is what we desired[.][25]

Since the will-to-life is a blind striving, which cannot be finally calmed, sexual desire can never be fully satisfied. Nor therefore can the love that arises out of it. Like all human desire it is doomed to frustration, for once gratified it wells up anew: 'every satisfied desire gives birth to a new one'.[26] Our nature is never to be content with pleasures, but quickly to seek fresh ones.

To will – to live – is to suffer. When our drives are satisfied (though this can only be temporary), we will suffer from boredom; when they are not we will suffer from despair. With skill and luck we can navigate a passage between boredom and despair. But we will still have to contend with the reality that such pleasure as we find arises merely from the fulfilment of a lack. For pleasure and happiness are not positive things. They are the relief of removing a pain.

And so the will-to-life is a treadmill that, as long as we succumb to it, will generate endless and ultimately pointless suffering. For this reason it would have been better, Schopenhauer famously says, if we hadn't been born in the first place. Second best, though, is to die:

death is the great opportunity no longer to be I . . . Dying is the moment of
that liberation from the one-sidedness of an individuality which does not
constitute the innermost kernel of our true being[.][27]

Will-to-life, in turn, manifests what, for Schopenhauer, is ultimate reality: the
general Will behind everything, a cosmic striving that, like the old conception of
God, is one and eternal, and so neither exists in space and time, nor is vulnerable
to change through causal laws. Unlike the old God, though, this impersonal
Will has no overall purpose and no concern for us as individuals. We neither
matter for our own sake, nor in a sense have any separate existence: we are all
merely manifestations of the Will and only wishful thinking causes us to believe
otherwise.

This is why we needn't fear death, because we have nothing to lose – except
our illusions of individuality. When we die all that happens is that the particular
manifestation of the general Will that each of us is, vanishes. But the Will itself,
which we experience above all in our sexual desire, does not die. The true source
of our being is indestructible and immortal.

In saying that everything is a manifestation of one underlying Will,
Schopenhauer is insisting on our essential unity, to that extent, with the animals
and all of nature. He is pulling back from those powerful traditions that connived
to make us utterly distinct from and superior to other creatures: the biblical tradition that places humans above the rest of creation; the Greek heritage that sees
reason or contemplation, the monopoly of human beings, as raising us above the
beasts; the modern, post-seventeenth-century, image of nature as a machine that
the human mind might understand and control.

Which brings us back to sex. For it is sex that connects the individual to the
universal Will behind everything. Sex is a voice of the will-to-life of the species
that speaks through each of us. And that will-to-life, in turn, manifests the
cosmic Will that is the innermost essence of everything.

Nonetheless, sex cannot be for Schopenhauer, as it is for so many Romantics,
the beginning of a mystical journey, which leads the individual from desire for
another person to 'consciousness of the identity of one's own inner being with that
of all things'.[28] He could never agree with Friedrich Schlegel that through erotic
love human nature can return to its original state of divinity. On the contrary, sex,
like all desire, obstructs the attainment of this redeeming consciousness in which
we see through the prison of individuality to grasp the oneness of all life. Since

sexual desire traps one in the delusions of individuality and so in endless suffering, salvation lies in denying its urgings – in refusing to identify with them; in calming and rising above them.

As a result, Schopenhauer concludes, our existence will have value only if we deny the will-to-life from which sexual desire springs; only if we refuse the striving of the ego, the promptings of the genitals, the hunger for gratification, and even the yearning for offspring. Christianity, Brahmanism and Buddhism all agree, so he thinks, on this renunciation of life – in total distinction from the Jews, whose Old Testament says that God saw the world and found it very good: 'the spirit of the Old Testament is diametrically opposed to that of the New; the former is optimistic, and the latter pessimistic'.[29]

✦ ✦ ✦

But if sex and romantic love must lead to suffering and can never bring about salvation there is a form of love that *can* redeem us from the life of desire; indeed that eventually leads to the blessed state in which the will-to-life is surrendered. This is the agape that we encountered earlier in this chapter. Agape (or *caritas*) has such redemptive power because its 'origin and nature'[30] is to see through the deception of individuality – the deception that I am distinct from you – and so to recognise ourselves and our will in everybody else, indeed in all animate things.

In dissolving the distinction between us and others, such insight enables us to feel their suffering almost as intimately as our own.[31] Their well-being becomes ours. To violate them is out of the question, for it would effectively be to violate ourselves. And so we are moved to alleviate their suffering – though agape, in its clear-sightedness, perceives that the joy this engenders is the result merely of removing a pain and never of creating positive happiness.

Agape's insight is, in other words, nothing but compassion. Indeed, Schopenhauer announces, agape *is* itself compassion.[32] Works of love are 'the inevitable and infallible symptom'[33] of knowing that our true self exists not only in our own person, but in everything that lives. Such knowledge is immediate, not the result of reason or argument. We cannot 'decide' to gain it, or to attain the love which expresses it, or to achieve the surrender of the will to which it eventually leads. These blessings seem to come to us unbidden, like a gift:

> *self-suppression of the will* comes from knowledge, but all knowledge and insight as such are independent of free choice, [consequently] that denial of

willing, that entrance into freedom, is not to be forcibly arrived at by intention or design, but comes from the innermost relation of knowing and willing in man; hence it comes suddenly, as if flying in from without. Therefore, the Church calls it the *effect of grace*[.][34]

In all this Schopenhauer closely follows the Christian account of agape, as it had developed since at least Augustine. We are to identify with the neighbour, regardless of who he or she is. Selflessness and resignation are the basis of compassion. Worldly pleasures bring suffering; and the striving for them depends on delusion. Grace is crucial to activating the human power to love, or even to making it possible at all. The value of truth lies in its capacity to lead one to this salvation. Spiritual achievement depends on a correct relation between correct perception and correct willing.

And so for this atheist philosopher, who sees sex as the force behind passionate love's highest ideals and as our most powerful drive, salvation lies in the condition of those ascetics, saints and mystics who have mortified the flesh and in whom the will has negated itself. The ideal he posits is 'empty nothing-ness', the state of enlightenment that Buddhism calls Nirvana. Then we will

see that peace that is higher than all reason, that ocean-like calmness of spirit, that deep tranquillity, that unshakeable confidence and serenity . . . beside which the miserable and desperate nature of our own [state] appears in the clearest light . . . [W]hat remains after the complete abolition of the will is, for all who are still full of the will, assuredly nothing. But also conversely, to those in whom the will has turned and denied itself, this very real world of ours with all its suns and galaxies, is – nothing.[35]

14

Love as affirmation of life
Nietzsche

A deep dilemma cuts through the history of Western love from its earliest sources in Hebrew Scripture and Greek philosophy: Is it nobler for the highest love to affirm the worldly or to repudiate it? Should love seek its perfections in the desiring and striving of this world – or beyond it? The world, that is, in which suffering and loss are inevitable. In which nothing timeless can exist. In which, as Schopenhauer noted, ambitions will, in the end, be in vain and peace will never be secured. This is the world into which we are born and the only world we can know.

For example: Is God's commandment to Israel to love him with *all* its heart, soul, and strength also, in effect, a commandment not to be detained by love of the world? Or does it, on the contrary, empower Israel to love a treacherous world – a world in which home cannot be guaranteed and peace might never be found?

Is love in Plato a longing to escape life's transience and loss into an ideal realm of permanence and perfection? Or is it also a way of taking possession of precisely this everyday world by focusing on the beauty and goodness instantiated in it in so many ways?

Is Christian love an affirmation of this life and our neighbour – wholly good insofar as they are the work of God, who has himself deemed his created life good? Or is it a repudiation of this world in the name of the Kingdom of Heaven, and so ultimately a yearning for death?

Is Romantic love, especially of the sort that we saw in Schlegel and Novalis, a form of despair about love – and about all desire: namely that it cannot be finally satisfied or 'consummated' in this finite and time-bound world of individuals? Or is its heaven-storming ambition, its ideal of dissolving into the infinite, rather an expression of optimism, and ultimately therefore of belief in the value of desire itself?

It is easy to forget that all these traditions affirm the world, if only to the extent that, despite its horrors, it is a place blessed by love and goodness. This very much includes mainstream Christianity, which never wished to give up entirely on this world and indeed had persecuted and triumphed over heretics, like the Gnostics of the second century CE, who despised the material world as evil. Augustine, for example, insists that all things created by God have measure, form and order, and to that extent are good.[1]

Love, whether it is religious in inspiration or not, will find the world hateful only insofar as it seeks what the world in its very nature cannot provide: eternity, completeness, and an end to loss and suffering. To the extent that even a naturalist or atheist has such ambitions for love, he or she will be ambivalent about the value of ordinary life. Thus Spinoza, who affirms the beauty and good-ness of nature and wishes love to do so too, cannot unreservedly affirm ordinary life; for he is still too wedded to the Platonic idea that the highest love sets its sights beyond mortal, changeable individuals and so beyond the world as we find it.

The only way of avoiding this obsessive ambivalence about whether love should trust or mistrust the world is to give up the idea that there is a state of affairs more perfect than time-bound human life can attain; and that love is the route which gets us there.

✦ ✦ ✦

The task of clearing our attitude to the world of this wrenching ambivalence is at the heart of Friedrich Nietzsche's philosophy. His life's work was to under-stand and overcome the impulse to seek salvation or moral perfection in a condi-tion purified of evil, loss, change and suffering. Instead, he attempts to discover what it would be for the very opposite impulse to reign: the impulse to say yes to *everything* that exists – not only to everything about our individual life, but to the whole chain of happenings that has led up to just the person that each of us is.

In doing so he invites us to imagine that our life – its miseries as well as its joys, and all the events that preceded it – will recur infinitely; and asks if our love of it is sufficient to be able to say yes even to this infinite recurrence. He wants us to see ourselves again as an inextricable part of nature and to abandon all half-heartedness about the actual existence we have and all thoughts about how it might be better or other than it is. This is the attitude of *amor fati* (love of fate):

> that one wants nothing to be different, not forward, not backward, not in all eternity. Not merely bear what is necessary, still less conceal it ... but *love* it.[2]

Nietzsche (1844–1900) has a strange significance in the history of love. He provides the basis for a revolution in our conception of love while saying almost nothing new about it. He does so by attacking the whole system of Platonic-Christian thinking that has structured Western values for over two thousand years and so has, in effect, dominated Western attitudes to love. This is the system that made love seek the ideal of eternity without change, good without bad, the spiritual without the physical. It culminates in the Romanticism of the nineteenth century that yearns to escape life's terribleness through exalted and passionate feeling and ultimately through death. Always expressing itself with great vehemence, Romanticism concocted two sorts of escape: either into peacefulness or else into frenzy: either 'rest, stillness, calm seas, redemption ... through art and knowledge, or intoxication, convulsions, anaesthesia, and madness.'[3]

The vehemence of Romanticism is motivated, Nietzsche comes to think, not by an abundance of life but by an *'impoverishment of life'*.[4] Its high spirits are suspect and not genuine. Its yearning for tranquillity reflects resignation. Its frenzy is born of exhaustion rather than vitality. Though much Romanticism claims to be anti-Christian he sees in its spirit merely a late manifestation of Christianity – that greatest of all popularisers of the ideal that this world be transcended.

Christianity – or 'Platonism for "the people" '[5] as Nietzsche deridingly describes it – has the brilliant cunning to turn denial of life into a *moral* duty. It enforces this duty by damning as evil the worldly, the bodily, and the assertion of one's natural power and strength. Christianity, he claims, teaches us to feel guilty about all this and instead to value their opposites: selflessness and humility. It invents a God who saves the weak and condemns the strong; concepts like 'original sin' that make us feel guilty about who we inescapably are; and 'gifts' like free will by which we can supposedly choose to repudiate the desires that are part and parcel of being human.

The result is to set us against ourselves. We are incited to hate what is real – our own nature and the world of change and adversity in which it is located – and to love what is unreal: a permanent, unchanging state free of loss and pain and time. This is precisely the state that Schopenhauer characterises as 'Nothing', that Christianity calls 'God', and that, through much of its history, love sanctifies as its supreme object.

Such mad desire for the unreal, the non-existent, Nietzsche calls the 'will to nothingness', the desperate 'last will' of man.[6] He diagnoses it as the fundamental will behind not only two millennia of Christianity but also the secular world it has left in its wake:

> We can no longer conceal from ourselves *what* is expressed by . . . this hatred of
> the human, and even more of the animal, and more still of the material . . . this
> longing to get away from all appearance, change, becoming . . . all this means –
> let us dare to grasp it – *a will to nothingness*, an aversion to life, a rebellion against
> the most fundamental presuppositions of life . . .[7]

But why would human beings want to will nothingness? Out of what motive would we repudiate what is natural and well-constituted and real, and instead create a tortured, self-hating inner world that hankers after the unreal? Though this question might seem to have little to do with love it actually has everything to do with it: for the will to nothingness is the will that, according to Nietzsche, sustains all attempts to find meaning in human life by 'Judeo-Christian' civilisation and its secular successors – a meaning to which love has been and remains central.

So why would anyone want to seek meaning by willing nothingness? The answer is: out of fear of suffering. This fear can get, and historically has got, so out of hand that the will turns against life itself[8] – in other words against the entire world of which suffering is an inescapable part. Which means, of course, against the only world there is.

In particular, Nietzsche says, this fear fastens on two causes of our suffering: our weakness and our losses. It fosters resentment of those who have strengths that make us feel weak; and of the loss to which all life is vulnerable. The loss of parents, children, and friends; of possessions and achievements; of life itself.

And so our culture becomes geared to eliminating the reality of suffering, the sight of suffering, and the causes of suffering. Its dominant values and virtues – very much including love – are obsessively directed at this goal. Its religion promises a world to come where there will be no more suffering and where all our earthly travails will be redeemed and rewarded. Its science and ethics, its politics and society, are geared to minimising risk and danger, and achieving a state of undisturbed well-being. Its watchwords are comfort, convenience, predictability.

✦ ✦ ✦

One value, above all, is fostered by resentment of suffering, of loss, and of all who are stronger and more fortunate. That value is pity: pity for suffering.

One might wonder what the problem is here. Can't such pity, as Rousseau and Schopenhauer claimed, be the noblest of values and definitive of love – at least if not abused to gain power over others? Can't it affirm and protect the lives of those we care about? Isn't it a cause for celebration that, amidst so much selfishness and indifference, human beings should also be moved by the suffering of others? And, more pragmatically, isn't pity essential to human flourishing, a basic disposition that enables us to live together – to form friendships, marriages, families, communities?

Absolutely not, Nietzsche insists. Pity isn't what it appears to be. Though it seems 'kind' it is an intrusive, even brutal, demand that the other cease to suffer because the sight of suffering – its very existence as a phenomenon – is unbearable. Though it appears humble, it arrogantly assumes that it knows what is best for the pitied, and refuses to recognise that 'one simply knows nothing of the whole inner sequence and intricacies that are distress for *me* or for *you*'.[9] Though it appears altruistic it is all too often motivated by a desire to escape one's own suffering and responsibility for oneself. Though it masquerades as 'giving' it really wants control:

> When we see somebody suffer, we like to exploit this opportunity to take possession of him; those who become his benefactors and pity him . . . call the lust for a new possession that he awakens in them 'love'; and the pleasure they feel is comparable to that aroused by the prospect of a new conquest.[10]

These concealed aims of pity are deeply perverse – as therefore is placing it at the heart of loving relationships. For only through suffering do we grow and mature; 'only *this* discipline has created all enhancements of man so far';[11] 'all becoming and growing – all that guarantees a future – involves pain'.[12] Whereas the state of undisturbed well-being that most pity seeks 'makes man ridiculous and contemptible', mean-spirited and fearful.

And the 'insane' aim of abolishing suffering (or, failing that, of concealing it) weakens not only the pitied but the pitier too. Unfortunately, nothing is more tempting than to lose oneself in the suffering of others so as not to focus on mastering one's own life. Nietzsche confesses to finding that temptation overwhelming:

> All such arousing of pity . . . is secretly seductive, for our 'own way' is too hard and demanding and too remote from the love and gratitude of others, and we do not really mind escaping from it – and from our very own conscience – to flee into the conscience of the others and into the lovely temple of the 'religion of pity'.[13]

This, too, is the purpose to which 'love for neighbour' has so often been put: 'You flee to your neighbour from yourselves and would like to make a virtue out of that'.[14] Which is why, Nietzsche thinks, pity and the biblical command were natural partners in crime.

One should trust the pity only of someone who is by nature strong and sovereign – someone who will not use it to flee himself or to enfeeble his neighbour. *His* pity will be for whatever weakens his neighbour – including a life dedicated to the avoidance of suffering.[15]

It sounds a hard, even obsessive, message. But for Nietzsche pity is not 'an isolated question mark'. It is emblematic of the will to nothingness itself: 'It was precisely here that I saw the *great* danger to mankind, its sublimest enticement and seduction – but to what? to nothingness?'[16] And so to ask what pity is really up to is to ask, in the starkest possible way, about the value of the whole system of morality inherited from Judaism and Christianity.[17]

✦ ✦ ✦

Love that originates in such a moral universe – one dominated by fear of suffering, loss, and weakness; one ruled by the morality of pity – is love that originates in resentment and hatred.

This is Nietzsche's most spectacular claim about the tradition of love that evolves from Judaism and Christianity: it grows out of hatred. He is not repeating the commonplace that love and hate go together – for example that love easily nurses hate when its hopes are disappointed, or even in anticipation of their disappointment. Rather, he is suggesting that hatred of nature, of strength, of life itself, *drives* 'the religion of love'. That from

> the profoundest and sublimest kind of hatred, capable of creating ideals and reversing values, the like of which has never existed on earth before – there grew something equally incomparable, a *new love*, the profoundest and sublimest kind of love[.][18]

Indeed, Nietzsche asks, 'from what other trunk *could* it have grown?'[19] How else could love, that most affirming of passions, come to repudiate the world and the very conditions of human flourishing if it were not driven by the thirst for revenge against the world? This ideal of love, far from opposing the thirst for revenge, is rather its 'triumphant crown',

> spreading itself farther and farther into the purest brightness and sunlight, driven as it were into the domain of light and the heights in pursuit of the goals of that hatred ... Jesus of Nazareth, the incarnate gospel of love, this 'Redeemer' who brought blessedness and victory to the poor, the sick, and the sinners – was he not this seduction in its most uncanny and irresistible form ...?[20]

When Nietzsche calls Christian love 'the profoundest and sublimest kind of love' he is, of course, being deeply ironical – but not entirely. Part of his subtlety as a philosopher is to see the potential for greatness in deformity and for health in sickness. We are, he memorably says, ennobled through degeneration.[21] A human being, terrified of a world of suffering, resentful of his helplessness, divided against himself, loathing what he inescapably is, hating the very conditions of his own flourishing – pain and suffering – while also craving to flourish: this is also a human being who will strive hard to invent imaginary, fantastic, worlds of which he *can* be master. Christian self-cruelty, with all its guilt and bad conscience, has been 'the womb of all ideal and imaginative phenomena' and has brought to light 'an abundance of strange new beauty and affirmation'.[22] Indeed its underlying resentment was what first made human beings really *interesting*.[23]

Nature, however, cannot be made to disappear. It will always reappear – if in monstrous guises. Which is what happened to Eros at the hands of Christianity, its sworn enemy: 'Christianity gave Eros poison to drink: he did not die of it but degenerated – into a vice.'[24]

✦ ✦ ✦

So what sort of love does Nietzsche think is noble? What sort of love strengthens rather than weakens us, arises from generosity rather than hatred, affirms the world rather than repudiating it?

Nietzsche's answer is: self-love. Not in the sense of complacent or indulgent self-assertion, which he abhors, but in the sense of severe reverence for oneself, and especially for oneself as possessing nobility worthy of one's respect. This, Nietzsche insists, is the precondition of our love for others and indeed for the world in general. Without it human beings lapse into precisely the destructive resentment that is expressed in the 'will to nothingness'. And so, Nietzsche insists: 'one thing is needful: that a human being should *attain* satisfaction with himself . . . Whoever is dissatisfied with himself is continually ready for revenge'.[25]

To say that we need to love ourselves if we are to love others would hardly be radical. What is radical is Nietzsche's insistence that any love for others not based on hard self-love is based on hate: hate for oneself and hate for others; his insistence that, as we saw earlier, 'selfless' Christian love arises – and can only arise – from the desire for revenge, and so isn't love at all.

And what is also radical is the thought that to love yourself – or indeed anyone or anything – is also to love fate *in general*. Which is precisely the step that Nietzsche seems to take when he says of each of us that 'one is a piece of fatefulness, one belongs to the whole, one is in the whole'. If your loved one belongs to the whole, you cannot love him in isolation from it. Since he is an inextricable part of existence in general, to love him *is* to love all of existence. 'The fatality of his essence is not to be disentangled from the fatality of all that has been and will be . . .'[26]

Of course we tend to experience passionate love, and especially sexual love, in what seems to be the opposite way: as exclusively focused on one person so that 'to the lover himself the whole rest of the world appears indifferent, pale, and worthless, and he is prepared to make any sacrifice, to disturb any order, to subordinate all other interests'.[27] But there is no contradiction here: the lovers' tremendous attention to each other might shut out the rest of the world beyond them; but this very attention is also the deepest possible affirmation of the whole to which they each belong.

Perhaps, then, it is one of love's great illusions that it is consummated in seclusion from the world. Perhaps, on the contrary, love has nowhere to hide. A strong love would affirm luck, chance, and necessity, rather than seek protection from them.

Which would mean that to love someone is not merely to be able to overcome the desire to 'change' them, but also to overcome the desire to change the world of which they are an inextricable part. That if love 'forgets the world' it forgets itself.

✦ ✦ ✦

Yet sexual or romantic passion is not the sort of love between two people that most interests Nietzsche. Beyond it, he says, there is a much rarer love 'in which this possessive craving of two people for each other gives way to a new desire and lust for possession – a *shared* higher thirst for an ideal above them. But who knows such love? Who has experienced it? Its right name is *friendship*.'[28]

Here Nietzsche seems to praise something very like the classical conception of *philia* that we saw in Aristotle and Montaigne. And, again like Aristotle and Montaigne, he believes that to love well takes mastery and practice. Love is not a 'spontaneous' emotion that springs ready-formed from us. All love – even for ourselves – is learned.

> *One must learn to love.* – This is what happens to us in music: First one has to *learn to hear* a figure and a melody at all, to detect and distinguish it, to isolate and delimit it as a separate life. Then it requires some exertion and good will to *tolerate* it in spite of its strangeness, to be patient with its appearance and expression, and kindhearted about its oddity. Finally there comes a moment when we are *used* to it, when we wait for it, when we sense that we should miss it if it were missing; and now it continues to compel and enchant us relentlessly until we have become its humble and enraptured lovers who desire nothing better from the world than it and only it.
>
> But that is what happens to us not only in music. That is how we have *learned to love* all things that we now love. In the end we are always rewarded for our good will, our patience, fair-mindedness, and gentleness with what is strange; gradually, it sheds its veil and turns out to be a new and indescribable beauty.

That is its *thanks* for our hospitality. Even those who love themselves will have learned it in this way; for there is no other way. Love, too, has to be learned.[29]

Learning to love, Nietzsche suggests, involves more than mere 'acceptance'. Since many aspects of the world – and indeed of our loved ones – are, frankly, ugly, to learn to love them is to learn to see them, and specifically their fatedness, as beautiful. For the beautiful *'arouses the will'*.[30]

Which brings us back to *amor fati* – love of fate – the attitude towards the world that Nietzsche sees as most fundamentally opposed to Christianity. As he says of himself and his ambition to be an affirmer:

> I want to learn more and more to see as beautiful what is necessary in things; then I shall be one of those who make things beautiful. *Amor fati*: let that be my love henceforth! I do not want to wage war against what is ugly. I do not want to accuse; I do not even want to accuse those who accuse. *Looking away* shall be my only negation. And all in all and on the whole: some day I wish to be only a Yes-sayer.[31]

This resembles Plato's insight that love is inspired by the beautiful. But it repudiates Plato's insistence that love selectively focuses on what is in itself beautiful – and instead suggests that love must also *make* things beautiful. Love, in other words, is like an artist who creates or interprets the object to which he attends in such a way that he can see the whole as beautiful. His affirmation of his work is powerful precisely because he is able to see it, down to its last detail, as necessary – as a fated product of his own life.

✦ ✦ ✦

Nietzsche's philosophy poses challenges to contemporary love that it has still not faced. What would love be like if it did not desire eternity, peace, safety – and instead affirmed their opposites? How can love find a way out of the labyrinth it has created for itself by being the ultimate repository of our yearning to escape the uncertainties of fate and loss and chance? What new possibilities would love have if it were freed of the burden of rescuing us from suffering?

These questions have become all the more pressing – and possible – because of an extraordinary event, famously announced by Nietzsche: the 'death of God'.[32] For Nietzsche the death of God is not only about the impossibility of continuing to believe in the all-powerful father-figure worshipped in monothe-istic religions, or in a heaven where the sufferings and sins of the righteous would be redeemed, or in the whole apparatus of guilt and reward that sustains this theology. Nor, more broadly, is it merely about freedom from the dark forces of superstition and religious authority, or about a delightful gift of personal empowerment and political liberty.

The death of God in the ultimate sense involves, in addition, the end of even deeper beliefs: that there is a state of timeless peace for which it is worth striving; that what is constant and enduring is more valuable than what is transient and in flux; that our sufferings can be justified in terms of some greater and indestruc-tible good to which they contribute – such as happiness, art, knowledge, liberty, or indeed love itself.

Nietzsche never got round to asking about how the death of God in this ulti-mate sense would change the nature of love. But his entire attack on the idea that there are values or states of being conceived as unconditional and eternal begs this question. How might love be enriched if it were freed from servitude to these beliefs? What would it be for love to overcome the sickness that Nietzsche sees in Western civilisation: its obsession with escaping suffering and loss and its whole religion of comfortableness? This is a challenge posed by Nietzsche to the modern world that he did so much to bring into being – a challenge that has yet to be seriously addressed.

15

Love as a history of loss
Freud

Nietzsche had enthroned psychology as 'the queen of the sciences' and 'the path to the fundamental problems'.[1] By this he meant that the key to discovering who we moderns are, and what the best life is for the type of person that each of us is fated to be, is to uncover our deepest – often unconscious – drives, instincts, and desires. And, above all, to harness their complex urges for power in a way that affirms life and fate.

Only in these psychological depths can we determine what ends, what values, what virtues will enable us to flourish. Only down there – rather than in asking what is morally the right thing to do, or what will maximise happiness, or what favours reproductive fitness, or what religions and other ideologies command – can we understand why we 'choose' the values we do, what functions they really play in our lives, and which values might be better suited to us.

As Nietzsche was succumbing to his final madness, two writers were in the early stages of a lifetime's work that would give dazzling form to this prophecy – and would do so in a manner that was in effect a declaration of war on the dominant Western conception of love, reaching back through Romanticism and Christianity to Plato and biblical Judaism. They were Sigmund Freud (1856–1939) and Marcel Proust (1871–1922).

Both these poet-thinkers of Jewish descent remain fascinating, however unfashionable their theories have become, because they fearlessly explore the minority view that sees love as animated by crude drives that can never be stably satisfied or cured of their potential for destruction; a view that finds intimate human attachments puzzling and, in many ways, sinister; a view, too, that has thoroughly eliminated God from its world picture.

Freud and Proust deny that human separateness can be overcome; or that we can really heed or affirm the other person for who they are; or that love is the place to look for pure goodness and harmony; or that its joys dwarf and even make good the trials of living. In this, their trail had already been blazed by Lucretius, as well as by Schopenhauer's recasting of romantic love as the expression of relentless sexual desire. But they go far beyond Lucretius and Schopenhauer in the psychological detail that fills their vast narratives of love's repeatedly frustrated and often violent search for satisfaction – and in their tracing the workings of erotic love back to childhood attachments and our anguished need for warmth and security, initially through the attentive presence of our mother. Above all they refuse the consolation that human love can ever transcend its fundamental selfishness.

But what exactly is the nature of this selfishness?

In his earlier thought Freud[2] suggests that *all* love is the expression of sexual energy that desires release and pleasure. Though he calls this energy 'libido', and conceives it as a drive that pervades human existence, its core aim is tactile stimulation, which by a certain age comes to be concentrated in the desire for intercourse.

He doesn't mince his words: the 'nucleus' of love, of whatever sort, consists in 'sexual love with sexual union as its aim'. He explicitly includes here self-love, love for parents and children, friendship, and love for humanity in general – as well as devotion to concrete objects and to abstract ideas.[3]

Sexual desire – like, for Freud, all drives – is both innate and insatiable: it neither needs an external stimulus to get it going nor can any satisfaction finally calm it. Its gratification produces pleasure and its frustration pain – pleasure and pain being, in this scheme, the twin masters of human action. Indeed, because of its power in human life and the numerous obstacles to its satisfaction, Freud comes to see libido as our main source of psychic tension and pain.

When it does encounter objects that satisfy it, libido will tend to form attachments to them – what Freud calls 'cathexes'; and this satisfaction is accompanied, he says, by the most intense pleasure available to our bodies: that of genital gratification. Once we find this out sex becomes a model for all gratification and the central drive of our life:

> man's discovery that sexual (genital) love afforded him the strongest experiences
> of satisfaction, and in fact provided him with the prototype of all happiness, must

have suggested to him that he should continue to seek the satisfaction of happiness in his life along the path of sexual relations and that he should make genital erotism the central point of his life.[4]

What is going on here? It seems absurd to claim that we crave intercourse with ourselves, with a landscape, or with humanity as a whole; and only slightly less strange that sexuality should be the 'nucleus' of our love for siblings and parents.

But Freud doesn't think this is necessarily absurd. All love, he suggests – although very vaguely – exhibits sexuality's core *desire* for union or its tendency to self-sacrifice. In the many situations where sexual intimacy is either taboo – as between parents and their children – or outright impossible – as in love for nature or abstract ideas – libido must be diverted from its naïve aim of genital union and instead find non-sexual outlets. This is 'aim-inhibited' love and its expressions are 'sublimations' of the original energy – in other words, a channelling of love's energy towards higher, more creative, more refined ends, such as art and thought, or political and social organisation. Sublimation for Freud (as before him for Nietzsche) is therefore a powerful engine of civilisation, and the absolute need to inhibit erotic desire is behind many of humanity's greatest achievements.

Aim-inhibition begins in earliest childhood. It is a matter of survival to check our libidinal drive when it could arouse the hostility of those on whose love and protection we depend: at first our mother, then both our parents, then the other carers of childhood, later society more broadly. Life, so Freud's early thought goes, is an unrelenting contest between the needs of self-preservation, driven by what he called 'ego-instincts', and the insistent demand of the libido for sexual gratification.

◆ ◆ ◆

Unconsciously, though, every relationship of love remains unabashedly sexual in its motivation. Libido can be restrained or retrained with the full might of taboo, self-preservation, and sublimation, but beneath it all it lives on: 'Love with an inhibited aim was in fact originally fully sensual love, and *it is so* still in man's unconscious.'[5] Left to their natural devices, the thought implies, all our love relationships – with parents, friends, children, the lot – would seek sexual satisfaction.

Indeed sexuality is so fundamental for Freud, at least in his earlier thinking, that the development of the infant is inexplicable without it. The 'first and most

significant of *all* sexual relations',[6] he says, is the infant's relationship to his
mother's breast. As the child emerges from infancy and encounters other people
who protect and satisfy it, its relationship to them, too, 'is on the model of, and
a continuation of, their relation as sucklings to their nursing mother.'[7] Freud
claims that a 'child's intercourse with anyone responsible for his care affords him
an unending source of sexual excitation and satisfaction from his erotogenic
zones' – especially when the carer, beginning with his mother, 'herself regards
him with feelings that are derived from her own sexual life: she strokes him,
kisses him, rocks him and quite clearly treats him as a substitute for a complete
sexual object.'[8]

In saying all this, Freud doesn't mean that the infant actually desires genital
intercourse with his mother. At that very early stage such a specific aim – indeed
desire in any meaningful sense, with its intentionality and its notions of another
person from whom one expects something – cannot yet have formed. His or
her emphasis is much more on the pleasures of tactile stimulation. These are
experienced first through the oral and anal areas, which are highly sensitive to
stimulation, and later in almost any area of the body. Freud thinks that a focus
on non-genital intimacy by the infant marks a specific stage in our development,
which, like all stages, remains in the adult. (But in the fetishist, he speculates, it
survives in fixations that replace genital intimacy and prevent the development
of full sexual relationships.)

Yet this immense emphasis on sexuality to explain human attachment seems
unwarranted and restrictive – and Freud himself came to admit nearly complete
confusion about what exactly his theory of libido was trying to say. In the first
place it does not succeed in explaining why the infant's pleasure in receiving
warmth and nourishment is sexual, rather than related to the broader delights of
intimacy, or why his mother experiences their bond, including its physical
aspects, in sexual terms. Nor is it clear that the primitive relationship with which
all his later loves resonate is with the mother's breast, rather than the whole
spectrum of relatings between infant and mother. The many forms of touching,
seeing, hearing, protecting, connecting, and nurturing must all be important
ways in which intimacy between a child and his parents can be experienced and
symbolised.

In adult relationships, too, it isn't plausible that libidinal energy can account
for such diverse phenomena as the longing for proximity between friends and
the love of humanity or of abstract objects; nor is it clear how it might explain

the complexities of trust and jealousy. Our needs for tenderness, kindness and solidarity are not reducible to libido that is inhibited from its natural aim of genital gratification. And to see all love as either aim-inhibited or aim-uninhibited libido fails to do justice to the rich motives for intimacy that we have seen in the history of love.

✦ ✦ ✦

Freud's account of human development is much more powerful when he comes to explore how love and its loss forge our sense of selfhood: how they enable us to recognise our independent existence as individuals, separate from others.[9]

At first, he suggests, the infant has no sense of being a self. Though he gets sensual satisfaction and emotional comfort at his mother's breast, he can't *experience* his mother and her breast as their source or himself as their recipient. In his state of 'primary narcissism' he can't yet distinguish his own existence from people or things beyond him. Or to put it in more up-to-date language:[10] if the child receives good enough care from his mother, he will come to experience her as under his omnipotent control, though separate from him in other respects.

A proper sense of self in other words of being the subject of his own experiences – arises, Freud suggests, out of the first trauma that afflicts every human being: the loving mother isn't always available for the infant when he wants her. The infant gradually learns that neither the physical satisfaction he receives at the mother's breast nor her responsiveness to his needs is controllable, and so must be distinct from his desire:

> An infant at the breast does not as yet distinguish his ego from the external world as the source of the sensations flowing in upon him. He gradually learns to do so, in response to various promptings. He must be very strongly impressed by the fact that some sources of excitation, which he will later recognise as his own bodily organs, can provide him with sensations at any moment, whereas other sources evade him from time to time – among them what he desires most of all, his mother's breast . . . In this way there is for the first time set over against the ego an 'object', in the form of something which exists 'outside' and which is only forced to appear by a special action.[11]

Later this lesson is reinforced by yet another rupture: his learning that he has a competitor for his mother – in the form of his father, towards whom he develops deeply ambivalent feelings, both admiring and fearing him[12] (indeed fearing him to the point where, according to Freud's notion of the Oedipus Complex, he wishes to kill him). Still later, at around the age of five, he begins to realise that his parents, at whom he has directed so much libidinal energy, aren't available to provide the degree of gratification that he craves.

These ruptures force upon us the sense that an external world exists, which doesn't respond perfectly to our wishes; and so a boundary is formed around our own person:

> originally the ego includes everything, later it separates off an external world from itself. Our present ego-feeling is, therefore, only a shrunken residue of a much more inclusive – indeed, an all-embracing – feeling which corresponded to a more intimate bond between the ego and the world about it.[13]

We therefore become individuals through the constant (and often disappointed) struggle to secure loved ones – in the first place our mother, and then our father – whose loss or power terrifies us, and whose independent reality, indeed selfhood, we eventually have to concede.

✦ ✦ ✦

But we concede it only up to a point. The battle to control these crucial individuals by whose loss and power we feel relentlessly threatened continues by another means: internalising (or 'introjecting') them. We domesticate them by taking them psychically into ourselves. By making them part of us.

This is the process that Freud calls 'identification' and he pictures it as the 'cannibalistic incorporation of the other person'.[14] It is a picture of great power, for eating another person is a symbol of violent, perhaps total, possession; and the stage of development at which this begins (the 'oral' phase) is when our relationship to our world – in other words to our mother – is still mediated by our mouth.

The point is clearly not to destroy our loved ones, but to preserve them – for ourselves. Plato had, of course, already seen love as a craving for permanent possession of the good. But Freud knows that however well our objects of love reciprocate this craving it is unfulfillable. The very essence of love is to fail. Permanent possession of what we desire – of what we deem to be a great good – is impossible. This is love's tragic nature.

Love's refusal to accept this failure must lead to violence. Though wise individuals might come close to acceptance, the infant (and the infantile in the adult) obviously cannot. And so, wracked by a feeling of impotence, he is tender towards loved ones, yet brutal in his desire for them. He affirms them, whether or not they love him back; yet when they don't, he also thirsts for revenge.

Revenge, of course, needn't be directed at the original cause of his suffering. Everyday experience all too often confirms Freud's claim that 'acts of revenge can be directed against the wrong people' because punishment 'must be exacted even if it does not fall upon the guilty'.[15] If love is sufficiently frustrated, Freud implies, it will always be on the lookout for scapegoats.

+ + +

Such contradictory feelings towards our primal objects of love are not in themselves 'pathological'. To seek to possess someone who is all-powerful over us; to feel both tender and vengeful towards them; to identify with them both insofar as they gratify us and insofar as they frustrate us; to cannibalise them and yet to set them up as our inner lords and masters – all this belongs to love.

And to the individual's formation. The selfhood that began to be forged when we recognised our parents as distinct from us is developed by turning them into ourselves. Specifically, we appropriate their values and methods of parenting to the point where we form that inner moral policeman or conscience that Freud calls the 'super-ego'. Then we love in ourselves the very things we love in them. We reproach ourselves for the very things that we reproach in them. And, in a peculiar inversion in the direction of aggressiveness, we also reproach ourselves for the very things *they reproach in us*. As Freud remarks, 'identification endeavours to mould a person's own ego after the fashion of the one that has been taken as a model'.[16] (As so often: to possess is to be possessed.)

In other words, identification with our parents creates the foundation of our values and so of how we judge and relate to ourselves. Freud expresses this thought by claiming that our identification with mother and father is crucial to establishing the ruling 'ego ideal by which the ego measures itself, which it emulates, and whose demand for ever greater perfection it strives to fulfil.' 'There is no doubt', he adds, 'that this ego ideal is the precipitate of the old picture of the parents, the expression of admiration for the perfection which the child then attributed to them.'[17]

Here lies the origin of so much of our identity and self-esteem. And here, too, lies the source of guilt and self-punishment when we fail to live up to the ruling ideal.

Self-punishment, Freud notes in one of his brilliant asides, is not only painful but also affords the sort of pleasure to be gained from a stern and protective father. It is at the threshold of that strange world of masochism – satisfaction at being the object of violence and humiliation – which, Freud suspects, is, like sadism, 'strongly alloyed with eroticism'.[18] Thus, self-punishment pleasurably combines with the erotic instinct, so that 'even the subject's destruction of himself cannot take place without libidinal satisfaction'.[19]

And then there is the world beyond our parents: society with *its* values and strictures. Freud sees its relation to us in very similar terms to our mother and father: as a great authority, whose protection and love are crucial to our survival, and whose values and severity we also internalise, under the ever-present watch of our super-ego (or conscience). This internal enforcer can become incomparably more brutal than society, for not only our actions but also every passing intention and desire comes under its merciless scrutiny – potentially provoking equally merciless feelings of guilt.[20]

The stakes couldn't be higher. The extent to which our super-ego can love rather than hate our ego is crucial to our sense of being safe and indeed alive: 'To the ego,' Freud says, 'living means the same as being loved – being loved by the super-ego'.[21] If the ego is not adequately loved it will abandon the will to live, become melancholic, and eventually be overwhelmed by fear of death. Freud's technical language should not obscure his moving thought:

> The fear of death in melancholia only admits of one explanation: that the ego gives itself up because it feels itself hated and persecuted by the super-ego . . . The super-ego fulfils the same function of protecting and saving that was fulfilled in earlier days by the father and later by Providence or Destiny. But, when the ego finds itself in an excessive real danger which it believes itself unable to overcome by its own strength . . . [it] sees itself deserted by all protecting forces and lets itself die. Here, moreover, is once again the same situation as that which underlay the first great anxiety-state of birth and the infantile anxiety of longing – the anxiety due to separation from the protecting mother.[22]

In his talk of identification, and also of internalising the norms of the society in which we live and on which our very life depends, Freud expresses an ancient insight in psychoanalytic terms: love and law are indissolubly linked. As we saw in the Old Testament and also, contrary to much received wisdom about the New, in what Jesus himself said, the source of love is also the source of law. 'If you love me you will keep my commandments' (John 14:15). Protection and recognition come from the same place as the dictates of commandment and conscience.

In short: as we develop and grow we accumulate a succession of incorporated loved ones. All of whom we will also have experienced as lost, at least from time to time, and as bringing with them the ever-present possibility of further loss. (As we already saw in Plato, love desires possession; so if this is impossible there is no love without loss.)

These loved-and-lost ones become part of the 'stuffing' of which our individuality is formed. Through our internalisation of them, we increasingly experience ourselves as a locus of doings and actions, as a centre of responsibility. They are key to structuring our emerging selves: our self-regard, our ethics, our capacity to be agents. As Freud puts it: 'the character of the ego is a precipitate of abandoned object-cathexes and . . . it contains the history of those object-choices'.[23] To a great extent the 'I' is constituted by the history of its loves – and, most powerfully, by the history of its disappointed loves.

✦ ✦ ✦

This brings us to one of Freud's most influential ideas: our earliest loves also provide the model for our *future* loves. In adult life we remain stubbornly faithful to our identification with mother and father. Whom we love and how we love is shaped by the ideals that we once took over from our parents.

Especially by those ideals that we haven't managed to live up to ourselves. Freud's answer to the question 'Why her?' is more subtle than saying that we see in her a copy of our parents. It is that she

> serves as a substitute for some unattained ego ideal of our own. We love it [the object of our love] on account of the perfections which we have striven to reach for our own ego, and which we should now like to procure in this roundabout way as a means of satisfying our narcissism.[24]

We are scarcely aware, of course, that we are trying to live our unattained parental ideals through our loved one (and, as a result, that we are failing to see her for who *she* is). We have too perfectly internalised our parents to have the perspective needed for such awareness. Indeed, we began to assimilate mother and father so long before we had developed into anything recognisably like an 'I' that there *never was* a time at which we had a self uncolonised by their presence.

And so, no matter how individual and distinctive we have succeeded in becoming in adulthood, once we are in love regression to the primal and most familiar source of comfort is always on the cards.

By regression Freud doesn't mean that our development is unwound, or that our adult personality is dissolved back into something primitive – say, before we had a self at all. On his archaeological picture of the mind all our earlier stages of development tend to be preserved alongside its latest form.[25] The psyche and its instincts are astoundingly conservative, with a clear 'compulsion to repeat' established patterns.[26] So it is quite possible for earlier, less differentiated, stages to be suddenly reactivated – say, by falling in love – while leaving the later, more organised, ones perfectly intact. His assumption is 'that in mental life nothing which has once been formed can perish – that everything is somehow preserved and that in suitable circumstances (when, for instance, regression goes back far enough) it can once more be brought to light.'[27]

No feeling better exemplifies this possibility of regression, Freud suggests, than the rapturous union that lovers experience when the boundaries between them 'threaten to melt away' and they are overwhelmed by an 'oceanic' sense of being at one with the universe. Time stands still and their bond feels immortal. When lovers say that 'nothing else matters', they feel this, so Freud's theory implies, because they inhabit an undifferentiated psychic universe in which, in a sense, nothing else *could* matter. In the state to which they have regressed an 'I' has not yet developed that can experience itself as an individual distinct from an external world.

This sense of the unbounded – and so of the immortal – is not unlike religious or mystical feelings in which we also seem to stand outside our usual limited mode of being. Unlike religion, though, Freud doesn't consider love's regression pathological; for it is only a temporary blurring of the boundary between the ego and the external world – merely a phase in which we attribute to the external world things that clearly originate in our own ego.[28] Whereas in religious belief, Freud thinks, regression is more than an episode: it is a way of life.

Nonetheless, the regression that occurs in love is hardly a harbinger of sweetness and goodness. It recalls an infantile state where the other cannot yet be experienced as a distinct person with their own needs. The lovers might seem tenderly devoted to one another's welfare, but, in reality, Freud suggests, they are each seeking an essentially narcissistic satisfaction. Each is ruthlessly determined to possess the other as the object of his or her gratification; each is hell-bent on eliminating the anxiety of losing the other. Worse: because they have regressed to such a primitive stage of development, they are unaware of this tyranny; their emotional world is not one in which they could be concerned about another whom they can harm. It is a grim but extraordinary reinterpretation of what is going on in the loving merger, celebrated for centuries as the apogee of submission to the loved one; as the moment in which, in the cliché, we 'give ourselves' to her with all our 'body and soul'; as the most spiritual intimacy of which human beings are capable.

All illusions, Freud thinks. The very opposite is the case.

But love is Janus-faced: it points forwards – not just backwards. As well as stimulating regression to less individuated psychic states and causing psychic disruption, the erotic instincts also 'seek to combine more and more living substance into ever greater unities'.[29] Their main purpose, Freud says in his later thought, is that of 'uniting and binding'.[30]

Here Freud sees love less in terms of a sexual drive aiming at gratification and more as a drive towards unification. Love integrates our inner life by propelling us towards increasingly complex identification with the objects 'out there' in the world on which it fixes. As our libido invests the external world and its objects with value, they become real and significant for us; also richer in detail and more integrated in structure.

Key to this process of integration is that we claim, and affirm as our own, the basic instincts and values that drive us. If we develop successfully, those instincts don't get stuck as part of a split-off super-ego that behaves like a tyrannical moral censor before whom we feel helplessly guilty. Nor is our life hijacked by a libido-drive that charges ahead in its autonomous way, a libido-drive that originates in the chaotic, entirely unconscious, instinctual realm that Freud calls, in his late writing, 'das Es', the 'it' or (as commonly translated) the 'id'. Instead, such instincts and drives are brought within the fold of a unified and differentiated realm, 'das Ich', the 'ego', which is able to affirm them as its own and so exercises the sovereign responsibility of a master rather than the enforced responsibility of a slave.[31]

Such integration is the goal of psychoanalysis. Freud alludes to it in his clarion call: 'Where id was, there ego shall be' (*Wo Es war, soll Ich werden*).[32] In other words, whereas the id is wracked by contradictory drives 'which pursue their own purposes independently and regardless of one another', the ego tries to resolve such contradictions by abandoning one drive or urge in favour of another (as well as by sublimating or redirecting them) – in short by organising the drives into an integrated hierarchy.

Only when the ego is successful in this striving is it capable of genuine self-love.[33] A high level of psychic organisation – and the truces and harmonies between drives that this involves – would make possible a fresh attachment to oneself for becoming once again, if only to a limited extent, the self-sufficient source of one's own gratification.[34] To love oneself would be to achieve just such a self-attachment.

✦ ✦ ✦

If there is one theme that threads its way through Freud's thought on love it is this: the fundamental ambivalence of the lover. I love another insofar as he is a source of gratification, but I will hate him insofar as he inevitably proves unreliable in providing it. I recognise him as an independent self – surely a precondition for any developed relationship with him – only because of this unreliability, as a result of which I also hate him. Since love's possessive ambitions cannot be perfectly or finally fulfilled, anger and destruction are always latent in its desiring. Indeed the more powerful the love, the greater its potential for fury.

In his late writings Freud vastly expands the scope and nature of this ambivalence, turning it into something like a cosmic principle. All life, he speculates, is governed by the struggle between a drive towards unification and a drive towards disintegration. The unifying drive binds individuals – in pairs, families, nations, races, and ultimately in the whole that we call 'mankind'. And the disintegrative drive opposes this unification, aims at releasing the tension inherent in unities, and leads what is living back into an inorganic state.

Freud no longer calls the drive for unification 'libido', but renames it 'Eros' (and wrongly takes it to be identical to Plato's concept of the same name.[35]) And the opposing drive he calls the 'death instinct':

> Only by the concurrent or mutually opposing action of the two primal instincts – Eros and the death instinct – never by one or the other alone, can we explain the rich multiplicity of the phenomena of life.[36]

The death instinct, Freud claims, expresses the 'dominating tendency of mental life, and perhaps of nervous life in general . . . to reduce, to keep constant or to remove internal tension'.[37] To the extent that the state in which all such tension has been abolished is death, '*the aim of all life is death*'.[38]

Why did Freud feel the need to introduce the death instinct? Essentially because he came to believe that principles such as pleasure and self-preservation, regression and integration, though they could explain a great deal of human behaviour, could not account for a huge reality: the *scale* of human destructiveness. A reality, it would follow, that any attempt to explain love, whether for others or for oneself, has to take into account.

Towards themselves, Freud noted, people could behave in ways that cannot be explained by the aim of maximising pleasure or preservation. They might compulsively repeat painful traumas, returning again and again to the original scene of terror, just as 'There are people in whose lives the same reactions are perpetually being repeated uncorrected, to their own detriment'.[39] Not to mention, one might add, the many other ways in which people sabotage their own flourishing and success – and in the process suffer twice: from the failure and from its self-infliction.

Towards others, he rightly observed, destructive impulses are everywhere to be seen. History is an almost unbroken record of violence, from massacres and wars to less visible scenes of annihilation, in which urges to exploit, abuse, humiliate, torture and kill one's neighbour are on constant display. When the normal restraints on such cruelty are out of action, Freud says, it 'manifests itself spontaneously and reveals man as a savage beast to whom consideration towards his own kind is something alien':

> Anyone who calls to mind the atrocities committed during the racial migrations or the invasions of the Huns, or by the people known as Mongols under Jenghiz Khan and Tamerlane, or at the capture of Jerusalem by the pious Crusaders, or even, indeed, the horrors of the recent [First] World War – anyone who calls these things to mind will have to bow humbly before the truth of this view.[40]

One must seriously doubt whether the death instinct is needed to explain, in general, the intensity of human aggression or, in particular, behaviour towards oneself that violates the pleasure principle. What matters here, though, is how it entrenches Freud's vision of love's inextricable relation to hate and destruction. As so often, he articulates an ancient myth – that is, an ancient structure of explanation – in his new language of psychoanalysis. This structure of explanation is present in, among other places, Zoroastrianism (the religion dating from the sixth century BCE, or earlier, and deriving from the Iranian prophet Zoroaster), which held that we live in a moral universe in which good – embodied in a God who is also a force for unity – is in constant struggle with evil, a force for destruction and disintegration. It is present, as Freud recognises, in the cosmology of Empedocles (*c.* 492–*c.* 432 BCE), the Greek thinker who saw the whole universe as being governed by love and strife, whose struggle keeps nature in constant flux.[41] It is there in mainstream Christian notions, so ridiculed by Freud, of God and Satan (notions that were themselves influenced by Zoroastrianism). And it is there in Manicheism, also Zoroastrian in many of its elements, which arose in the third century CE and to which St Augustine belonged before he became a Christian.

There are wider problems with Freud's picture of the human soul, such as his immense emphasis on sexuality to explain love (and generally our interest in the world) – an emphasis that he himself eventually conceded was unsatisfactory; or his convoluted notions of how intention works in sexual desire; or the extent to which he seeks to explain the richness of human attachment in terms of the gratification of basic drives. Many things that I have ignored, such as his patriarchal bias, are, to put it mildly, questionable.

These sorts of problems, and a litany of further unsatisfactory assertions, have been assaulted by armies of critics, many of them brilliant, who rightly accuse Freud of making false claims to scientific accuracy, when it is quite obvious that there is no way of testing psychoanalytic theory that can begin to have the rigour of disciplines like physics, chemistry and biology.

But our concern here is not with scientific accuracy. If it were we could ignore almost the entire history of love as unverifiable nonsense, from the Jewish belief in a God who places love for him at the head of his commands to his people, to Plato's idea that love is a search for absolute beauty, to almost all Christian love that isn't based on Aristotle, to love-mysticism from the Renaissance to the Romantic period, and to any theory of sex that sees it as the beginning of a great ethical journey. Our concern is rather with how our Western conceptions of love have slowly been assembled. We want to know how, with all their internal incoherence and absurdity, they have come to have a grip over us so powerful that almost no contemporary relationship is free of their influence; and whether they really enable us to find the ontological grounding through forms of intense intimacy, which, I claim in this book, is love's deepest goal.

Here Freud is a figure whom we cannot ignore; indeed who still speaks more powerfully to our age than any other psychologist and perhaps any other thinker of the last hundred years. Concepts such as repression, regression, repetition, sublimation, projection, internalisation and libido saturate our language and structure the whole way in which we think of ourselves and our relations to others. The idea that childhood experiences, especially in love, form patterns that are repeated later in life is a hallowed cliché.

Freud is also of towering importance – and deeply plausible – in getting us to think about how an individual is constituted by the history of his loves and losses. How he might move back and forth between the various stages of this history. How mature love involves freeing oneself from infantile patterns and the ways in which they hold intimacy hostage to the terror of loss. How frustrated desire – be it sexual or otherwise – can be redirected into seemingly unrelated behaviour. How close normal sexual desire is to abnormal. How perversions easily become part of the fabric of our psyche. How hatred and anger are not only central to the development of love – if only because of the frustration and helplessness it involves – but pervade loving relationships and so imprison them in fundamental ambivalence. How love is the wellspring of the greatest ideals as well as being utterly amoral at its childish core. How the lover both gives to the loved one and is possessive of him to the point of cannibalising his psyche. How our capacity to love depends not upon innocence but upon loss of innocence.

These are fearsome thoughts. They issue in a tragic view of love as doomed to sabotage what it most wants. As lovers we crave union with another, whom we set up constantly to disappoint us (by projecting onto them ideals derived from the internalisation of our parents); whom we subject to the primitive urges of regressive states; and who, by virtue of their proximity and our desire for them, are inevitably on the receiving end of the vast forces of human destructiveness. And so 'almost every intimate emotional relation between two people which lasts for some time – marriage, friendship, the relations between parents and children – contains a sediment of feelings of aversion and hostility, which only escapes perception as a result of repression.'[42]

Though Lucretius and Schopenhauer to some extent anticipate Freud's thought, as do tragedians from Sophocles to Shakespeare, and Racine to Zola, he goes further than any other writer in suggesting that lovers not only cannot create a cocoon in which they are safe from humanity's murderous impulses, but inevitably nourish these very horrors within the confines of their intimacy. Because such horrors belong to the essence of life in general and of intimacy in particular. Worse: they belong there largely unknowingly, especially in love's most ecstatic unions.

Here Freud provides a necessary challenge to the cosy and in many ways complacent optimism of what love can be, which has prevailed at least since early Christianity – an optimism that, despite the difficulties it recognises in getting there, sees a consummation marked by perfection, bliss, harmony, understanding, cooperation, benevolence, truthfulness, and innocence.

Jesus is reported as saying that 'unless you change and become like children, you will never enter the kingdom of heaven' (Matthew 18:3). Insofar as the Kingdom of Heaven is taken to be the kingdom of love, this has been interpreted down the ages as meaning that to love well we must love as children do. In fact Jesus was talking about the need for humility and praising children's capacity for that.[43] But whether or not his followers misunderstood him, the belief that children's love is the most pure, unselfish, and giving – and that a loss of innocence harms rather than helps our capacity to love – has become a powerful view on love in the West. It is a view to which Freud's entire body of work stands in magisterial opposition, and which he has defied with a degree of imagination, detail, and conviction unmatched by any other thinker.

16

Love as terror and tedium
Proust

In Marcel Proust (1871–1922) we find a vivisection of love's protracted struggles to secure the ungraspable but fervently desired being of another, which is without parallel in the Western tradition. Beset by and forged out of a myriad illusions, associations and memories, love is revealed as a remorseless dialectic of anxiety and disappointment, hope and tedium, delight and dread – a dialectic resolved into some sort of stable attachment only by the final loss of the loved one, if at all.

Fear of isolation and helplessness structures love and gives it its tremendous urgency. Born in fear, living in fear and sometimes dying from fear, love chases the impossible goal of possessing a stranger whom we frantically and in many ways arbitrarily anoint as 'the one', even though she might not actually be to our taste. We see her as offering our life a new berth, and lunge at this vision – often a mere mirage – with a will stymied by its own ruthlessness and confusion.

If we nonetheless manage to live harmoniously with her, this is the result less of genuine appreciation of her merits, or of our honesty and openness with one another, than of something quite different: the genius of habit, which can bless and stabilise almost any situation in which we have trapped ourselves.

Indeed, whether she is honest and open with us might have little effect on whether we love her: 'A person has no need of sincerity, nor even of skill in lying, in order to be loved. Here I mean by love reciprocal torture.'[1] Thus speaks Marcel, the narrator of Proust's monumental work, *A la recherche du temps perdu*, of his relationship with Albertine, the woman he craves, despises, desires, suspects, admires, disdains, and misunderstands.

And yet, like almost the whole Western tradition before him, the Narrator cannot resist seeing in love *the* great opportunity for life's redemption. To read Proust is not only to have our eyes opened to the power and resourcefulness of love's immoralism; not only to see how profoundly love is structured by suffering, animated by deceit, and anaesthetised by boredom; not only to find unsurpassed portrayals of jealousy, cruelty, indifference, and narcissism. It is also to be reminded of the tremendous, perhaps insuperable, Western craving for life's sufferings to be redeemed in a supreme good: in this case, in a work of art that will incorporate and justify the pain described by the Narrator over nearly three thousand pages and that could not have been created without it.

Thus a narrative whose virtuosic pessimism appears to struggle against the dominant Western love tradition and its furious desire for harmony, security, eternity and unconditional affirmation, turns out to perpetuate that tradition by other means.

❖ ❖ ❖

The torture might be redeemable in the end, but if it is so protracted what keeps the Narrator riveted to Albertine? Even after he has repeatedly decided that she is feckless, manipulative, a deceiver, and uninteresting to boot? What is the hope that gives love its stupendous persistence?

The answer seems to be nothing less than to discover and possess ultimate being – in another human being, in nature, in things in general.[2] And so to feel complete: 'Love, in the pain of anxiety as in the bliss of desire, is a demand for a whole' (3:102). It arises from the corrosive pain of aloneness, which yearns to be assuaged by the absolute presence of a loved one. If all human beings have an urge to love and be loved it is because all human beings suffer from isolation and helplessness.

Love's insane desire is therefore to possess the loved one so perfectly that all vulnerability will be abolished. It pursues this dream by every means – seduction, kindness, cajoling, persuasion, domination, cruelty, imagination, and not least by that uniquely powerful attempt at union: sexual intercourse.

But the hope of possessing another is doomed to disappointment. Does anyone, or for that matter anything, have an ultimate reality to possess? And even if they do, and even if we could locate that reality, aren't other people too capricious, too self-absorbed, too opaque, to be possessible? They might love us back, but they still live their own lives and disappear from time to time in ways that we can't predict or control.

◆ ◆ ◆

Like Freud, Proust traces our need for primal security and its inevitable frustration back to the infant's anxious longing for mother – and its dawning realisation that it lives in a world of individuals whose attentiveness isn't constant: who arrive only to vanish again.

The Narrator recalls how, as a boy, he had yearned for his mother's goodnight kiss and waited expectantly for her to come to his bedroom; how even before he had received the comfort he craved he had feared its ending – her departure:

> My sole consolation when I went upstairs for the night was that Mamma would come in and kiss me after I was in bed. But this good night lasted for so short a time, she went down again so soon, that the moment in which I heard her climb the stairs . . . was for me a moment of the utmost pain; for it heralded the moment which was bound to follow it, when she would have left me and gone downstairs again. So much so that I reached the point of hoping that this good night which I loved so much would come as late as possible, so as to prolong the time of respite during which Mamma would not yet have appeared (1·13–14)

Later in life, the Narrator draws an explicit parallel between the pain he felt as a child on those occasions when his mother would leave him at night with at best a tepid kiss, and his agonies when, after they have argued, Albertine does the same thing. On these occasions, she, like his mother, seems frighteningly detached; even if he gets a kiss from her she is absent from it. Yet, as an adult, he cannot demand that she appease his anguish in the way that he used to ask of his mother:

> It was no longer the peace of my mother's kiss . . . that I felt when I was with Albertine on these evenings, but, on the contrary, the anguish of those on which my mother scarcely bade me good-night, or even did not come up to my room at all, either because she was cross with me or was kept downstairs by guests . . . But if I felt the same anguish as in my childhood, the different person who caused me to feel it, the difference in the feeling she inspired in me, the very

transformation in my character, made it impossible for me to demand its appeasement from Albertine as in the old days from my mother. I could no longer say: 'I'm unhappy.' . . . As in the old days . . . when my mother had left me without soothing me with her kiss, I wanted to rush after Albertine, I felt that there would be no peace for me until I had seen her again[.] (3:107–8)

Adult love doesn't exactly repeat childhood patterns. It is more ambitious and more unstable. It seeks, in a way that the infant couldn't, the essence of the loved one – and a union with that essence which will feel 'complete'. It seeks to know and understand the other, and repeatedly comes up against their maddening obscurity. Yet for all the fury of its desire to possess, it is, like the rhythm of sexual arousal and satiety, ambivalent through and through: the person it craves one minute it casts aside the next; the anxieties that it yearns to be free of it also clings to; it yo-yoes between desire and disgust.[3]

And so the adult cannot expect to be loved back with the clarity of a mother's love – for him love is less satisfying than for the child, though he has more possible sources of reassurance (there are, in theory at least, various lovers to choose from as well as non-human loves, such as nature, learning, and work). Eros can be as mercurial as it is powerful. It is a force of staggering complexity and flux.

The Narrator doesn't, therefore, see the adult's desire for union as involving a regression to the infant's need for mother and so to a more primitive form of psychic structure. Nor is he ever tempted to see all our concern with the world as an investment of *sexual* energy in it[4] (though he does ascribe desire a role in all our artistic and intellectual endeavours,[5] and sexual images are prominent in his depictions of physical objects[6]). Proust isn't reheated Freud. Instead, the infant's desire for mother is merely the first, if most powerful, expression of this universal human search for security.

✦ ✦ ✦

To read Proust is to feel that of all life's great projects none is beset by such a gulf between ends and means as is love – between vaulting ambition and the confused, cack-handed ways in which we pursue it.

The obstacles to success in love, and especially in 'romantic' love, begin with the arbitrariness of our choices. We somehow alight on one person, in whom we invest all our hopes – until we are disillusioned and think of moving on to the next. Why do we pick her out before we can possibly know that there is a 'fit' between us? Before we have the faintest sense of who she – or he – is?

The Narrator sees a little band of girls on the beach at Balbec, 'as noble as if it had been composed of Hellenic virgins' (1:853). They walk 'with the control of gesture that comes from the perfect suppleness of one's own body and a sincere contempt for the rest of humanity' (1:847). They are beautiful, hard, and frivolous; all are confident to the point of insolence (1:848). And at first he is smitten with all of them: as goddesses of beauty presiding over a magically carefree world they are interchangeable for him. One will do as well as the next.

Then he notices one, pushing a bicycle, 'with brilliant, laughing eyes and plump, matt cheeks . . . using slang terms so typically of the gutter' (1:850). Unexpectedly she throws him a 'smiling, sidelong glance, aimed from the centre of that inhuman world which enclosed the life of this little tribe, an inaccessible, unknown world wherein the idea of what I was could certainly never penetrate or find a place' (1:851).

Though the Narrator finds her common, juvenile and lacking in virtue – very contrary, in other words, to his rather refined tastes; though he feels that he could never be understood by her; though it seems impossible that there could be a real meeting of spirits with this girl, or with anyone in that crowd – nonetheless, as when Dante encountered Beatrice, this one glance is all he needs to fall in love with her, and so to desire to possess her and her whole life:

I knew that I should never possess this young cyclist if I did not possess also what was in her eyes. And it was consequently her whole life that filled me with desire; a sorrowful desire because I felt that it was not to be fulfilled, but an exhilarating one because what had hitherto been my life having ceased all of a sudden to be my whole life, being no more now than a small part of the space stretching out before me which I was burning to cover and which was composed of the lives of these girls . . . (1:852)

If the Narrator has any explanation for his fixation on this unknown girl (who turns out to be Albertine), it is that her mysterious world – full of things he doesn't have, like confidence, diffidence, laughter, and youth – might arouse in his sated soul a new thirst 'akin to that with which a parched land burns' (1:852). She offers relief from familiarity with himself.

But no sooner has this reason occurred to him than he recalls that, actually, his 'inaccessible ideal' (1:852) is a woman with reddish hair – whereas she has dark hair. But where did *that* strange ideal come from? Not from a love of reddish hair as such, he tells us, but because a girl with such hair, named Gilberte, whom he had desired a long time ago, had been the friend of an author called Bergotte, whom the Narrator venerated and into whose literary world he longed to enter. Because he venerated Bergotte he fell in love with Gilberte, and because she had red hair, this became his ideal.

So why then does he fall in love with Albertine? Because, it seems, she is the first to look at him, and he rejoices in this glance not because of anything peculiar to her but because it promises to introduce him to all the *other* girls, one of whom he might one day befriend. Perhaps his passion isn't after all for Albertine as such but for the intoxicating reality to which she gestures. Perhaps he loved Bergotte for the same reason. And Gilberte. As the Narrator says quite explicitly:

> The belief that a person has a share in an unknown life to which his or her love may win us admission is, of all the prerequisites of love, the one which it values most highly . . . (1:108)

So there might be a dreadful combination of randomness and fatedness about our choices in love. What is fated – or at least far from arbitrary – is the 'unknown life' into which we wish to enter. What is random is the person we choose to lead us to this life.

Proust writes that the *sort* of person we love is determined by our own fixed temperament which seeks out those who are either opposite or complementary to ourselves. Above all, 'the coupling of contrary elements is the law of life . . . As a rule we detest what resembles ourselves' (3:103).[7] The cultured might seek the uncultured; the sensitive the hard; the nervy the calm. We desire that being who affords us 'that prolongation, that possible multiplication of oneself, which is happiness' (1:852).

✦ ✦ ✦

Thus we lie in wait, perhaps for years, for the person whose unknown world will, we imagine, delight and affirm us. Then someone turns up who appears to be her. Like the girls on the beach she is tantalisingly unattainable. Her enchanted world feels hermetically cut off from us. Her inner life is a mystery. We can hardly believe that this nymph could desire just *us*.

This elusiveness is exactly what sets our imagination on fire:

> This evanescence of persons who are not known to us . . . urges us into that state of pursuit in which there is no longer anything to stem the tide of imagi- nation. To strip our pleasures of imagination is to reduce them to their own dimensions, that is to say to nothing. (1:853)

We are 'sick with despair' at the thought that we might never be able to sample such beauty; that instead we will be forced to console ourselves by demanding pleasure from 'women whom we have not desired, so that we die without ever having known what that other pleasure was' (1:855). The loved one – unknown, unknowable, the embodiment of 'all that is most mysterious in the beauty which we desire' (1:855) – inspires cascades of images in our mind, many of them ill- defined but all promising supreme happiness.

There is no chance that we will see her for who she is: 'it is the tragedy of other people that they are merely showcases for the very perishable collec- tions of one's own mind' (3:568). And by 'finding' in her exactly what we have been seeking, our love for her seems inevitable – how else could it be that we encountered this one person in a million? Though of course it *isn't* inevitable, as the Narrator later realises of his love for Albertine: 'it was not therefore – as I so longed, so needed to believe – absolutely necessary and predestined' (2:408).

But what if no one shows up who promises to satisfy our desires, however long we wait? What then?

Well, the Narrator suggests, we can simply invent her. In other words we can fall in love with someone who exists solely in our imagination. He remembers a walk he used to take as a child through the countryside, along the Méséglise way. Overcome by its beauty, he wanted to express his rapture, but found that all he could manage were pathetically inadequate gestures: '. . . seeing upon the water, and on the surface of the wall, a pallid smile responding to the smiling sky, I cried aloud in my enthusiasm, brandishing my furled umbrella: "Gosh, gosh, gosh, gosh!"' (1:169–70). The inarticulacy of his delight made him feel helpless: 'my shouts of happiness,' he says, were 'no more than expressions of the confused ideas which exhilarated me, and which had not achieved the repose of enlightenment, preferring the pleasures of a lazy drift towards an immediate outlet rather than submit to a slow and difficult course of elucidation' (1:169).

An immediate outlet would be a woman who, at a stroke, makes him one with this nature and spares him the effort of discovering his own relationship to it. Since no one is actually to hand, he duly conjures up a peasant girl whom he might clasp with his whole being. She personifies the landscape that so enchants him. Its beauty belongs to her alone and only she, he convinces himself, can disclose its mysteries: 'to wander thus among the woods of Roussainville without a peasant-girl to embrace was to see those woods and yet know nothing of their secret treasure, their deep-hidden beauty' (1:171). And, he assures himself, these beauties of nature which she vouchsafes him will, in their turn, enlarge 'what I might have found too restricted in the charms of the woman' (1:171).[8]

✦ ✦ ✦

'What I might have found too restricted in the charms of the woman'. These last words are key to Proust's understanding of love. The peasant girl has barely taken shape in the Narrator's mind before he worries about being restricted by her. She has to point to, and be enriched by, some bigger reality – the magnificence of the surrounding nature – in order for the thought of grasping her, which just a moment ago had been his fervent desire, to be tolerable. The urge to possess, he suggests, is undermined by its own success.

Which is what happens in real life for the Narrator. When he eventually gets Albertine he is soon oppressed by boredom. The reason is clear: 'love is kept in existence only by painful anxiety . . . It is born, and it survives, only if some part remains for it to conquer. We love only what we do not wholly possess' (3:102). This is a variant of the old adage that love is about the chase and not the quarry: the adage that is every day confirmed by the many men and women who are attracted only to the unavailable – only, say, to someone married or unresponsive – and who lose interest as soon as he or she can be attained.

To fall out of love with someone doesn't, however, ensure that we will now see her 'realistically'. On the contrary: one set of illusions will merely replace another, so that rather than overrating her we will underrate her. Instead of being dazzled by her perfection we are likely to be horrified by her dullness. Instead of being unable to believe our good fortune, we will feel unfairly lumbered with misfortune. Instead of feeling that she is 'made' for us she will come to seem alien. As Swann, another great lover in Proust's novel, says: 'To think that I've wasted years of my life, that I've longed to die, that I've experienced my greatest love, for a woman who didn't appeal to me, who wasn't even my type!' (1:415). This is not unlike the Narrator's attitude to Albertine when he feels he has finally secured her.

And so elusiveness and boredom are the twin masters of their love, the driving forces of its gruesome dialectic – a distant echo of Plato's suggestion that Poverty and Plenty (which also induce desire and satiety) are the parents of Eros. Both these terrors contribute to love's despair. Elusiveness arouses possessiveness. Familiarity generates indifference.

Worse: possessiveness and indifference can succeed each other at a moment's notice. Desperate longing can abruptly give way to the desire to escape. At one point the Narrator is convinced that he no longer loves Albertine. He has looked into his heart, examined it minutely, and the verdict is clear. He finds her vapid, tedious; it is time to seek other women. How little self-knowledge he really has, how difficult it is for a lover to read his own heart, becomes clear minutes later when he is abruptly told that 'Mademoiselle Albertine has gone!' His decision to leave her is at once replaced by certainty that he loves her.

> A moment before, in the process of analysing myself, I had believed that this separation without having seen each other again was precisely what I wished, and, comparing the mediocrity of the pleasures that Albertine afforded me with the richness of the desires which she prevented me from realising ... I had felt that I was being subtle, had concluded that I no longer wished to see her, that I no longer loved her. But now these words: 'Mademoiselle Albertine has gone,' had produced in my heart an anguish such that I felt I could not endure it much longer[.] (3:425)[9]

Love, so often taken as the gold standard of constancy, is subject to the wildest swings. Only the pain of the other's unattainability keeps it in being. But attaining her also causes pain – the pain of boredom. Either way we suffer. Suffering is the destiny of love. As the Narrator remarks, 'I must choose to cease from suffering or to cease from loving' (3:101).

✦ ✦ ✦

We might love only what we do not wholly possess; but can we, in fact, ever be said to 'possess' anybody? The answer seems to be a resounding no.

The first problem is that if our loved ones 'are merely showcases for the very perishable collections of one's own mind' (3:568) then what we are trying to possess exists not in them but merely in our own imagination. In pursuing them we are chasing our own shadow. Their reality barely enters into it.

And there is a deeper problem: the very idea of possession depends upon a conception of the human self as something compact, with a stable core that defines it and that we can, almost literally, 'grasp'. The lover assumes that even if the other person can't be fully known, or is unpredictable, they have an enduring 'core' that can somehow be embraced. This is what the Narrator believes when he thinks that Albertine is his.

But what if a better picture of a person – at least when we are in love with them – is a being 'scattered in space and time, . . . a series of events on which we can throw no light, a series of insoluble problems, a sea which, like Xerxes, we scourge with rods in an absurd attempt to punish it for what it has engulfed' (3:99–100)? How is possession supposed to work then? Do we think we can possess events scattered in space and time? '[W]e cannot touch all these points' (3:95), says the Narrator. And even if we could, new events, new points in space and time, will soon burst into being, and perhaps just where we didn't expect them. We will have gained 'possession' of aspects of our lover's existence – only for the continuous flux that is a human life to have already moved on. Possession of a life – of 'the whole' – will be, in principle, impossible.

So too will be that hallowed virtue of love: sincerity. Sincerity assumes that we have a coherent and stable self which we can accurately express. And moreover a self that we wish to know – and can know, or else how could we be sure that we are expressing our 'real' feelings?

If, however, we don't have such a coherent self, if we are like moving points scattered in space and time, with no fixed or even definable dimensions – or, to change the image, if we are successive selves that come and go without discernible logic – then isn't sincerity another of those pious fictions that obscure our lack of mastery over living – and loving? Moreover, supposing we could catch and know one of these fleeting forms, would we really want to do so? For we are – and strive to remain – a stranger to ourselves, in fact the stranger 'to whom we lie the most because he is the one whose contempt would be most painful to us' (2:907).

And there is another, perhaps more obvious, impediment to sincerity: even in those rare moments when we are able and willing to know our feelings, it is extraordinarily difficult to give accurate expression to them. Recalling his walks on the Méséglise way the Narrator realises that

> most of our attempts to translate our innermost feelings do no more than relieve us of them by drawing them out in a blurred form which does not help us to identify them. When I try to reckon up all that I owe to the Méséglise way, all the humble discoveries of which it was either the fortuitous setting or the direct inspiration and cause, I am reminded that it was in that same autumn . . . that I was struck for the first time by this discordance between our impressions and their habitual expression. (1:169)

What of sex? The whole person might be elusive, but can we not be said to possess a loved one in some way through sex?

Again the answer is no. The intimacy of sex tantalises us with the vast hinterland of the other person, but gives us almost no access to it. We might experience love-making as a moment of possession, but in reality, the Narrator says, we possess nothing. This is already obvious in that first step: the kiss. As soon as we press our lips to somebody we hit a barrier that reminds us of the impossibility of attaining their depths:

> a pair of lips, designed to convey to the palate the taste of whatever whets their appetite, must be content, without understanding their mistake or admitting their disappointment, with roaming over the surface and with coming to a halt at the barrier of the impenetrable but irresistible cheek. (2:377–8)

The Narrator's presentation of the way sexual exploration is brought to such an abrupt halt is almost comical.[10] And, he makes clear, any hope that we will somehow secure the ultimate reality of the other is further dashed by the ways in which sex, like all love, is perverted by the lovers' egotism and despair, illusion and greed, fear and rivalry.

And by sadism. In an event which he recounts just after his recollection of the walks near Roussainville, the Narrator is lying in some bushes and happens to see a young woman, Mlle Vinteuil, and her lesbian lover lustily desecrating the portrait of Mlle Vinteuil's recently-dead father. The old man, a village music teacher, had apparently sacrificed everything for his daughter; and she, the custodian of his memory and supposedly in mourning for him, incites her 'vicious' friend to this act of impiety:

> This photograph was evidently in regular use for ritual profanations, for the friend replied in words which were clearly a liturgical response: 'Let him stay there. He can't bother us any longer. D'you think he'd start whining, and wanting to put your overcoat on for you, if he saw you now with the window open, the ugly old monkey?' . . . [Mlle Vinteuil] could not resist the attraction of being treated with tenderness by a woman who had shown herself so implacable toward the defenceless dead, and, springing on to her friend's lap she held out a chaste brow to be kissed precisely as a daughter would have done, with the exquisite sensation that they would thus, between them, inflict the last turn of the screw of cruelty by robbing M. Vinteuil, as though they were actually rifling his tomb, of the sacred rights of fatherhood. (1:177–8)

The scene culminates with Mlle Vinteuil daring her lover to spit on her father's photo.

What is all this about? Is this just a woman, whom we learn has essentially a 'virtuous mind' and much goodness and gentleness besides, self-consciously enjoying a taste of cruelty? (Cruelty is a usually unseen leitmotif of our relations with one another, but in the play of sex it is easier to imagine it as merely a joke.) Or, by contrast, is the Narrator right to wonder whether she was *failing* to discern in herself – alongside her virtue, her respect for the dead, and her filial affection – 'that indifference to the sufferings one causes which . . . is the most terrible and lasting form of cruelty' (1:180)? Indeed, as I suggested in my discussion of Rousseau in chapter 11, our hearts might be hardest – we might be least capable of pity – towards precisely the suffering that we ourselves inflict.

And isn't there something else at work too, something that the Narrator doesn't mention: the desire to spit on one's own love – on one's own desire for 'that possible multiplication of oneself, which is happiness'? That desire makes one vulnerable, sometimes desperately so – especially to those who answer it. Perhaps Mlle Vinteuil is happy for her father's photo to be spat on – and to delegate its desecration to her lover – not despite her gratitude to the old man and all he sacrificed for her, but because of it. To spit on his memory is to spit on the burden of her need for him; on the burden of her debt to him; on the pain of her love for him. That is why she holds out 'a chaste brow to be kissed precisely as a daughter': to make light of her daughterly need; to feign indifference to what she really craves and no longer gets: the security that only a parent can give.

✦ ✦ ✦

Does all this – the arbitrariness of our choices; the impossibility of possessing another's life; the inconstancy of love – suggest that we are prone to choose our loved ones badly? And that we cannot be sure we love them – or they us?

It seems so. The Narrator's choice of Albertine rests on trivia that speak of no fundamental 'goodness' to which his love is a response. Her glance. A pleasing physical form. A mysterious smile. He realises that he cannot know her depths, nor she his: we are inscrutable to each other (and to ourselves). His desire for her, far from being clear-sighted, is driven by ever-changing images of memory and imagination, and by torments of jealousy and isolation. He wishes to penetrate to the essence of someone who might not even be to his taste. Is she a stand-in for a more primal object of desire that his helplessness is groping to define? Such as his original mother? Or a Mother Earth? Or 'invisible forces' or 'obscure deities' (2:1165) with which he seeks contact and with which his lover puts him in touch as if she were a lightning rod? Or some other symbol of wholeness?

Though it seems simplistic to suggest, as the Narrator often does, that only the failure to possess the woman we desire, and so the persistence of doubt, can sustain our love for her, no one has revealed the serpentine workings of jealousy in more detail than Proust. Jealousy is the searchlight that we obsessively train on the dark realm of the other's life. Even when love's needs are momentarily satisfied, jealousy is always a step ahead – ever alert to what might go wrong, to what might not be as it seems. The Narrator speaks of the pain of imagining

> the unknown evil element in her [Albertine's] life, of the places, impossible to identify, where she has been, where she still goes perhaps during the hours when we are not with her, if indeed she is not planning to live there altogether, those places in which she is separated from us, does not belong to us, is happier than when she is with us. (3:98)

Such is the torment of this ignorance about the loved one's feelings and doings that, the Narrator says, a man might prefer his mistress or wife 'to go out by herself . . . with the man whom he knows to be her lover, preferring to the unknowable this torture which at least he knows!' (3:100).

And so jealousy is 'a demon that cannot be exorcised' (3:98). It not only feeds on ignorance; it also creates ignorance, thus moving in a vicious circle of its own making:

> Jealousy, which is blindfold, is not merely powerless to discover anything in the darkness that enshrouds it; it is also one of those tortures where the task must be incessantly repeated, like that of the Danaides, or of Ixion [tied to his turning wheel for eternity]. (3:147–8)

Yet these doubts, this constant wondering about what the other is up to, sustain love in another way too: they maintain our openness to the loved one. Through this openness, the Narrator muses, the other can flow into us and appear, briefly, to give us what love wants: to fill the emptiness of our own being with theirs.

> It was right, I told myself, that by incessantly asking myself what she could be doing, thinking, wishing, at every moment, whether she intended, whether she was going to return, I should keep open that communicating door which love had opened up in me, and feel another person's life flooding through open sluices to fill the reservoir which must not again become stagnant. (3:459)

We suffer if we doubt and we suffer if we don't. If all doubts could be assuaged, we would then be ridden with 'despair at having obtained fidelity only by force, despair at not being loved' (3:99). But doubts cannot be assuaged for long – if we are honest with ourselves that we can never keep track of where our loved one is, or even of who she is.

✦ ✦ ✦

What of friendship? Isn't this a form of love that is less prone to lying and self-ishness? Or to the fruitless attempt to escape from oneself into the world of another? Wouldn't the Narrator be bound to recommend it for precisely those reasons?

Absolutely not. He castigates friendship as 'an abdication of self . . . devoid of virtue', which is especially dangerous to those people – namely, artists – who are able to create their own life and works, and so have 'a duty to live for themselves' (1:968).

Friendship, he suggests, is intimacy for cowards. It might offer us relief from solitude, but at the price of abandoning our own inner reality and its development. Thus, 'the artist who gives up an hour of work for an hour of conversation with a friend knows that he is sacrificing a reality for something that does not exist' (3:909). This something is little more than the 'vague, sentimental glow' (2:410) that our superficial self enjoys at being able to lean on another person as a convenient prop, and to draw from them the comfort and consolation that we cannot find within ourselves.

Yet we easily succumb to the illusion that the communication afforded by friendship is real, noble and enriching. We want to believe that what our friend says to us has moved us – has added something valuable to our substance as a person. We imagine that deep conversation with him is precious because it enables each of us to relate to, delight in, and affirm the core of the other; but, in fact, 'conversation, which is friendship's mode of expression, is a superficial digression which gives us nothing worth acquiring. We may talk for a lifetime without doing more than indefinitely repeat the vacuity of a minute' (1:968).

This is not a truthful bond. Unlike love based on erotic desire, friendship, the Narrator implies, trades on 'the lie which seeks to make us believe that we are not irremediably alone', the lie 'that prevents us from admitting that, when we chat, it is no longer we who speak, that we are fashioning ourselves then in the likeness of other people and not of a self that differs from them' (1:969).

In the history of love, we are at the opposite end of the spectrum to Aristotle, Cicero, Montaigne and even Nietzsche (despite his praise of solitude), all of whom see friendship as the arena in which love finds its supreme possibilities – possibilities founded, in the Aristotelian tradition, on shared virtues of character. Their esteem for friendship assumes that friends *can* know much about each other, at least ethically; and that a conversation between their lives does enable them to flourish as individuals. Indeed, Montaigne insists that our self is enhanced, not impoverished, by sacrificing *all* our other loyalties for our friend.

Such assumptions are anathema to Proust's Narrator. For him, a genuine human bond is hostile to virtues like respect, understanding, empathy, sobriety, and goodwill – hallmarks of friendship as classically conceived. He suggests that these aren't virtues to which a lover should aspire, but refuges from love and its struggles. He makes us wonder whether trusting another whose nature and intentions we cannot fathom isn't just to give ourselves a break from the real business of love. Whether trust, in this context, far from being the mark of love, isn't in fact alien to love.

It would not be hard to criticise Proust's Narrator for his (professed) pessimism about love – and for failing to acknowledge that there is much more to love than he allows: that reciprocal and life-enhancing intimacy is possible, which two people experience as 'exchanging souls', or as being 'second selves' to each other; that love can involve a stable concern for the other's welfare and a glorifying of her worth which is sane and accurate; that jealousy and vulnerability can be calmed by trust; that the ultimate separateness of the other need not be a cause solely for anxiety but can occasion wonder and delight and even reassurance.

But there is little point in listening to an extraordinary voice in the hope of learning to experience things afresh, only to complain that he hasn't allowed room for conventional wisdom; only to demand that he domesticate his narrative with more emotional and ethical nobility. Like many great writers, Proust pursues his particular truths into their last hiding places, even if the cost is painful one-sidedness.

His merciless insight is that love is born of and in suffering; lives in and through suffering; and, if it (in other words the insatiable neediness that powers it) ever dies, then it dies from and in suffering. As a result of this suffering love can, perversely perhaps, both fail to see the *particular* reality of the feared and elusive loved one, and yet see deeply into the *general* structure of the world. 'Love is space and time made perceptible to the heart' (3:392). Far from suspending or transcending time, love is the very structure of time.

Indeed the Narrator seems to be contemptuous of happiness, except insofar as it leads to suffering. Happiness 'is really useful to us in one way only, by making unhappiness possible' (3:945).

But who wants to see such hard realities? And who needs to, when we have that superbly effective instrument of concealment called habit?

> Habit! that skilful but slow-moving arranger who begins by letting our minds suffer for weeks on end in temporary quarters, but whom our minds are none the less only too happy to discover at last, for without it, reduced to their own devices, they would be powerless to make any room seem habitable. (1:9)

Thanks to its genius for the banal, habit keeps the ship of our life stable in the seas of vicissitude, protecting it from shocks, truths and all experiences that don't console.

Habit: 'the ballast that chains the dog to his vomit', as Samuel Beckett remarked in his study of Proust.[11] Normal life, Beckett continues, is little else. 'Or rather life is a succession of habits, since the individual is a succession of individuals,' and the dangerous moments, when we are briefly unprotected by this 'guarantee of a dull inviolability', come in periods of transition when we morph from one individual to the next. These transitions are 'precarious, painful, mysterious and fertile, when for a moment the boredom of living is replaced by the suffering of being' – that is, by the 'free play of every faculty'.[12]

What can better foster such a fertile transition than the horrors of love?

It would have been interesting if the Narrator had left his spellbinding account of love, or of one sort of loving, right there. He has forced us to reckon with the possibility that passionate love – including that which seems stable and well-founded and to promise so many delights – in fact strives to secure and manipulate the loved one using all expedient means, including altruism; that this striving foments anger, jealousy and grief when it isn't fulfilled and satiety and boredom when it is; that the people we most love are the people whose reality we are often least willing to concede, let alone to nurture and affirm; that we project our fears and fantasies onto the loved one, whom we are able to see only through the prism of our own ideals; that we can become obsessed with our love for someone who otherwise doesn't really appeal to us. What thinkers like Lucretius and Spinoza and Rousseau and Plato diagnosed as pathologies and never elaborated with anything like the Narrator's forensic insight, he presents as the heart of love's fanatical desiring, which we daily conceal from ourselves with our protean powers of habit and delusion.

But Proust's Narrator is also too Western a figure, too saturated with the thought of Plato and Christianity, to resist the temptation to seek redemption from life's suffering – and, in the end, to find it.

Almost literally in the end. After nearly three thousand pages filled with pain, hope, misunderstanding, illusion, revulsion, anger, cruelty, deception, mourning, fear, intermittent joys, histrionic outbursts, tenderness, treachery, humour, yearning and indifference, the Narrator suggests, in a strange final section of

Proust's book entitled 'Time Regained' (*Le Temps retrouvé* – which might more appropriately be called 'Time Redeemed'), that release from the trap of an impossible desire to possess another individual is indeed available. At least for the few who have the will and the talent. Such release – or resurrection – is to be found through a project of creative insight that, in Platonic fashion, transcends the everyday and reaches for the truth about the whole – in this case about our life taken as a whole and the general form of our loves that it reveals:[13]

> every individual who makes us suffer can be attached by us to a divinity of which he or she is a mere fragmentary reflection, the lowest step in the ascent that leads to it, a divinity or an Idea which, if we turn to contemplate it, immediately gives us joy instead of the pain which we were feeling before – indeed the whole art of living is to make use of the individuals through whom we suffer as a step enabling us to draw nearer to the divine form which they reflect . . . (3:935)

Not surprisingly, perhaps, for a man deeply shaped by Romantic ideas, this reaching for the true and the whole is to be attained in art, and specifically in narrative art.[14] In an echo of Nietzsche, we hear that life is to become literature; the individual is to incorporate his painful experiences into a narrative that subsumes and masters them, and through which he is able to find freedom. And joy. In this way time's ravages, which love has made perceptible to the heart, are vanquished. Time, as Beckett puts it, can be 'a condition of resurrection because an instrument of death'.[15]

The work of narrative art might be fictional, but that doesn't mean that we can simply make it up. On the contrary, 'it pre-exists us and therefore we are obliged . . . to discover it' within us (3:915). This isn't so easy. Ordinarily our inner nature remains 'for ever unknown to us'. We avoid 'the discovery of our true life, of reality as we have felt it to be', though it ought to be more precious to us than anything in the world (3:915). We fail to look inside ourselves, to read 'the inner book of unknown symbols' (3:913) – 'the only one which has been dictated to us by reality' (3:914).

We fail to look because the task is lonely. To decipher this inner book is 'an act of creation in which no one can do our work for us or even collaborate with us' (3:913). Most of the time we look away from ourselves, inventing any number of grandiose excuses to do so: the need to attend to great public events;

to pursue 'the triumph of justice'; to 'restore the moral unity of the nation' (3:913). But the artist who turns his life into literature isn't free to do this:

> This work of the artist, this struggle to discern beneath matter, beneath experience, beneath words, something that is different from them, is a process exactly the reverse of that which, in those everyday lives which we live with our gaze averted from ourself, is at every moment being accomplished by vanity and passion and the intellect, and habit too, when they smother our true impressions, so as entirely to conceal them from us, beneath a whole heap of verbal concepts and practical goals which we falsely call life. (3:932)

For the artist almost any experience – painful and pleasant, good and bad, noble and ignoble, frivolous and serious, indolent and diligent – can be grist to the creative mill. Indeed, if we are to extract general understanding from our experiences, which is the goal and redemptive purpose of art, we must have as many of them as possible and must suffer as much as possible.

Yet we cannot know until the time is ripe what form the narrative will take and what relevance to it our experiences will have. To paraphrase Kierkegaard: we can only live life forwards and understand it backwards.[16] And so when the Narrator finally sees 'that the work of art was the sole means of rediscovering Lost Time', he notices of his experiences up to then that

> I had stored them up without divining the purpose for which they were destined or even their continued existence any more than a seed does when it forms within itself a reserve of all the nutritious substances from which it will feed a plant . . . I began to perceive that I had lived for the sake of the plant without knowing it . . . And thus my whole life up to the present day might and yet might not have been summed up under the title: A Vocation. (3:935–6)

To achieve this summing up we must unhook ourselves from our loves, 'however much it hurts us' (3:933), so that we can each grasp the general form of our love 'and give this love, the understanding of this love, to all, to the universal spirit, and not merely first to one woman and then to another with whom first one and then another of the selves that we have successively been has desired to be forever united' (3:934).

As in the Platonic ascent our attachment must move from the particular to the universal. Any engagement with a particular loved one will trigger the same suffering again. To seek satisfaction of such a desire is

> as naïve as to attempt to reach the horizon by walking straight ahead. The further the desire advances, the further does real possession recede. So that if happiness, or at least the absence of suffering, can be found, it is not the satisfaction, but the gradual reduction and the eventual extinction of desire that one should seek. One seeks to see the beloved object, but one ought to seek not to: forgetfulness alone brings about the ultimate extinction of desire. (3:458)

We recognise this particular version of the Platonic ascent from Schopenhauer, who also sees the quieting of desire as the wisest response to a tyranny that cannot be finally satisfied. But Proust's Narrator is bleaker than even this great ascetic: he seems to hold that we are fundamentally on our own. There is no other form of intimacy with human beings – no agape or compassion of the sort to which Schopenhauer looks – in which we can find consolation for the failures of passionate love. The reason? 'The bonds between ourselves and another person exist only in our minds':

> Memory as it grows fainter loosens them, and notwithstanding the illusion by which we want to be duped and with which, out of love, friendship, politeness, deference, duty, we dupe other people, we exist alone. Man is the creature who cannot escape from himself, who knows other people only in himself, and when he asserts the contrary, he is lying. (3:459)

17

Love reconsidered

For much of its history love has been captive to an obsession with opposites. It is either self-seeking or self-giving; either possessive or submissive; either illusion-creating or truth-seeking; either conditional or unconditional; either inconstant or enduring; either mired in fantasy or a privileged window onto reality. And in every case it is taken to be the apogee, the paradigm, of the quality in question.

For the majority, especially since Luther, genuine love is to the right of each of these divisions: self-giving, truth-seeking, submissive, unconditional, enduring. While lesser love (if one can call it love at all) is to the left.

By contrast, a small band of rebels insists that all genuine love, especially love with an erotic content, is ineluctably self-interested, possessive and mercurial. Ovid, at least in his *Art of Love*, celebrates love's delight in power and pleasure and play. Nietzsche echoes this more stridently, and disparages selflessness as the sickness of a soul consumed by fear and resentment. 'Pessimists' like Freud and Proust's Narrator see love's neediness, fantasies and ruptures as inevitable, yet are with the majority to this extent: these qualities overwhelmingly issue in pain and disappointment. Though, especially with Proust, there might be comedy and delight too, as well as energy and raw material for thought, art and self-creation, they don't doubt that in our relationships with each other we sabotage the constancy, understanding and intimacy that we claim to want so badly.

You know you are on ideological territory when the world is portrayed in terms of Manichean opposites of good and bad, optimistic and pessimistic. My experience, necessarily impressionistic, is that our age not only sustains this centuries-old ideology but clearly pitches its tent on the side of Luther and his successors (a tent in which religious believers and atheists, metaphysicians and naturalists, happily and perhaps unwittingly crowd in together). In particular, it sees genuine love as unconditional, enduring and selfless; and when these expectations are disappointed it easily lurches to the opposite extreme, bitterly resenting loved ones in whom so much hope had been invested and writing-off love as brutal or impossible.

In the first chapter I suggested a theory of love – of what it is, and of what inspires and sustains it – that both avoids such deluded expectations and throws out the false dichotomies on which they trade. In concluding, I will pick up some key elements of this theory – most of which we have encountered in the intervening chapters. But, before doing so, it is worth reminding ourselves how deeply entrenched these expectations are in Christian traditions – as preserved and even intensified by our secular age.

ILLUSION 1: LOVE IS UNCONDITIONAL

Despite insufficient scriptural support, Christianity offers a clear logic for the idea that humans can love – God or each other – unconditionally (even if, as I argued in chapter 7, it is a flawed logic):

(i)   God is, by definition, absolutely sovereign. Nothing beyond God can therefore condition his acts of love (acts of love like the Creation, the Covenant with Israel, and the incarnation and sacrifice of Jesus).

(ii)   All genuine human love depends on, and is to imitate, God (with much disagreement over how and to what extent). Therefore:

(iii)   All genuine human love must be unconditional.

The aspiration to model human love on divine love is already present in both of Christianity's major sources. We see the germs of it in the Hebrew Bible's call to imitate God's ways – 'Be holy, for I the Lord your God am holy' (Leviticus 19:2) – and in the Platonic account of the lover's ascent to a godlike state of contemplation. And we see it immeasurably strengthened by the formula 'God is Love' (1 John 4:8 and 16); for if God is love then *imitatio dei* must centrally involve the ideal of loving as God does.

Remarkably, the mantra of unconditional love is reiterated even by contemporary philosophers of love writing in an entirely secular vein. Irving Singer, for example, speaks of love as involving a 'bestowal', which is a 'spontaneous gift of the lover, not a conditioned response' and 'not elicited by goodness in the beloved'[1] – precisely the sort of language used by mainstream Christian traditions to describe God's agapeic love, but language which verges on the meaningless when torn from that vital context.

For love, like everything human, is conditioned. If you are a religious believer and hold that God's grace can enable humans to love in a divine way, then the concept of 'unconditional love' makes at least theoretical sense. In practice, though, it booby-traps relationships with an impossible expectation, which is fundamentally untrue to the nature of human love.

ILLUSION 2: LOVE IS ETERNAL

To model human love on divine love also spawns the illusion that it is in the very nature of genuine love to be, like God's, enduring – and even in some sense eternal. If human love ever wanes, so the thought goes, then it wasn't love in the first place. ('Love is not love/ Which alters when it alteration finds'.)

But human beings are not God.

Genuine human love will last only for as long as the lover sees in the loved one the supreme good that inspires his love – whatever he takes that good to be. (Thomas Aquinas even says this of human love for God: that if God were not good we would have no reason to love him.) In addition, love will last only for as long as the lover can sustain the attentiveness towards the loved one that is love's principal virtue and the precondition for its development. Perhaps, too, it will endure only if lovers develop the shared living, the dialogue of their two lives that, Aristotle reminds us, is essential if love's potential is to be actualised. (Aristotle is, we recall, one of the few thinkers explicitly to acknowledge that love can die.)

But attentiveness is fragile and imperceptibly surrenders to inattentive habit. Genuine love is an achievement which can be sporadic at best. What we think of as our constancy is often merely habit, that 'guarantee of a dull inviolability', as Samuel Beckett puts it.

Habit's genius is to keep us ignorant of this self-deception. We imagine we have found an intimate and easy-going harmony in our relationship; we support and participate in each other's projects; yet we have merely manoeuvred ourselves into a limbo of dependence, secured by unspoken rules whose secret mutual acceptance itself seems a sign of our closeness. Indeed, habit even succeeds in deluding us about *its own* nature: it convinces us that it is, if anything is, practical and down-to-earth. But it is a chain of illusions that ties us to a fantasy: 'the ballast that chains the dog to his vomit'.

ILLUSION 3: LOVE IS SELFLESS

Those who deem selfless love to be the most genuine are not confined to religious thinkers, like Luther and Nygren. Here we also find atheists like Schopenhauer and a contemporary philosopher such as Harry Frankfurt, who claims that love 'consists most basically in a disinterested concern for the well-being or flourishing of the person who is loved'[2] – a secular variant of the selflessness emphasised by Christian tradition, though it throws out the theology that is needed to make sense of the notion of love's disinterestedness.[3]

But the virtues of genuine love – attentiveness to the reality of the other; submission to her lawfulness and what it is calling on us to do; devotion to her as a second self – demand self-possession, self-interest in our flourishing, and so selfhood of the most developed kind. These virtues are achievements of a self whose powers of perception and engagement are dedicated to these tasks in the highest possible degree. This is particularly so since love is so future-oriented, involving sustained relationship with an evolving life that is largely unknowable and unpredictable.

Perhaps God's love can give without being motivated by need and interest; but here again we see the folly, even the idolatry, of modelling human love on divine love, especially when this model is torn from the religious context to which alone it belongs.

◆ ◆ ◆

Though these three illusions depend on a model of love that originates in religious thought and practice, I have suggested throughout this book that this model becomes ever more dominant as the authority of religion declines; even the religious have mostly accepted religion's narrower role, since the Enlightenment, in explaining natural events, in prescribing and enforcing values, and in politics and education. As that decline has progressed, so men and women have increasingly expected their love to take over where God's left off. And in imputing to human nature powers to love that were once reserved for

God, they have cast aside the humility and patience on which religious traditions insist, and to which concepts such as 'grace' give voice.

There have been idolatrous and sometimes horrific attempts to impute this divine role to a community or nation or state or ethnic group, and to make these the principal source and focus of its members' love – above all Nazism's worship of Führer and Volk. Ultimately, though, the group hasn't been able to compete with the overwhelming moral value placed on achieving intimacy with one's inner nature and on recovering or discovering a genuine individuality uncorrupted by cravings for status and social acceptance. Since the eighteenth century, and thanks in part to Rousseau (despite the collectivist tendencies of his thought), love has increasingly played a starring role in this particular search for moral value: in enabling each of us to become an authentic being amidst a crumbling and spiritually insufficient collective identity.

Indeed, every increase in individualism fuels the prestige of love. The more independent our identity is of political, religious, national or community loyalties, so the more we turn to love as the ultimate source and sign of belonging – a sign that people display today as eagerly as in previous eras they displayed their fidelity to church or state. And the more individualistic we become the more we expect love to be a secular journey for the soul, a final source of meaning and freedom, a supreme standard of value, a key to the problem of identity, a solace in the face of rootlessness, a desire for the worldly and simultaneously a desire to transcend it, a redemption from suffering, and, a promise of eternity. Or all of these at once.

In short: love is being overloaded.

✦ ✦ ✦

But the sacred can't be had on the cheap. From the beginnings of Western love in God's Covenants with Abraham and Moses, his command to love him with all one's powers despite the horrors he sporadically inflicts on his people, his turbulent relationship with Israel, and – in the New Testament – his sacrifice of his son to a violent and humiliating death, we are warned that patience for suffering, self-discipline and loss mark the highest love. Not because love seeks obstacles for their own sake, as Denis de Rougemont insists, but because love's goal is so elusive (in almost every one of its definitions that we have encountered in this short history), its ambition so urgent, and the path towards it so treacherous. As the people of Israel found in their relationship with God, this ambition will inspire terror and joy, either of which can overwhelm mere mortals.

Which is what we remain: mere mortals. Love should be modelled on how humans are commanded to love God, not on how God is said to love humans. Unlike God, everything humans do is thoroughly conditioned, interested, time-bound, and dependent on our building a robust self amid the vagaries of fate and vulnerability. And we have a supreme need, that God by definition doesn't, indeed that he was 'invented' to fulfil: to be united with (what we take to be) the ground of our being; to experience our life as indestructibly secure, vivid and anchored; to find a home. These are all ways of trying to articulate 'ontological rootedness', the search for which, I first suggested in chapter 1, is what love is ultimately about.

Love and the Quest for Home

Love is the rapture we feel for people who (or things that) inspire in us the experience or hope of ontological rootedness – a rapture that triggers and sustains the long search for a vital relationship between our being and theirs. We experience their mere presence as grounding – or as a promise of grounding – because it seems to be receptive to, to recognise, to echo, to provide a powerful berth to, what we regard as most essential about us. Which very much includes our origins, and the strengths, vulnerabilities, sensibility and fate with which they endow us. And which, far from being purely private, is deeply influenced by models that we absorb from our parents, society and peers.

Sometimes a loved one will actually have a common origin with us. But they needn't. What matters is that, for us, their presence symbolises or develops earlier sources of security that we have experienced; and is open to an ontological dialogue with us. This dialogue turns on these earlier sources of security, and infuses our existence with vividness and reality that feel 'as strong as death' (Song of Songs 8:6). As strong as the fear of extinction.

It is hardly surprising, then, that love can be so confusing. Its aim – groundedness, rootedness, at-homeness – is hard to define (though not necessarily much harder to define than 'beauty' or 'goodness' or 'truth' or 'wholeness' – those concepts that have so far dominated Western ideas about the object and inspiration of love). We can't be sure that we have attained such rootedness at all, let alone stably. It can be aroused by very diverse people (and things), for whom we might otherwise have little affinity. Our imagination, impatient to impose clarity on our expectations of the other and heavily influenced by prevailing images of what is desirable and what isn't, immediately gets to work when love is in the offing, idealising those who seem to ground us and repelling us from whoever fails to do so.

As a result, we are often slow to recognise someone who can be a source of rootedness for us – and even slower to submit to this peculiarly intangible power. Our faith in the loved one as such a source can never be deluded – though we can be greatly deluded about how far, how reliably, and in what manner the promise will be fulfilled. And of course about whether and how our love will be requited.

Passionate attachment that isn't love

By contrast, we won't love anybody who fails to inspire in us a promise of onto-logical rootedness – no matter how beautiful or good she is; no matter how generous or altruistic or empathetic or compassionate or protective or respectful we might otherwise be to each other; no matter how interested in each other's lives and projects we are; no matter how much we share the same values.

For these qualities don't in themselves inspire love. Though they are natural responses to love, once kindled, and though they certainly enrich the shared life that people who love each other lead and fill it with delight and harmony and fascination, they are not what love fundamentally seeks. We can remain cold to someone who bestows them all on us or love another who fails to do so; indeed much unhappy love is about just that.

◆ ◆ ◆

Esteem, too, is less important to love's inspiration than it might seem to be. We can fall in love with someone who is indifferent or contemptuous towards us or whom we don't esteem beyond their ontological significance to us. To do so is not perverse or foolish: the esteem of others cannot ground us, though it might temporarily appear to do so. Which is why it never suffices to make our life feel secure and real – why we always need more of it.

And why it is so dangerous to evaluate the strength of our love relationships by how much we respect and value one another. This error causes us not only to misunderstand the resilience of our bond but also to expect esteem to enhance it – and when it doesn't to look for yet more. And when *that* doesn't work, to mistrust its sincerity. But to look to esteem to strengthen love is to look in the wrong place.

This also means that love isn't, in the first instance, about valuing 'the whole person', or the loved one 'in her full particularity', including all the qualities and projects that matter to her. Let alone, to use the cliché, about loving the whole person 'for her own sake'. It isn't even about liking her. Indeed, we might brutally resist qualities or projects of hers even where we desire them – her sexuality, her beauty, her artistry, her interests, her kindness – if we imagine that she is offering us these in lieu of, or to withhold from us, the one thing to which we really want a firm relation: that mysterious kernel of her being in which we discover the promise of ontological rootedness.

BEAUTY AS A CONSEQUENCE, NOT CAUSE, OF LOVE

Such is the power of Plato's thought in its many guises that it has become axiomatic to think that love is inspired by beauty – whether of body or of soul or of character.

But is this really the case?

We manifestly don't love everyone and everything that we find beautiful, or even all beauty that we ourselves lack. Plato's conception of beauty as the real object of love has encouraged a tremendous inflation of the use of the word 'love' – which has contributed to the confusion about what we mean by it and when we genuinely feel it. Whereas, in most cases, what is really getting inspired are other forms of intimacy, esteem, devotion, possessiveness and attachment: forms that lack love's ontological relation and motivation.

Indeed we can also love what is ugly. Not because it is ugly but because it puts us in touch with something primordial, something earthily vital about (our) life as it is – which can't be reduced to 'the beauty we see in the ugly'. It is not absurd to find this in, for example, Berg's opera *Wozzeck* and to love it. Nor is it absurd to find Richard Strauss's tone poems overwhelmingly beautiful and yet not to love them. The grim and the coarse and the degraded can have a power of being that is not conveyed at all by the tone poems – indeed that the latter seem, equally mysteriously, to tear one from.

This is to suggest that the relationship between love and beauty is the other way around to Plato's conception of it. To find beauty – or goodness – in an object of love is a consequence rather than the cause of love. The rapture aroused by the promise of grounding, of rootedness and of home will cause us to experience its source as beautiful – and as good. (Indeed the rapture is identical with the judgement of beauty.) But not everyone or everything that we find beautiful or good will offer that promise.

WHAT INSPIRES LOVE VERSUS WHAT DEVELOPS LOVE

So when we talk of love as involving a desire for possession (as Plato and Proust do) or when we characterise the loving attitude as receptivity, or acceptance, or submission, or self-giving, or compassion, or empathy, or patience, or emptying of the self (as various traditions in Judaism, Christianity and their secular successors do), or when we see love as idealising the loved one (as Rousseau, Schopenhauer and many others do) or as identifying with her as a 'second self' (as Aristotle and Montaigne do), we need to be careful not to put the cart before the horse. Love, once aroused by the promise of ontological rootedness, elicits these feelings; but it cannot be reduced to them.

Indeed such feelings express key virtues of love – and, when perverted by other motives (such as the desire to flee from oneself into the life of another; or the urge to manipulate another through, for example, offering her pity or submission or acceptance), its key vices. Possession or submission or self-giving or idealisation secure and express intimacy with loved ones *once* love for them has been kindled in us. They are, when judiciously practised, conditions for bedding down relationships with the objects of our love after these have inspired the rapturous hope of a grounding that feels indestructible. They are modes of attention that love, if it is to relate successfully to its objects, must continuously develop. Indeed, as many innovators in love from Plato to the troubadours to Rousseau have pointed out, the key virtues of love need to be learned and trained.

WHY LOVE, THOUGH NEEDY, DOESN'T INSTRUMENTALISE

Love, I have so far claimed, is distinguished from all other passionate attachments in this sole respect: that its focus is the ontological rootedness inspired by the loved one; and that the dialogue which develops and deepens it is ontological in character.

This is so, whether the love is romantic, filial, sibling, parental, the perfect friendship described by Aristotle, or even directed at nature, art, money, status, wine, and other things that cannot requite our feelings. The love that animates these relationships is not of different sorts but rather expresses in different ways the same need to experience our beingness in the world as rooted, and so as finding an affirmative echo. In this sense no emotion is needier than love, no matter how much it gives and shares. And no emotion is more conditional. To repudiate love for being either needy or conditional would be to repudiate love itself. (Socrates reports – intriguingly – that love is always poor and needy.)

All of which might sound dreadfully cold – as if the loved one is seen as a mere instrument for satisfying a deep need. But this isn't the case at all. To experience the other – or rather: our relationship to the other – as grounding our being presupposes that we see him as radically distinct from us in his being – as the foundation of a home that, in its nature, isn't an extension of us and needs to be cared for in its separateness. Just as the believer cannot successfully turn to God for ontological grounding unless she reveres his ultimate sovereignty, so all love is stillborn if the loved one isn't encountered as ungraspable. To be deeply at home with someone's being is an experience that, in its nature, can't be instrumental – and will be immediately undermined by any thoughts of him as a means to an end. The loved one seems, in that unnerving combination typical of love, to be both identical with us and alien; both familiar and unreachable.

But love isn't instrumentalising for another reason too. *Once* aroused by the promise of ontological rootedness we will – in the healthy situation, where love is able to develop – open ourselves to loved ones with such overwhelming joy and gratitude and generosity, with an attachment and commitment of such power, with concern for their demands and welfare and projects so unhesitating, and with a desire to intertwine our life with theirs so consuming, that our relationship with them will then seem utterly unconditional.

And not merely seem unconditional. It will be unconditional to the extent that no *further* condition need be satisfied to go on loving them, and nothing they do could possibly kill our love. We will love them in spite of almost any destructiveness, indifference, mean-spiritedness, and vindictiveness they might show us. And, contrary to Aristotle, in spite of separation, mistrust, or decline in their excellences of character. Unless – and this is the only circumstance in which love can be killed – they stop being the sort of person who can arouse in us the hope of ontological rootedness.

LOVE IS JANUS-FACED

Among the most persistent expressions of love's search for home is its craving to 'return'. And above all to recover an origin that we take to define who we are but from which we feel alienated: God, nation, ethnic group, family, nature, mother, father. Love and piety for origins are deeply connected. (One reason, perhaps, why people so often fall in love with those of similar background, even without social pressure to do so.)[4]

We find powerful expressions of this theme of return at key moments in the tradition that we have surveyed.

Plato says in the *Phaedrus* that the soul yearns to fly back to its spiritual source, while in the *Symposium* he has Aristophanes recount the story of love's search for a lost unity with our other half.

Genesis narrates the loss of an original paradise, the Garden of Eden, in which humans had been one with nature and God; and much subsequent religious tradition presents man's redemption through love as the overcoming of this original separation from God. (The doctrine of 'original sin', though it appears distasteful when viewed as a condemnation of human nature, is nonetheless a powerful metaphor for the reality that we are all born estranged from precisely this greatest good: the discovery of a home in relation to which our life might be grounded and our specific being determined – a good to which much of a well-lived life will be dedicated.)

Augustine characterises genuine love as the soul seeking to return to its spiritual origin in God, who offers us the good of being – as opposed to sin, which Augustine regards as a state of non-being.

St Bonaventure describes spirituality as finding a way to the original Creator – so that ultimately we encounter the completeness of being that is God.

Friedrich Schlegel says that through love 'human nature returns to its original state of divinity'.

Freud speaks of the 'regression' that takes place in the lovers' experience of union with one another, and he speculates that our adult loves are animated by, and in a sense rediscover, our early libidinal attachments to our primary care-giver, generally our mother. At times he wonders whether *all* instincts don't seek to restore an earlier state of affairs; whether, to put it in terms of his late thought, both Eros and the 'death instinct' aren't fundamentally conservative.[5] (Indeed the death instinct, much derided by commentators, is interesting precisely as a metaphor for our overpowering instinct to recover the very beginning – here pictured as the inorganic state that pre-existed even life itself.)

As well as looking to the past, though, love is a movement towards the future. Thus, the *Symposium* articulates not only the backward pull, expressed in Aristophanes' myth, but also the forward urge, described in Diotima's account of the ascent of love to contemplating absolute beauty. Christian narratives picture a motion towards God through a transformation by divinely-inspired love: the same Augustine who speaks of love as a return to our spiritual roots also sees it as always related to the future – as striving for our 'sufficiency', by which he means for maximum being. For Spinoza, love – which he defines as pleasure associated with its cause – always strives for greater 'perfection'; in other words for more being, or greater fulfilment of our being. Rousseau and the Romantic tradition that he inaugurates describe love as a journey inwards: towards discovering and becoming who one individually is. Nietzsche's ideal of *amor fati* affirms not only the path backwards – the chain of events, in all their contingency, which has made us just the person we now are and which at the limit is the whole history of existence – but also wills the future which that chain of events determines. For Freud love catalyses not only regression but also development: the differentiation and integration of psychic states in which the erotic instincts have combined more and more living substance into ever greater unities.

Love therefore looks simultaneously to past and future. Differently put: its spirit is, at once, nostalgic and utopian, conservative and idealistic. To that extent, love is Janus-faced: both a recovery and a discovery.[6]

LOVE AS IMPERSONAL

This experience of a movement back to an origin or forward to a future completion speaks of a key feature of love: its tendency, perhaps even urge, to 'overshoot' its immediate object, to look beyond it, and to that extent to be impersonal. And to do so precisely when it is most personal: when it is most intensely focused on the particularity of the loved one; when her promise of ontological grounding is greatest, and when her lover has therefore dedicated himself most fully to her existence and flourishing.

For such grounding easily comes to be experienced as pointing to, or even as identical with, that whole to which love is often thought to lead us. This whole, or supreme good, has been conceived as, for example, God (Judaism; Christianity); absolute beauty (Plato); divine creation (Ficino); Nature (Spinoza); the indivisible, eternal world (Schlegel); the unity of all living things (Schopenhauer); fate (Nietzsche); and narrative (Proust). When love wants to grasp the whole – or to imagine the relationship between two people *as* the whole – it risks demanding from the loved one far more than they can possibly be.

This isn't a demand for which we should criticise love, primly insisting that it abandon its ambitions for the whole and stay focused on the particularity of the loved one. For love's nature is to seek grounding in the world in and through the individual loved one, and in doing so it can hardly help having a double orientation. It will look intently at her particularity (though without omniscient pretensions to see her 'as such', in her 'full' particularity, or in 'all' her complexity, as much contemporary wisdom would have it). And – inspired precisely by this particularity and its promise of ontological grounding – love will look beyond her to a universe in which the lover now feels he or she can be at home.

If this sounds mysterious, it necessarily is. Ontological grounding can best be expressed through myths of an original source and sustainer of life. The nature of its special power over us will remain a secret – a secret that casts a spell over us, and that we often play with, intentionally or not, when we seduce another into a genuine love relationship.

COLLAPSING THE OLD OPPOSITES

We have seen that conditional love – aroused by a very particular good that the lover seeks, namely a promise of ontological rootedness, and maybe at first unmoved or even repelled by everything about the loved one that isn't good in *this* way – is the prerequisite for, and not the opposite of, unconditional commitment to her. By the same token self-seeking, possessive love (often referred to as 'Eros-love') is the prerequisite for self-giving, submissive love (often called 'agape'), and not, as most tradition insists, its necessary opposite. In fact, the more powerful agape-love is, the *more* powerful must be Eros-love, on whose searching energy agape feeds.

But if we take a closer look at Eros and agape we see that they aren't, in fact, just stages in the progress of love from desire to self-giving, but are both, in their developed form, modes of attending constantly to the loved one, with the same aim: assimilating her presence. This presence can be grasped only by attending to its innate lawfulness and what it demands of us – just as assimilating and interpreting a piece of music demands such attention. In love as in music, to submit and give ourselves is the only way genuinely to possess. (Real possession, in which the other floods us with their being and its lawfulness and to that extent becomes our being and our lawfulness, has nothing to do with what is sometimes called 'possession':

the attempt to swallow up and annihilate the threatening independence of the other; the attempt that is so superbly articulated by Freud and Proust.)

Plato's account of Eros, as attributed to Diotima, so clearly recognises this need for attentiveness – indeed is so clearly *about* achieving an ever larger and more refined attentiveness – that it was simply an error for Eros to be conceived by some Christian traditions, especially post-Reformation, as crudely egoistic desire, incompatible with openness and generosity to the loved one. Equally its desire to possess in no way seeks to control or swallow up the object of love, in the manner of Marcel and Albertine, since it is clear that Diotima is talking about nothing of the sort.

We might more profitably use words like 'Eros', 'agape' and *'philia'* to name not distinct types of love, but rather three modes of love's mature attentiveness (which can also be three stages in the development of love's attentiveness).[7] We should then say that Eros is the desire for a loved one who inspires ontological rootedness and whose presence in our life we strive to secure (though not in the self-defeating sense of crude possessiveness); that this encounter triggers agape, passionate surrender to her presence and above all to the lawfulness of her being, which makes no further conditions; and that as this surrender develops it also comes to have the character of *philia*, now considered purely as a mode of attention (which, *contra* Aristotle, need not be founded in or directed at uniquely ethical qualities): an intimate, and necessarily reciprocal, identification with the unfolding and unpredictable life of the other, experienced as a second self. We experience her as a second self not only, or even primarily, because we have similar virtues, but much more broadly because we have a similar understanding of our projects, goods, sensibilities, histories and origins.[8]

LOVE FOR OUR NEIGHBOUR

But surely, one might protest, self-interest and selflessness do come apart at some point? Surely the volunteer who risks her life to help hungry orphans or earthquake victims is doing so purely out of self-giving love and not because she is seeking any sort of grounding for her own life?

But here too altruism can be seen as motivated by a powerful desire for rootedness – in this case experienced as oneness with one's community, or even with humanity or nature as a whole: the sense of unity that, for example, Francis of Assisi, Spinoza, Schopenhauer and Friedrich Schlegel express in their very different ways. Instead of identifying with just one other person as a second self, any fellow member of the community or of humanity seems like a second self.

Since Christian Scripture is often thought to be the unambiguous source of an ideal of universal self-giving love, it is worth recalling the places in the New Testament in which love's scope is principally the community in which the lover's life and commitments are anchored – whether it be, as Jesus puts it, 'those who hear the word of God and do it' or, as we read in the letters and Gospel of John, the inner circle of a particular Christian community to whose identity and defence love between its members is considered crucial. And in which there is no suggestion that the self is somehow emptied or disinterested. Indeed the interest is clear: love is directed in the first instance to those with kindred beliefs. The first circle of love, as St Paul suggests, comprises fellow Christians: 'as we have opportunity, let us do good to all people, especially to those who belong to the family of believers' (Galatians 6:10).

FEAR IS CONSTITUTIVE OF LOVE

Beyond food, water, shelter and affectionate recognition, there is no greater human need than to feel that our life is securely rooted. This ontological need – the vulnerability that it expresses and also creates – fills love with a degree of fear that marks it out from all other sorts of passionate attachment – and all other forms of giving, submitting, caring and valuing.

Why is the ontological relation so frightening? Most obviously because we fear losing the loved one. Her life remains, in many ways, a mystery to us: we will never fully fathom the laws that govern her – including her loyalty to us. We fear the unreliability of her promise, whether she has explicitly made it to us – as God has extended the Covenant to his people – or whether we have imputed it to her. We fear her parting even before she has gone, as Proust's Narrator describes in the childhood scene with his mother; and we dread rejection, which, as St John of the Cross puts it, is 'among the sternest ordeals'. Freud suggests that such fears can be traced back to earliest infancy: love develops through long experience of, reaction to, and anticipation of, loss – beginning with loss of our mother's attentiveness.

Then there is fear of the loved one's destructiveness, which can never be ruled out, even if she more than reciprocates our love. Hebrew Scripture's accounts of divine wrath and Jesus's talk of eternal damnation remind us of the devastation and vengeance that God can inflict on the creation he loves.

Devastation that might be predictable – punishment for wrongs committed – but that, more frighteningly still, might be unpredictable and incomprehensible: the sufferings of Job.

But there is a yet more fundamental reason why fear is constitutive of love. Someone who possesses power over our sense of existing will inspire awe that threatens to overwhelm us, even if we believe they will never abandon or destroy us. Like Kant's concept of the sublime we stand, exalted and humbled, before the 'absolutely great'. Its grandeur makes us feel powerful and powerless – not just to possess the loved one, but in our existence itself: the existence which we yearn for love to anchor. Almost every religious mystic has borne witness to this painful ambivalence.

If we were to experience the same object without love we could attempt to grasp or understand it, and relate to it as an equal. But the greater its ontological significance to us the more it frustrates such attempts; and the more it threatens to flood us with its reality – a reality whose power feels as if it could either secure our life or destroy it. (Its illumination of our own existence also leaves us nowhere to hide from ourselves – always the reality from which we most urgently seek exile. Indeed, the more successful love is the more mercilessly it reveals our solitude.)

This is just the experience that the Hebrew prophets speak of in relation to God – who is, by definition, the maximum possible source of ontological rooted-ness. It is the terror of Moses, told by God that 'you cannot see my face; for no one shall see me and live' (Exodus 33:20) – the terror of the finite human being before the infinite and urgently desired presence of God. It is the fear of Abraham and of Job, which the stories of their trials so eloquently express.

What is most frightening is *seeing* God – not losing him, or being punished by him. Even a loved one who we believe will never desert us, who is all-loving and ever-present, will inspire fear. Perhaps particularly fear.

LOVE, FEAR AND HATE

Fear, of course, quickly leads to hate – unless the lover can genuinely accept his vulnerability to the loved one. (Anger and anxiety are inflamed by our not believing we are entirely powerless; when our options don't seem closed.)

When the loved one is the monotheistic God, the lover, for all his arguing and pleading with God, ultimately has no choice but acceptance. The relationship of human to God, of creature to all-powerful creator, of contingent being to the source of all being, is one of absolute vulnerability. Indeed the believer affirms this vulnerability, rather than resents it, for it belongs to the very structure of his faith. Hate for God will not arise and if it should briefly do so, say for his disappearance in an hour of great need, then it is still tempered by the absence of all recourse. Thus, in relationship to him, fear and love can coexist.

But when the loved one is another human being, we are never impotent-by-definition. There is, in principle, always scope to manipulate her into loving us. As Socrates reports, love is relentlessly scheming, a skilful magician, 'always devising tricks like a cunning huntsman'. Why accept our vulnerability if it might be provisional and if the balance of need, power and availability between two lovers is shifting and unclear? And so, in love for other humans, unlike love for God, fear easily leads to hate – a hate that can eventually conceal (though it can never extinguish) the love.

DISGUST, NOT HATE, IS THE OPPOSITE OF LOVE

But hate is not the opposite of love. For hate still exemplifies love's cardinal virtue: attentiveness to the other person. Indeed hate often fosters it, riveting us to the other, and precisely to those qualities that exert the greatest ontological power over us – in other words precisely to the qualities that can evoke love.

We can expect the opposite of love to be that feeling towards another in which the conditions of love – what inspires it and enables it to develop into a transformative relationship – are completely absent. A feeling which, unlike hate, cannot coexist with love.

That feeling is disgust. Someone towards whom we feel disgust not only can't inspire love in us (whereas someone we hate can) – can't, in other words, inspire the promise of ontological rootedness – but, on the contrary, exacerbates our *insecurity* in precisely this respect. His existence seems to corrupt everything around him that matters to us, and make it weightless, illegitimate, unmoored, unclean, disoriented. We must escape him to safeguard our sense of our own reality. His power to induce such emotions is uncanny, for he doesn't need to do or say anything against us to make the ground under our feet seem to melt away. Indeed his attitude towards us might be genuinely benign, even loving.

Disgust reacts overwhelmingly to seemingly trivial stimuli – in just the opposite direction to love. A gesture or act that in itself is neither harmful nor even aimed at us, a dribbling mouth or a minor lie, can make us feel unsafe to our foundations. Disgust always tends to the extreme, detecting a hidden world of danger beyond whatever aroused it and responding with a revulsion that, at the limit, is at once physical, aesthetic, ethical and intellectual.

In short, disgust is, in the direction of its reactions, the antithesis of love. Where love is aroused by another's promise of ontological rootedness, disgust responds to something (equally hard to define) about their presence that seems to undermine the very possibility of rootedness. Where love responds to the promise of the other with maximum attentiveness and patience, disgust responds by an immediate turning away that eschews all attentiveness and patience. Where love seeks to bed down a relationship through possession or submission or listening or seeing or self-giving or compassion, disgust is an ontological fight-and-flight reaction that shuts down every one of these relations. Where love idealises the other, disgust shrinks him to a nothing. Unlike hate, vengeance or jealousy, which can involve a complex, even obsessive, preoccupation with another's life, disgust wants him out of the way: out of mind and beyond sight, hearing, smell, touch, and – in every sense – taste. Until he exists neither as subject nor even as object – but only as a shudder banished to the past. Hate was never this ambitious.

Do we necessarily love our children?

Finally, I need to develop a point I made earlier: we can be deeply devoted to the well-being of people and things without loving them; that is without seeing a promise of ontological rootedness in them.

This often feels perverse: we value *just* this person, enjoy her beauty, admire her life, thrill to her projects and care about her flourishing. We are grateful to her for some extraordinary kindness or help or pleasure. Mutual empathy is hardly lacking. Nonetheless, something is missing.

Just as, conversely, we can be locked in relationships that offer few such delights – and yet we don't cease to love the other.

Many, perhaps most, people will recognise this distinction between love and other forms of passionate identification or attachment. They will admit its possibility, if reluctantly, in the case of their spouses or friends or siblings or sexual partners or parents.

But not in the case of their children. Here, as nowhere else, we are deep in ideological territory, where unconditional (and equal) love must be professed – indeed, is experienced as a biological and moral given.

In fact, this sanctification of love for our children dates from no earlier than the eighteenth century.[9] Before then parental love for children certainly existed, as did 'childhood'; but the elevation of the relationship to a litmus test of genuine love, and in particular of unconditional love, is considerably more recent.

Good parents will, of course, protect, defend and nurture the lives of all their children equally, indeed fiercely so; and, in that sense, they will be no more loyal or dutiful to one than to the other. But to protect and defend, or to respect and admire, a child's – or anyone's – life is not the same as to love it.

In reality, it is as with all love: the parent will love those children most who give him the greatest sense of ontological rootedness – those with whom he feels most grounded and at home; perhaps because they poignantly echo the qualities that, for him, define his life and its origins; perhaps for more mysterious reasons. They might be unreliable, feckless, and a cause of great sadness to him; but he will love them regardless.

In both Hebrew and Christian Scripture we see a much truer picture of love for children and its dreadful inequality. We see how, through the unequal and unmerited conferral of grace, the God of the Old *and* New Testaments elects some and not others; how the parable of the marriage feast tells us that 'many are called, but few are chosen', while the story of the labourers, also in Matthew's Gospel, proclaims that 'the last will be first, and the first will be last'; how God loves David over Saul, though ethically Saul is undoubtedly the better person; how the Prodigal Son is celebrated *more* than his virtuous brother – the one who is generous, supportive and loyal to his father (if love for children were equal he might at least be celebrated in the same way); how, though 'God so loved the world that he gave his only Son', some of his children, Jesus himself tells us, will nonetheless be consigned to the eternal damnation of Hell; how Jacob had twelve sons, and loved one of these – Joseph – above all the others (which, given that Jacob is the father of the twelve tribes of Israel, is hardly a favouritism that can be brushed aside); how Jacob in turn had been the favourite son of Rebekah; and how he had taken second place to Esau in the eyes of their father, Isaac. And so on . . .

✦ ✦ ✦

The moral is not that it is perverse to love a God who behaves in such a way, or to adhere to religions whose founding myths portray the 'injustice' of love so mercilessly. The moral is that love – as distinct from care, devotion and protection – cannot, even in principle, be equal or universal or unconditional. And that though children, with their acute sensitivity to the difference between care and love, will do everything possible to try to evoke love in their parents when it isn't naturally there, they will fail.

These myths warn us, too, that love must learn to accept that it might be unrequited. The only basis for successful mutual love is the attitude of the courtesan, Philine, in Goethe's *Wilhelm Meister*: 'Wenn ich Dich liebe, was geht's Dich an?' If I love you, what business is it of yours? The lover then makes herself available to the loved one – parent or friend or child or romantic lover or God – without regarding him as obliged to reciprocate. And aware that we are anyway too opaque to one another to be sure of the nature and extent of the other's love for us.

LOVE AND IMMORALITY

If the yearning for ontological rootedness is as powerful as I have suggested, the upshot is clear: the stronger love is – which means: the more vivid the promise of such rootedness is – the more the lover will sacrifice everything he holds dear to the law of the loved one.

Including everything moral. This is where love's potential to condone or ignore immorality really lies: *not* in the violence of jealousy or possessiveness, nor in the stalking and capture of loved ones, but on the contrary in the lover's obedience to them.

The greater the ontological power of the loved one the more clearly his demands will trump all morality by which the lover otherwise feels bound. This is why submission to the monotheistic God – as the maximum possible ontological presence – or to his secular successors, such as Communism, Freedom, Progress, or Nation, can open the door to maximum inhumanity.

As we saw in chapter 2, the supreme example of love is Abraham's for God – precisely at the moment when God orders him to sacrifice Isaac. Yes, he loves God more than he loves his own son. Not for a mysterious reason but because God is the ground of his being (and of course the ground of Isaac's – whose failure to protest is rather less commented upon but equally significant).

What God is testing in Abraham are those central attributes of love: fear of, and obedience to, one whom you recognise as grounding your being. But God is not interested in fear and obedience that lead to a crumbling of the self – to a lover who is rendered chaotic, confused and paralysed by God's ontological power. Rather he is interested in a self that can act decisively – that has the self-mastery (of which courage is only one element) to take responsibility for his command, including to sacrifice everything else one loves to it. Which means: to sacrifice every other dictate of conscience or justice.

Abraham understands this, and acts unflinchingly. He experiences God's command not as extrinsic, but rather as his own innermost law. His loyalty to God – his meticulous attention to what God wants of him – is not passive but self-willed.

And so love can be both commanded and free. One is attentive to the command to put everything – all one's heart and soul and might – into the loving relationship, because one already freely loves. Abraham has already fallen in love with the vast ontological presence that is the Hebrew God, and has already received the Covenant from God, when he is put to the ultimate test.

✦ ✦ ✦

The attentiveness with which humans are called on to love the Hebrew and the Christian God is, I have argued throughout this book, the model for all love. The monotheistic God is the maximum being that can be conceived, and the source and sustainer of all other beings; and so by definition he fulfils love's single condition: the promise of ontological rootedness. But he does not root us merely by existing: we need to seek relationship with him, which demands patient cultivation of the three modes of attention that I suggested we designate 'Eros', 'agape' and 'philia'.

Such relationship can thrive only if we are prepared for injustice, cruelty, and abandonment – a preparedness on which all sustainable intimacy depends. It is marked by fear, especially the fear of success, for nearness to a loved one, with his ontological power over us, can overwhelm us more than his loss. We hope for requital but we are ready to do without it (sure that God does not need us, just as in Plato's *Symposium* the highest object of love – absolute beauty – cannot reciprocate). We strive to know the loved one and train ourselves really to look and listen; yet without the omniscient pretence that we – with our partial perspectives, distorted by need, anxiety, habit and history – can ever understand him 'as such', or 'in all his complexity', or 'as he is in himself'. And so we place ourselves at his disposal, trying to understand what the law of his being calls on us to do.

This is the template for all genuine human relationships. Instead of the hubris of modelling human love on how God is, questionably, said to love us, we are better off looking at how we are to love him. The command to love God is a way of saying that our flourishing is founded upon a lifelong search for a powerful relationship to the ground of our being – and that, whether it takes religious or secular form, such a search is the ultimate purpose of a well-lived life.

Notes

PREFACE

1. I variously use he/his/him, she/her, or they/them/their as a pronoun for the loved one.

CHAPTER 1 LOVE PLAYS GOD

1. Friedrich Nietzsche, *The Antichrist*, sect. 19, in *The Portable Nietzsche*, trans. W. Kaufmann (New York, 1954), p. 586.
2. I owe this formulation to Irving Singer, *The Nature of Love* (Chicago, 1984–87), vol. II, p. 294.
3. For example, Harry Frankfurt claims that love 'consists most basically in a disinterested concern for the well-being or flourishing of the person who is loved. It is not driven by any ulterior purpose but seeks the good of the beloved . . . for its own sake' (*The Reasons of Love*, Princeton, NJ, 2004, p. 79, cf. pp. 42 and 52). Irving Singer, in his trilogy, *The Nature of Love*, repeatedly distinguishes love as 'appraisal' of value in the loved one from love as spontaneous or gratuitous 'bestowal' of value – a distinction that, as we will see, is just another expression of the old Eros/agape dichotomy, though it rejects the religious framework from which such distinctions derive and in which alone they make full sense. He goes on to admonish any thinker, beginning with Plato and Aristotle, who fails to recognise the importance of bestowal, which he considers the greater of the two (again on the conventional lines of the traditional prioritisation of agape). Another example of this remarkable respect for received wisdom by leading contemporary thinkers is Martha Nussbaum's criticism of Proust for failing to subscribe to what are, in effect, contemporary clichés, without pausing to ask whether Proust might have reason to do so. Thus she raises three 'worries' about what is lacking in Proust's account of love: 'a worry about compassion, a worry about reciprocity, and a worry about the individual'. The latter is a worry about any thinker (Plato is another) who fails to see that love must recognise that people are 'qualitatively distinct and, especially separate, having their own lives to live', a recognition that must 'embrace the very fact of difference' (*Upheavals of Thought*, Cambridge, 2001, pp. 496–9 *passim*). And she adds that 'a lover who focuses on objects as sources of good and well-being will be unlikely to love them in all their full particularity' (ibid., p. 527). But at no point do these three philosophers – three of the small minority who write about love at all – really investigate whether love is fundamentally about such worthy ambitions; and, if it is, whether such omniscient-sounding claims as being able to love others 'in all their full particularity' are possible or even meaningful.
4. Philip Larkin, 'An Arundel Tomb', l. 42, in *Collected Poems* (London, 2003), p. 117.

5. I owe the points on Hindu texts, Plotinus and Rumi to Singer, *The Nature of Love*, vol. I, pp. 216–19.
6. Benedict XVI, Encyclical Letter, *Deus Caritas Est* (2005), Part I, sect. 11.

CHAPTER 2 THE FOUNDATION OF WESTERN LOVE: HEBREW SCRIPTURE

1. The dating of Deuteronomy and Leviticus, with their love commandments, is highly controversial, but is almost certainly not later than, respectively, the seventh and sixth centuries BCE – so substantially before Plato, Aristotle or Jesus lived. At the same time the final redaction of the traditions witnessed in the Torah (the first five books of the Hebrew Bible) could not have occurred earlier than the fifth century BCE. See Alexander Rofé, *Introduction to the Literature of the Hebrew Bible*, Jerusalem Biblical Studies, vol. 9 (Jerusalem, 2009), pp. 214–49.
2. All translations from the Bible (Hebrew and New Testament) are taken from the New Revised Standard Version (NRSV), Anglicised Edition (Oxford, 1995), except where otherwise stated. This expression in Deuteronomy 6:5 is emphasised further in Deuteronomy 10:12: 'So now, O Israel, what does the Lord your God require of you? Only to fear the Lord your God, to walk in all his ways, to love him, to serve the Lord your God with all your heart and with all your soul'. It is also found in Deuteronomy 11:1 and in Joshua 22:5. In critical scholarship this requirement, and its terminological relationship to expressions of loyalty found in Neo-Assyrian treaty oaths, has been demonstrated by Moshe Weinfeld in *Deuteronomy and the Deuteronomic School* (Oxford, 1972), pp. 59–146, and in his article 'The Loyalty Oath in the Ancient Near East' (1976), pp. 379–414. See more recently: Udo Rütersworden, 'Die Liebe zu Gott im Deuteronomium', in *Die deuteronomistischen Geschichtswerke: Redaktions- und religionsgeschichtliche Perspektiven zur 'Deuteronomismus'-Diskussion in Tora und Vorderen Propheten*, ed. Markus Witte et al. (Berlin, 2006), pp. 229–38. I thank Sandra Jacobs for pointing this out to me.
3. Leviticus 19:18 states: 'You shall not take vengeance or bear a grudge against any of your people, but [you] shall love your neighbour as yourself: I am the Lord'.
4. The most frequently used Hebrew word for love is אהבה (*ahavah*), which covers not only love for God and neighbour but also the intimacy of friends, of parents and children, as well as of lovers. Erotic love is also referred to by the Hebrew term דוד (*dod*); while חסד (*hesed*) refers to something akin to friendship-love and its qualities of loyalty, loving kindness and identification with the other as a second self. The use of some of these words varies significantly, however, between the different biblical texts.
5. From Maimonides, 'Laws of Repentance', ch. X, para. 5, in *Mishneh Torah, The Book of Adoration by Maimonides*, ed. and trans. Moses Hyamson (Jerusalem and New York, 1975), p. 92b. I owe this citation to *The Code of Maimonides: Book II, The Book of Love*, trans. Menachem Kellner (New Haven and London, 2004), p. xvi.
6. This is indicated also in post-biblical literary sources, such as Jubilees 36:4: 'And among yourselves, my sons, be loving of your brothers as a man loves himself, with each man seeking for his brother what is good for him, and acting together on earth, and loving each other as themselves'. See 'Jubilees', trans. O.S. Wintermute, in *The Old Testament Pseudepigrapha*, vol. 2, ed. James H. Charlesworth (New York, 1985), p. 124.
7. I owe this point about equality and the citation from the Jerusalem Talmud (*Hagigah* ch. 2: Mishnah 1) to Lenn Goodman in *Love Thy Neighbor As Thyself* (New York, 2008), p. 12. I am much indebted to his illuminating discussion of this commandment and its implications. The Jerusalem Talmud (Hebrew: *Talmud Yerushalmi*) is also commonly known as the Palestinian Talmud. For an analytic translation see *The Talmud of the Land of Israel*, vol. 20 (*Hagigah* and *Moed Qatan*), trans. Jacob Neusner (Chicago, 1986), p. 50.
8. As discussed in Goodman, *Love Thy Neighbor*, pp. 15–17.
9. According to Proverbs 11:17, 'Those who are kind reward themselves, but the cruel do themselves harm'.

10. Mishnah, 'The Fathers' (*Avot*), ch. 2, Mishnah 10, in *The Mishnah*, trans. Herbert Danby (London, 1958), p. 447. This tractate is also known as 'The Ethics of the Fathers'.

11. Nahmanides on Leviticus 19:18, cited in Goodman, *Love Thy Neighbor*, p. 13.

12. The Hebrew word גר (*ger*) is translated as both 'alien' and 'stranger'.

13. Normative rabbinic tradition takes the word 'alien' to refer to the convert in the Bible, but there is no clear basis for this. I owe this point to Graham Davies (personal communication).

14. We should note the very different tradition in Nahum 1:2: 'A jealous and avenging God is the Lord, the Lord is avenging and wrathful; the Lord takes vengeance on his adversaries and rages against his enemies'.

15. The NRSV says, 'You shall not profit by the blood of your neighbour', but recognises in a footnote that the literal translation is, rather, 'You shall not stand against the blood of your neighbour'.

16. This is the view of those parts of Deuteronomy pervaded by a 'militaristic spirit and the unyielding commandment to destroy by the ban all the land's inhabitants' (Rofé, *Introduction*, p. 204). In the Hebrew Bible, as in the ancient Near East, war and the establishment of social order were perceived in a cosmological context. Here the relationship between the (divine) gods and the (human) king represented the king's military activities as part of the cosmic struggle against the forces of chaos. As such, national warfare was understood not only as 'morally tolerable but as morally imperative', as argued in C.L. Crouch, *War and Ethics in the Ancient Near East: Military Violence in Light of Cosmology and History* (Berlin and New York, 2009), p. 194.

17. Cf. Genesis 1:26, 5:1; and Hebrews 1:3. In this context it is interesting that in comparative Mesopotamian tradition expressions such as 'the image of the god Marduk' and 'the image of the god Nergal' represent the presence of the god in his temple and city. See Moshe Weinfeld, *The Place of the Law in the Religion of Ancient Israel* (Leiden and Boston, 2004), pp. 106–9; and V.A. Hurowitz, 'The Divinity of Mankind in the Bible and the Ancient Near East: A New Mesopotamian Parallel', in *Mishneh Todah: Studies in Deuteronomy and Its Cultural Environment in Honor of Jeffrey H. Tigay*, ed. N. Sacher Fox, D.A. Gilat-Gilad and M.J. Williams (Winona Lake, IN, 2009), pp. 263–74. I thank Sandra Jacobs for pointing this out to me.

18. Cf. Micah 6:8.

19. Babylonian Talmud, *Shabbat* 133b, quoted in Goodman, *Love Thy Neighbor*, p. 16. See *Shabbath II*, in the Babylonian Talmud, ed. and trans. I. Epstein (London, 1935–48).

20. Cf. Leviticus 25:35–8, Proverbs 22:22–3 and Proverbs 17:5, which states: 'Those who mock the poor insult their Maker'.

21. As indicated in Leviticus 6:2–7, which ordains that trespass against one's neighbour incurs a repayment to the person concerned of one fifth more than the value of the item stolen as well as a guilt offering to the priest to atone for the sin to the Lord.

22. Babylonian Talmud, *Ta'anit* 20b. I owe the references in this paragraph to Goodman, *Love Thy Neighbor*, p. 17.

23. I owe this comment to Michael Harris (personal communication). The Greek translation 'I AM EXISTENCE', or 'I AM THE EXISTING ONE' is evocative of divine beingness, but unfaithful to the Hebrew (Graham Davies, personal communication).

24. For a valuable discussion of the use of the divine name here (and in relation also to Exodus 6:3) see Thomas L. Thompson, 'How Yahweh Became God: Exodus 3 and 6 and the Heart of the Pentateuch', *Journal for the Study of the Old Testament*, vol. 68, 1995, pp. 57–74.

25. See *The Concise Dictionary of Classical Hebrew*, ed. D.J.A. Clines (Sheffield, 2009), p. 148; and יהוה in Brown, F., Driver, S.R. and Briggs, C.A., *The Brown-Driver-Briggs Hebrew and English Lexicon of the Old Testament* (Peabody, MA, 2000), pp. 217–18.

26. See 'Imitatio Dei and the Nature of God', in Menachem Kellner, *Maimonides on Human Perfection*, Brown Judaic Studies, vol. 202 (Atlanta, 1990), pp. 59–60.

27. Harold Bloom remarks, with splendid understatement, that 'The largest paradox of Christianity in Luke, John and nearly all that comes after is the simultaneous dismissal of the Jewish people as obsolete (at the best), while still relying all but totally upon a revisionary interpretation of the Hebrew Bible.' Harold Bloom, *Jesus and Yahweh: The Names Divine* (New York and London, 2005), p. 165.

28. Similarly in Psalms 145:20 ('The Lord watches over all who love him') and Psalms 31:23.

29. Song of Songs (also known as the Song of Solomon) 8:6.
30. This exegesis on Deuteronomy 11:13 is provided by the early (anonymous) rabbinic commentators in *Sifre: A Tannaitic Commentary on the Book of Deuteronomy*, trans. R. Hammer (New Haven, 1986), Piska 41, p. 85.
31. Mishnah, 'The Fathers' (*Avot*), ch. 1, Mishnah 2, in *The Mishnah*, p. 446.
32. 'Thou shall love thy neighbour as thyself', R. Akiva said, 'is the fundamental principle of the Torah', as recorded in *Sifra: An Analytic Translation*, vol. III, trans. Jacob Neusner (Atlanta, 1988), p. 109. Compare Romans 13:8: 'Owe no one anything, except to love one another, for the one who loves another has fulfilled the law'; and also Matthew 22:39–40.
33. Babylonian Talmud, *Shabbat* 31a. Hillel the Elder flourished in Jerusalem in the latter half of the first century BCE and the beginning of the first century CE. For a discussion of the comparative expression in the early Aramaic (Palestinian) Targum, see Serge Ruzer, 'From "Love Your Neighbour" To "Love Your Enemy": Trajectories in Early Jewish Exegesis', *Revue Biblique*, vol. 109, no. 3, 2002, p. 378.
34. Cf. Luke 6:31. See also John 13:34–5; Matthew 19:19, 22:39–40; Mark 12:31; Luke 10:27; Romans 13:8–9; Galatians 5:14; and James 2:8.
35. Tessa Rajak, *Translation and Survival: The Greek Bible of the Ancient Jewish Diaspora* (Oxford and New York, 2009), pp. 7–10.
36. Henry Chadwick, *The Early Church* (London, 1967), p. 42.
37. In the Septuagint, agape is not yet associated exclusively with 'unconditional' love as opposed to Eros-love, but embraces maternal or paternal love in, for example, Genesis 22:2 and 28:28; neighbourly love in, for example, Leviticus 19:18; love between husband and wife in, for example, Genesis 24:67, 29:18 and 29:30; and erotic desire, as in Shechem's lust for Dinah reported in Genesis 34:3, and in Amnon's desire for his half-sister, Tamar, reported in 2 Samuel 13:1, 4 and 15.
38. In chapter 7 I will argue that even in the New Testament agape is not sharply and consistently distinguished from Eros-love – a distinction that is, instead, read back into the New Testament many centuries later, above all by the Reformation and its successors.
39. Erotic love is also referred to by the Hebrew term דוד (*dod*) and is used, often synonymously, with 'my beloved'. See also Song of Songs 1:13, 14, 16; 2:16; and 6:3.
40. As Isaiah 6:3 reveals: 'Holy, Holy, Holy is the Lord of Hosts; the whole earth is full of His glory'.
41. For a different perspective on the ritual status of eunuchs see Isaiah 56:3–5.
42. 'Jonathan stripped himself of the robe that he was wearing, and gave it to David, and his armour, and even his sword and his bow and his belt' (1 Samuel 18:4). This gesture foreshadows David's displacement of Jonathan as the monarch, seemingly by symbolic consent of the prince.
43. And similarly in 20:17: 'Jonathan made David swear again by his love for him: for he loved him as he loved his very own life'.
44. In contrast to Scripture, the rabbinic tradition refers to Jonathan's devotion to David as an example of unconditional love, and to Amnon's desire for Tamar as conditional love (2 Samuel 13:1–20). See Mishnah, *Avot*, ch. 5, *Mishnah* 16, in *The Mishnah*, p. 457.
45. Martin Buber, *On Judaism* (New York, 1967), p. 210.
46. This sense of what it is right and just to do amounts, in this context, to what we would today call a conscience; and, though 'conscience' is not a biblical word, I will use it in what follows.
47. For example, Exodus 20:12–17, 23:1; Leviticus 18:6–23, 19:11.
48. Psalm 51:15–17, cited in Augustine, *City of God*, trans. Henry Bettenson (London, 2003), p. 377.
49. Job 1:12, 2:6. My discussion of Job is indebted to Singer, *The Nature of Love*, vol. I, pp. 254–5.
50. Cf. Romans 9:15.
51. This marvellous sentence reads: 'For I know that my Redeemer lives,/ and that at the last he will stand upon the earth;/ and after my skin has been thus destroyed,/ then in my flesh I shall see God,/ whom I shall see on my side,/ and my eyes shall behold, and not another' (Job 19:25–7).

52. Job 2:9, where she asks: 'Do you still persist in your integrity? Curse God, and die'.
53. Regarding prayer, Job 42:10 states only: 'And the Lord restored the fortunes of Job when he had prayed for his friends; and the Lord gave Job twice as much as he had before'.
54. Disloyalty to God can evoke his wrath and destructiveness, as the story of Noah's Ark suggests – the Ark being reserved for the faithful Noah, whose love for God is contrasted with 'the wickedness of humankind [that] was great on the earth' (Genesis 6:5).
55. Immanuel Kant, *Critique of Judgement*, trans. J.C. Meredith (Oxford, 1952), sect. 25, p. 94.
56. Though later rabbinic Judaism will connect it to the merit of the Patriarchs (a point I owe to Menachem Kellner, personal correspondence).
57. Harold Bloom characterises God's untameable nature in Shakespearean terms: 'Yahweh fuses aspects of Lear, Falstaff, and Hamlet: Lear's unpredictable furies, Falstaff's surging vitalism, and Hamlet's restlessness of consciousness'. Bloom, *Jesus and Yahweh*, p. 169.
58. For example, we see such intercession in the aftermath to the 'Golden Calf' story in Exodus 33–4. With some of the Prophets, such as Hosea and Jeremiah, matters are otherwise and – unlike in the Torah – God is said to reach out to Israel even when it has transgressed and prior to any reform. (I thank Graham Davies for pointing this out to me – personal communication.)
59. I am not assuming that such people are merely stand-ins or metaphors for our parents.

CHAPTER 3 FROM PHYSICAL DESIRE TO PARADISE: PLATO

1. I owe this point to Martha Nussbaum, *The Fragility of Goodness: Luck and Ethics in Greek Tragedy and Philosophy* (Cambridge, 1986), *passim*.
2. For more on Empedocles' idea of love as a cosmic force, see Jonathan Barnes, *The Presocratic Philosophers* (London, 1982), pp. 309–10 and 419–20.
3. See Barnes, *Presocratic Philosophers*, p. 241.
4. Sophocles, *Antigone*, ll. 881–7, in *The Three Theban Plays: Antigone, Oedipus the King, Oedipus at Colonus*, trans. Robert Fagles and Bernard Knox (London, 1984), p. 101.
5. Plato, *The Symposium*, trans. Walter Hamilton (Harmondsworth, 1951), 177C, p. 40.
6. Though Plato excludes love between the sexes from this goodness.
7. Beauty for the Greeks – *kalon*, sometimes translated as 'fine' – was something very broad, encompassing both aesthetic beauty and ethical beauty, and so is exemplified by everything of value.
8. Plato, *Symposium*, 209C–D and 212A, pp. 91–4.
9. I owe this speculation and the quotation from Baudelaire that follows it to A.W. Price, *Love and Friendship in Plato and Aristotle* (Oxford, 1997), p. 228.
10. Kenneth Dover, in his major (though no longer unchallenged) study, *Greek Homosexuality* (Cambridge, MA, 1978), expresses amazement that the penis of the passive young man 'remains flaccid even in circumstances to which one would expect the penis of any healthy adolescent to respond willy-nilly'. Quoted in Nussbaum, *The Fragility of Goodness*, p. 188.
11. In two of Plato's late works, the *Republic* and the *Laws*, he takes a hard line against homosexuality, castigating it as unnatural. See Plato, *The Republic*, trans. Desmond Lee (London, 2003), 403B–C, pp. 99–100; Plato, *The Laws*, trans. Trevor J. Saunders (Harmondsworth, 1975), 636C–E and 838E, pp. 61–2, 336–7. See also Plato, *Phaedrus* 250E and 255E–256E, in *Euthyphro, Apology, Crito, Phaedo, Phaedrus*, trans. Harold North Fowler (Cambridge, MA, 2005), pp. 484–7, 500–1.
12. Plato, *Charmides*, 155C–D, in *Early Socratic Dialogues*, trans. Trevor J. Saunders (London, 1987), p. 179.
13. Plato, *Symposium*, 191D, p. 62.
14. Plato, *Symposium*, 192E, p. 64.
15. Plato, *Symposium*, 193C, p. 65.
16. Plato, *Symposium*, 191C, p. 61.
17. Roger Scruton elegantly describes the nature of a myth, and its enduring power, when (in the context of a discussion of Wagner's operas) he says that it 'is not a fable or religious doctrine but a vehicle for human knowledge. The myth acquaints us with ourselves and our condition,

using symbols and characters that give objective form to our inner compulsions.' In *Death-Devoted Heart: Sex and the Sacred in Wagner's* Tristan and Isolde (New York, 2004), p. 5.

18. Cf. Plato, *Symposium*, 191D–192B, pp. 62–3.
19. Sigmund Freud, *Inhibitions, Symptoms and Anxiety*, vol. XX, p. 122 (1959), in *Standard Edition of the Complete Psychological Works of Sigmund Freud*, trans. and ed. James Strachey, vols. I–XXIV (London, 1953–74).
20. Plato, *Symposium*, 193C, p. 65.
21. Plato, *Symposium*, 192D–E, pp. 63–4.
22. Plato, *Symposium*, 201A, p. 78.
23. Plato, *Symposium*, 205E, pp. 85–6.
24. Plato, *Symposium*, 201A, p. 78.
25. Plato, *Symposium*, 205E, pp. 85–6.
26. Plato, *Symposium*, 199E, p. 76.
27. Plato, *Symposium*, 200A, p. 76.
28. Marcel Proust, *Remembrance of Things Past*, trans. C.K. Scott Moncrieff and Terence Kilmartin (Harmondsworth, 1983), vol. 2, p. 637.
29. In the translation of the *Symposium* by Robin Waterfield (Oxford, 1994), 203B, p. 44.
30. Plato, *Symposium*, 203C–D, p. 82.
31. Plato, *Symposium*, 206C–E, p. 86.
32. It is unclear whether to procreate in beauty means to procreate in the presence of beauty or to procreate from out of beauty – or both.
33. Plato, *Symposium*, 203E, p. 82.
34. Plato, *Symposium*, 212A, p. 95.
35. Plato, *Symposium*, 211A–B and D–E, pp. 93–5.
36. Plato, *Symposium*, 202E, p. 81.
37. Plato, *Symposium*, 212A–B, p. 95.
38. Plato, *Symposium*, 210A, p. 92.
39. Plato, *Symposium*, 210B, p. 92.
40. Plato, *Symposium*, 210D, pp. 92–3.
41. Plato, *Symposium*, 212B, p. 95.
42. Plato, *Symposium*, 212A, p. 95.
43. Plato tells us elsewhere that the highest good is like the sun; it is the source of light that reveals all other things as they really are. This presumably means that, like the sun, it cannot be seen clearly by directly looking at it. See Iris Murdoch's discussion of the Platonic Good in *The Sovereignty of Good* (London, 1970), especially pp. 46–76.
44. W.H. Auden, *The Age of Anxiety: A Baroque Eclogue* (New York, 1947), p. 35.

CHAPTER 4 LOVE AS PERFECT FRIENDSHIP: ARISTOTLE

1. The word that Aristotle uses is *eudaimonia*, sometimes (and inadequately) translated as 'happiness'.
2. Apart from perfect *philia*, based on the friends' goodness, Aristotle also uses the term *philia* in two other senses, which will not concern us here: to denote relationships based on utility – such as business relationships, where these are cooperative rather than competitive – and to denote those based on pleasure.
3. Proust, *Remembrance*, vol. 1, p. 968.
4. Character, for Aristotle as for many other Greeks, is a far more significant determinant of a person's life than it tends to be for us today. For them virtues of character – like courage, benevolence, reliability, truthfulness, self-command, wisdom or generosity – dictate the entire capacity of a person to fulfil his human potential. 'Man's character is his fate', says Heraclitus (flourished *c.* 500 BCE), one of the founders of Greek thought. Charles H. Kahn, *The Art and Thought of Heraclitus* (Cambridge, 1979), fragment CXIV (Diels-Kranz fragment 119), p. 81.

5. Though, of course, the Platonic love that leads *another* up the ladder (as is explicit in the *Phaedrus* and implicit in the *Symposium*) requires his cooperation. I thank A.W. Price for reminding me of this.

6. Price, *Love and Friendship*, p. 108.

7. Nussbaum, *The Fragility of Goodness*, pp. 358–9. Cf. A.W. Price, who, similarly, makes the point that since 'the self is primarily realised in its choices', the best love is based on a very broad sharing of the activities by which these choices are manifested. See Price, *Love and Friendship*, p. 107.

8. Nussbaum, *The Fragility of Goodness*, p. 358.

9. Sonnet 116, in William Shakespeare, *The Sonnets and a Lover's Complaint* (London, 1995), p. 134.

10. Nussbaum, *The Fragility of Goodness*, p. 360.

11. '. . . if the absence is of long duration it appears to bring about forgetfulness of the love itself.' Quoted in Nussbaum, *The Fragility of Goodness*, p. 360.

12. Nussbaum, *The Fragility of Goodness*, pp. 338–9.

13. Aristotle, *Nicomachean Ethics* (hereafter *NE*), 1165b15, in *The Complete Works of Aristotle*, ed. Jonathan Barnes (Princeton, NJ, 1984), vol. II, p. 1842.

14. *NE*, 1165b23–5, p. 1844.

15. *NE*, 1165b26–30, p. 1842.

16. *NE*, 1156b12, p. 1827.

17. *NE*, 1155b32, p. 1826. Cf. Price, *Love and Friendship*, p. 107.

18. See *NE*, 1168b7, p. 1847; 1170b6, p. 1850; 1245a34–5, p. 1974. For an excellent discussion of this idea of 'another self' or 'second self' or 'single soul', see Price, *Love and Friendship*, pp. 110–11 and 123–4.

19. *NE*, 1156b7 8, p. 1827.

20. 'Now equality and likeness *are* friendship': *NE* 1159b3, p. 1832, my italics.

21. Relationships between husbands and wives belong, for Aristotle, to intrinsically unequal relationships (*NE*, 1158b13–19, p. 1831), and in these the better party should be loved more than he loves and the worse less than he loves (*NE*, 1158b24–8, p. 1831).

22. *NE*, 1158b13–14, p. 1831.

23. '*Qua* slave then, one cannot be friends with him. But *qua* man one can' (*NE*, 1161b4–8, p. 1835). Cf. C.C.W. Taylor, 'Politics', in *The Cambridge Companion to Aristotle*, ed. Jonathan Barnes (Cambridge, 1995), pp. 256–7.

24. *NE*, 1159b12–13, p. 1832.

25. *NE*, 1155b7, p. 1826. Aristotle himself says that 'like is dear to like': *NE*, 1165b16–17, p. 1842.

26. See, for example, David M. Buss, *Evolutionary Psychology: The New Science of the Mind* (Boston, MA, 1999), p. 130.

27. '. . . goodwill [*eunoia*] when it *is* reciprocal being friendship'. *NE*, 1155b33, and 1156a3–5, p. 1826. See John M. Cooper, 'Aristotle on Friendship', in *Essays on Aristotle's Ethics*, ed. Amélie Oksenberg Rorty (Berkeley and Los Angeles, 1980), pp. 308–11. My discussion is greatly indebted to Cooper's chapter.

28. *NE*, 1155b31–2, p. 1826.

29. *NE*, 1164a3–13, p. 1839.

30. As Martha Nussbaum, to whom this section is much beholden, puts it: 'unlike Plato, he does not appear to believe that intense sexual desire or excitement plays any essential role in the values and benefits of love'. Nussbaum, *The Fragility of Goodness*, p. 358.

31. *NE*, 1159a11–12, p. 1832.

32. John M. Cooper suggests that, for Aristotle, 'in loving and valuing the other person for his own sake one becomes able to love and value oneself' ('Aristotle on Friendship', p. 333).

33. 'For there is nothing so characteristic of friends as living together'. *NE*, 1157b19–20, p. 1829.

34. *NE*, 1170a4–11, especially 5–6, p. 1849.

35. I owe this interpretation of what Aristotle means by 'living together' to Nussbaum, *The Fragility of Goodness*, pp. 358–9.

36. *NE*, 1170b12–13, p. 1850.

37. *NE*, 1156b4–5, p. 1827; 1157b11–12, p. 1829.
38. Aristotle, *Eudemian Ethics*, 1245b18–19, in *The Complete Works of Aristotle*, ed. Jonathan Barnes (Princeton, NJ, 1984), vol. II, p. 1974.
39. Aristotle, *Politics*, 1253a28–9, in *The Complete Works of Aristotle*, ed. Jonathan Barnes (Princeton, NJ, 1984), vol. II, p. 1988.
40. My discussion here is much indebted to Cooper, 'Aristotle on Friendship', pp. 320–4.
41. *NE*, 1105a29–33, p. 1746.
42. Aristotle, *Magna Moralia*, 1213a16–17, in *The Complete Works of Aristotle*, ed. Jonathan Barnes (Princeton, NJ, 1984), vol. II, p. 1920.
43. Friedrich Nietzsche, *On the Genealogy of Morals*, in *The Basic Writings of Nietzsche*, trans. W. Kaufmann (New York, 1968), p. 451 (Preface, sect. 1).
45. Aristotle, *Magna Moralia*, 1213a20–6, p. 1920. Cf. *NE*, 1169b28–1170a3, p. 1849, and *Eudemian Ethics*, 1245a35–6, p. 1974: 'Therefore, to perceive a friend must be in a way to perceive one's own self and to know a friend is to know one's self.' Some scholars doubt that *Magna Moralia* is really by Aristotle, but the passage cited here is typically Aristotelian.
46. In Kahn, *Art and Thought*, fragment XLIV (Diels-Kranz fragment 94), p. 49.

CHAPTER 5 LOVE AS SEXUAL DESIRE: LUCRETIUS AND OVID

1. This chapter is much indebted to Singer, *The Nature of Love*.
2. Lucretius, *De Rerum Natura* (henceforth *DRN*, followed by book and line number), translated with an introduction by C.H. Sisson (New York, 2003), IV: 1054–7, p. 131. (I owe this reference to Singer, *The Nature of Love*, vol. I, p. 132.) I have used the Sisson translation of Lucretius because its English is less archaic than that of the superior translation by W.H.D. Rouse, revised by M.F. Smith (Cambridge, MA, 1975).
3. Lucretius, *DRN* IV: 1089–90, p. 132.
4. Lucretius, *DRN* I: 4–5, p. 15.
5. Lucretius, *DRN* I: 21–5, pp. 15–16.
6. Lucretius, *DRN* IV: 1110–11, p. 133.
7. Lucretius, *DRN* IV: 1079–83, p. 132.
8. Lucretius, *DRN* IV: 1155–64, p. 134.
9. I am indebted here to Singer, *The Nature of Love*, vol. I, p. 133 and *passim*.
10. Epicurus, *Epicurus: The Extant Remains*, ed. and trans. Cyril Bailey (Hildesheim and New York, 1970), p. 89. I am indebted to M.F. Smith's remarks on Epicurus in his Introduction to W.H.D. Rouse's translation of *De Rerum Natura*.
11. Epicurus, *The Extant Remains*, p. 123.
12. Epicurus, *The Extant Remains*, p. 101.
13. Epicurus, *The Extant Remains*, p. 95.
14. Epicurus, *The Extant Remains*, p. 95.
15. As Lord Illingworth quips in Oscar Wilde's *A Woman of No Importance* (London, 1996), Act III.
16. Lucretius, *DRN* IV: 1240–7 *passim*, p. 136.
17. Lucretius, *DRN* IV: 1261–2, p. 137.
18. Lucretius, *DRN* IV: 1265–8, p. 137.
19. Lucretius, *DRN* IV: 1269–77 p. 137.
20. Lucretius, *DRN* IV: 1063–7, p. 132.
21. Cited in Stuart Gillespie and Philip Hardie, eds., *The Cambridge Companion to Lucretius* (Cambridge, 2007), pp. 6–7.
22. Alfred, Lord Tennyson, 'Lucretius', ll. 14–23, in *The Major Works*, ed. Adam Roberts (Oxford, 2009), pp. 380–1.
23. Singer, *The Nature of Love*, vol. I, p. 140.
24. Ovid, *The Art of Love*, trans. Rolfe Humphries (Bloomington, 1957), Book 2, ll. 233–4.
25. Here I paraphrase Octavio Paz, who praises Catullus's capacity to convey how 'Our flesh covets what our reason condemns'. In *The Double Flame: Essays on Love and Eroticism*, trans. Helen Lane (New York, 1995), p. 48.

26. Paz, *Double Flame*, p. 47. Politically, though, women were hardly emancipated, despite a slow development in their autonomy as the Roman Empire developed. As Augusto Fraschetti remarks, 'Women's lives often interwove stories of political intrigue (a sphere from which they were excluded) with romantic intrigue (in which they were chief players). . . . If some women . . . seem to burst in (and they do so with force) upon this exclusively male sphere, it must be noted that their actions are described by the sources not just as acts of intrigue, but as very harmful acts as well, damaging not only the men who were involved with them, but the city as a whole.' In Augusto Fraschetti, ed., *Roman Women*, trans. Linda Lappin (Chicago and London, 2001), p. 16.

27. Ovid, *The Art of Love*, Book 3, ll. 793–4.

28. Ovid, *The Art of Love*, Book 2, ll. 153–8. I owe this reference to Singer, *The Nature of Love*, vol. I, p. 129.

29. Ovid, *The Art of Love*, Book 1, ll. 35–6.

30. Ovid, *The Art of Love*, Book 1, ll. 89–92.

31. Ovid, *The Art of Love*, Book 1, ll. 269–70.

32. Ovid, *The Art of Love*, Book 1, ll. 365–6.

33. Ovid, *The Art of Love*, Book 1, ll. 459–62.

34. Ovid, *The Art of Love*, Book 1, ll. 509, 513, 520–24 *passim*.

35. Ovid, *The Art of Love*, Book 1, ll. 579–80.

36. Ovid, *The Art of Love*, Book 1, ll. 601–2.

37. Ovid, *The Art of Love*, Book 1, ll. 659–62.

38. Ovid, *The Art of Love*, Book 2, ll. 109–23 *passim*.

39. Ovid, *The Art of Love*, Book 3, ll. 95–6.

40. Ovid, *The Art of Love*, Book 3, ll. 193–4.

41. Ovid, *The Art of Love*, Book 3, l. 201.

42. Ovid, *The Art of Love*, Book 3, l. 280.

43. Ovid, *The Art of Love*, Book 3, ll. 475–7.

44. Ovid, *The Art of Love*, Book 3, ll. 529–31.

45. Ovid, *The Art of Love*, Book 3, ll. 773–6 *passim*.

46. Ovid, *The Art of Love*, Book 3, ll. 795–6.

47. Ovid, *The Art of Love*, Book 3, ll. 797–8.

48. Ovid, *The Art of Love*, Book 1, l. 342.

49. Ovid, *Metamorphoses*, trans. F.J. Miller (Cambridge, MA, 1951), Book IV, ll. 376–9. I owe this reference to the myth of Salmacis and Hermaphroditus to Singer, *The Nature of Love*, vol. I, p. 127.

CHAPTER 6 LOVE AS THE SUPREME VIRTUE: CHRISTIANITY

1. Christianity obviously embraces a broad and diverse set of beliefs and practices, and so we need to be extremely careful about attributing anything very precise to it, rather than its various texts, denominations and thinkers. But if we try to stand back from the complexity and ask what its great innovations in love are, these, I think, are the two that present themselves.

2. Augustine, *Tractates on the Gospel of John, 55–111* (Washington, DC, 1994), p. 131.

3. The Synoptic Gospels are those under the names of Matthew, Mark and Luke, which are similar enough in specific content and narrative structure to be profitably viewed side-by-side ('syn-optically'). Most of Mark appears – often word for word – in Matthew and Luke, and Matthew and Luke share material not in Mark. These three Gospels present the appearance in the main of being composed from arranging short 'pericopes' – stories and sayings of Jesus circulating in the early Church. The fourth Gospel, John's, is strikingly different, not least in what it says on love but also in the lengthier discourses and dialogues through which Jesus is presented. John is generally held to have been written significantly later than the Synoptics – by some estimates sixty-five years after Jesus's death.

4. Matthew 5–7, cf. Luke's shorter parallel 'Sermon on the Level Place', 6:17–49.

5. As we saw in chapter 2, Hillel's version of this principle is cast negatively: 'What is hateful to you do not do to your neighbour; that is the whole *Torah*. The rest is commentary' (Babylonian Talmud, *Shabbat* 31a). Hillel was a dominant figure behind the Pharisee party in first-century Palestine, a party of religious interpreters that the Jesus of the Synoptic Gospels both shares much with and sharply opposes.

6. Of the Synoptic Gospels, Matthew most clearly presents Jesus as devoted to the law. Matthew goes on to say that anyone who relaxes any of the commandments will be the least in the Kingdom of Heaven (Matthew 5:19–20). Even in the other Gospels – and in St Paul – where the body of Jewish law seems less authoritative, the law is fulfilled in God's command to love.

7. Anders Nygren, *Agape and Eros*, trans. Philip S. Watson (Philadelphia, 1953), p. 251.

8. Augustine, *St Augustine: On the Spirit and the Letter*, trans. W.J. Sparrow-Simpson (London, 1925), p. 69.

9. John Rist, 'Faith and Reason', in *The Cambridge Companion to Augustine*, ed. Norman Kretzmann and Eleonore Stump (Cambridge, 2001), p. 36.

10. Werner G. Jeanrond, *A Theology of Love* (London, 2010), p. 79.

11. Augustine, 'Letters 100–155', *The Works of Saint Augustine* (New York, 2003), p. 413.

12. Augustine, *City of God*, pp. 636–7.

13. This is especially true for the early Luther – before 1525 – though I try to reflect his later thought too in what follows.

14. In Nygren, *Agape and Eros*, p. 720 n. 1.

15. In Nygren, *Agape and Eros*, p. 734 n. 2.

16. In Rudolf Otto, *Mysticism East and West: A Comparative Analysis of the Nature of Mysticism*, trans. Bertha L. Bracey and Richenda C. Payne (New York, 1932), p. 194.

17. In Nygren, *Agape and Eros*, p. 734. I originally encountered most of the citations in this paragraph in Singer, *The Nature of Love*, vol. I, pp. 312–42. My discussion of Luther is indebted to Singer.

18. Augustine, 'Sermon 192: On Christmas Day', *The Works of Saint Augustine* (New York, 1993), p. 46.

19. Augustine, 'Sermon 121: On the Words of the Gospel of John 1:10–14: The World Was Made through Him', *The Works of Saint Augustine* (New York, 1992), p. 234.

20. The idea that the flourishing individual self is structured by a hierarchy of capacities, attained only by the few and only after the most intense and prolonged preparation, has had a very long run in the history of ideas, and is still seen in such typically modern thinkers as the self-proclaimed 'Antichrist', Friedrich Nietzsche (e.g. *On the Genealogy of Morals*, Essay II, sect. 2, pp. 494–6).

21. Bonaventure, *The Soul's Journey into God, the Tree of Life and the Life of St Francis*, trans. Ewert H. Cousins (New York, 1978), p. 79. I am indebted to the discussion of Bonaventure and mysticism in Singer, *The Nature of Love*, vol. I, pp. 179–81.

22. See Jeanrond, *A Theology of Love*, p. 77.

23. I thank Liz Carmichael for comments on Aquinas's conception of the human capacity for friendship with God (personal communication).

24. Cited in Jeanrond, *A Theology of Love*, p. 82. These remarks on Aquinas are indebted to Jeanrond, pp. 77–83.

25. I owe this formulation of the point to Jeanrond, *A Theology of Love*, p. 108.

26. Augustine, 'Confessions', *The Works of Saint Augustine* (New York, 1997), p. 39.

27. Plato, from whom Augustine draws so heavily, has his teacher Socrates recount the myth of the human soul as a horseman whose pure steed pulls him upward to the roof of the cosmos despite also being pulled down into genesis or history by the motions of the impure steed (*Phaedrus*, p. 246, in Plato, *Euthyphro, Apology, Crito, Phaedo, Phaedrus*, pp. 471–5). Of course, Plato has no comparable doctrine of grace by which the ascent is to be inspired and directed, but the idea of the soul as pulled in two directions clearly has its roots in him. I am grateful to Stanley Rosen for pointing this out.

28. Cited in Nygren, *Agape and Eros*, p. 528, n. 3 (Nygren's translation). The quote is from Augustine's 'Answer to the Pelagians, III: Unfinished Work in Answer to Julian', *The Works*

of Saint Augustine (New York, 1999), p. 342, where the translation reads: 'Rather, the grace of God makes them willing from unwilling.'

29. Cited in Oliver O'Donovan, *The Problem of Self-Love in St Augustine* (New Haven, 1980), p. 128. The quote is from Augustine's 'The Trinity'. The New City Press translation (Augustine, 'The Trinity', *The Works of Saint Augustine*, New York, 1991, p. 209) reads 'We are bidden to imitate this mutuality by grace, both with reference to God and to each other . . .'

30. Augustine expresses this thought in a metaphor: 'Purify this love, then, divert onto your garden the water that is going down the drain, let the current that drove you into the arms of the world be redirected to the world's Maker.' Augustine, 'Exposition 2 of Psalm 31', *The Works of Saint Augustine* (New York, 2000), p. 367.

31. Through this vanity love is 'curving in on itself' (*curvatus in se*), as Augustine puts it, and so failing to be *caritas*.

32. Augustine, *Treatises on Various Subjects*, trans. Mary Sarah Muldowney (Washington, DC, 1952), p. 252.

33. Martin Luther, 'Second Christmas Sermon: Early Christmas Morning Service, Titus 3:4–8', *Sermons of Martin Luther*, vol. 6 (Grand Rapids, MI, 1995), p. 145.

34. Cited in Singer, *The Nature of Love*, vol. I, p. 327. My remarks on Luther and the citations from him that I have chosen are greatly indebted to Singer.

35. Cited in Singer, *The Nature of Love*, vol. I, p. 327.

36. Cited in Nygren, *Agape and Eros*, p. 733.

37. Luther, 'Second Christmas Sermon', p. 145.

38. Cited in Nygren, *Agape and Eros*, p. 734 n. 2.

39. Nygren, *Agape and Eros*, p. 734.

40. Meister Eckhart, *The Works of Meister Eckhart*, trans. C. de B. Evans, ed. Franz Pfeiffer (Kila, MT, 1992), pp. 381–2. I owe this reference to Singer, *The Nature of Love*, vol. I, p. 225.

CHAPTER 7 WHY CHRISTIAN LOVE ISN'T UNCONDITIONAL

1. For example, Augustine, *Tractates on the Gospel of John*, pp. 127–8.

2. St John of the Cross, *A Spiritual Canticle of the Soul and the Bridegroom Christ*, trans. David Lewis (London, 1919), pp. 172–3. Here John of the Cross echoes St Paul when the apostle considers the body's existing for the Lord (Jesus) and to be a member of Christ. Whereas he who joins himself to a prostitute becomes one body with her, says Paul, 'anyone united to the Lord becomes one spirit with him' (1 Corinthians 6:17vv.).

3. St John of the Cross, *A Spiritual Canticle of the Soul*, p. 239. I encountered these passages originally in Singer, *The Nature of Love*, vol. I.

4. St Teresa of Avila, *The Interior Castle or the Mansions* (London, 1921), p. 272. I owe this reference to Singer, *The Nature of Love*, vol. I, p. 222.

5. St John of the Cross, *Dark Night of the Soul*, trans. E. Allison Peers (New York, 1959), p. 52.

6. St John of the Cross, *Dark Night of the Soul*, p. 55.

7. Meister Eckhart, *The Essential Sermons, Commentaries, Treatises and Defense*, trans. Edmund Colledge and Bernard McGinn (New York, 1981), p. 78. I owe this reference to Denis de Rougemont, *Love in the Western World*, trans. Montgomery Belgion (Princeton, NJ, 1983), p. 156.

8. Eckhart, *The Works of Meister Eckhart*, p. 176. I owe this and the following reference to de Rougemont, *Love in the Western World*, p. 155.

9. Eckhart, *The Works of Meister Eckhart*, p. 186.

10. Cf. John the Evangelist: 'Do not love the world or the things in the world. The love of the Father is not in those who love the world' (1 John 2:15).

11. Clifton Wolters, Introduction in Julian of Norwich, *Revelations of Divine Love*, trans. Clifton Wolters (Harmondsworth, 1966).

12. See Jeanrond, *A Theology of Love*, p. 72.

13. Bernard of Clairvaux, *Bernard of Clairvaux: Selected Works*, trans. G.R. Evans (New York, 1987), p. 198. I owe this and the following citation to Singer, *The Nature of Love*, vol. I, p. 191.

14. Bernard of Clairvaux, *Selected Works*, pp. 196–7.
15. Thomas Aquinas, *Summa Theologiae*, vol. 34: *Charity*, trans. R.J. Batten (London, 1975), pp. 93–5; cited in Jeanrond, *A Theology of Love*, p. 80.
16. 'Do not be conformed to this world, but be transformed by the renewing of your minds' (Romans 12:2).
17. 'We will not all die, but we will all be changed . . . For the trumpet will sound, and the dead will be raised imperishable, and we will be changed' (1 Corinthians 15:51–2).
18. The writer of the later letter to the Ephesians – frequently held to be a follower of Paul writing in his name – finds an image of Christ and the Church in the becoming one flesh of a man and a woman (Ephesians 5:31). But Paul has no clear line in praise of the 'sanctity of marriage' that we find in later Christianity.
19. This formulation, repeatedly used in the Sermon on the Mount, almost certainly refers to Hebrew Scripture.
20. Leviticus 20:10; Deuteronomy 17:7, cf. 22:22.
21. John 8:1–11 cites Jesus demanding forgiveness of the woman taken in adultery.
22. *Dikaiosune* – also translatable as 'justice'.
23. 'The meek' – which is to say the gentle, but also with the sense of 'the afflicted' – are those who suffer at the hands of others. Jesus is directly quoting Psalm 37, which commands the righteous to 'Be still before the Lord, and wait patiently for him;/ do not fret over those who prosper in their way,/ over those who carry out evil devices.' Verses 10–11: 'Yet a little while, and the wicked will be no more;/ though you look diligently for their place, they will not be there./ But the meek shall inherit the land,/ and delight in abundant prosperity./ The wicked plot against the righteous,/ and gnash their teeth at them:/ but the Lord laughs at the wicked,/ for he sees that their day is coming.'
24. This echoes Sirach (Ecclesiasticus), which proclaims that 'the beginning of pride is sin' (10:13).
25. This is what Samuel Huntington calls the core ethic that binds the United States and its immigrants from other faiths and nations into one. See Samuel P. Huntington, *Who Are We?: The Challenges to America's National Identity* (New York, 2004), pp. 59ff.
26. Is the connection between sexual prudery and the accumulation of power and wealth fortuitous? Probably not. As the sociologist Max Weber pointed out, ascetic self-denial is closely connected to a focus on wealth creation: 'For when asceticism was carried out of monastic cells into everyday life . . . it did its part in building the tremendous cosmos of the modern economic order.' See Max Weber, *The Protestant Ethic and the Spirit of Capitalism*, trans. Talcott Parsons (Mineola, 2003), pp. 155–83.
27. John 3:16; cf. 1 John 4:9vv.
28. Thomas Aquinas, *Summa Theologiae*, vol. 16: *Purpose and Happiness*, trans. Thomas Gilby (London, 1969), p. 139.
29. Anthony Kenny, *What is Faith?: Essays in the Philosophy of Religion* (Oxford, 1992), p. 66.
30. Augustine, 'Letter 194: Augustine to Sixtus', *The Works of Saint Augustine* (New York, 2004), p. 296.
31. See Augustine, 'The Trinity', pp. 252, 421; and Oliver O'Donovan, *The Problem of Self-Love in St Augustine*, pp. 130, 135.
32. John Calvin, 'Articles concerning predestination', in *Theological Treatises*, p. 179, quoted in Vincent Brümmer, *The Model of Love: A Study in Philosophical Theology* (Cambridge, 1993), p. 189.
33. Mark 10:27; Matthew 19:26; Luke 18:27; cf. also Luke 1:37.
34. Aquinas, *Summa Theologiae*, vol. 34: *Charity*, p. 135.
35. For an illuminating discussion of the scope of love in Luke and in the Johannine community, see Jeanrond, *A Theology of Love*, pp. 36–7.
36. Martin Gilbert's *The Righteous: The Unsung Heroes of the Holocaust* (London, 2003) is a necessary corrective to the view that the Pope and the Vatican were indifferent to the fate of the Jews. Gilbert mentions, for example, the clergy in France who were outspoken in their condemnation of the deportations and the many churchmen in Italy, including leading Jesuits, who saved Jews from deportation.

37. Martin Rhonheimer, 'The Holocaust: What Was Not Said', *First Things*, no. 137, 2003, p. 18.
38. Even treatments of this subject that are more even-handed than Daniel Goldhagen's *A Moral Reckoning: The Role of the Catholic Church in the Holocaust and Its Unfulfilled Duty of Repair* (New York, 2002) still tend to explain the Church's behaviour in terms of either pragmatism or anti-Semitism or both.
39. The expression has its earliest extant source in 1 Corinthians 11:25. Paul delivers what he 'received from the Lord' concerning the institution of the Eucharist: after supper, Jesus took the cup, 'saying "This cup is the new covenant in my blood".' Cf. Luke 22:20. Mark and Matthew omit the word 'new' from their accounts of Jesus's words on this occasion.
40. Nonetheless, to invoke these crimes as an argument against all religious belief is absurd: secularism has also spawned incalculable bigotry and violence, and the evil of a creed is hardly a simple function of the numbers executed in its name.
41. Thomas Aquinas, *Summa Theologiae*, vol. 9: *Angels*, trans. Kenelm Foster (London, 1968), p. 197.
42. Aquinas, *Summa Theologiae*, vol. 9: *Angels*, p. 203.
43. Cited in Nygren, *Agape and Eros*, p. 642.

CHAPTER 8 WOMEN AS IDEALS: LOVE AND THE TROUBADOURS

1. The French medievalist, Gaston Paris, coined the term '*amour courtois*' in 1883.
2. Friedrich Nietzsche, *Beyond Good and Evil*, in *The Basic Writings of Nietzsche*, trans. W. Kaufmann (New York, 1968), sect. 260, p. 398.
3. The coincidence of *fin' amor* and the cult of the Virgin in medieval Europe is a most remarkable and mysterious moment in the Western world's relationship to the feminine. See the final footnote of this chapter.
4. I am indebted to the work of L.T. Topsfield, *Troubadours and Love* (Cambridge, 1975); see p. 39.
5. Today known more commonly as William IX, Duke of Aquitaine and Count of Poitiers.
6. Cited in Linda M. Paterson, 'Development of the courtly *canso*', in *The Troubadours*, ed. Simon Gaunt and Sarah Kay (Cambridge, 1999), p. 36.
7. Where they are not cited in works of secondary literature mentioned below, English translations of troubadour poems are from Alan R. Press (ed. and trans.), *Anthology of Troubadour Lyric Poetry* (Edinburgh, 1971). These lines are from p. 13.
8. Press, *Anthology of Troubadour Lyric Poetry*, p. 15.
9. C.S. Lewis, in his classic and still influential study *The Allegory of Love*, regards adultery as one of the four major features of courtly love; but the strictures against adultery of some troubadours from the second generation onwards suggest that it isn't by any means an invariable feature, even if adulterous desire itself is.
10. I owe this point to Catherine Léglu, 'Moral and satirical poetry', in *The Troubadours*, ed. Simon Gaunt and Sarah Kay (Cambridge, 1999), pp. 49–50.
11. Léglu, 'Moral and satirical poetry', p. 49.
12. Cited in Linda M. Paterson, *The World of the Troubadours* (Cambridge, 1993), p. 235.
13. Cited in Singer, *The Nature of Love*, vol. II, p. 80, to which this chapter owes a great debt; cf. de Rougemont, *Love in the Western World*, p. 34. It is unclear, however, whether Courts of Love actually existed, at least as early as the twelfth century, or whether they were, at that stage, merely textual fictions.
14. I thank Stephen Jaeger for illuminating comments on this matter (personal correspondence). This formulation is also indebted to Singer, *The Nature of Love*.
15. Press, *Anthology of Troubadour Lyric Poetry*, p. 19.
16. Press, *Anthology of Troubadour Lyric Poetry*, p. 69.
17. I am grateful to Simon Gaunt for drawing my attention to misogynistic sentiments in Bernart de Ventadorn's '*Can vei la lauzeta mover*' (private correspondence).
18. Press, *Anthology of Troubadour Lyric Poetry*, p. 79, my italics.

19. I owe this translation to Paterson, 'Development of the courtly *canso*', p. 31.
20. Press, *Anthology of Troubadour Lyric Poetry*, p. 79.
21. Press, *Anthology of Troubadour Lyric Poetry*, p. 67.
22. Press, *Anthology of Troubadour Lyric Poetry*, p. 81.
23. I owe this point to Paterson, 'Development of the courtly *canso*', pp. 31–2.
24. Press, *Anthology of Troubadour Lyric Poetry*, p. 183.
25. Press, *Anthology of Troubadour Lyric Poetry*, p. 187.
26. Press, *Anthology of Troubadour Lyric Poetry*, p. 313.
27. For example, de Rougemont, *Love in the Western World*, pp. 35, 76.
28. Cited in Topsfield, *Troubadours and Love*, p. 11 – though it is unclear how reliable such biographical accounts of the troubadours are.
29. Press, *Anthology of Troubadour Lyric Poetry*, p. 189.
30. This paragraph is indebted to Singer's discussion of jealousy in *The Nature of Love*, vol. II, p. 27.
31. Topsfield, *Troubadours and Love*, pp. 221–2. My remarks on jealousy are much indebted to Topsfield.
32. Topsfield, *Troubadours and Love*, p. 32; cf. pp. 28–33.
33. Topsfield says that *jois* 'is an inner force which seeks enjoyment in life, powerful and self-perpetuating but needing an object on which to crystallise.' *Troubadours and Love*, pp. 123–4.
34. Press, *Anthology of Troubadour Lyric Poetry*, p. 197.
35. Press, *Anthology of Troubadour Lyric Poetry*, p. 69.
36. This interpretation of courtly love as masochistic-narcissistic has been advanced by the most diverse authors, from Denis de Rougemont in *Love in the Western World*, to Slavoj Žižek, drawing heavily on Lacan, in 'Courtly Love, or Woman as Thing', *The Žižek Reader*, ed. Elizabeth Wright and Edmond Wright (Oxford, 1999).
37. It is fascinating that the idolisation of the lady (*ma domna*, or *midons*) in courtly love coincides with the eruption of Mary-worship (*Madonna*) in the twelfth and thirteenth centuries. Bernard of Clairvaux (1090–1153), the abbot and mystic whom we encountered in chapter 7, was an almost exact contemporary of the first known troubadour, Guilhem de Peitieu. While Guilhem was paying homage to his married mistresses Bernard was fostering a chaste, but nonetheless passionate, veneration of Mary.

CHAPTER 9 HOW HUMAN NATURE BECAME LOVEABLE: FROM THE HIGH MIDDLE AGES TO THE RENAISSANCE

1. Some of these love letters were discovered about a century after Abelard and Heloise died; the rest came to light only at the end of the twentieth century. Historians are divided about their authenticity, and especially about whether the recently discovered correspondence is by Abelard and Heloise.
2. Abelard and Heloise, *The Lost Love Letters of Heloise and Abelard: Perceptions of Dialogue in Twelfth-Century France*, trans. Constant J. Mews and Neville Chiavaroli (Basingstoke, 2001), p. 229.
3. Abelard and Heloise, *The Letters of Abelard and Heloise*, trans. Betty Radice (Harmondsworth, 2003), p. 69.
4. Abelard and Heloise, *The Letters of Abelard and Heloise*, p. 11.
5. Abelard and Heloise, *The Letters of Abelard and Heloise*, p. 12.
6. I owe this point to Singer, *The Nature of Love*, vol. II, p. 102, and much of my discussion here is indebted to him.
7. Scruton, *Death-Devoted Heart*, p. 32.
8. Gottfried von Strassburg, *Tristan*, trans. A.T. Hatto (London, 1960), pp. 262–3.
9. Gottfried, *Tristan*, p. 263.
10. Gottfried, *Tristan*, p. 264, cited in Singer, *The Nature of Love*, vol. II, pp. 105–6.
11. I owe this point to Singer, *The Nature of Love*, vol. II, p. 106.
12. Gottfried, *Tristan*, p. 43.
13. Gottfried, *Tristan*, p. 265.

14. Gottfried, *Tristan*, pp. 267–8.
15. de Rougemont, *Love in the Western World*, pp. 133–4.
16. St Francis of Assisi, *Francis and Clare: The Complete Works*, trans. Regis J. Armstrong and Ignatius C. Brady (New York, 1982), p. 39.
17. This paragraph and the quote are indebted to Ingrid D. Rowland, 'The Renaissance Revealed', *From Heaven to Arcadia: The Sacred and the Profane in the Renaissance* (New York, 2008), pp. 3–4.
18. Bamber Gascoigne, *A Brief History of Christianity* (London, 2003), p. 62. This section on St Francis is much indebted to Gascoigne.
19. Friedrich Nietzsche, *On the Genealogy of Morals*, Essay III, sect. 28, p. 598.
20. Augustine, *City of God*, pp. 375–6.
21. For example, as Ingrid Rowland points out, when Titian painted his *Assumption of the Virgin* in 1518 'he could entrust the portrayal of religious ecstasy entirely to the realm of physical bliss'. 'Titian: the Sacred and the Profane', in *From Heaven to Arcadia: The Sacred and the Profane in the Renaissance* (New York, 2005), pp. 129–30.
22. Marsilio Ficino, *Platonic Theology*, trans. Josephine L. Burroughs, *Journal of the History of Ideas* vol. 5, no. 2 (1944), p. 238. Cited in Richard Tarnas, *The Passion of the Western Mind* (London, 1991), p. 214.
23. Giovanni Pico della Mirandola, 'The Dignity of Man', in *The Portable Renaissance Reader*, ed. J.B. Ross and M.M. McLaughlin (New York, 1977), p. 478. Cited in Tarnas, *The Passion of the Western Mind*, p. 215.
24. Singer, *The Nature of Love*, vol. II, pp. 170–1. My discussion of love in the Renaissance is much indebted to Singer.
25. I owe these points to Singer, *The Nature of Love*, vol. II, pp. 171–2.
26. Again I am indebted to Singer, *The Nature of Love*, vol. II, pp. 173–5 *passim*.
27. Cited in Singer, *The Nature of Love*, vol. II, p. 180.
28. Michel de Montaigne, *The Complete Essays*, trans. M.A. Screech (London, 1993). This quote is from 'On Affectionate Relationships' (also translated as 'On Friendship'), p. 212.
29. Montaigne, *The Complete Essays*, p. 212.
30. Montaigne, *The Complete Essays*, p. 208.
31. Montaigne, *The Complete Essays*, p. 212.
32. Montaigne, *The Complete Essays*, p. 215.
33. Montaigne, *The Complete Essays*, pp. 212–13.
34. Montaigne, *The Complete Essays*, p. 215.
35. Montaigne, *The Complete Essays*, p. 214.
36. Montaigne, *The Complete Essays*, p. 217.
37. Montaigne, *The Complete Essays*, p. 210.
38. Montaigne, *The Complete Essays*, p. 207.
39. *Homo sum, humani a me nihil alienum puto.* Quoted in Peter Burke, *Montaigne* (Oxford, 1981), p. 9.
40. Montaigne, *The Complete Essays*, p. 1251.
41. I owe this formulation to M.A. Screech, *Montaigne and Melancholy: The Wisdom of the Essays* (London, 1991), p. 122.
42. Montaigne, *The Complete Essays*, p. 1268.
43. Quoted in Burke, *Montaigne*, p. 12.
44. Montaigne, *The Complete Essays*, p. 1261.
45. Quoted in Burke, *Montaigne*, p. 10; cf. Montaigne, 'On educating children'.
46. Montaigne, *The Complete Essays*, p. 1269.
47. Montaigne, *The Complete Essays*, p. 1268.
48. Montaigne, *The Complete Essays*, p. 1261.
49. Montaigne, *The Complete Essays*, p. 1267.
50. Montaigne, *The Complete Essays*, p. 1268, my translation.

CHAPTER 10 LOVE AS JOYFUL UNDERSTANDING OF THE WHOLE: SPINOZA

1. Baruch (Benedict de) Spinoza, *Ethics*, ed. and trans. G.H.R. Parkinson (London, 1989), Part II, proposition xlviii, p. 75. (Henceforth references give Part and proposition number.)
2. Spinoza, *Ethics*, I, xxix, p. 25.
3. Spinoza, *Ethics*, I, xxxiii, p. 27.
4. Since, for Spinoza, God is not a creator separate from creation, God cannot be thought of as creating the world and then, without further interference, letting it function according to the laws and mechanisms that he created. God is continuously active as the on-going cause of all events and things.
5. Spinoza, *Ethics*, V, xxiv, p. 213.
6. Spinoza, *Ethics*, IV, xlii, p. 223.
7. Spinoza, *Ethics*, III, xiii, pp. 94–5.
8. Spinoza, *Ethics*, III, xxxi, p. 105.
9. Spinoza, *Ethics*, III, xxxi, p. 106.
10. Cited in Spinoza, *Ethics*, III, xxxi, p. 106.
11. Spinoza, *Ethics*, V, vi, p. 204.
12. Spinoza, *Ethics*, V, iii, p. 202.
13. Spinoza, *Ethics*, V, xv, p. 208.
14. I am grateful to Sue James for comments on an earlier draft of this chapter and am also indebted to Henry E. Allison, *Benedict de Spinoza* (New Haven and London, 1987), and Stuart Hampshire, *Spinoza* (Harmondsworth, 1987).

CHAPTER 11 LOVE AS ENLIGHTENED ROMANTICISM: ROUSSEAU

1. Jean-Jacques Rousseau, *The Reveries of the Solitary Walker*, in The Reveries of the Solitary Walker, *Botanical Writings and Letter to Franquières*, trans. Charles Butterworth (Hanover, NH, 2000), p. 89. I owe this citation to Singer, *The Nature of Love*, vol. II, p. 343.
2. Jean-Jacques Rousseau, *Emile, or On Education*, trans. Allan Bloom (New York, 1979), p. 433.
3. Rousseau, *The Reveries of the Solitary Walker*, pp. 89–90.
4. Rousseau, 'Discourse on the Origins of Inequality' in *Discourse on the Origins of Inequality (Second Discourse), Polemics, and Political Economy*, trans. Judith R. Bush and Roger D. Masters (Hanover, NH, 1992), p. 38.
5. Rousseau, 'Discourse', p. 36.
6. Rousseau, 'Discourse', p. 42.
7. Rousseau, *Emile*, p. 212.
8. Rousseau, *Emile*, p. 213.
9. Rousseau, 'Discourse', p. 76.
10. Rousseau, 'Discourse', p. 91.
11. Rousseau, 'Discourse', p. 63.
12. Rousseau, 'Discourse', p. 36.
13. Rousseau, 'Discourse', p. 36 (added in the 1782 edition).
14. I thank Nicholas Dent for pointing this out to me (private communication).
15. Rousseau, 'Discourse', p. 36.
16. Rousseau, 'Discourse', pp. 38–9.
17. François de la Rochefoucauld (1613–1680), *Maxims*, trans. Leonard Tancock (Harmondsworth, 1982), p. 54.
18. Rousseau, 'Discourse', p. 86.
19. I owe this point to Bloom, *Love and Friendship*, p. 65.
20. Jean-Jacques Rousseau, *Julie, or the New Heloise*, trans. Philip Stewart and Jean Vaché (Hanover, NH, 1997), p. 294. I owe this reference to Ernst Cassirer, *The Question of Jean-Jacques Rousseau*, trans. and ed. Peter Gay (New Haven and London, 1989), p. 93.
21. Rousseau, *Emile*, p. 235.
22. Bloom, *Love and Friendship*, p. 57. This whole paragraph owes a great deal to Bloom, especially pp. 44–6, 56–7, and 61.

23. Rousseau, *Emile*, pp. 333–4. I owe this reference to Bloom, *Love and Friendship*, p. 93.
24. Rousseau, *Confessions*, in *The* Confessions *and Correspondence, Including the Letters to Malesherbes*, trans. Christopher Kelly (Hanover, NH, 1995). p. 91.
25. Bloom, *Love and Friendship*, p. 47.
26. Bloom, *Love and Friendship*, p. 47.
27. My remarks on Rousseau and pity owe much to Bloom, *Love and Friendship*, pp. 67–71.
28. Rousseau, *Emile*, p. 329, quoted in Bloom, *Love and Friendship*, p. 91.
29. Rousseau, *Emile*, p. 391, quoted in Bloom, *Love and Friendship*, pp. 112–13.

CHAPTER 12 LOVE AS RELIGION: SCHLEGEL AND NOVALIS

1. Friedrich Schlegel, *Lucinde*, in *Friedrich Schegel's* Lucinde *and the Fragments*, trans. Peter Firchow (Minneapolis, 1971), p. 113. Quoted in Singer (*The Nature of Love*, vol. II, pp. 386–7), to whom my discussion and choice of citations are much indebted.
2. Schlegel, *Lucinde*, p. 47.
3. Friedrich Schlegel, 'On Philosophy: To Dorothea', in *Theory as Practice: A Critical Anthology of Early German Romantic Writings*, ed. and trans. J. Schulte-Sasse et al. (Minneapolis, 1991), pp. 423–4.
4. Schlegel, *Lucinde*, p. 49.
5. Friedrich Schlegel, 'Athenaeum Fragments', in *Friedrich Schlegel's* Lucinde *and the Fragments*, trans. Peter Firchow (Minneapolis, 1971), no. 34, p. 165.
6. Schlegel, *Lucinde*, p. 46.
7. Schlegel, 'Athenaeum Fragments', no. 34, pp. 165–6.
8. Schlegel, *Lucinde*, p. 108.
9. Schlegel, 'On Philosophy: To Dorothea', p. 427.
10. Schlegel, *Lucinde*, p. 113, my italics.
11. Schiller, letter to Goethe, 19 July 1799, *Friedrich Schiller: Werke und Briefe, Band 12, Briefe II: 1795–1805*, ed. N. Oellers (Frankfurt, 2002), p. 467.
12. Schlegel, *Lucinde*, p. 113. I owe this reference to Singer, *The Nature of Love*, vol. II, p. 386.
13. Schlegel, *Lucinde*, p. 48. I owe this reference to Thomas Mann, *Pro and Contra Wagner*, trans. Allan Blunden (London, 1985), p. 124.
14. I owe this formulation to Singer, *The Nature of Love*, vol. II, p. 294.
15. Schlegel, *Lucinde*, p. 48.
16. This paragraph is indebted to Singer, *The Nature of Love*, vol. III, pp. 18–19.
17. Novalis is the pen-name of Friedrich von Hardenberg. He met Sophie von Kühn in November 1794, when he was aged twenty-two and she twelve. They became engaged the following year, but she fell ill and died in 1797 (two days after her fifteenth birthday). Novalis himself died of tuberculosis at twenty-nine. My discussion of Novalis and choice of citations is indebted to Mann, *Pro and Contra Wagner*.
18. Novalis, *Hymns to the Night*, in *Hymns to the Night and Other Selected Writings*, trans. Charles E. Passage (Indianapolis, 1960), p. 4.
19. Novalis, *Hymns to the Night*, p. 6.
20. Novalis quoted in Mann, *Pro and Contra Wagner*, p. 124. This sentence comes from a note which is attached to the German edition of Novalis's 1797 Journal, but is not included in the English translation. ['Im Tode ist die Liebe, am süßesten; für den Liebenden ist der Tod eine Brautnacht – ein Geheimniß süßer Mysterien.'] Source. Novalis, *Schriften*, vol. 4, ed. Richard Samuel (Stuttgart, 1975), p. 50. The English translation of the Journal is to be found in *The Birth of Novalis: Friedrich von Hardenberg's Journal of 1797, with Selected Letters and Documents*, trans. Bruce Donehower (Albany, NY, 2007), pp. 79–97.
21. Novalis, *Hymns to the Night*, pp. 6–7.
22. Emily Dickinson, letter to Louise and Frances Norcross, late May 1863. In *The Letters of Emily Dickinson*, ed. Thomas H. Johnson (Cambridge, MA, 1997), p. 425.

23. Novalis, 'Faith and Love', sect. 16, p. 39, in *The Early Political Writings of the German Romantics*, ed. and trans. Frederick Beiser (Cambridge, 1996). 'Faith and Love', published in July 1798, is a short text written for the coronation of Friedrich Wilhelm III and his wife Luise.
24. Novalis, 'Faith and Love', sect. 4, pp. 35–6.
25. Novalis, *Hymns to the Night*, p. 4.
26. Novalis, *Hymns to the Night*, p. 4.
27. Schlegel, *Lucinde*, p. 127, cited in Mann, *Pro and Contra Wagner*, p. 125. Mann draws attention to the remarkable parallel between these words and the text of Wagner's *Tristan und Isolde*, to which I am indebted.

CHAPTER 13 LOVE AS THE URGE TO PROCREATE: SCHOPENHAUER

1. Arthur Schopenhauer, *The World as Will and Representation* (hereafter *WWR*), trans. E.F.J. Payne (New York, 1966), vol. II, p. 513.
2. Schopenhauer, *WWR*, vol. II, p. 513.
3. Schopenhauer, *WWR*, vol. II, pp. 512–13.
4. Schopenhauer, *WWR*, vol. II, pp. 513–14.
5. Schopenhauer, *WWR*, vol. II, p. 513.
6. Schopenhauer, *WWR*, vol. II, pp. 533–4.
7. Schopenhauer, *WWR*, vol. II, p. 531.
8. Schopenhauer, *WWR*, vol. II, p. 534.
9. Schopenhauer, *WWR*, vol. II, p. 542.
10. Schopenhauer, *WWR*, vol. II, p. 545.
11. Schopenhauer, *WWR*, vol. II, p. 544.
12. Schopenhauer, *WWR*, vol. II, p. 545.
13. Schopenhauer, *WWR*, vol. II, p. 544.
14. Schopenhauer, *WWR*, vol. II, p. 543.
15. I translate *Wille zum Leben* as 'will-to-life', rather than 'will-to-live' (as it is rendered in Payne's English translation), since 'will-to-life' captures better the desire not merely to persevere as an individual but to survive through my offspring.
16. Schopenhauer, *WWR*, vol. II, p. 571.
17. Schopenhauer, *WWR*, vol. II, p. 542.
18. Schopenhauer, *WWR*, vol. II, p. 536.
19. Schopenhauer, *WWR*, vol. II, p. 216.
20. Schopenhauer, *WWR*, vol. II, p. 205.
21. Schopenhauer, *WWR*, vol. II, p. 209.
22. Schopenhauer, *WWR*, vol. II, p. 216.
23. Schopenhauer, *WWR*, vol. II, pp. 216–17.
24. Schopenhauer, *WWR*, vol. II, p. 217.
25. Schopenhauer, *WWR*, vol. II, pp. 209–10.
26. Schopenhauer, *WWR*, vol. II, p. 573.
27. Schopenhauer, *WWR*, vol. II, pp. 507–8.
28. Schopenhauer, *WWR*, vol. II, p. 613.
29. Schopenhauer, *WWR*, vol. II, p. 621.
30. Schopenhauer, *WWR*, vol. I, p. 374.
31. Schopenhauer, *WWR*, vol. I, pp. 372, 375.
32. Schopenhauer, *WWR*, vol. I, p. 374.
33. Schopenhauer, *WWR*, vol. I, p. 373.
34. Schopenhauer, *WWR*, vol. I, p. 404.
35. Schopenhauer, *WWR*, vol. I, pp. 411–12.

CHAPTER 14 LOVE AS AFFIRMATION OF LIFE: NIETZSCHE

1. Cited in John Hick, *Evil and the God of Love* (London, 1985), p. 51.

2. Friedrich Nietzsche, *Ecce Homo*, in *The Basic Writings of Nietzsche*, trans. W. Kaufmann (New York, 1968), p. 714.

3. Friedrich Nietzsche, *The Gay Science*, trans. W. Kaufmann (New York, 1974), sect. 370, p. 328.

4. Nietzsche, *The Gay Science*, sect. 370, p. 328.

5. Nietzsche, *Beyond Good and Evil*, Preface, p. 193.

6. Nietzsche, *On the Genealogy of Morals*, Essay III, sect. 14, p. 558.

7. Nietzsche, *On the Genealogy of Morals*, Essay III, sect. 28, pp. 598–9.

8. Nietzsche, *On the Genealogy of Morals*, Preface, sect. 5, p. 455.

9. Nietzsche, *The Gay Science*, sect. 338, p. 269.

10. Nietzsche, *The Gay Science*, sect. 14, p. 88.

11. Nietzsche, *Beyond Good and Evil*, sect. 225, p. 344.

12. Friedrich Nietzsche, *Twilight of the Idols*, in *The Portable Nietzsche*, trans. W. Kaufmann (New York, 1954), p. 562 ('What I owe to the Ancients', sect. 4).

13. Nietzsche, *The Gay Science*, sect. 338, p. 270.

14. Nietzsche, *Thus Spoke Zarathustra*, Part I, sect. 16, in *The Portable Nietzsche*, trans. W. Kaufmann (New York, 1954), p. 172.

15. Nietzsche, *Beyond Good and Evil*, sect. 293, pp. 420–1.

16. Nietzsche, *On the Genealogy of Morals*, Preface, sect. 5, p. 455.

17. Nietzsche, *On the Genealogy of Morals*, Preface, sect. 6, p. 456.

18. Nietzsche, *On the Genealogy of Morals*, Essay I, sect. 8, p. 470.

19. Nietzsche, *On the Genealogy of Morals*, Essay I, sect. 8, p. 470, my italics.

20. Nietzsche, *On the Genealogy of Morals*, Essay I, sect. 8, p. 471.

21. Friedrich Nietzsche, *Human, All Too Human*, trans. R.J. Hollingdale (Cambridge, 1986), vol. I, sect. 224, p. 107.

22. Nietzsche, *On the Genealogy of Morals*, Essay II, sect. 18, pp. 523–4.

23. Nietzsche, *On the Genealogy of Morals*, Essay I, sect. 6, pp. 468–9.

24. Nietzsche, *Beyond Good and Evil*, sect. 168, p. 282.

25. Nietzsche, *The Gay Science*, sect. 290, p. 233.

26. Nietzsche, *Twilight of the Idols*, p. 500 ('The Four Great Errors', sect. 8).

27. Nietzsche, *The Gay Science*, sect. 14, p. 89.

28. Nietzsche, *The Gay Science*, sect. 14, p. 89.

29. Nietzsche, *The Gay Science*, sect. 334, p. 262.

30. Nietzsche, *On the Genealogy of Morals*, Essay III, sect. 6, p. 541.

31. Nietzsche, *The Gay Science*, sect. 276, p. 223.

32. Nietzsche, *The Gay Science*, sect. 125, pp. 181–2.

CHAPTER 15 LOVE AS A HISTORY OF LOSS: FREUD

1. Nietzsche, *Beyond Good and Evil*, sect. 23, p. 222.

2. This chapter owes a great debt to Jonathan Lear's *Love and Its Place in Nature* (New York, 1990), which has much influenced its argument and choice of citations, and to Sebastian Gardner, Ken Gemes, and Bernard Reginster (personal communications).

3. Sigmund Freud, *Group Psychology and the Analysis of the Ego*, vol. XVIII (1955), p. 90. *Standard Edition of the Complete Psychological Works of Sigmund Freud*, trans. and ed. James Strachey, vols. I–XXIV (London, 1953–74 [hereafter *SE*]).

4. Sigmund Freud, *Civilization and Its Discontents*, *SE*, vol. XXI (1961), p. 101.

5. Freud, *Civilization and Its Discontents*, pp. 102–3, my italics.

6. Sigmund Freud, *Three Essays on Sexuality*, *SE*, vol. VII (1953), p. 222, my italics.

7. Freud, *Three Essays on Sexuality*, pp. 222–3.

8. Freud, *Three Essays on Sexuality*, p. 223.

9. Again, my argument is indebted to Lear, *Love and Its Place in Nature*, e.g. pp. 160–3.

10. The notion of 'primary narcissism' has been largely discredited by empirical research in early child psychology.

11. Freud, *Civilization and Its Discontents*, pp. 66–7.
12. Sigmund Freud, *The Future of an Illusion*, SE, vol. XXI (1961), p. 24.
13. Freud, *Civilization and Its Discontents*, p. 68.
14. Sigmund Freud, *New Introductory Lectures on Psycho-Analysis*, lecture 31, SE, vol. XXII (1964), p. 63.
15. Sigmund Freud, *The Ego and the Id*, SE, vol. XIX (1961), p. 45.
16. Freud, *Group Psychology*, p. 106.
17. Freud, *New Introductory Lectures*, lecture 31, p. 65.
18. Freud, *Civilization and Its Discontents*, p. 120.
19. Sigmund Freud, *The Economic Problem of Masochism*, SE, vol. XIX (1961), p. 170.
20. Freud, *Civilization and Its Discontents*, pp. 126–8. This thought is strikingly prefigured in Nietzsche's *On the Genealogy of Morals*, Essay II, where the development of conscience is explained in almost identical terms.
21. Freud, *The Ego and the Id*, p. 58.
22. Freud, *The Ego and the Id*, p. 58, quoted in Lear, *Love and Its Place in Nature*, pp. 154–5, to which my discussion is indebted.
23. Freud, *The Ego and the Id*, p. 29, cited in Lear, *Love and Its Place in Nature*, p. 164, n. 24.
24. Freud, *Group Psychology*, pp. 112–13.
25. Freud, *Civilization and Its Discontents*, pp. 71–2.
26. Freud, *Civilization and Its Discontents*, p. 118. See also Freud, *New Introductory Lectures*, p. 106.
27. Freud, *Civilization and Its Discontents*, p. 69.
28. Freud, *Civilization and Its Discontents*, p. 66.
29. Freud, *New Introductory Lectures*, lecture 32, p. 107.
30. Freud, *The Ego and the Id*, p. 45.
31. This formulation is indebted to Lear, *Love and Its Place in Nature*, p. 176.
32. Freud, *New Introductory Lectures*, lecture 31, p. 80; cf. Freud, *The Ego and the Id*, p. 56.
33. This thought is excellently developed in Lear, *Love and Its Place in Nature*, pp. 164–72.
34. I owe this formulation to Bernard Reginster (personal communication).
35. Clearly there are big differences between Plato's and Freud's concepts of Eros; for example, Freud in no way believes that the sexual instinct drives a search for a timeless, transcendent good, and so he wildly exaggerates when he claims that in 'its origin, function, and relation to sexual love, the "Eros" of the philosopher Plato coincides exactly with the love-force, the libido of psycho-analysis . . .' See Freud, *Group Psychology*, p. 91; cf. Freud, *The Resistances to Psycho-Analysis*, SE, vol. XIX (1961), p. 218.
36. Sigmund Freud, *Analysis Terminable and Interminable*, SE, vol. XXIII (1964), p. 243; cf. Freud, *New Introductory Lectures*, p. 107.
37. Sigmund Freud, *Beyond the Pleasure Principle*, SE, vol. XVIII (1955), p. 55.
38. Freud, *Beyond the Pleasure Principle*, p. 38.
39. Freud, *New Introductory Lectures*, pp. 106–7.
40. Freud, *Civilization and Its Discontents*, p. 112.
41. See chapter 3.
42. Freud, *Group Psychology*, p. 101. Freud suggests that only a mother's relationship to her son might be an exception to this rule.
43. Similar passages in the other Gospels also don't identify children with a special capacity to love. Mark's Gospel says 'receive the kingdom as a little child to enter it' (Mark 10:15), without explaining at all what it is about being like a child that Jesus is valuing. Even humility isn't explicitly mentioned.

Chapter 16 Love as terror and tedium: Proust

1. Marcel Proust, *Remembrance of Things Past*, vols. 1, 2 and 3, trans. C.K. Scott Moncrieff and Terence Kilmartin (Harmondsworth, 1983), vol. 3, p. 105. Volume and page numbers now cited in text.

2. I am influenced in this formulation by Singer, *The Nature of Love*, vol. III, pp. 161–2.
3. I am indebted to Malcolm Bowie, *Proust Among the Stars* (London, 1998), p. 262.
4. I owe the formulation of this sentence to Lear, *Love and Its Place in Nature*, p. 133.
5. I thank Alison Finch for pointing this out to me (personal communication).
6. I owe this point to Alison Finch, 'Love, sexuality and friendship', in *The Cambridge Companion to Proust*, ed. Richard Bales (Cambridge, 2001), p. 169. This chapter is much indebted to her article. Bowie (*Proust Among the Stars*, pp. 263–4) also emphasises the 'thoroughgoingly erotic' textures of Proust's writing, in the sense not of some simple pan-sexuality but rather of the complexity, discrimination, intensity and vulnerability of desire – and 'desirous thinking'.
7. I owe this reference to André Maurois, *The Quest for Proust*, trans. Gerard Hopkins (London, 1962), p. 210.
8. I am indebted to Singer's discussion of this scene in Singer, *The Nature of Love*, vol. III, pp. 170–1.
9. This passage is superbly analysed by Martha Nussbaum, to whom I am indebted. See *Love's Knowledge: Essays on Philosophy and Literature* (Oxford and New York, 1990), pp. 261–85.
10. I thank Alison Finch for emphasising the comic side of Proust (personal communication) overlooked by many commentators, especially, perhaps, by philosophers.
11. Samuel Beckett, *Proust* (London, 1970), pp. 19–20.
12. Beckett, *Proust*, p. 19.
13. This section, and especially the idea of redeeming the suffering of love for individuals through a Platonic 'ascent', owes a particular debt to Martha Nussbaum, *Upheavals of Thought*, especially pp. 511–26. A similar account is offered in her 'People as Fictions: Proust and the Ladder of Love', in *Erotikon*, ed. Shadi Bartsch and Thomas Bartscherer (Chicago and London, 2005), especially pp. 229–38. My choice of citations is also indebted to her. I also acknowledge Finch, 'Love, sexuality and friendship', e.g. p. 169.
14. Nussbaum, 'People as Fictions', p. 229.
15. Beckett, *Proust*, p. 35.
16. Kierkegaard remarks that 'Philosophy is perfectly right in saying that life must be understood backwards. But then one forgets the other clause – that it must be lived forward.' *Søren Kierkegaard's Journals and Papers*, vol. 1, A–E, ed. and trans. Howard V. Hong and Edna H. Hong (Bloomington and London, 1967), p. 450.

Chapter 17 Love reconsidered

1. Singer, *The Nature of Love*, vol. I, p. 96; cf. vol. I, p. 5 (value is bestowed on the loved object 'regardless of its capacity to satisfy interests') and p. 15 ('Love is sheer gratuity. It issues from the lover like hairs on his head . . . it cannot be derived from outside').
2. Frankfurt, *The Reasons of Love* (Princeton, NJ, 2004), p. 79.
3. For example, if you believe, with Augustine, that only God can genuinely love and that unaided human love will always be perverted by selfishness and evil, then we need to strive for selflessness so that God's love can work through us. But if you have jettisoned such beliefs, then disinterested concern will never supply the passion and engagement that characterise real love.
4. Indeed, this is why genuine love of all sorts is so remarkably conservative. For even when love seeks unfamiliar worlds, even when it craves 'difference', it does so, we might conjecture, because these are worlds with which the lover senses an unexplored affinity and that he wishes to claim as his rightful inheritance, rather than – as Proust's Narrator suggests – because he is seeking something fundamentally different to himself.
5. Freud, *New Introductory Lectures*, pp. 107–8.
6. As are love's twin virtues of repentance and forgiveness, which, properly conceived, also have the character of return-and-renewal. Repentance is crucial to any loving relationship because it is needed for love's task of grounding or homing: of bringing the individual back to himself,

back to the real ground of his being. It reboots him, so to speak, so that he wins his liberty from past betrayals of himself and specifically of genuine relationship to the ground of his being – betrayals which made it impossible to relate and speak freely to his loved one.

Forgiveness is the loved one's acceptance of this act, and the renewed intimacy that it makes possible. It welcomes the lover back into the mode of being where the other can be a home or ground for him. Like love itself, forgiveness-and-repentance has a circular motion where a movement into the past is also a movement into the future. As if love really experiences time not as a purely linear movement towards some moment of final 'consummation' or salvation, but as endlessly circular.

7. In other words, as modes of attentiveness, Eros, agape and *philia* can be synchronic as well as diachronic.

8. In chapter 2 I suggested that we see all three modes of attention in the love of Jonathan for David and of Ruth for Naomi. More importantly, we see all three in the Hebrews' love for God, sometimes spoken of in rapturous-erotic tones redolent of the Song of Songs, sometimes in terms of the devotion and favour extended to a friend and inspired by his goodness, sometimes in terms of unreserved submission to the will of the other.

9. I thank Jay Belkin for a stimulating discussion on the history of 'childhood'.

Bibliography

Abelard and Heloise, *The Lost Love Letters of Heloise and Abelard: Perceptions of Dialogue in Twelfth-Century France*, trans. Constant J. Mews and Neville Chiavaroli (Basingstoke: Palgrave Macmillan, 2001).
—— *The Letters of Abelard and Heloise*, trans. Betty Radice (Harmondsworth: Penguin, 2003).
Allison, Henry E., *Benedict de Spinoza* (New Haven and London: Yale University Press, 1987).
Aquinas, Thomas, *Summa Theologiae*, vol. 9: *Angels*, trans. Kenelm Foster (London: Eyre & Spottiswoode, 1968).
—— *Summa Theologiae*, vol. 16: *Purpose and Happiness*, trans. Thomas Gilby (London: Eyre & Spottiswoode, 1969).
—— *Summa Theologiae*, vol. 34: *Charity*, trans. R.J. Batten (London: Eyre & Spottiswoode, 1975).
Aristotle, *Eudemian Ethics, Magna Moralia, Nicomachean Ethics* and *Politics*, in *The Complete Works of Aristotle*, vol. II, ed. Jonathan Barnes (Princeton, NJ: Princeton University Press, 1984).
Auden, W.H., *The Age of Anxiety: A Baroque Eclogue* (New York: Random House, 1947).
Augustine, 'Answer to the Pelagians, III: Unfinished Work in Answer to Julian', in *The Works of Saint Augustine*, Part I, vol. 25 (New York: New City Press, 1999).
—— *City of God*, trans. Henry Bettenson (London: Penguin, 2003).
—— 'Confessions', in *The Works of Saint Augustine*, Part I, vol. 1 (New York: New City Press, 1997).
—— 'Exposition 2 of Psalm 31', in *The Works of Saint Augustine*, Part III, vol. 15 (New York: New City Press, 2000).
—— 'Letter 194: Augustine to Sixtus', in *The Works of Saint Augustine*, Part II, vol. 3 (New York: New City Press, 2004).
—— 'Letters 100–155', in *The Works of Saint Augustine*, Part II, vol. 2 (New York: New City Press, 2003).
—— *St Augustine: On the Spirit and the Letter*, trans. W.J. Sparrow-Simpson (London: Macmillan Co., 1925).
—— 'Sermon 121: On the Words of the Gospel of John 1:10–14: The World Was Made through Him', in *The Works of Saint Augustine*, Part III, vol. 4 (New York: New City Press, 1992).
—— 'Sermon 192: On Christmas Day', in *The Works of Saint Augustine*, Part III, vol. 6 (New York: New City Press, 1993).
—— 'Teaching Christianity', in *The Works of Saint Augustine*, Part I, vol. 11 (New York: New City Press, 1996).
—— 'The Trinity', in *The Works of Saint Augustine*, Part I, vol. 5 (New York: New City Press, 1991).

—— *Tractates on the Gospel of John, 55–111* (Washington, DC: Catholic University of America Press, 1994).

—— *Treatises on Various Subjects*, trans. Mary Sarah Muldowney, The Fathers of the Church vol. 16 (Washington, DC: Catholic University of America Press, 1952).

Babylonian Talmud, ed. and trans. I. Epstein (London: Soncino Press, 1935–48).

Barnes, Jonathan, *The Presocratic Philosophers* (London: Routledge, 1982).

Beckett, Samuel, *Proust* (London: Calder & Boyars, 1970).

Benedict XVI, Encyclical Letter, *Deus Caritas Est (God is Love)* (Vatican: Libreria Editrice Vaticana, 2005).

Bernard of Clairvaux, *Bernard of Clairvaux: Selected Works*, trans. G.R. Evans (New York: Paulist Press, 1987).

Bible, New Revised Standard Version, Anglicised Edition (Oxford: Oxford University Press, 1995).

Bloom, Allan, *Love and Friendship* (New York: Simon & Schuster, 1993).

Bloom, Harold, *Jesus and Yahweh: The Names Divine* (New York and London: Riverhead Books, 2005).

Bonaventure, *The Soul's Journey into God, the Tree of Life and the Life of St Francis*, trans. Ewert H. Cousins (New York: Paulist Press, 1978).

Bowie, Malcolm, *Proust Among the Stars* (London: HarperCollins, 1998).

Brown, F., Driver, S.R. and Briggs, C.A., *The Brown-Driver-Briggs Hebrew and English Lexicon of the Old Testament* (Peabody, MA: Hendrickson Publishers, 2000).

Brümmer, Vincent, *The Model of Love: A Study in Philosophical Theology* (Cambridge: Cambridge University Press, 1993).

Buber, Martin, *On Judaism* (New York: Schocken Books, 1967).

Burke, Peter, *Montaigne* (Oxford: Oxford University Press, 1981).

Buss, David M., *Evolutionary Psychology: The New Science of the Mind* (Boston, MA: Allyn & Bacon, 1999).

Calvin, John, *Calvin: Theological Treatises*, ed. and trans. J.K.S. Reid (Philadelphia: Westminster Press, 1954).

Cassirer, Ernst, *The Question of Jean-Jacques Rousseau*, ed. and trans. Peter Gay (New Haven and London: Yale University Press, 1989).

Chadwick, Henry, *The Early Church* (London: Penguin, 1967).

The Concise Dictionary of Classical Hebrew, ed. D.J.A. Clines (Sheffield: Sheffield Phoenix Press, 2009).

Cooper, John M., 'Aristotle on Friendship', in *Essays on Aristotle's Ethics*, ed. Amélie Oksenberg Rorty (Berkeley and Los Angeles: University of California Press, 1980).

Crouch, C.L., *War and Ethics in the Ancient Near East: Military Violence in Light of Cosmology and History*, Beihefte zur Zeitschrift für die alttestamentliche Wissenschaft (Berlin and New York: Walter de Gruyter, 2009).

Dickinson, Emily, *The Letters of Emily Dickinson*, ed. Thomas H. Johnson (Cambridge, MA: Harvard University Press, 1997).

Dover, Kenneth, *Greek Homosexuality* (Cambridge, MA: Harvard University Press, 1978).

Eckhart, Meister, *The Essential Sermons, Commentaries, Treatises and Defense*, trans. Edmund Colledge and Bernard McGinn (New York: Paulist Press, 1981).

—— *The Works of Meister Eckhart*, ed. Franz Pfeiffer, trans. C. de B. Evans (Kila, MT: Kessinger, 1992).

Epicurus, *Epicurus: The Extant Remains*, ed. and trans. Cyril Bailey (Hildesheim and New York: Georg Olms Verlag, 1970).

Ficino, Marsilio, *Platonic Theology*, trans. Josephine L. Burroughs, *Journal of the History of Ideas*, vol. 5, no. 2 (April 1944), pp. 227–42.

Finch, Alison, 'Love, sexuality and friendship', in *The Cambridge Companion to Proust*, ed. Richard Bales (Cambridge: Cambridge University Press, 2001).

Francis of Assisi, *Francis and Clare: The Complete Works*, trans. Regis J. Armstrong and Ignatius C. Brady (New York: Paulist Press, 1982).

Frankfurt, Harry G., *The Reasons of Love* (Princeton, NJ: Princeton University Press, 2004).

Fraschetti, Augusto, ed., *Roman Women*, trans. Linda Lappin (Chicago and London: University of Chicago Press, 2001).

Freud, Sigmund, *Standard Edition of the Complete Psychological Works of Sigmund Freud*, trans. and ed. James Strachey, vols. I to XXIV (London: Hogarth Press, 1953–1974):

—— *Analysis Terminable and Interminable*, vol. XXIII (1964).

—— *Beyond the Pleasure Principle*, vol. XVIII (1955).

—— *Civilization and Its Discontents*, vol. XXI (1961).

—— *The Economic Problem of Masochism*, vol. XIX (1961).

—— *The Ego and the Id*, vol. XIX (1961).

—— *The Future of an Illusion*, vol. XXI (1961).

—— *Group Psychology and the Analysis of the Ego*, vol. XVIII (1955).

—— *Inhibitions, Symptoms and Anxiety*, vol. XX (1959).

—— *New Introductory Lectures on Psycho-Analysis*, vol. XXII (1964).

—— *The Resistances to Psycho-Analysis*, vol. XIX (1961).

—— *Three Essays on Sexuality*, vol. VII (1953).

Gascoigne, Bamber, *A Brief History of Christianity* (London: Constable & Robinson, 2003).

Gaunt, Simon and Kay, Sarah, eds., *The Troubadours* (Cambridge: Cambridge University Press, 1999).

Gilbert, Martin, *The Righteous: The Unsung Heroes of the Holocaust* (London: Black Swan, 2003).

Gillespie, Stuart and Hardie, Philip, eds., *The Cambridge Companion to Lucretius* (Cambridge: Cambridge University Press, 2007).

Goldhagen, Daniel, *A Moral Reckoning: The Role of the Catholic Church in the Holocaust and Its Unfulfilled Duty of Repair* (New York: Random House, 2002).

Goodman, Lenn E., *Love Thy Neighbor as Thyself* (New York: Oxford University Press, 2008).

Gottfried von Strassburg, *Tristan*, trans. A.T. Hatto (London: Penguin, 1960).

Hampshire, Stuart, *Spinoza* (Harmondsworth: Penguin, 1987).

Hick, John, *Evil and the God of Love* (London: Macmillan, 1985).

Huntington, Samuel P., *Who Are We?: The Challenges to America's National Identity* (New York: Simon & Schuster, 2004).

Hurowitz, V.A., 'The Divinity of Mankind in the Bible and the Ancient Near East: A New Mesopotamian Parallel', in *Mishneh Todah: Studies in Deuteronomy and Its Cultural Environment in Honor of Jeffrey H. Tigay*, ed. N. Sacher Fox, D.A. Gilat-Gilad and M.J. Williams (Winona Lake, IN: Eisenbrauns, 2009).

Hyamson, Moses, ed. and trans., *Mishneh Torah, The Book of Adoration by Maimonides* (Jerusalem and New York: Feldheim, 1975).

Jeanrond, Werner G., *A Theology of Love* (London: T. & T. Clark, 2010).

John of the Cross, *Dark Night of the Soul*, trans. E. Allison Peers (Garden City, NY: Image Books, 1959).

—— *A Spiritual Canticle of the Soul and the Bridegroom Christ*, trans. David Lewis (London: T. Baker, 1919).

Julian of Norwich, *Revelations of Divine Love* (Harmondsworth: Penguin, 1966).

Kahn, Charles H., *The Art and Thought of Heraclitus* (Cambridge: Cambridge University Press, 1979).

Kant, Immanuel, *Critique of Judgement*, trans. J.C. Meredith (Oxford: Oxford University Press, 1952).

Kellner, Menachem, *Maimonides on Human Perfection*, Brown Judaic Studies, vol. 202 (Atlanta: Scholars Press, 1990).

Kenny, Anthony, *What is Faith?: Essays in the Philosophy of Religion* (Oxford: Oxford University Press, 1992).

Kierkegaard, Søren, *Søren Kierkegaard's Journals and Papers*, vol. 1, A–E, ed. and trans. Howard V. Hong and Edna H. Hong (Bloomington and London: Indiana University Press, 1967).

Larkin, Philip, *Collected Poems* (London: Faber & Faber, 2003).

Lear, Jonathan, *Love and Its Place in Nature* (New York: Farrar, Straus & Giroux, 1990).

Leclercq, Jean, *Monks and Love in Twelfth-Century France* (Oxford: Oxford University Press, 1979).

Léglu, Catherine, 'Moral and satirical poetry', in *The Troubadours*, ed. Simon Gaunt and Sarah Kay (Cambridge: Cambridge University Press, 1999).

Lindemann, Albert S., *Anti-Semitism before the Holocaust* (Harlow: Longman, 2000).

Lucretius, *De Rerum Natura*, trans. C.H. Sisson (New York: Routledge, 2003). Also trans. W.H.D. Rouse, rev. M.F. Smith (Cambridge, MA: Harvard University Press, 1975).

Luther, Martin, 'Second Christmas Sermon: Early Christmas Morning Service, Titus 3:4–8', in *Sermons of Martin Luther*, vol. 6 (Grand Rapids, MI: Baker Books, 1995).

Maimonides, Moses, *The Code of Maimonides: Book II, The Book of Love*, trans. Menachem Kellner (New Haven and London: Yale University Press, 2004).

Mann, Thomas, *Pro and Contra Wagner*, trans. Allan Blunden (London: Faber & Faber, 1985).

Maurois, André, *The Quest for Proust*, trans. Gerard Hopkins (London: Penguin, 1962).

The Mishnah, trans. Herbert Danby (London: Oxford University Press, 1958).

Montaigne, Michel de, *The Complete Essays*, trans. M.A. Screech (London: Penguin, 1993).

Murdoch, Iris, *The Sovereignty of Good* (London: Routledge, 1970).

Nietzsche, Friedrich, *The Antichrist, Thus Spoke Zarathustra* and *Twilight of the Idols* in *The Portable Nietzsche*, trans. W. Kaufmann (New York: Viking, 1954).

—— *Beyond Good and Evil, Ecce Homo* and *On the Genealogy of Morals* in *The Basic Writings of Nietzsche*, trans. W. Kaufmann (New York: The Modern Library, 1968).

—— *The Gay Science*, trans. W. Kaufmann (New York: Vintage, 1974).

—— *Human, All Too Human*, trans. R.J. Hollingdale (Cambridge: Cambridge University Press, 1986).

Novalis, 'Faith and Love', in *The Early Political Writings of the German Romantics*, Cambridge Texts in the History of Political Thought, ed. and trans. Frederick Beiser (Cambridge: Cambridge University Press, 1996).

—— *Hymns to the Night*, in *Hymns to the Night and Other Selected Writings*, trans. Charles E. Passage (Indianapolis: Bobbs-Merrill, 1960).

—— Journal, in *The Birth of Novalis: Friedrich von Hardenberg's Journal of 1797, with Selected Letters and Documents*, trans. Bruce Donehower (Albany, NY: State University of New York Press, 2007).

—— *Schriften*, vol. 4, ed. Richard Samuel (Stuttgart: Kohlhammer, 1975).

Nussbaum, Martha, *The Fragility of Goodness: Luck and Ethics in Greek Tragedy and Philosophy* (Cambridge: Cambridge University Press, 1986).

—— *Love's Knowledge: Essays on Philosophy and Literature* (Oxford and New York: Oxford University Press, 1990).

—— 'People as Fictions: Proust and the Ladder of Love', in *Erotikon*, ed. Shadi Bartsch and Thomas Bartscherer (Chicago and London: University of Chicago Press, 2005).

—— *Upheavals of Thought* (Cambridge: Cambridge University Press, 2001).

Nygren, Anders, *Agape and Eros*, trans. Philip S. Watson (Philadelphia: Westminster Press, 1953).

O'Donovan, Oliver, *The Problem of Self-Love in St Augustine* (New Haven: Yale University Press, 1980).

Otto, Rudolf, *Mysticism East and West: A Comparative Analysis of the Nature of Mysticism*, trans. Bertha L. Bracey and Richenda C. Payne (New York: Macmillan, 1932).

Ovid, *The Art of Love*, trans. Rolfe Humphries (Bloomington: Indiana University Press, 1957).

—— *Metamorphoses*, trans. F.J. Miller (Cambridge, MA: Harvard University Press, 1951).

Paterson, Linda M., 'Development of the courtly *canso*', in *The Troubadours*, ed. Simon Gaunt and Sarah Kay (Cambridge: Cambridge University Press, 1999).

—— *The World of the Troubadours* (Cambridge: Cambridge University Press, 1993).

Paz, Octavio, *The Double Flame: Essays on Love and Eroticism*, trans. Helen Lane (New York: Harcourt Brace, 1995).

Pico della Mirandola, Giovanni, 'The Dignity of Man', in *The Portable Renaissance Reader*, ed. J.B. Ross and M.M. McLaughlin (New York: Penguin, 1977).

Plato, *Charmides*, in *Early Socratic Dialogues*, trans. Trevor J. Saunders (London: Penguin, 1987).

—— *Euthyphro, Apology, Crito, Phaedo, Phaedrus*, trans. Harold North Fowler (Cambridge, MA: Harvard University Press, 2005).

—— *The Laws*, trans. Trevor J. Saunders (Harmondsworth: Penguin, 1975).

—— *The Republic*, trans. Desmond Lee (London: Penguin, 2003).

—— *The Symposium*, trans. Walter Hamilton (Harmondsworth: Penguin, 1951). Also trans. Robin Waterfield (Oxford: Oxford University Press, 1994).

Press, Alan R., ed. and trans., *Anthology of Troubadour Lyric Poetry* (Edinburgh: Edinburgh University Press, 1971).

Price, A.W., *Love and Friendship in Plato and Aristotle* (Oxford: Oxford University Press, 1997).

Proust, Marcel, *Remembrance of Things Past*, vols. 1, 2 and 3, trans. C.K. Scott Moncrieff and Terence Kilmartin (Harmondsworth: Penguin, 1983).

Rajak, Tessa, *Translation and Survival: The Greek Bible of the Ancient Jewish Diaspora* (Oxford and New York: Oxford University Press, 2009).

Rhonheimer, Martin, 'The Holocaust: What Was Not Said', *First Things*, no. 137 (2003), pp. 18–27.

Rist, John, 'Faith and Reason', in *The Cambridge Companion to Augustine*, ed. Norman Kretzmann and Eleonore Stump (Cambridge: Cambridge University Press, 2001).

Rochefoucauld, François de la, *Maxims*, trans. Leonard Tancock (Harmondsworth: Penguin, 1982).

Rofé, Alexander, *Introduction to the Literature of the Hebrew Bible*, Jerusalem Biblical Studies, vol. 9 (Ein-Kerem, Jerusalem: Simor, 2009).

Rougemont, Denis de, *Love in the Western World*, trans. Montgomery Belgion (Princeton, NJ: Princeton University Press, 1983).

Rousseau, Jean-Jacques, *Confessions*, in *The Confessions and Correspondence, Including the Letters to Malesherbes*, The Collected Writings of Rousseau, vol. 5, trans. Christopher Kelly (Hanover, NH: University Press of New England, 1995).

—— 'Discourse on the Origins of Inequality', in *Discourse on the Origins of Inequality (Second Discourse), Polemics, and Political Economy*, The Collected Writings of Rousseau, vol. 3, trans. Judith R. Bush and Roger D. Masters (Hanover, NH: University Press of New England, 1992).

—— *Emile, or On Education*, trans. Allan Bloom (New York: Basic Books, 1979).

—— *Julie, or the New Heloise*, The Collected Writings of Rousseau, vol. 6, trans. Philip Stewart and Jean Vaché (Hanover, NH: University Press of New England, 1997).

—— *The Reveries of the Solitary Walker*, in *The Reveries of the Solitary Walker, Botanical Writings and Letter to Franquières*, The Collected Writings of Rousseau, vol. 8, trans. Charles Butterworth (Hanover, NH: University Press of New England, 2000).

Rowland, Ingrid D., 'The Renaissance Revealed' and 'Titian: The Sacred and the Profane', in *From Heaven to Arcadia: The Sacred and the Profane in the Renaissance* (New York: New York Review of Books Collections, 2005).

Russell, James C., *The Germanization of Early Christianity: A Sociohistorical Approach to Religious Transformation* (New York: Oxford University Press, 1994).

Rüterswörden, Udo, 'Die Liebe zu Gott im Deuteronomium', in *Die deuteronomistischen Geschichtswerke: Redaktions- und religionsgeschichtliche Perspektiven zur 'Deuteronomismus'-Diskussion in Tora und Vorderen Propheten*, ed. Markus Witte et al. (Berlin: Walter de Gruyter, 2006).

Ruzer, Serge, 'From "Love Your Neighbour" To "Love Your Enemy": Trajectories in Early Jewish Exegesis', *Revue Biblique*, vol. 109, no. 3 (2002), pp. 371–89.

Schiller, Friedrich, *Werke und Briefe, Band 12, Briefe II: 1795–1805*, ed. N. Oellers (Frankfurt: Deutscher Klassiker Verlag, 2002).

Schlegel, Friedrich, *Lucinde* and 'Athenaeum Fragments', in *Friedrich Schlegel's* Lucinde *and the Fragments*, trans. Peter Firchow (Minneapolis: University of Minnesota Press, 1971).

—— 'On Philosophy: To Dorothea', in *Theory as Practice: A Critical Anthology of Early German Romantic Writings*, ed. and trans. J. Schulte-Sasse et al. (Minneapolis: University of Minnesota Press, 1991).

Schopenhauer, Arthur, *The World as Will and Representation*, trans. E.F.J. Payne, vols 1 and 2 (New York: Dover, 1966).

Screech, M.A., *Montaigne and Melancholy: The Wisdom of the Essays* (London: Penguin, 1991).

Scruton, Roger, *Death-Devoted Heart: Sex and the Sacred in Wagner's* Tristan and Isolde (New York: Oxford University Press, 2004).

Shakespeare, William, *The Sonnets and a Lover's Complaint* (London: Penguin, 1995).

Sifra: An Analytic Translation, vol. III, trans. Jacob Neusner (Atlanta: Scholars Press, 1988).

Sifre: A Tannaitic Commentary on the Book of Deuteronomy, trans. R. Hammer (New Haven: Yale University Press, 1986).

Singer, Irving, *The Nature of Love,* vols. I, II and III (Chicago: University of Chicago Press, 1984–87).

Sophocles, *Antigone,* in *The Three Theban Plays: Antigone, Oedipus the King, Oedipus at Colonus,* trans. Robert Fagles (London: Penguin, 1984).

Spinoza, Baruch (Benedict de), *Ethics,* ed. and trans. G.H.R. Parkinson (London: J.M. Dent & Sons, 1989).

The Talmud of the Land of Israel, vol. 20 (*Hagigah* and *Moed Qatan*), trans. Jacob Neusner (Chicago: University of Chicago Press, 1986).

Tarnas, Richard, *The Passion of the Western Mind* (London: Random House, 1991).

Taylor, C.C.W., 'Politics', in *The Cambridge Companion to Aristotle,* ed. Jonathan Barnes (Cambridge: Cambridge University Press, 1995).

Tennyson, Alfred (Lord), *The Major Works,* ed. Adam Roberts (Oxford: Oxford University Press, 2009).

Teresa of Avila, *The Interior Castle or the Mansions* (London: T. Baker, 1921).

Thompson, Thomas L., 'How Yahweh Became God: Exodus 3 and 6 and the Heart of the Pentateuch', *Journal for the Study of the Old Testament,* vol. 68 (1995), pp. 57–74.

Topsfield, L.T., *Troubadours and Love* (Cambridge: Cambridge University Press, 1975).

Weber, Max, *The Protestant Ethic and the Spirit of Capitalism,* trans. Talcott Parsons (Mineola: Dover Publications, 2003).

Weinfeld, Moshe, *Deuteronomy and the Deuteronomic School* (Oxford: Clarendon Press, 1972).

—— 'The Loyalty Oath in the Ancient Near East', *Ugarit-Forschungen,* 8 (1976), pp. 379–414.

—— *The Place of the Law in the Religion of Ancient Israel,* Supplements to Vetus Testamentum (Leiden and Boston: Brill, 2004).

Wilde, Oscar, *A Woman of No Importance* (London: Penguin, 1996).

Wintermute, O.S., trans., 'Jubilees', in *The Old Testament Pseudepigrapha,* vol. 2, ed. James H. Charlesworth (New York: Doubleday, 1985).

Wolters, Clifton, introduction in Julian of Norwich, *Revelations of Divine Love,* trans. Clifton Wolters (Harmondsworth: Penguin, 1966).

Žižek, Slavoj, 'Courtly Love, or Woman as Thing', in *The Žižek Reader,* ed. Elizabeth Wright and Edmond Wright (Oxford: Blackwell, 1999).

Index